A Historical Source Book
for the Ottawa Valley

A Historical Source Book for the Ottawa Valley

by Enoch Padolsky and Ian Pringle

The Linguistic Survey of the Ottawa Valley
Carleton University, Ottawa

First published 1981 by the Linguistic Survey of the Ottawa Valley, Carleton University, Ottawa

ISBN 0-7709-0115-8

TABLE OF CONTENTS

vi

ix

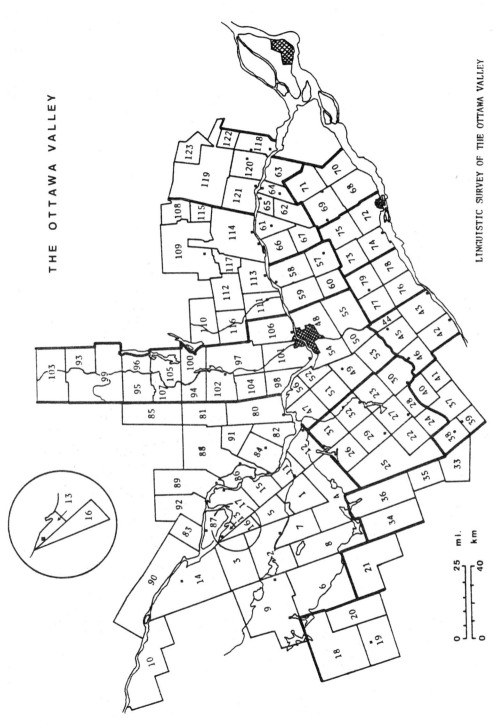

THE OTTAWA VALLEY

LINGUISTIC SURVEY OF THE OTTAWA VALLEY

MAP 1

Introduction

This is not a history book. It is a book of materials from which history books, in part at least, are written. These materials were collected to provide a historical context for The Linguistic Survey of the Ottawa Valley, a project studying the varieties of English spoken in Eastern Ontario and Western Quebec. Because of the close connection between language and history, these historical materials have proved to be of continuous value to us in our work. The scope of the information collected, however, goes beyond our own narrow uses, and at the urging of a number of our historian friends we have decided to make our materials available as a *Source Book* for those who are working on or simply interested in the history of the Ottawa Valley.

The chief innovation of this book is that it makes available for the first time a large amount of demographic information (on population, ethnic groups, and religions) and an area-specific bibliography for the entire Ottawa Valley, that is on both the Ontario and Quebec sides of the Ottawa River. The specific area covered can be seen in Map 1, "The Ottawa Valley." The total area covered is 15,067 square miles and in 1971 it had a population of 709,625. Though the study area corresponds generally to the area drained by the Ottawa River and its watershed, it is undoubtedly somewhat larger than what is traditionally called "The Ottawa Valley." This is intentional. If the "Valley" has a character of its own, it can only be discovered in its context. We in our work, and others no doubt in theirs, are interested in knowing where in fact the Valley "boundaries" are and what is on the other side of them in contrast. The city of Ottawa (including Vanier and Rockcliffe Park) has been *excluded* throughout: we felt it is a separate subject area, and many studies and additional sources of information on it are already available. The rest of the Valley, so rich in history and people, has not received the attention it deserves. For reference purposes, it should therefore be noted that the excluded area (Ottawa, Vanier, and Rockcliffe Park) totaled 44.33 square miles in 1971 and had a population in that year of 326,956. The city of Hull and other areas of the Census Metropolitan Area of Ottawa-Hull are *included* in the study area.

The materials presented in this book are mainly of two sorts: 1) bibliographical information, and 2) information drawn from the Canada Census. The bibliographical information is quite straightforward. Bibliographical references appear as part of the *Notes* to each area, and in an extensive bibliography at the end of the book. This bibliography began as an attempt to list every serious historical work which discusses all or part of the region under consideration. Like all bibliographies, ours is no doubt incomplete. In particular, primary materials, documents, and so on have not normally been listed. We are also sure that we have missed many small pamphlets published privately. With these exceptions, however, we hope that it is reasonably complete up to 1978. It has been updated in part subsequently.

The period covered by the census data goes back to 1851 and forward to 1971, or sometimes 1976. The census information is presented in a number of ways. In some places actual figures are used, in others percentages are given. The data appear not only in lists but also in a large number of graphs and maps. The aim has been to allow students, local historians, and other users of the book to make historical judgments about individual areas, combinations of these areas, or the Valley as a whole. In order to make best use of this book, users are therefore encouraged to read carefully the important explanations which follow. They present the precise nature of the materials and detail the ways they are presented and how they can be used.

I THE INTEGRAL UNIT

Since most of the book is organized to put the emphasis on individual areas in the Valley, it is important to establish from the outset the exact nature of these areas. A glance at the base map (Map 1) shows that there are 123 of these, 79 in Ontario and 44 in Quebec. These individual areas which we call "integral units," ("IU's" for short), form the basis of the information given in the book. We call them "integral" because their boundaries are geographically fixed and historically stable over time, regardless of any internal divisions or changes that may have occurred. The units formed with these stable boundaries can thus be compared historically over time. The IU's were formed by combining in one unit all census subdivisions that were ever grouped together in any census year from 1851 (or creation date, if after 1851) to 1971. For example, IU 9 consists of 5 townships in Renfrew county: Burns, Hagarty, Jones, Richards, and Sherwood. In recent years, these townships have appeared in the census in two groups: 1) Hagarty and Richards; and 2) Sherwood, Jones, and Burns. In earlier years however (1881 for example), they appeared as: 1) Hagarty and Jones; and 2) Sherwood, Richards and Burns. In order to be able to make consistent comparisons between all census years, therefore, the five townships were grouped together as one "integral" unit. Note as well that the IU always includes the incorporated municipal villages, towns, and cities. The case of IU 9, for example, contains Barry's Bay and Killaloe Station. Many of these latter entities were incorporated after 1851 and from then on listed separately in the census. In order to make comparisons to the time before they were so listed, it is necessary to re-combine them in the IU. In terms of the format of this book, (see Format below) the IU's are presented in the "Main File" and internal groupings—townships, villages, etc.—in the "Subfiles." In much of Ontario, the IU corresponds with township boundaries or collections of townships, along with any villages, towns, and cities found therein. In Quebec, the IU includes, in addition, a number of parishes and undesignated census subdivisions. Finally, to put it in the most recent Statistics Canada vocabulary, the IU corresponds either to a consolidated census subdivision (CCS) or those combinations of CCS's which can be traced historically from 1851 (or creation date) to 1971.

Even IU boundaries, however, and sometimes the data on IU's, can be problematic, especially in Quebec. Though IU changes are noted (see **Main Files**, *Changes*, below), the maps, for example, do not always reflect boundary shifts. Nor is it always possible to be sure, given name changes, county boundary changes, etc., that census geographical changes have been properly recorded by us or by the census, especially in the earlier years. Readers are therefore advised to use caution in their interpretations and to keep the changes in mind. But these problems should not be over stressed. The difficulties with the Quebec material are amply compensated by being able to make comparisons on both sides of the Ottawa River, and the general problems are minor relative to the value of being able to make comparisons over the thirteen census years since 1851.

II THE CENSUS INFORMATION

The information collected from the census and presented in this book falls into 3 main categories: population, main ethnic groups, and main religious groups. Many other categories of information are of course available in the census, but these three are undoubtedly among the most central in studying the demography of the Ottawa Valley. The notes which follow explain the nature of the categories and any special problems in the data.

1. Population and Area

The population figures were collected for all IU's and their various components from 1851 (or creation date if after 1851) to 1971. The only areas presented are those of 1971, though area changes are noted for each case. It should be noted that the 1971 population figures are based on the short form used by the census, i.e. the 100% basis. These figures may differ slightly from the long form (1/3 sample) totals of Ethnicity and Religion for that year.

2. Ethnicity

The study has collected only the major ethnic groups in the Valley. These include: English, Scottish, Irish, French, German-Dutch, and Polish-Russian. In addition there are two special categories: British, and British North-American. For convenience, these are listed below along with their abbreviations and graph symbols:

◈	BR	British
◇	BNA	British North-American
▽	ENG	English
×	SCOT	Scottish
+	IR	Irish
▣	FR	French
▲	GD	German-Dutch
⊙	PR	Polish-Russian

The following important details should be noted about each of the categories.

British ethnic groups

After 1941, the census does not provide a breakdown of the British ethnic groups on the basis of our IU's. There is thus no way of documenting ENG, SCOT, and IR for those last three census years. (In most census years prior to 1951, the breakdown of the British groups is available and we have collected and presented these figures. In addition, however, we have totaled these figures and listed them in the BR category—on graphs, etc.—for the sake of convenience and comparability.) It should also be noted that in 1851 and 1861, the British ethnic labels (ENG, etc.) refer to place of birth rather than ethnic origin. In addition, for those years only, there is the category of British North-American, which we have also included in the BR total. The BNA group includes the following census categories for 1851 and 1861: "Natives of Canada - Not French," those from the Maritime Provinces, and those from the United States. For those two years, then: BR = ENG + SCOT + IR + BNA. It should also be noted that other British groups (eg. Manx, Welsh) have always been included by us under English in the few places where they are found.

French

This category includes those from France in addition to French-Canadians, wherever this distinction is made in the census. There are, however, very few of the former in the Valley, even in the earliest census years.

German-Dutch

This category includes along with German those listed in the census as ethnically from the Netherlands. The reasons for this combination are well known to those who have worked previously with census ethnicity data. (See N.B. Ryder, "The Intepretation of Origin Statistics," *The Canadian Journal of Economics and Political Science*, Vol. XXI [1955], 466-479.) Combining of the two groups in early censuses, shifting answers by "Germans" during the war years and immediately after, and the confusion over time between "Dutch" and "Deutsch", all necessitate the joint category. In fact, actual Dutch ethnic representation in the Ottawa Valley is relatively low and those wishing to interpret GD as mainly German would not in most cases be too far off the mark. For example, in Renfrew County, where there is a large GD population, the 1941 war-time census gave the following county figures: German 11,125, Dutch 255. This population is corroborated by the mother tongue language figures for that year: German 6,122, Dutch 39.

Polish-Russian

This is another joint category made necessary mainly because until 1911 the two groups were combined in the census. It should be noted that in 1861 Prussian switches from Russian to German. In fact, almost all PR in the Valley is actually Polish, indeed Kashubian Polish. In Renfrew County, where most of the PR population is concentrated, the 1941 ethnicity figures show the following: Polish 5,176, Russian 37. Mother tongue figures were: Polish 3,990, Russian 15.

Other Ethnic Groups

Unlike the case of religious groups, where Other Religions appear in the graphs, there is no line for the other ethnic groups in the Ethnicity graphs. The main reason for this omission is the limitation of space on the graphs. As a result, the total of the graphed ethnic groups does not always equal 100%.

There are a number of other important points to keep in mind when using ethnic figures:

a) *There are no figures for ethnic origin available for the 1891 census.* The lack of data is indicated in the graphs by a dotted line or series of dashes.

b) The precise definition of ethnic origin changes over time with differing degrees of stress on race, ancestral country of origin, cultural affiliation, and language. The degree to which these shifting definitions invalidate the category depends in part of course on the region of Canada in question and the use to which one intends to put the figures. In addition, ethnic origin is consistently traced through the male (paternal) side only. Nevertheless, it seems to us that with some caution, census ethnic figures can be used to reflect some sort of group claim or community affiliation, keeping in mind the changing sense of ethnicity over the period in question. In addition, it is likely that the Ottawa Valley is less problematic than many other areas in Canada. (For a discussion of these problems, see the Ryder article referred to earlier.)

c) The 1971 census gives the following note: "In 1971 respondents were asked the question: 'To what ethnic or cultural group did you or your ancestor (on the male side) belong on coming to this continent?' If applicable, the language spoken at that time by the person or by the paternal ancestor was used as a guide in determining the person's ethnic group." (*Statistics Canada Catalogue 92-774 Special Bulletin 1971 Census: Population: Specified Ethnic Groups, Introduction*)

d) The 1971 ethnicity figures are from the long form, collected on a 33 1/3% sample basis and are randomly rounded to the nearest 5 or 0. The totals do not therefore necessarily accord exactly with the totals for either population or religion though the differences are usually not significant.

e) For those wishing to check ethnic figures in this book or to work further in this area, the following is a list of our sources:

1851-1881   Volume 1 of the respective census.
1891   Data on ethnic origin not available.
1901-1921   Volume 1 of the respective census.
1931-1941   Volume 2 of the respective census.
1951   Data at the census subdivision level is not available in the printed census. We obtained our figures directly from Statistics Canada.
1961   Catalogue No. 92-526 (SP-2) Population by Specified Origins.
1971   Catalogue No. 92-774 (SP-4) Population: Specified Ethnic Groups.

3. Religion

The study has collected only the major religious affiliations in the Valley. These include: Anglican, Roman Catholic, Presbyterian, Methodist, Baptist, and Lutheran. For convenience, these are listed below along with their abbreviations and graph symbols:

+	ANG	Anglican
▼	RC	Roman Catholic
▣	PRES	Presbyterian
✕	METH	Methodist
◈	BAP	Baptist
▲	LUTH	Lutheran
⊙	OTHREL	Other Religions

The following important details should be noted about each of the categories.

Anglican and Roman Catholic
In 1891 Anglican includes Reformed Episcopal. These two groups also appear in the census under other names, for example, Church of England and Church of Rome.

Presbyterian
No attempt has been made to distinguish in early years between Church of Scotland and the various non-established Presbyterians. The category includes all groups under the

Presbyterian label in the census. From the 1931 census on, Presbyterian refers to those "free" Presbyterians who did not join the United Church in 1925.

Methodist

Again, all types of Methodists which appear separately in early census years have been grouped under this label. From 1931 on. METH = United Church and includes all those former Presbyterians who participated in the church union of 1925. This important change in status is not indicated by us on the Religion graphs but should be kept in mind.

Baptist and Lutheran

Again, this category groups all types of Baptists and Lutherans wherever they are distinguished in the census. It should be noted that Baptist and Lutheran were collected by us only where these groups were present in proportionately significant numbers. In those places and times where BAP and LUTH are proportionately small, they are included in the Other Religions category. In the graphs, these uncollected figures are considered missing numbers and are assigned a value of 0. In the subfiles these missing figures are shown by blank spaces. If the figures are missing, it can be assumed that these groups form only a minimal percentage of the population of the area.

Other Religions

This category was not collected separately but was calculated by subtracting the sum of collected religious groups from the total population. As a result, the category may represent a range of other religious responses, as for example: Evangelical, Greek Orthodox, Jewish, No response, No Religion, and in the places and years in which they were not collected, Baptist and Lutheran.

The following notes should be kept in mind when using the Religions information:

a) The 1971 religion figures, like those for ethnicity, are from the census long form collected on a 33 1/3% sample basis and are randomly rounded to the nearest 5 or 0. The totals do not therefore necessarily accord exactly with the totals for either population or ethnicity though the differences are usually not significant.

b) For those wishing to check religion figures in this book or to work further in this area, the following is a list of our sources:

1851-1901	Volume 1 of the respective census.
1911	Volume 2 of the 1911 census.
1921	Volume 1 of the 1921 census.
1931-1941	Volume 2 of the respective census.
1951	Data at the census subdivision level are not available in the printed census. We obtained our figures directly from Statistics Canada.
1961	Catalogue No. 92-527 (SP-3) Population: Religious Denominations
1971	Catalogue No. 92-775 (SP-5) Population: Specified Religious Denominations

III THE FORMAT OF THIS BOOK

In this section of the Introduction we wish to familiarize readers with the format used in this book and to provide a number of details necessary in interpreting the information presented. There are three divisions in the main body of the book:

1. Ottawa Valley Integral Units: Main Files and Subfiles.
2. Two Graphs of Ottawa Valley Demographic Features.
3. A Selection of Demographic Maps of the Ottawa Valley.

Finally, there is the Bibliography and Index of Place Names. Specific comments on how to use Sections 2 and 3 (Graphs and Maps) have been placed in the introductory remarks to each of those sections. However, the comments which follow on section 1 (Ottawa Valley IU's) and the earlier comments on the nature of the census information may also be important for the proper interpretation of the graphs and maps.

Ottawa Valley Integral Units

This section of the book presents the main core of information collected on the 123 individual areas of the Ottawa Valley. For each of these areas (IU's), there is a Main File, and where more detailed information is available, a Subfile, both of which have fixed formats. Notes particular to the Subfiles format follow the discussion of the Main File format below. The IU's are grouped by county and at the beginning of each county there is a county map and a headnote which lists general bibliographical sources, census sources, and county wide data.

Main Files

Each main file has the following headings: ID Number, Name(s), Area, 1971 Density, Type, Population, Changes, Subfiles, and Notes. In addition, each IU main file includes three graphs which show the development over time in the IU of: Population, Ethnicity, and Religion. Immediately following the main file is the subfile of that IU, where such subfiles exist.

ID Number

Every integral unit is identified by a seven digit coded number. The first two digits of the ID number indicate the county, the next three digits identify the IU, and the last two digits give the type of the area. The county segments follow this code:

Ontario					*Quebec*
01	Renfrew	06	Leeds	11 Glengarry	14 Pontiac
02	Hastings	07	Grenville	12 Stormont	15 Gatineau-Hull
03	Lennox and Addington	08	Carleton	13 Dundas	16 Papineau
04	Lanark	09	Russell		17 Argenteuil
05	Frontenac	10	Prescott		

As the above list indicates, county names and boundaries are generally those of 1971. There are, however, some notable exceptions: Cumberland Township for example, is included in its historical place in Russell County rather than in its new place in Carleton (R.M. of Ottawa-Carleton). Some notes on county boundaries appear throughout the main files. The middle three digits of the ID Number, which indicate the IU, run from 001 to 123 and can be found located on the base map (Map 1) along with a somewhat abbreviated list of names. The last 2 digits of the ID Number are either 00 or 99. These indicate the type: 00 = Rural, 99 = Combined. (See *Type*, below.)

Name(s)
The name or names used for each IU are generally those of all the consolidated census subdivisions of 1971 found in the IU. There are a few minor exceptions as for example in 1611499, where the name [Petite Nation] is added since that historical seigneury makes up the bulk of that area. No names of villages, towns, or cities appear in the IU name except where they happen to be the same as the subdivision names.

Area
The 1971 area in square miles is listed under this heading. Any differences in area in earlier census years are noted under the *Changes* heading. (See below.)

1971 Density
Under this heading the population density for the IU is given for the year 1971.

Type
The main function of this heading is to indicate whether the IU includes any incorporated villages, towns, or cities. There are thus only 2 types, Rural and Combined. Rural IUs do not contain and have not contained any incorporated villages, etc. in their census history; Combined IUs presently contain one or more incorporated villages, etc., and may also have contained them in earlier census years. Though the Rural or Combined-type of IU may very roughly correspond to general notions of "rural" and "urban," the type-tags should be used with a great deal of caution. Though all rural-type IUs have indeed been "rural" by census definition for much of their history, some such as Nepean (0805400) or Gloucester (0804800) have clearly become heavily "urban" in recent years. The type-tag may thus not in itself be used for urban/rural analysis in any one census year. Similarly, though the Combined-type IU label indicates the presence of incorporated villages, etc. for some census years, it need not imply official census "urban" status since the required population and population density may not be present. For an updated picture of the Rural/Urban status of all Ottawa Valley IUs according to current census definitions, see Map 2 below: "Rural-Urban 1976." It should also be noted that the type-tag does not comment on the internal make-up of the IU except insofar as the incorporated villages, etc., are concerned. A Combined IU need not consist of more than one township (though it may), and a Rural IU may contain more than one township (though it need not). Thus, though all Combined IU's are assured of having subfiles, many Rural ones have them as well. (See *Subfiles*, below.)

Population
This heading gives the total population for the IU normally for 4 years: 1851, 1881, 1941 and 1971. IUs created after 1851 will of course have later and/or fewer dates. The years 1851 (or date of creation, if later) and 1971 were chosen to represent the earliest and latest figures available. The choice of 1881 and 1841 was dictated by a number of different factors. A full explanation can be found in the introduction to the Maps section, below, p. 430.

Changes

Under this heading, a list of the changes which have affected the IU over time is given, along with the census date at which the changes took place. These changes include: annexations or losses of territory, any rare omissions or additions of territory for a particular year, some of the more important name changes, and the dates of incorporation of villages, towns, and cities in the IU. County name changes or boundary changes are not usually listed since they do not affect the IU directly. Internal changes within the parts of the IU can be found in the "Changes" category of the subfile immediately following the main file. It is particularly important to check the IU "Changes" for any annexations or losses of territory when using the graphs that appear with each main file. Note that for convenience of use, the change dates given are the census year rather than the actual date of change. Thus, for example, in IU 17, Beachburg's incorporation in 1959 appears as a change for 1961.

Subfiles

Under this heading in the main file is provided a convenient list of the components of the IU for which additional information is given in the subfiles which follow immediately. See *Subfiles*, below, for a discussion of the format and use of the subfiles.

Notes

The information given under this heading includes annotations and page references to those historical works listed in the Bibliography which refer specifically to the IU, general geographical information, usually where historically significant, and additional census sources which could usefully be consulted on this IU. In some cases, especially around the Metropolitan Area of Ottawa-Hull, information and/or changes that appear in the 1976 Census are noted here. In those cases where striking shifts take place in some of the graph lines, explanations or comments are sometimes added. Other interpretive comments based on the information in the subfiles are also given occasionally in this section. Finally some attempt has been made to note the larger unincorporated places in the IU from the 1971 Census. Usually only those places of about 200 inhabitants and up are noted, unless the unincorporated place, though less than 200, forms a high percentage of the population of a small IU.

IU Graphs

As mentioned earlier, each main file includes three graphs for each IU: 1. Population, 2. Ethnicity, and 3. Religion. These graphs, computer drawn using the APL graphing package, require a few notes of explanation.

1. Population

This graph shows the population *in actual figures* for the IU from 1851 (or date of creation) to 1971. The vertical axis of the graph gives the population size on an evenly distributed scale adjusted to the minimum and maximum population of that IU. The horizontal axis gives the census year on a scale of 20 year intervals from 1840 to 1980. Since the vertical axis is adjusted to IU size, it should be remembered that population graphs which look alike do not necessarily reflect equal increases and decreases of population.

2. Ethnicity

This graph shows *in percentages* the distribution of the various major ethnic groups in the IU from 1851 (or date of creation) to 1971. The vertical axis of the graph gives the population *in percentages* on a scale of 10% intervals adjusted upward to the highest percentage for any line in the IU. Because of this adjustment, line size along the vertical axis is not necessarily equal in different graphs. This should be kept in mind when making comparisons between ethnicity graphs or between ethnicity graphs and religion graphs. The horizontal axis gives the census year on scale of 20 year intervals from 1840 to 1980. A guide to the graph symbols and abbreviated labels can be found on p. xiii of this Introduction. Since there are no census data for 1891, dotted straight lines connect 1881 to 1901 in all ethnicity graphs. The identifying graph symbol which appears at the 1891 year location has no data basis. For a full discussion of the data on the Ethnic groups shown on the graphs, see above, *The Census Information: 2. Ethnicity*. The reader should be reminded that the British graph line (BR) includes a number of other lines from 1851 to 1941 and that 1971 percentages are calculated from the population totals on the long form 33 1/3% sample basis.

3. Religion

This graph shows *in percentages* the distribution of the various major religious groups in the IU from 1851 (or date of creation) to 1971. The vertical axis of the graph gives the population *in percentages* on a scale of 10% intervals adjusted upward to the highest percentage for any line in the IU. Because of this adjustment, line size along the vertical axis is again not necessarily equal in different graphs. This should be kept in mind when making comparisons between religion graphs or between religion graphs and ethnicity graphs. The horizontal axis gives the census year on a scale of 20 year intervals from 1840 to 1980. A guide to the graph symbols and abbreviated labels can be found on p. xv of this Introduction. For a full discussion of the data on Religion groups shown on the graphs, see above, *The Census Information: 3. Religion*. The reader should be reminded that the Other Religions line (OTHREL) has been calculated by subtracting the sum of collected groups from the total population, that from 1931 onward the Methodist line (METH) = United Church, PRES = "free" Presbyterians, and that 1971 percentages are calculated from the population totals on the long form 33 1/3% sample basis.

Subfiles

The subfiles provide a further breakdown of information on 75 of the 123 individual areas (integral units) of the Ottawa Valley. Subfiles exist on all incorporated villages, towns, and cities and also on many IU components (townships, etc.) which have been listed separately in some census years. All Combined-type IU's (i.e. those having ID Numbers ending in 99) thus have subfiles on incorporated centres and, as in the case of some Rural-type IUs, may also have subfiles on other IU components. Since the subfile information often permits a closer view of the distributions represented in the graphs of the main file, subfiles are best used in concert with the main files. This is also advisable since information given in the main file is usually not repeated in the subfile.

Subfile Format

In general, the subfile format parallels that of the main file. The ID Number is the same as the Main File and each component of the subfile has information under the headings: Area, 1971 Density, and Population. As for the main files, population figures are normally given for the years 1851, 1881, 1941, and 1971. (For a discussion of the choice of these dates, see above *Main Files: Population* and the introduction to the Maps section, below p. 430). This pattern of dates is frequently broken in the subfiles, however, because of the unavailability of figures or later dates of creation or incorporation of subfile components. Many of the components also have the *Changes* heading, where information on the internal changes of the IU appears (incorporation dates, internal annexations, etc.). Major external boundary changes which affect components are usually listed as well, as are former names for the component area where they are likely to be well known. In the latter cases, however, the Main File *Changes* should be consulted since the information given there is generally more complete. There are no *Notes* for the subfiles since pertinent information has been included in the Main Files *Notes*.

Each subfile component is given an identifying number (a, b, c, etc.) which is located on the Subfile Map which appears at the beginning of each subfile. Boundaries between subfile component areas are indicated on the maps by dotted lines. Because of limitations of space on the maps, it has not been possible to indicate smaller boundaries, such as township boundaries when a component consists of more than one township, and readers will have to consult more detailed maps for this information. Incorporated villages, etc. are indicated on the maps with small squares. These are of course representative only and do not indicate the actual area of the incorporated centres. The 1971 areas of these centres can be found under the relevant Area headings in the subfile.

The Subfile Names are the same as those of the main file except that some names are followed by a "Rural" or "Urban" tag. The "Rural" tag is added to those components from which an incorporated village, town, or city has been separated. Some care has been taken in positioning the "Rural" tag within the component name. Where known, the tag follows without a break precisely that component or sub-component in which the incorporated centre is located. For example, in Subfile a of IU 9 "Hagarty (Rural), Richards," the incorporated centre, in this case Killaloe Station, is shown to be located in Hagarty Township. In a few cases, however, this information is unknown, or the village, etc., has been incorporated from more than one sub-component. In these cases, the "Rural" tag appears at the end of a component name separated by a comma. An example of this is IU 111 where we have made no attempt to locate the villages and towns (b, c, and d in the Subfile) and the listing of component a appears as "Buckingham, Buckingham West, Buckingham South-East, L'Ange Gardien, (Rural)." The "Urban" tag appears *only* after the names of those incorporated centres which have the same name as the "Rural" component, as in Cornwall, for example. The restriction of the "Urban" tag to these cases may result in some uncertainty as to whether or not a component is an incorporated centre for those readers who are not familiar with the place. This can always be resolved by checking the subfile map where all incorporated places are indicated by a square. In addition, all those centres incorporated after 1851 will have an incorporation date listed under "Changes." It should be noted again that the terms "Rural" and "Urban" are being used in a traditional sense and do not imply official census status. For a discussion of this point, see above, *Main Files: Type.*

The remainder of the subfile provides, in tabular form, the actual population figures for the subfile components for the various ethnic groups and religions. The presentation of these figures under the "Ethnicity" and "Religion" headings is quite straightforward and requires perhaps only the following few notes. Where possible, information is always presented for the census years 1881 and 1941. (For a discussion of the choice of these dates, see the introduction to the Maps section, below, p. 000.) Many exceptions occur, however, because of the unavailability of figures or later dates of creation or incorporation. In any case, the census year 1891 is generally avoided since no ethnicity data are available for that year. In all cases, however, regardless of the problems, figures from at least 2 years are given so that some historical perspective, no matter how limited, can be gained. In the list of place names of the tables, the "Rural" tag is used only after the incorporation of the associated village, town, or city. For example, in IU 14, Petawawa appears without a "Rural" tag for 1951 and earlier, and with the tag in 1971 after the incorporation of the village of Petawawa in 1961. Occasionally, information in the Ethnicity and Religion tables is given for breakdowns or combinations of components other than those of the other headings and subfile maps. This minor change of format, always due to the way the information is available in the census, may cause a few problems such as locating sub-component areas on the maps or making consistent comparisons for some census years. We have tried to overcome the latter problem by double listing some information. Thus, for example, in IU 2, the Ethnicity and Religion information for 1881 is available only in combined form for components a and c (Algona North and Wilberforce Townships). To compensate for this, and to permit comparisons, we have also listed 1941 figures in combined form as well as separately. Readers are reminded that after 1941, information on ENG, SCOT, and IR is available only as a single BR (British) listing. Finally, the following two points should be kept in mind regarding the Religion tables: 1. Blank spaces in Baptist and Lutheran columns indicate that the information was not collected for those years because these groups did not represent a significant proportion of the population. 2. After 1931, the PRES column shows only those Presbyterians who did not join the United Church, and the METH/UC column shows the United Church.

Further Census Information on The Ottawa Valley

This book contains only a part of the census information collected by the Linguistic Survey of the Ottawa Valley. The graphs, maps, and tables presented here are drawn from a larger and more detailed data file which has been computerized in an SPSS systems file. The data exist in both raw figures and percentages for all 123 IUs and in "Rural" and "Urban" components for all Combined-type IUs. In addition, information is available on the same geographical basis on: Mother Tongue and Home Language for 1971, Age and Sex for 1971, and ENG, SCOT, IR as a percent of BR for 1851 to 1941. At the time this book is going to press, we are making arrangements for copies of the computer printouts of both raw data and percentage data files to be made available for consultation at the Social Science Data Archives, Loeb Building, Carleton University. Those wishing to consult the computer file itself should contact us directly at The Linguistic Survey of the

Ottawa Valley, English Department or Linguistics Department, Carleton University, Ottawa, Canada K1S 5B6.

Acknowledgements

A book like this could not have been made without the assistance of a large number of people. We should like to take this opportunity of thanking all those student research assistants who have worked on the project, and in particular Stan Staple who collected much of the data from the census, Teresa Plowright, who created the SPSS file, David Mills and Carmen Baggeley, who worked on the Bibliography, and Donna Campbell, John Carmichael, Misao Dean, Duncan Glendinning, Ann LeDressay, Marilyn McHugh, and Debbie McMahon, all of whom worked on the maps, graphs, and editing of this book. For their careful typing we should also like to thank Debbie Badali, Doreen Hallam and Beverly Riley. We should also like to thank those of our colleagues who contributed to this book by their valuable consultations and advice: John Clarke (Geography), Stan Mealing, Carman Bickerton, and John Taylor (History), Frank Vallee and John De Vries (Sociology), and Barbara Farrell (Map Library). We should like to thank Gilles Paquet (former Dean of Graduate Studies) and Naomi Griffiths (Dean of Arts) for their encouragement and support. We should also like to express our gratitude to Statistics Canada and the User Advisory Services for their help on a number of occasions. The research conducted for this book was made possible by grants from Carleton University and the Social Sciences and Humanities Research Council of Canada.

Errors in a book of this sort are bound to occur and for these we ourselves take full responsibility. Some have already been caught by random error checks and graph idiosyncracies, but some, such as the realization that Litchfield Township in IU 88 could have been a separate IU, came too late in the project to be changed. We would of course be delighted to receive from our readers a list of any errors found or any suggestions they would like to make on the book.

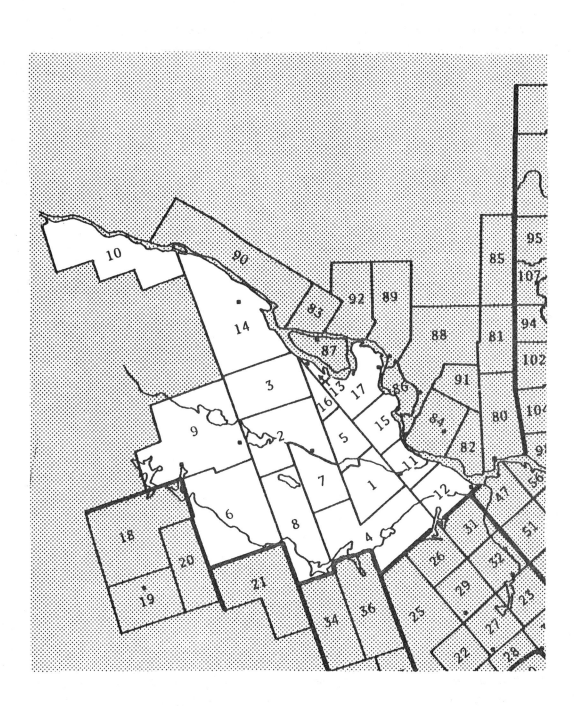

Integral Units   001 - 017

In addition to works dealing with particular areas of Renfrew
County, a number of studies deal with aspects of the whole County.
Perhaps most important is 276 (Fraser, n.d.); other major studies
are 164 (Kennedy, 1970) and 189 (Price and Kennedy, 181). Some
details of early history are given in 103 (Belden, 1880). The most
important single source on the forest industry is 212 (Whitton, 1944).
A number of studies discuss, in complementary ways, Polish settlement in the County, especially 78 (Radecki and Heyden Korn, 1976),
69b (Makowski, 1967), and 244 (Lee-Whiting, 1967). Economics and
geography are treated in 169 (Hardy, 1976) and 28 (Dean, 1969).

Considerable census information on Renfrew County is available in tables, maps, and analyses at the census division level. The
Indian Reserve in IU 2, excluded from our figures, had an area of
2.68 sq. miles and a population of 220 in 1971. County totals for
1971: population 90,875; area 2,952.00 sq. miles; density 30.78
persons/sq. mile.

ID: 0100100 <u>ADMASTON</u>

AREA: 126.31 sq. miles

1971 DENSITY:
   10.54 persons/sq. mile

TYPE:
   Rural

POPULATION:
   1851:   685
   1881: 2383
   1941: 1408
   1971: 1331

CHANGES: None

SUBFILES: None

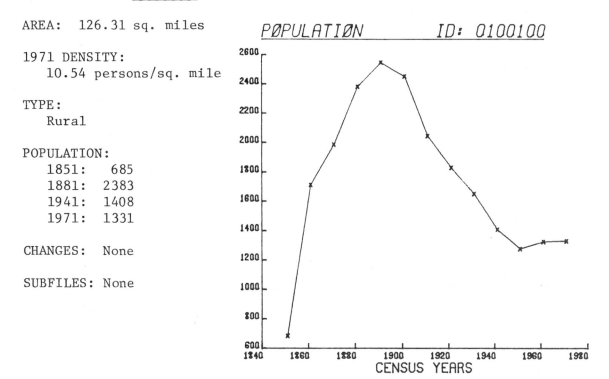

NOTES:

The Opeongo Road crosses Admaston.

The suitability of land in Admaston for farming is discussed in 163 (Keenan, 1964), p. 62. Fraser n.d. (276), p. 85, gives statistics relating to land use.

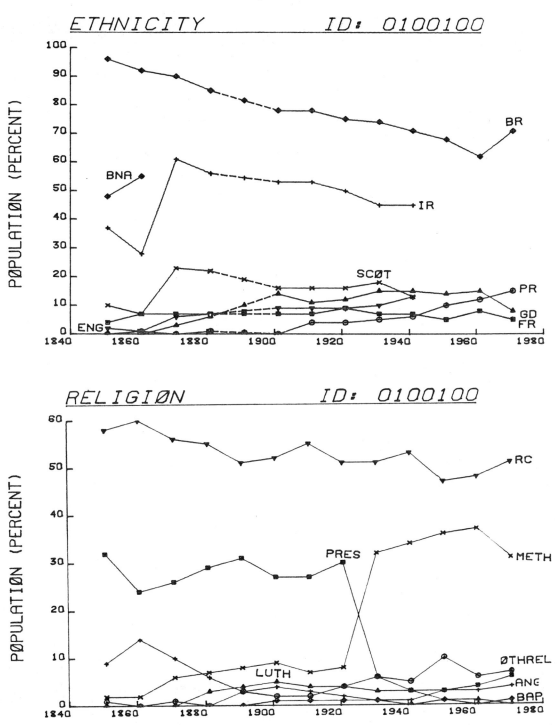

ID: 0100200   ALGONA NORTH, ALGONA SOUTH, WILBERFORCE

AREA: 190.47 sq. miles

1971 DENSITY:
    11.81 persons/sq. mile

TYPE:
    Rural

POPULATION:
    1851:   688
    1881:   3363
    1941:   2714
    1971:   2250

CHANGES: 1951 part of
    Wilberforce annexed
    to Eganville (in
    0100799).

SUBFILES:
    a. Algona North
    b. Algona South
    c. Wilberforce

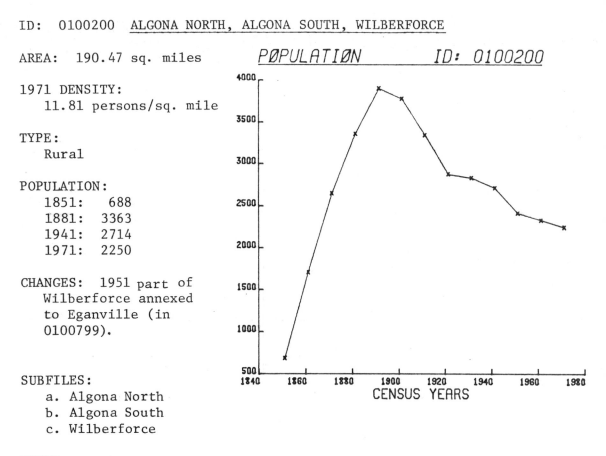

POPULATION   ID: 0100200

CENSUS YEARS

NOTES:

Kennedy, 1970 (164), pp. 187-188, discusses the Eganville area, and
134 (E.O.D.C., 1971) gives some information about the town.

These three townships are drained by the Bonnechère River. Eganville,
located at the Fifth Chute on the river, has been assigned by us to
Grattan township (0100799). The Algonquin Indian Reserve, on land
purchased by the Federal government in 1870, is located just east of
Golden Lake on the south shore of the Bonnechère. The unincorporated
village of Golden Lake (in Algona North) had a population of 229 in
1971. The Indian Reserve area (2.68 sq.miles in 1971) and population figures (220 in 1971) have not been included in the IU figures.

5

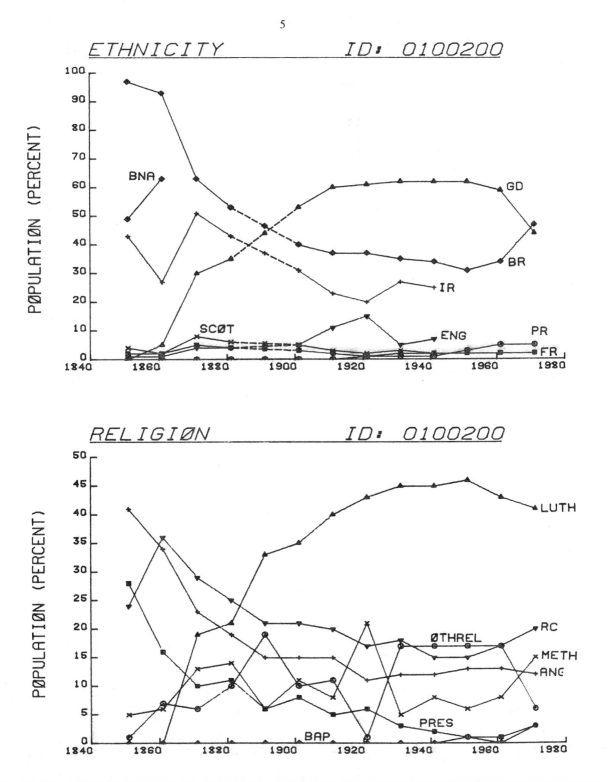

ID: 0100200 SUBFILES

a. ALGONA NORTH

AREA: 36.90 sq. miles

1971 DENSITY:
13.85 persons/sq. mile

POPULATION:
1901: 373
1941: 533
1971: 511

b. ALGONA SOUTH

AREA: 51.37 sq. miles

1971 DENSITY:
6.50 persons/sq. mile

POPULATION:
1901: 1080
1941: 654
1971: 334

CHANGES: 1951 part
annexed to Eganville
(in 0100799).

c. WILBERFORCE

AREA: 102.20 sq. miles

1971 DENSITY:
6.5 persons/sq. mile

POPULATION:
1901: 2327
1941: 1527
1971: 1405

ID: 0100200   SUBFILES   cont'd

ETHNICITY

PLACE	YEAR	ENG	SCOT	IR	FR	GD	PR
Algona N., Wilberforce	1881	117	190	1047	49	987	0
Algona N., Wilberforce	1941	175	66	489	47	1231	37
Algona North	1941	116	16	17	27	340	12
Wilberforce	1941	59	50	472	20	891	25
Algona South	1881	7	8	405	76	199	0
Algona South	1941	3	0	193	7	448	2

RELIGION

PLACE	YEAR	ANG	RC	PRES	METH/UC	BAP	LUTH
Algona N., Wilberforce	1881	608	329	345	428		545
Algona N., Wilberforce	1941	334	216	51	217		805
Algona North	1941	21	81	13	37		106
Wilberforce	1941	313	135	38	180		699
Algona South	1881	22	522	19	37		156
Algona South	1941	1	202	0	12		415

ID: 0100300 <u>ALICE, FRASER</u>

AREA: 172.56 sq. miles

1971 DENSITY:
    14.07 persons/sq. mile

TYPE:
    Rural

TOTAL POPULATION:
    1861:   727
    1881:   1912
    1941:   1538
    1971:   2428

CHANGES: 1861 created.

SUBFILES: None

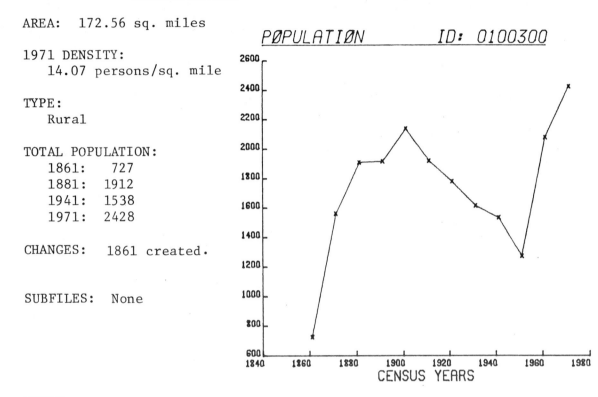

POPULATION   ID: 0100300

CENSUS YEARS

NOTES:

No sources listed in the bibliography deal specifically with Alice and Fraser.

The rugged terrain of Fraser Township makes it ill-suited for farming.

Alice Township, in close proximity to the city of Pembroke, is the more heavily settled of the two.

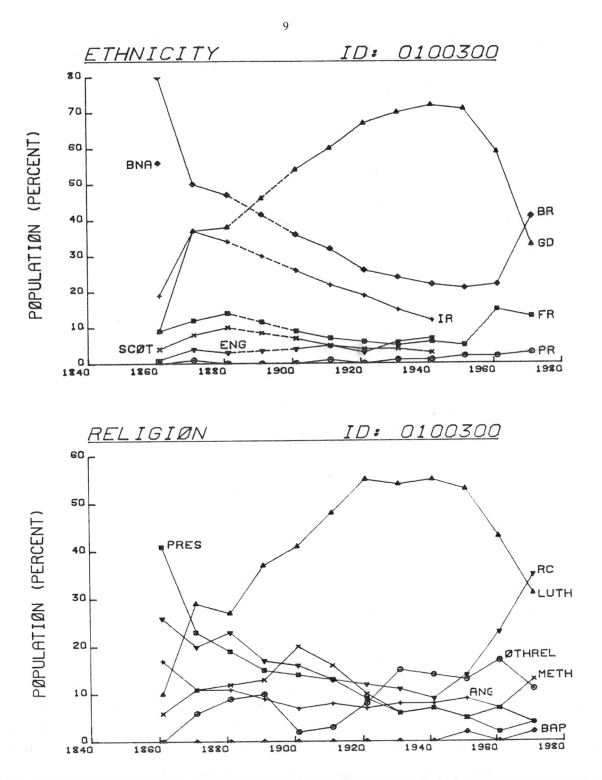

ETHNICITY   ID: 0100300

RELIGIØN   ID: 0100300

ID: 0100400   BAGOT, BLITHFIELD, BROUGHAM

AREA: 267.38 sq. miles

1971 DENSITY:
   4.70 persons/sq. mile

TYPE:
   Rural

TOTAL POPULATION:
   1851:   1372
   1881:   1700
   1941:   1548
   1971:   1257

CHANGES: None

SUBFILES:
   a. Bagot, Blithfield
   b. Brougham

POPULATION   ID: 0100400

CENSUS YEARS

NOTES:

The historically important mining operations in the area are discussed in 11b (Brown, 1978), pp. 188-190 and 164 (Kennedy, 1970), pp. 44-45. Hardy, 1978 (149), p. 23 gives details on farming and seasonal dwellings in the area in 1974.

Bagot and Blithfield contain Calabogie Lake and are crossed by the Madawaska River, which forms the southern boundary of Brougham. The unincorporated village of Calabogie, in Bagot township, had a population of 229 in 1971.

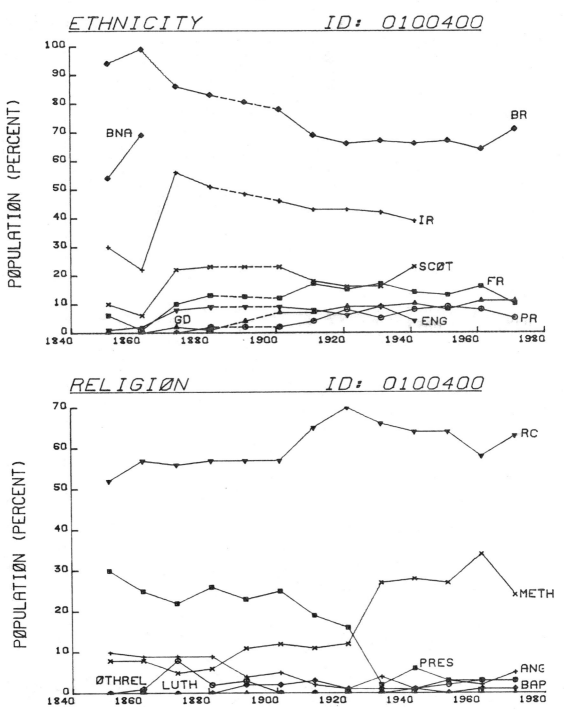

ID: 0100400 SUBFILES

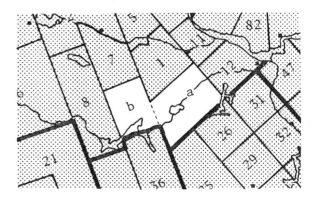

a. <u>BAGOT, BLITHFIELD</u>

   AREA: 163.14 sq. miles

   1971 DENSITY:
      6.44 persons/sq.
      mile

   POPULATION:
      1881: 1126
      1941: 1075
      1971: 1051

b. <u>BROUGHAM</u>

   AREA: 104.24 sq. miles

   1971 DENSITY:
      1.98 persons/sq.
      mile

   POPULATION:
      1881: 574
      1941: 473
      1971: 206

ID: 0100400   SUBFILES   cont'd

ETHNICITY

PLACE	YEAR	ENG	SCOT	IR	FR	GD	PR
Bagot, Blithfield	1881	133	363	472	106	19	33
Bagot, Blithfield	1941	53	323	361	156	61	92
Bagot	1941	53	323	349	156	61	92
Blithfield	1941	0	0	12	0	0	0
Brougham	1881	17	26	395	117	0	9
Brougham	1941	7	30	248	65	90	30

RELIGION

PLACE	YEAR	ANG	RC	PRES	METH/UC	BAP	LUTH
Bagot, Blithfield	1881	68	539	398	96		
Bagot, Blithfield	1941	7	596	52	414		
Bagot	1941	7	584	52	414		
Blithfield	1941	0	12	0	0		
Brougham	1881	81	437	47	0		
Brougham	1941	1	392	36	26	14	

ID: 0100500 <u>BROMLEY</u>

AREA: 81.31 sq. miles

1971 DENSITY:
  14.97 persons/sq. mile

TYPE:
  Rural

POPULATION:
  1851: 687
  1881: 1797
  1941: 1563
  1971: 1217

CHANGES: None

SUBFILES: None

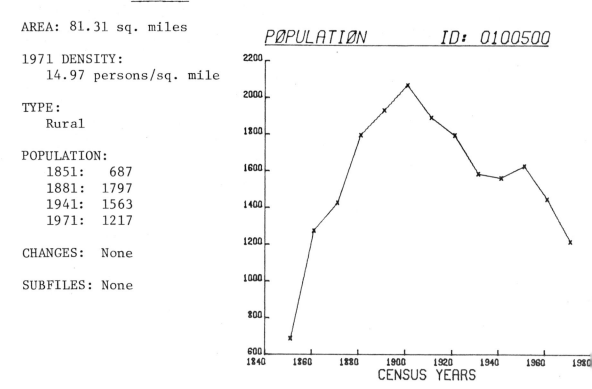

POPULATION   ID: 0100500

CENSUS YEARS

NOTES:

Land use in Bromley is discussed in 276 (Fraser, n.d.), p. 85, and 149 (Hardy, 1976), p. 23. Kennedy, 1970 (164), p. 186, discusses the history of Douglas.

Bromley is crossed by the Bonnechère River in the southwest corner and by the Snake River in the north. The unincorporated village of Douglas (1971 population 307) is located at the Third Chute on the Bonnechère, where the river falls 21 feet.

15

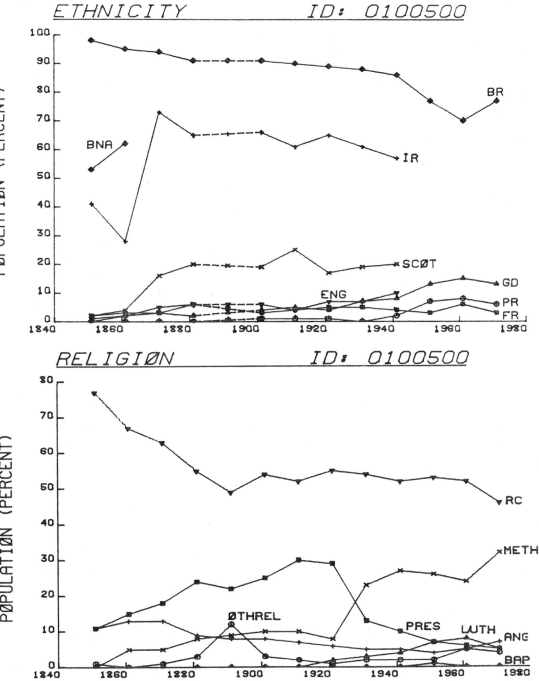

ID: 0100600 <u>BRUDENELL, LYNDOCH, RADCLIFFE, RAGLAN</u>

AREA: 344.04 sq. miles

1971 DENSITY:
 6.75 persons/sq. mile

TYPE:
 Rural

POPULATION:
 1861: 1023
 1881: 2148
 1941: 2538
 1971: 2323

CHANGES: 1861 created

SUBFILES:
 a. Brudenell, Lyndoch
 b. Radcliffe, Raglan

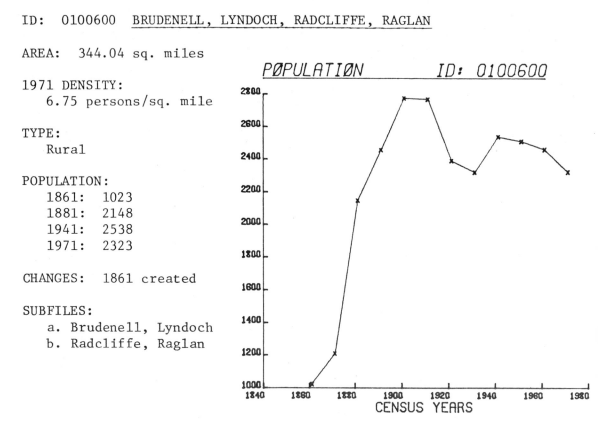

NOTES:

Kennedy, 1970 (164), pp. 174-177, discusses the important mining operations in the area. Brown, 1978 (11b) deals more particularly with the Craigmont Mine in Raglan Township (pp. 182-184) and with the community of Brudenell (pp. 131-132). See also 149 (Hardy, 1976), p. 23, for land use in the area.

The Opeongo Road crosses the area, passing through the middle of Brudenell. The largest ethnic group in Radcliffe is Polish; the Irish are concentrated in Brudenell; the Germans in Lyndoch and Raglan.

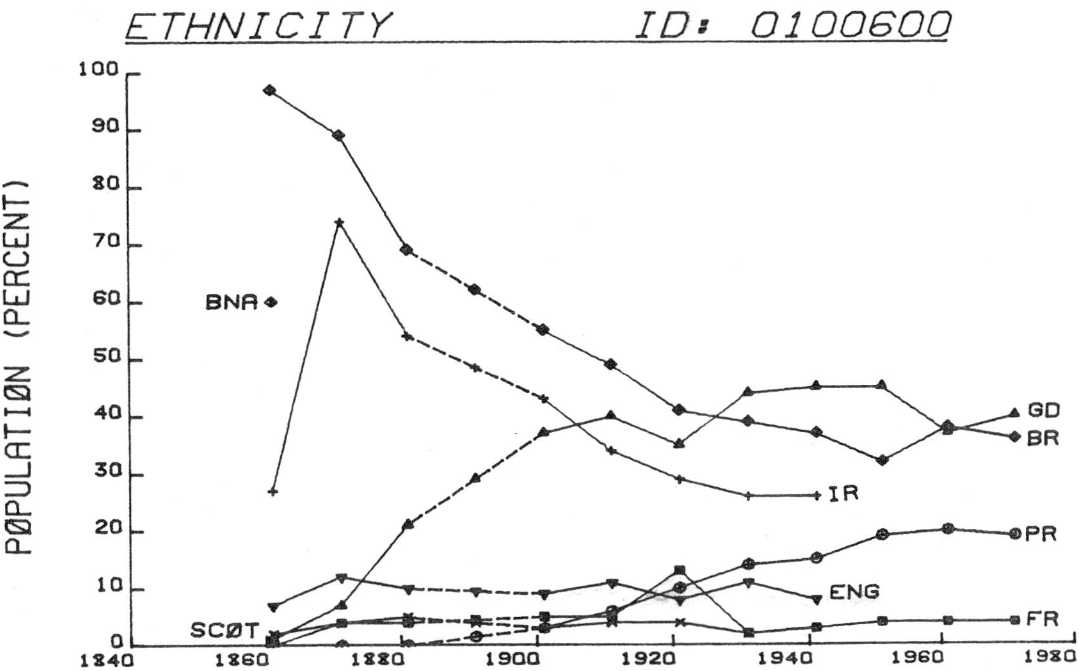
ETHNICITY
ID: 0100600
POPULATION (PERCENT)
100
90
80
70
60
50
40
30
20
10
0
1840
1860
1880
1900
1920
1940
1960
1980
BNA
GD
BR
IR
PR
ENG
FR
SCOT

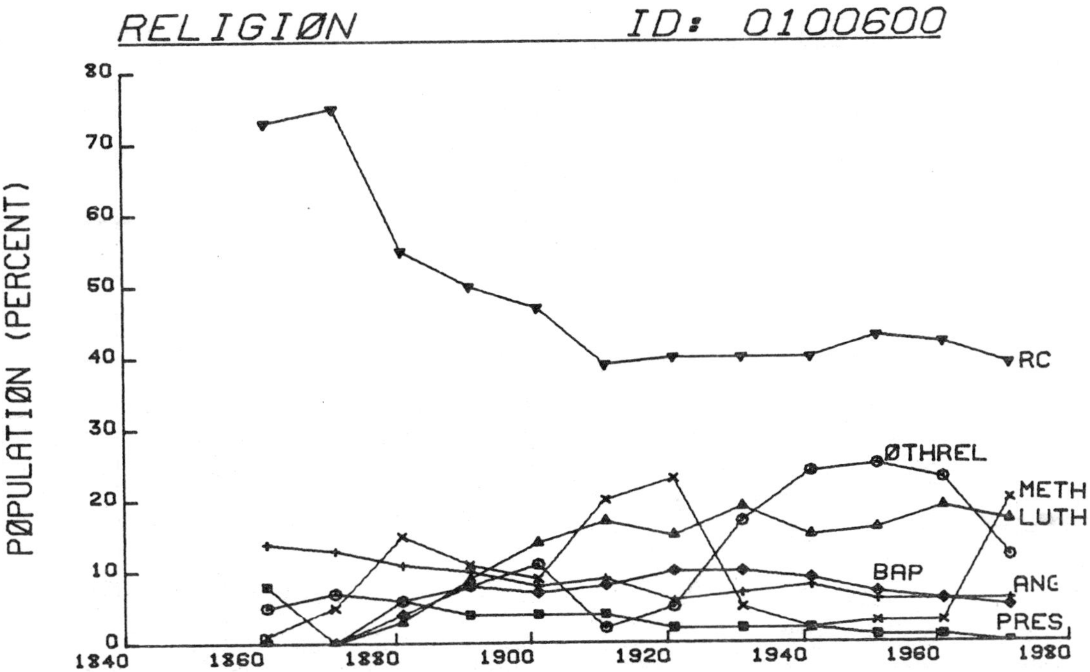
RELIGION
ID: 0100600
POPULATION (PERCENT)
80
70
60
50
40
30
20
10
0
1840
1860
1880
1900
1920
1940
1960
1980
RC
OTHREL
METH
LUTH
BAP
ANG
PRES

ID: 0100600   SUBFILES

a. BRUDENELL, LYNDOCH

   AREA: 171.39 sq. miles

   1971 DENSITY:
      4.92 persons/sq. mile

   POPULATION:
      1881:   1270
      1941:   1179
      1971:   843

b. RADCLIFFE, RAGLAN

   AREA: 172.65 sq. miles

   1971 DENSITY:
      8.57 persons/sq. mile

   POPULATION:
      1881:   878
      1941:   1359
      1971:   1480

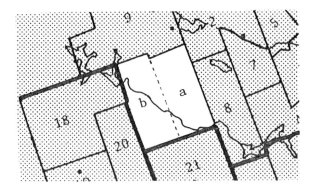

ID: 0100600   SUBFILES   cont'd

ETHNICITY

PLACE		YEAR	ENG	SCOT	IR	FR	GD	PR
Brudenell,	Lyndoch	1881	143	31	884	30	180	2
Brudenell,	Lyndoch	1941	115	4	444	16	539	61
Brudenell		1941	66	2	349	5	178	60
Lyndoch		1941	49	2	95	11	361	1
Radcliffe,	Raglan	1881	68	82	282	58	265	7
Radcliffe,	Raglan	1941	93	69	207	68	611	310
Radcliffe		1941	55	27	76	35	83	294
Raglan		1941	38	42	131	33	528	16

RELIGION

PLACE		YEAR	ANG	RC	PRES	METH/UC	BAP	LUTH
Brudenell,	Lyndoch	1881	130	913	38	99	61	
Brudenell,	Lyndoch	1941	52	537	4	20	221	144
Brudenell		1941	37	427	0	0	77	9
Lyndoch		1941	15	110	4	20	144	135
Radcliffe,	Raglan	1881	117	270	91	217	18	62
Radcliffe,	Raglan	1941	155	482	43	25	15	237
Radcliffe		1941	131	375	2	10	13	2
Raglan		1941	24	107	41	15	2	235

ID: 0100799 <u>GRATTAN</u>

AREA: 111.54 sq. miles

1971 DENSITY:
   23.94 persons/sq. mile

TYPE:
   Combined

POPULATION:
   1851:   554
   1881:   1893
   1941:   2488
   1971:   2670

CHANGES: 1891 Eganville
   incorporated; 1951 part
   of Wilberforce (in
   0100200) annexed to
   Eganville.

SUBFILES:
   a. Grattan (Rural)
   b. Eganville

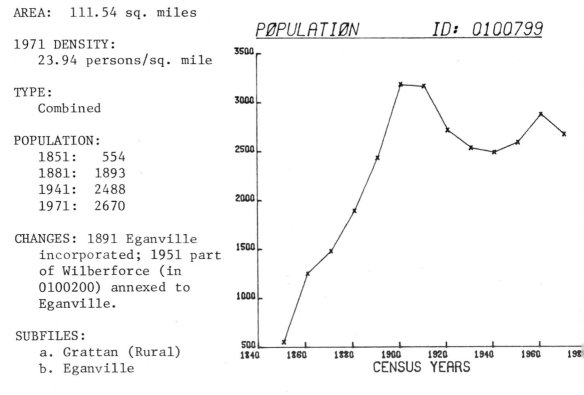

POPULATION   *ID: 0100799*

CENSUS YEARS

NOTES:

Lee-Whiting 1967 (245), discusses the granting of lots along the
Opeongo Road in 1844-46, and (246) the history of a sawmill in the
Township.

Note the steady increase in the German percentage from 1861 to 1961.

21

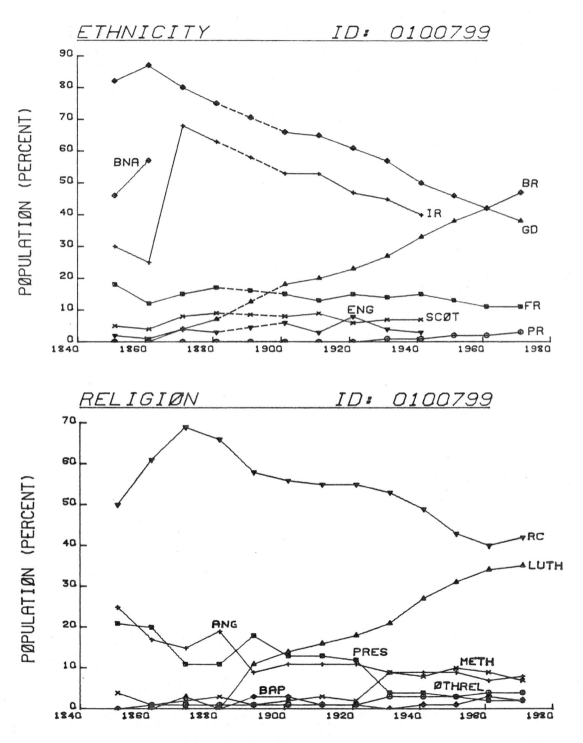

ID: 0100799 SUBFILES

a. GRATTAN (RURAL)

AREA: 110.62 sq. miles

1971 DENSITY:
11.53 persons/sq. mile

POPULATION:
1891: 1724
1941: 1400
1971: 1275

CHANGES: 1891 Eganville
incorporated.

b. EGANVILLE

AREA: 0.92 sq. miles

1971 DENSITY:
1516.30 persons/sq. mile

POPULATION:
1891:   710
1941: 1088
1971: 1395

CHANGES: 1891 incorporated; 1951 annexed part of Wilberforce
(in 0100200).

ID: 0100799 SUBFILES cont'd

ETHNICITY

PLACE	YEAR	ENG	SCOT	IR	FR	GD	PR
Grattan (Rural)	1901	116	134	1051	421	328	10
Grattan (Rural)	1941	37	102	553	310	381	12
Eganville	1901	65	111	632	50	231	1
Eganville	1941	44	72	441	72	428	18

RELIGION

PLACE	YEAR	ANG	RC	PRES	METH/UC	BAP	LUTH
Grattan (Rural)	1901	222	1272	220	20	60	284
Grattan (Rural)	1941	137	745	77	75	5	300
Eganville	1901	132	500	194	58	30	177
Eganville	1941	84	465	18	126	20	365

ID: 0100800   GRIFFITH, MATAWATCHAN, SEBASTOPOL

AREA: 214.16 sq. miles

1971 DENSITY:
    5.29 persons/sq. mile

TYPE:
    Rural

POPULATION:
    1861:   590
    1881:   1240
    1941:   907
    1971:   1132

CHANGES: 1861 created.

SUBFILES:
    a. Griffith,
        Matawatchan
    b. Sebastopol

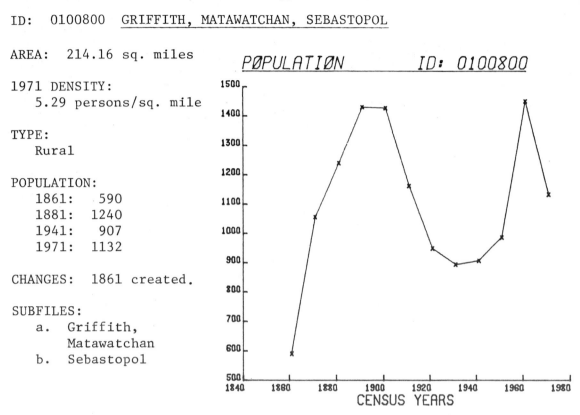

POPULATION   ID: 0100800

CENSUS YEARS

NOTES:

Lee-Whiting 1967 (245) mentions German settlement in Sebastopol in
1862. Kennedy, 1970 (164) mentions molybdenum operations in
Griffith, (45).

The Opeongo Mountain Range, an escarpment which in places rises
600 feet, cuts across Sebastopol. Lake Clear is also found in
Sebastopol.

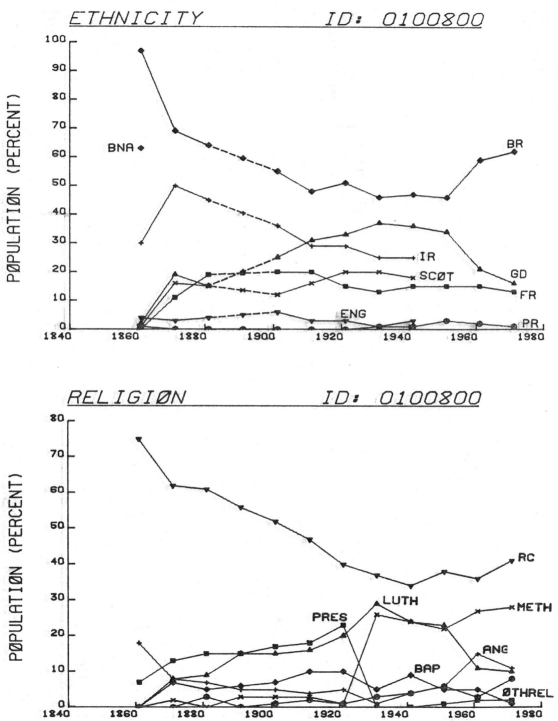

ETHNICITY   ID: 0100800

RELIGION   ID: 0100800

ID: 0100800   SUBFILES

a. GRIFFITH, MATAWATCHAN

   AREA: 144.48 sq. miles

   1971 DENSITY:
      2.27 persons/sq. mile

   POPULATION:
      1881: 614
      1941: 442
      1971: 328

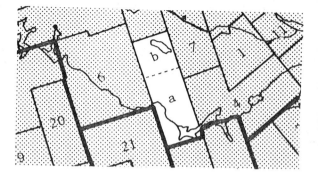

b. SEBASTOPOL

   AREA: 69.68 sq. miles

   1971 DENSITY:
      11.54 persons/sq.
      mile

   POPULATION:
      1881: 626
      1941: 465
      1971: 804

ID: 0100800   SUBFILES   cont'd

ETHNICITY

PLACE	YEAR	ENG	SCOT	IR	FR	GD	PR
Griffith, Matawatchan	1881	29	167	190	206	3	0
Griffith, Matawatchan	1941	25	164	89	121	33	5
Sebastopol	1881	17	16	372	32	189	0
Sebastopol	1941	3	2	141	12	297	4

RELIGION

PLACE	YEAR	ANG	RC	PRES	METH/UC	BAP	LUTH
Griffith, Matawatchan	1881	48	368	180	0		
Griffith, Matawatchan	1941	18	171	0	209	8	4
Sebastopol	1881	36	385	10	4	61	102
Sebastopol	1941	21	140	3	11	75	212

ID: 0100999   HAGARTY, BURNS, JONES, RICHARDS, SHERWOOD

AREA: 347.74 sq. miles

1971 DENSITY:
    14.85 persons/sq. mile

TYPE:
    Combined

POPULATION:
    1881:   1442
    1941:   4872
    1971:   5161

CHANGES: 1881 created;
    1911 Killaloe Station
    incorporated; 1941
    Barry's Bay incorpor-
    ated.

SUBFILES:
    a. Hagarty (Rural),
       Richards
    b. Sherwood (Rural),
       Jones, Burns
    c. Killaloe Station
    d. Barry's Bay

PØPULATIØN   ID: 0100999

CENSUS YEARS

NOTES:

Aspects of the Polish settlements in this area are discussed in 244
(Lee-Whiting, 1967), pp. 108-112; 69b (Makowski, 1967), pp. 56, 61-2,
64; 78 (Radecki and Heyden Korn, 1976), pp. 21-2.

Information relating to land use in the area is presented in 276
(Fraser, n.d.), p. 78 and 149 (Hardy, 1976), p. 23. See also 189
(Price and Kennedy, 1961), p. 94. Killaloe Station is the subject
of a monograph item 140 (Garvey, 1967).

Note the continuous Polish majority since 1901. Most of the population of the five townships resides in Hagarty and Sherwood. The
unincorporated village of Wilno, almost entirely Polish, had a
population of 190 in 1971. Round Lake Centre's population was 229.

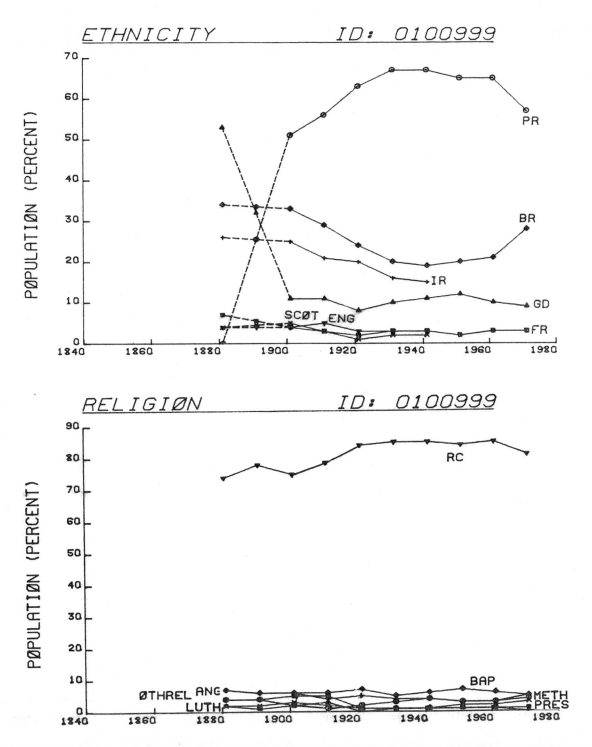

ETHNICITY   ID: 0100999

RELIGION   ID: 0100999

ID: 0100999 SUBFILES

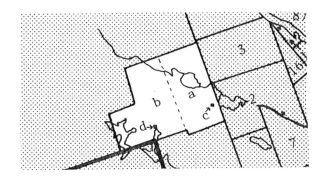

a. <u>HAGARTY (RURAL), RICHARDS</u>

   AREA: 154.51 sq. miles

   1971 DENSITY:
      9.0 persons/sq. mile

   POPULATION:
      1941: 1741
      1971: 1391

   CHANGES: 1911 Killaloe Station incorporated.

b. <u>SHERWOOD (RURAL), JONES, BURNS</u>

   AREA: 191.04 sq. miles

   1971 DENSITY:
      8.0 persons/sq. mile

   POPULATION:
      1941: 1305
      1971: 1528

   CHANGES: 1941 Barry's Bay incorporated.

c. <u>KILLALOE STATION</u>

   AREA: 1.19 sq. miles

   1971 DENSITY:
      810.0 persons/sq. mile

   POPULATION:
      1911: 435
      1941: 628
      1971: 810

   CHANGES: 1911 incorporated.

ID: 0100999   SUBFILES   cont'd

d. <u>BARRY'S BAY</u>

   AREA: 1.19 sq. miles

   1971 DENSITY:
     1203.36 persons/sq. mile

   POPULATION:
     1941:   1198
     1971:   1432

   CHANGES: 1941 incorporated.

<u>ETHNICITY</u>

PLACE	YEAR	ENG	SCOT	IR	FR	GD	PR
Hagarty (Rural)	1941	54	11	218	22	224	969
Richards	1941	9	4	32	27	28	143
Sherwood (Rural)	1941	2	2	19	4	9	987
Jones	1941	11	7	29	25	9	163
Burns	1941	1	0	0	5	0	26
Killaloe Station	1941	28	43	203	20	222	111
Barry's Bay	1941	30	11	217	40	26	852

<u>RELIGION</u>

PLACE	YEAR	ANG	RC	PRES	METH/UC	BAP	LUTH
Hagarty (Rural)	1941	62	1187	23	7	139	15
Richards	1941	48	175	1	0	6	0
Sherwood (Rural)	1941	2	1016	1	3	0	0
Jones	1941	17	219	6	1	0	2
Burns	1941	1	25	0	0	0	0
Killaloe Station	1941	29	369	5	4	126	11
Barry's Bay	1941	34	1144	1	15		1

ID: 0101000 HEAD, CLARA, MARIA

AREA: 308.91 sq. miles

1971 DENSITY:
   1.53 persons/sq. mile

TYPE:
   Rural

POPULATION:
   1871: 140
   1881: 953
   1941: 620
   1971: 474

CHANGES: Created 1871:
   Head only.

SUBFILES:
   a. Head
   b. Clara
   c. Maria

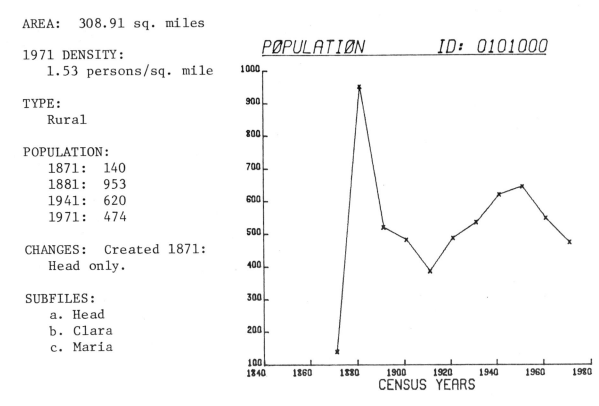

POPULATION   ID: 0101000

CENSUS YEARS

NOTES:

149   (Hardy, 1976), p. 23 gives details on land use in the area in
      1974.

In 1881 Clara and Maria Townships were added to Head.

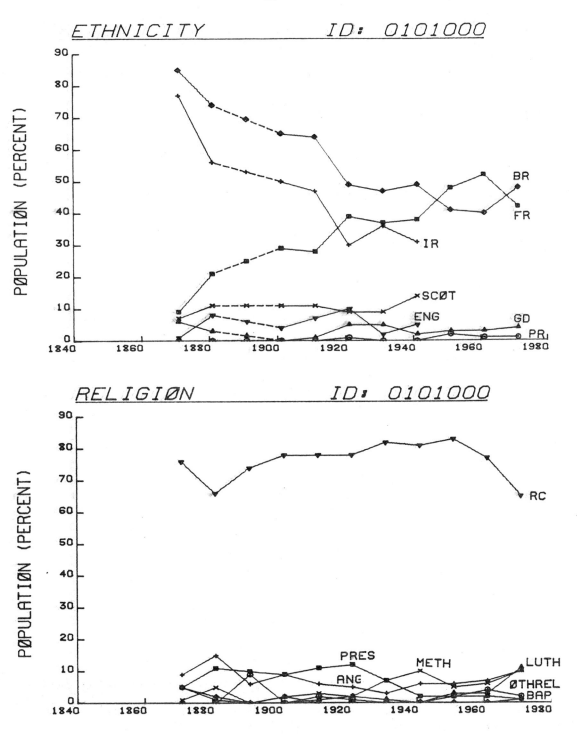

ID: 0101000 SUBFILES

HEAD, CLARA, MARIA

(Township Breakdown of Area,
Density and Population not
available for 1971)

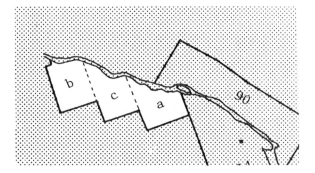

HEAD, CLARA, MARIA

ETHNICITY

PLACE	YEAR	ENG	SCOT	IR	FR	GD	PR
Head	1921	25	15	87	136	5	2
Head	1941	11	29	91	171	2	0
Clara	1921	8	19	49	42	20	0
Clara	1941	17	37	72	44	12	0
Maria	1921	15	12	11	11	1	2
Maria	1941	1	18	29	20	1	0

ID: 0101000 SUBFILES cont'd

<u>RELIGION</u>

PLACE	YEAR	ANG	RC	PRES	METH/UC	BAP	LUTH
Head	1921	2	263	24	2		0
Head	1941	4	310	8	6		2
Clara	1921	22	90	16	7		8
Clara	1941	32	131	2	53		1
Maria	1921	1	30	18	2		
Maria	1941	0	59	4	6		

ID: 0101199 <u>HORTON</u>

AREA: 65.85 sq. miles

1971 DENSITY:
   165.21 persons/sq. mile

TYPE:
   Combined

POPULATION:
   1851:   1142
   1881:   3115
   1941:   6659
   1971: 10879

CHANGES: 1861 Renfrew
   incorporated; 1971 part
   of rural area annexed to
   Renfrew.

SUBFILES:
   a. Horton (Rural)
   b. Renfrew

NOTES

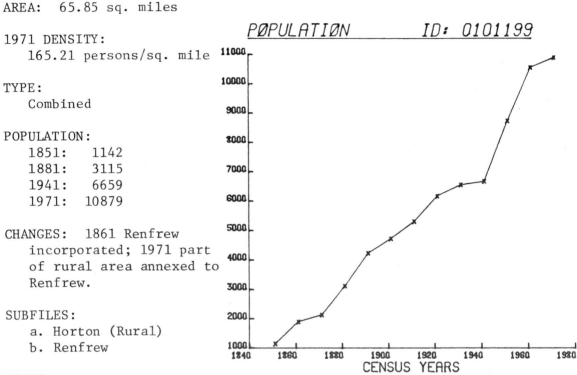

149 (Hardy, 1976), p. 23 gives details on land use in the rural area.
Aspects of Renfrew's economy are noted in 134 (E.O.D.C., 1971), p. 54;
(Dean, 1969), Plate 34; 149 (Hardy, 1976), p. 18.

The history of the town is summarized in 164 (Kennedy, 1970),
pp. 183-185.

Most of the population growth in the township has taken place in the
town of Renfrew.

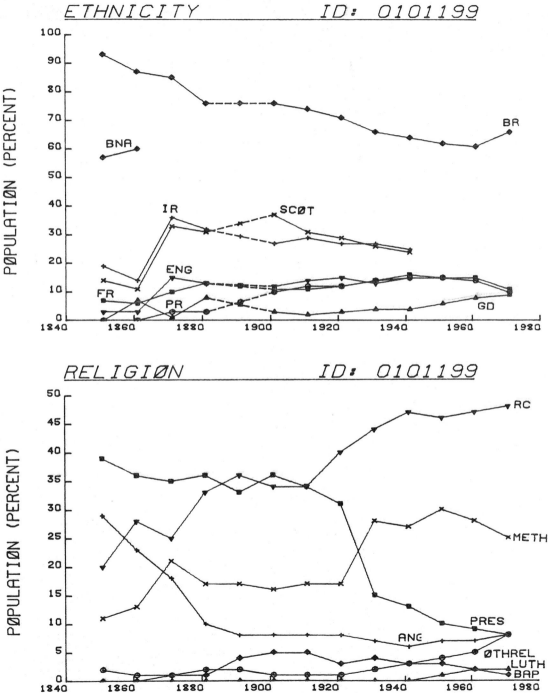

ETHNICITY   ID: 0101199

RELIGIØN   ID: 0101199

ID: 0101199 SUBFILES

a. HORTON (RURAL)

AREA: 61.28 sq. miles

1971 DENSITY:
27.84 persons/sq. mile

POPULATION:
1881: 1510
1941: 1148
1971: 1706

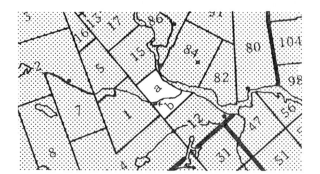

CHANGES: 1861 Renfrew incorporated; 1971 part annexed to Renfrew.

b. RENFREW

AREA: 4.57 sq. miles

1971 DENSITY:
2007.22 persons/sq. mile

POPULATION:
1881: 1605
1941: 5511
1971: 9173

CHANGES: 1861 incorporated; 1971 annexed part of Horton (Rural).

ID: 0101199 SUBFILES cont'd

ETHNICITY

PLACE	YEAR	ENG	SCOT	IR	FR	GD	PR
Horton (Rural)	1881	210	541	610	46	14	82
Horton (Rural)	1941	161	418	235	70	46	215
Renfrew	1881	191	420	399	345	220	0
Renfrew	1941	857	1151	1426	970	231	798

RELIGION

PLACE	YEAR	ANG	RC	PRES	METH/UC	BAP	LUTH
Horton (Rural)	1881	211	249	610	406		
Horton (Rural)	1941	40	313	238	453	24	
Renfrew	1881	114	781	515	136	23	
Renfrew	1941	366	2831	650	1334	192	19

ID: 0101299 McNAB

AREA: 104.08 sq. miles

1971 DENSITY:
  96.94 persons/sq. mile

TYPE:
  Combined

POPULATION:
  1851:   1513
  1881:   3266
  1941:   6965
  1971: 10089

CHANGES: 1861 Arnprior
  incorporated; 1931 Braeside incorporated; 1961
  part of rural area
  annexed to Arnprior.

SUBFILES:
  a. McNab (Rural)
  b. Arnprior
  c. Braeside

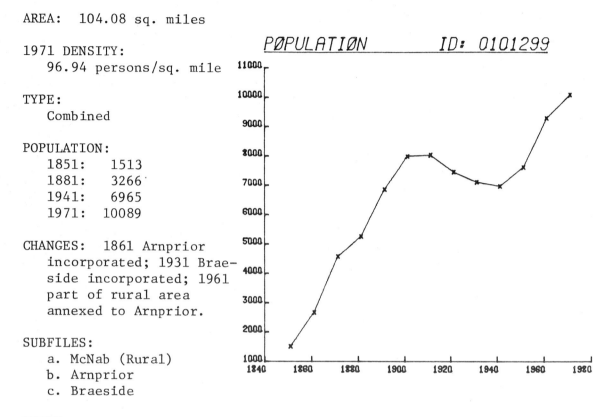

POPULATION   ID: 0101299

NOTES:

Fraser, 1914 (235) discusses the McNab settlement. Details on the
history of Arnprior are included in 212 (Whitton, 1943), pp. 62-4,
and 96b (Arnprior Centennial, 1962), especially pp. 72-8. Aspects of
the history of Braeside are discussed in 212 (Whitton, 1943),
pp. 62-5. Information relating to industry in the area is given in
28 (Dean, 1969), Plate 35, and 134 (E.O.D.C., 1971), pp. 5,6.

Considerable census information on McNab Township is available in
tables dealing with the Census Agglomeration of Arnprior. Urbanized
Core: Arnprior and the adjacent unincorporated area of Mansfield and
Dochart (1971 population 1128); Rural Fringe: Braeside and the rest
of McNab Township. The 1971 population of the unincorporated village
of White Lake was 217.

41

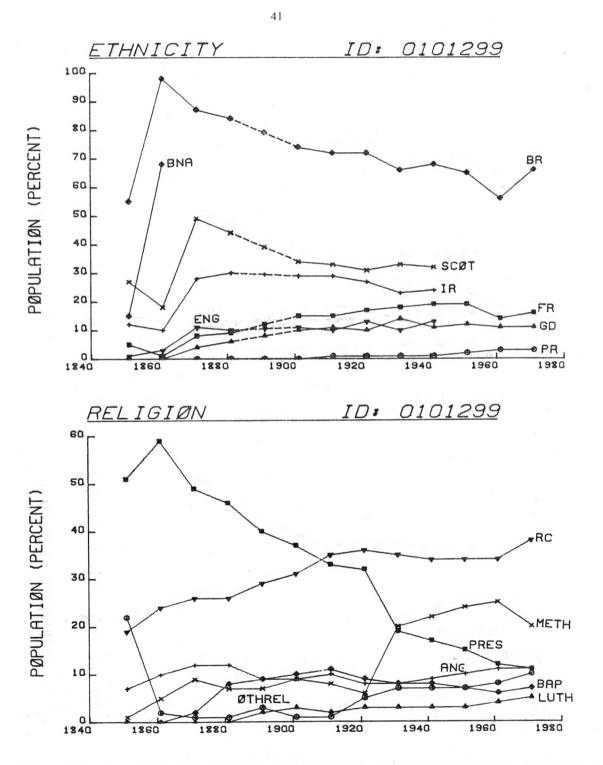

ID: 0101299   SUBFILES

a. McNAB (RURAL)

AREA: 99.97 sq. miles

1971 DENSITY:
   35.52 persons/sq. mile

POPULATION:
   1881: 3092
   1941: 2565
   1971: 3551

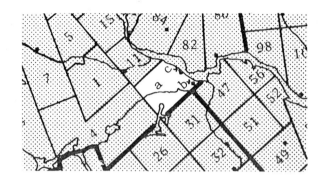

CHANGES: 1861 Arnprior incorporated; 1931 Braeside incorporated;
   1961 part annexed to Arnprior.

b. ARNPRIOR

AREA: 3.29 sq. miles

1971 DENSITY:
   1828.57 persons/sq. mile

POPULATION:
   1881: 2174
   1941: 3895
   1971: 6016

CHANGES: 1861 incorporated;
   1961 annexed part of McNab
   (Rural).

c. BRAESIDE

AREA: 0.82 sq. miles

1971 DENSITY:
   636.59 persons/sq. mile

POPULATION:
   1941: 505
   1971: 522

CHANGES: 1931 incorpor-
   ated.

ID: 0101299 SUBFILES cont'd

ETHNICITY

PLACE	YEAR	ENG	SCOT	IR	FR	GD	PR
McNab (Rural)	1881	216	1768	792	103	204	0
McNab (Rural)	1941	203	1290	497	246	292	18
Arnprior	1881	327	523	795	353	133	0
Arnprior	1941	609	723	1052	947	492	19
Braeside	1941	77	194	103	128	3	0

RELIGION

PLACE	YEAR	ANG	RC	PRES	METH/UC	BAP	LUTH
McNab (Rural)	1881	206	578	1851	119	315	
McNab (Rural)	1941	134	476	676	693	263	106
Arnprior	1881	416	768	586	247	108	
Arnprior	1941	498	1708	408	630	293	119
Braeside	1941	23	156	102	194	14	

ID: 0101399 <u>PEMBROKE</u>

AREA: 15.52 sq. miles

1971 DENSITY:
   1140.91 persons/sq. mile

TYPE:
   Combined

POPULATION:
   1851:   633
   1881:   3503
   1941:   11583
   1971:   17707

CHANGES: 1861 town of
   Pembroke incorporated;
   1961 annexed part of
   Stafford (0101600).

SUBFILES:
   a. Pembroke (Rural)
   b. Pembroke (Urban)

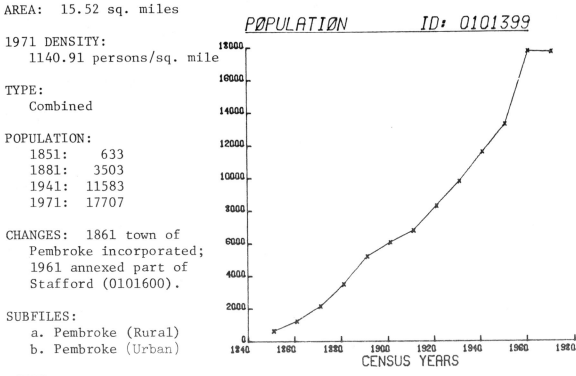

POPULATION   ID: 0101399

CENSUS YEARS

NOTES:

The area is featured extensively in the standard historical works on the Upper Ottawa Valley. It is also the subject of a monograph, 188b (Pembroke Centennial, 1958).

The recent economic circumstances of the town (or, since 1971, the city) of Pembroke are outlined in 28 (Dean, 1969), Plates 33, 34, and 134 (E.O.D.C., 1971), pp. 45-6.

Considerable census information on the city of Pembroke is available in tables dealing with the Census Agglomeration of Pembroke.

The large population growth in the township centres on the city of Pembroke and adjacent areas.

45

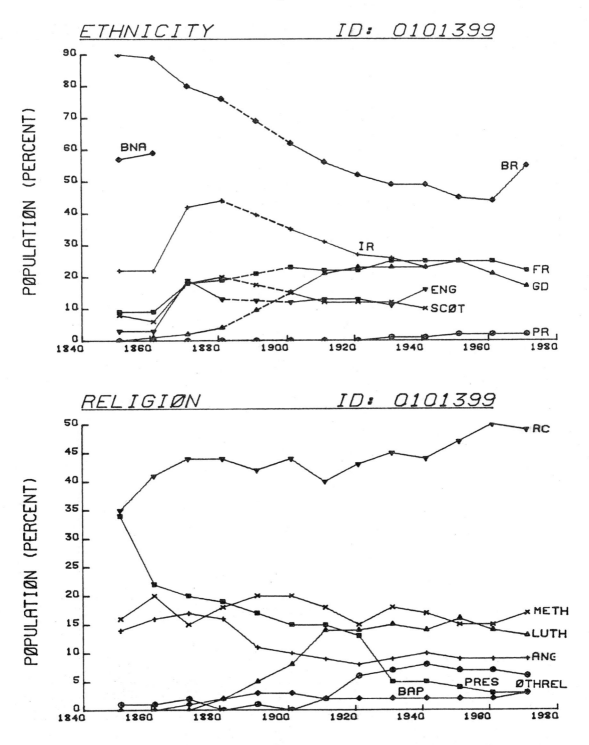

ID: 0101399   SUBFILES

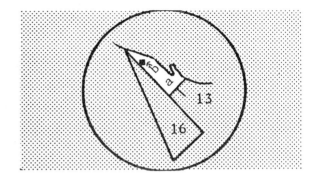

a. PEMBROKE (RURAL)

   AREA: 11.53 sq. miles

   1971 DENSITY:
      100.87 persons/sq. mile

   POPULATION:
      1881:   683
      1941:   424
      1971:   1163

   CHANGES: 1881 Pembroke incorporated; 1961 part annexed to
      Pembroke (Urban).

b. PEMBROKE (URBAN)

   AREA: 3.99 sq. miles

   1971 DENSITY:
      4146.37 persons/sq. mile

   POPULATION:
      1881:   2820
      1941:   11159
      1971:   16544

   CHANGES: 1861 incorporated; 1961 annexed parts of Pembroke (Rural)
      and Stafford (0101600).

ID: 0101399 SUBFILES cont'd

ETHNICITY

PLACE		YEAR	ENG	SCOT	IR	FR	GD	PR
Pembroke	(Rural)	1881	135	167	288	65	14	0
Pembroke	(Rural)	1941	45	48	189	75	66	1
Pembroke	(Urban)	1881	311	524	1243	591	135	1
Pembroke	(Urban)	1941	1824	1128	2425	2791	2626	161

RELIGION

PLACE		YEAR	ANG	RC	PRES	METH/UC	BAP	LUTH
Pembroke	(Rural)	1881	90	245	132	214		
Pembroke	(Rural)	1941	47	92	5	156	0	24
Pembroke	(Urban)	1881	457	1297	517	400	55	80
Pembroke	(Urban)	1941	1110	5030	536	1783	263	1608

ID: 0101499 PETAWAWA, BUCHANAN, McKAY, ROLPH, WYLIE

AREA: 357.67 sq. miles

1971 DENSITY:
   64.64 persons/sq. mile

TYPE:
   Combined

POPULATION:
   1861:   639
   1881:   1388
   1941:   3028
   1971: 23121

CHANGES: 1861 created;
   1951 Camp Petawawa
   included; 1961 Deep
   River, Chalk River and
   Petawawa incorporated.

SUBFILES:
   a. Petawawa (Rural)
   b. Buchanan (Rural),
      McKay, Rolph (Rural),
      Wylie
   c. Deep River
   d. Chalk River
   e. Petawawa (Urban)

POPULATION   ID: 0101499

CENSUS YEARS

NOTES:

Kennedy, 1970 (149), pp. 205, 207, 221-2, deals with the settlement of
the region and its subsequent history. Price and Kennedy, 1961 (189),
deals more particularly with Chalk River and Deep River (see pp. 94-6).
An article in the Globe and Mail (Sept. 12, 1978, p. 8) discusses the
economic circumstances of the area, and further information is given
in 149 (Hardy, 1976), pp. 23-6.

Considerable census information on Petawawa Township is available in
tables dealing with the Census Agglomeration of Petawawa. The northern half of the township is part of the Urbanized Core; the southern
half is Rural Fringe. The unincorporated village of Rolphton (in
Rolph township) had a population of 418 in 1971. The large increase
of population after 1941 is due mainly to the presence of the
military base and later nuclear installations.

49

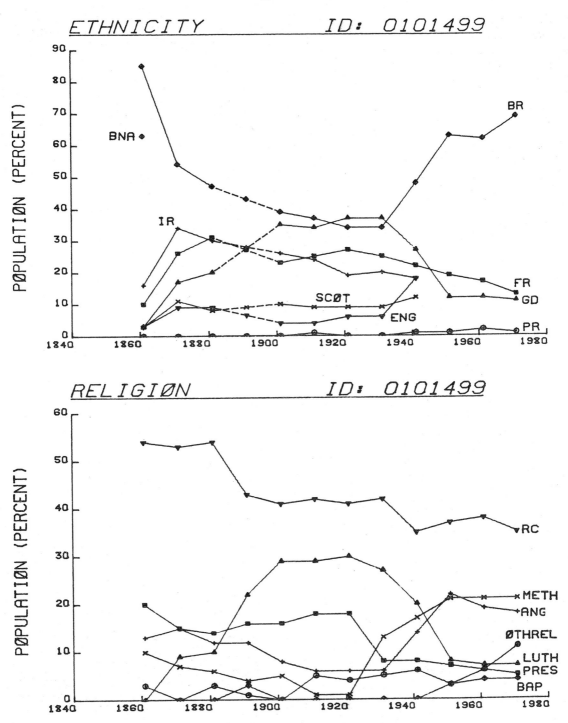

ID: 0101499 SUBFILES

a. PETAWAWA (RURAL)

   AREA: 69.06 sq miles

   1971 DENSITY:
     123.17 persons/sq. mile

   POPULATION:
     1951:   6200
     1971:   8506 (Rural)

   CHANGES: 1951 Petawawa Military Camp included; 1961 Petawawa
   incorporated.

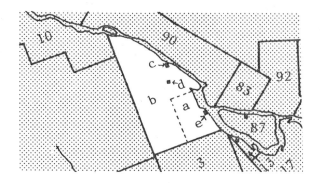

b. BUCHANAN (RURAL), McKAY, ROLPH (RURAL), WYLIE

   AREA: 266.0 sq. miles

   1971 DENSITY:
     7.77 persons/sq. mile

   POPULATION:
     1951: 2558
     1971: 2066

   CHANGES: 1951 Deep River excluded;
   1961 Deep River incorporated;
   Chalk River incorporated.

c. DEEP RIVER

   AREA: 19.57 sq. miles

   1971 DENSITY:
     289.78 persons/sq. mile

   POPULATION:
     1951: 2043
     1971: 5671

   CHANGES: 1951 separate entry;
   1961 incorporated.

d. CHALK RIVER

   AREA: 0.87 sq. miles

   1971 DENSITY:
     1257.47 persons/sq. mi.

   POPULATION:
     1971: 1094

e. PETAWAWA (URBAN)

   AREA: 2.17 sq. miles

   1971 DENSITY:
     2665.44 persons/sq. mi.

   POPULATION:
     1971: 5784

   CHANGES: 1961 incorporated.

ID: 0101499 SUBFILES cont'd

ETHNICITY

PLACE	YEAR	ENG	SCOT	IR	FR	GD	PR
Petawawa, McKay	1881	22	33	169	196	247	5
Petawawa, McKay	1941	449	212	227	272	588	13
Petawawa	1951	(British)	3984		1064	861	45
Petawawa (Rural)	1971	(British)	5710		1010	1240	165
Buchanan, Rolph, Wylie	1881	102	81	242	241	29	0
Buchanan, Rolph, Wylie	1941	87	144	333	387	219	4
Buchanan	1941	61	89	190	207	149	3
Rolph	1941	13	38	95	152	57	1
Wylie	1941	13	17	48	28	13	0
Buchanan, McKay, Rolph (Rural), Wylie	1951	(British)	1228		740	296	94
Buchanan (Rural), McKay, Rolph (Rural), Wylie	1971	(British)	1215		605	155	25
Deep River	1951	(British)	1645		196	89	30
Deep River	1971	(British)	4310		500	355	65
Chalk River	1971	(British)	690		245	115	5
Petawawa (Urban)	1971	(British)	3985		710	670	65

ID: 0101499 SUBFILES cont'd

RELIGION

PLACE	YEAR	ANG	RC	PRES	METH/UC	BAP	LUTH
Petawawa, McKay	1881	73	349	60	29		145
Petawawa, McKay	1941	338	440	178	248		490
Petawawa	1951	1571	2165	407	998	247	635
Petawawa (Rural)	1971	1620	3020	335	1685	525	970
Buchanan, Rolph, Wylie	1881	100	398	141	55		
Buchanan, Rolph, Wylie	1941	83	631	72	265		115
Buchanan	1941	49	326	34	200	1	95
Rolph	1941	10	245	38	41	5	12
Wylie	1941	24	60	0	24		8
Buchanan, McKay, Rolph (Rural), Wylie	1951	228	1291	153	557	24	204
Buchanan (Rural), McKay, Rolph (Rural), Wylie	1971	310	1065	120	320	30	65
Deep River	1951	539	529	151	671	44	29
Deep River	1971	1040	1690	240	1400	120	135
Chalk River	1971	145	575	45	210	20	65
Petawawa (Urban)	1971	970	2430	310	1170	255	410

ID: 0101599 ROSS

AREA: 88.42 sq. miles

1971 DENSITY:
  28.44 persons/sq. mile

TYPE:
  Combined

POPULATION:
  1851:   708
  1881: 2131
  1941: 2123
  1971: 2515

CHANGES: 1901 Cobden
  incorporated.

SUBFILES:
  a. Ross (Rural)
  b. Cobden

POPULATION   ID: 0101599

CENSUS YEARS

NOTES:

The historical importance of Cobden is explained in: 164 (Kennedy, 1970), p. 19. Figures relating to the economic base of the township are presented in 149 (Hardy, 1976), pp. 13, 23.

The unincorporated village of Forester's Falls had a population of 164 in 1971.

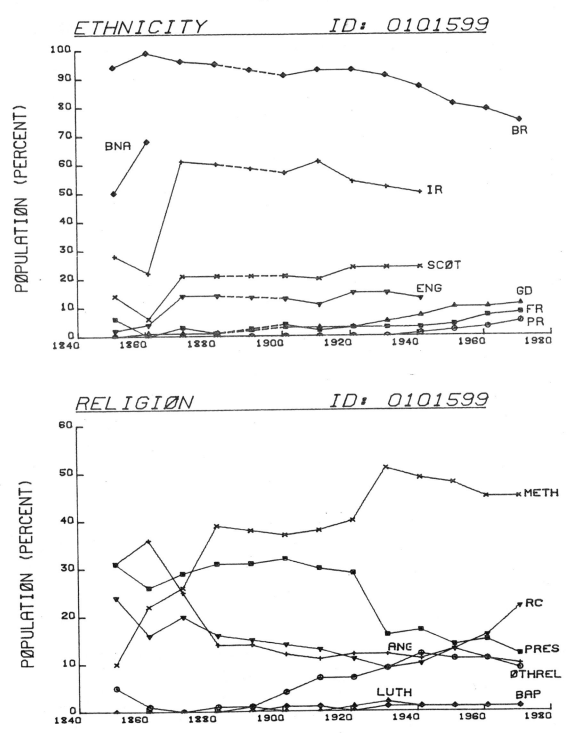

ID: 0101599   SUBFILES

a. ROSS (RURAL)

   AREA: 87.68 sq. miles

   1971 DENSITY:
      18.12 persons/sq. mile

   POPULATION:
      1901: 2269
      1941: 1467
      1971: 1589

   CHANGES: 1901 Cobden incorporated.

b. COBDEN

   AREA: 0.74 sq. miles

   1971 DENSITY:
      1251.35 persons/sq. mile

   POPULATION:
      1901: 734
      1941: 656
      1971: 926

   CHANGES: 1901 incorporated.

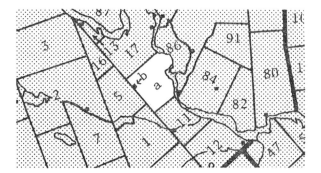

ID: 0101599 SUBFILES cont'd

ETHNICITY

PLACE	YEAR	ENG	SCOT	IR	FR	GD	PR
Ross (Rural)	1901	292	472	1330	57	93	9
Ross (Rural)	1941	191	355	739	37	129	8
Cobden	1901	106	162	373	57	4	0
Cobden	1941	87	152	328	37	29	4

RELIGION

PLACE	YEAR	ANG	RC	PRES	METH/UC	BAP	LUTH
Ross (Rural)	1901	180	260	791	910	25	8
Ross (Rural)	1941	101	108	258	790	7	19
Cobden	1901	168	148	170	214		
Cobden	1941	127	101	107	248	7	

ID: 0101600 <u>STAFFORD</u>

AREA: 34.79 sq. miles

1971 DENSITY:
  107.93 persons/sq. mile

TYPE:
  Rural

POPULATION:
  1851: 281
  1881: 1055
  1941: 1280
  1971: 3755

CHANGES: 1961 part annexed
  to Pembroke (Urban) in
  0101399.

SUBFILES: None

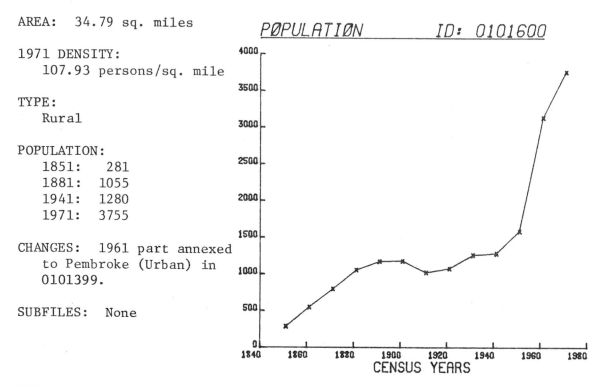

NOTES:

None of the sources examined deals particularly with Stafford Township.

Considerable census information on Stafford Township is available in the tables dealing with the Census Agglomeration of Pembroke. The northern tip of the township is part of the Urbanized Core, the remainder is Rural Fringe.

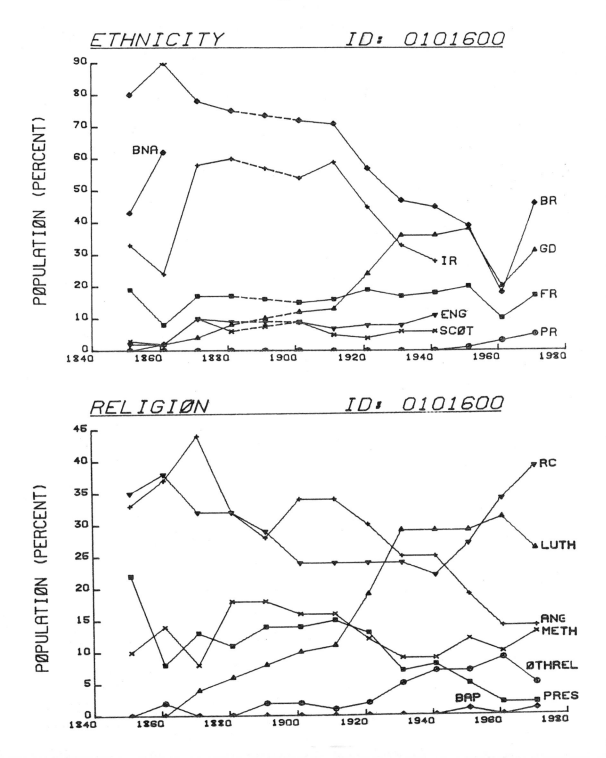

ID: 0101799   <u>WESTMEATH</u>

AREA: 118.57 sq. miles

1971 DENSITY:
   19.79 persons/sq. mile

TYPE:
   Combined

POPULATION:
   1851: 1152
   1881: 3220
   1941: 2715
   1971: 2346

CHANGES: Beachburg incorporated 1961.

SUBFILES:
   a. Westmeath (Rural)
   b. Beachburg

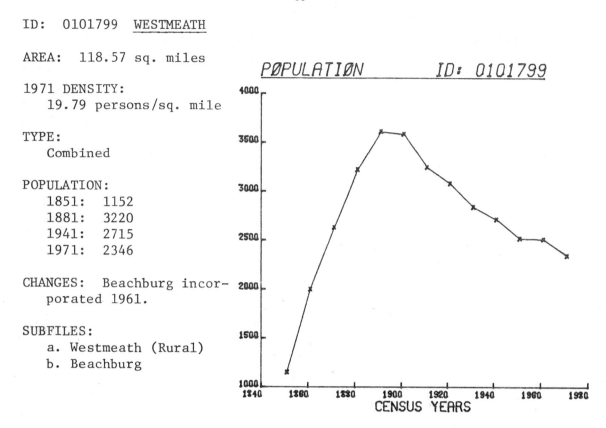

POPULATION   ID: 0101799

CENSUS YEARS

NOTES:

Mills (item 72), pp. 114-5, 126, discusses the Scottish element in Westmeath. Land use and the economic circumstances of the township are mentioned in 276 (Fraser, n.d.), p. 86; 149 (Hardy, 1976), pp. 13, 23; and 189 (Price and Kennedy, 1961), p. 92.

The unincorporated village of Westmeath had a population of 266 in 1971.

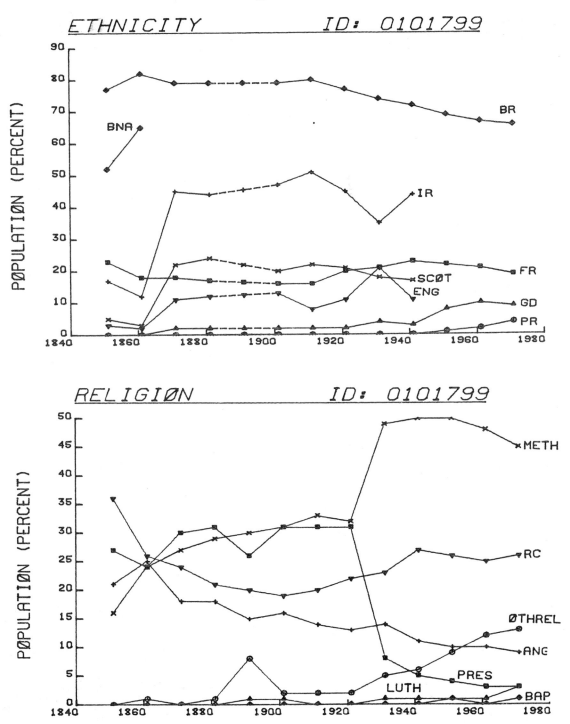

ID: 0101799 SUBFILES

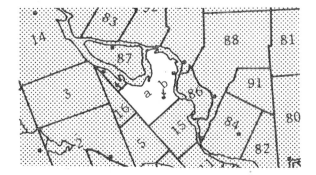

a. WESTMEATH (RURAL)

    AREA: 116.90 sq. miles

    1971 DENSITY:
      15.37 persons/sq. mile

    POPULATION:
      1961: 1972
      1971: 1797

b. BEACHBURG

    AREA: 1.67 sq. miles

    1971 DENSITY:
      328.74 persons/sq. mile

    POPULATION:
      1961: 542
      1971: 549

ID: 0101799 SUBFILES cont'd

ETHNICITY

PLACE		YEAR	ENG	SCOT	IR	FR	GD	PR
Westmeath	(Rural)	1961	(British)	1218		500	202	35
Westmeath	(Rural)	1971	(British)	1070		400	160	100
Beachburg		1961	(British)	459		18	58	6
Beachburg		1971	(British)	435		30	40	0

RELIGION

PLACE		YEAR	ANG	RC	PRES	METH/UC	BAP	LUTH
Westmeath	(Rural)	1961	138	625	62	871		31
Westmeath	(Rural)	1971	145	570	50	670	15	40
Beachburg		1961	111	14	9	346		
Beachburg		1971	70	20	25	345	15	20

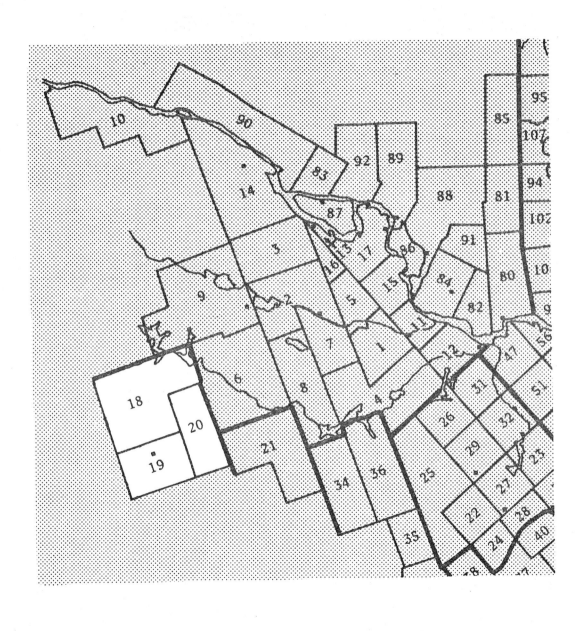

Only the northern townships of Hastings County fall within the
study area. As will be seen within, a small number of works deal
with some of these areas in some detail, but of the works listed
in the bibliography only 198 (Smith, 1956) and 263 (Richards, 1958)
deal with the whole of the portion of Hastings included in the study.
An important study of the whole County is 108 (Boyce, 1967), which
however emphasizes the southern townships.

The three IU's of the study area had a combined population of
7,578 in 1971, a combined area was 713.61 sq. miles, and a population density of 10.62. County wide totals for 1971: population
99,393; area 2,303.82 sq. miles; density 43.14 persons/sq. mile.

ID: 0201800 BANGOR, HERSCHEL, McCLURE, MONTEAGLE, WICKLOW

AREA: 381.16 sq. miles

1971 DENSITY:
    6.41 persons/sq. mile

TYPE:
    Rural

POPULATION:
    1871:   930
    1881:   1927
    1941:   2864
    1971:   2442

CHANGES: 1871 created.

SUBFILES:
    a. Bangor, McClure,
       Wicklow
    b. Herschel, Monteagle

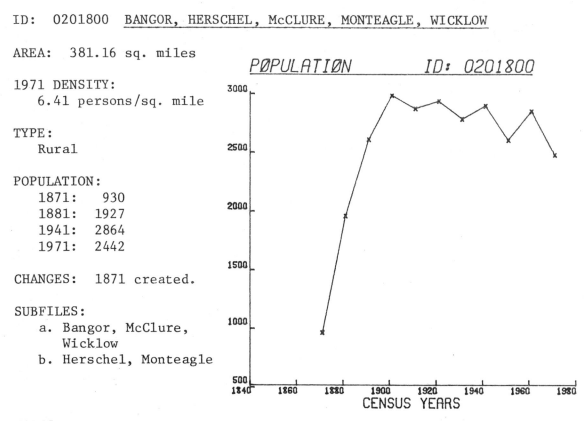

NOTES:

Monteagle, the most populated township of this group, contains the
unincorporated village of Maynooth (1971 population: 328). In 1941
the Irish were the largest British ethnic group in all five townships;
the Germans held the overall plurality in Bangor and Wicklow.

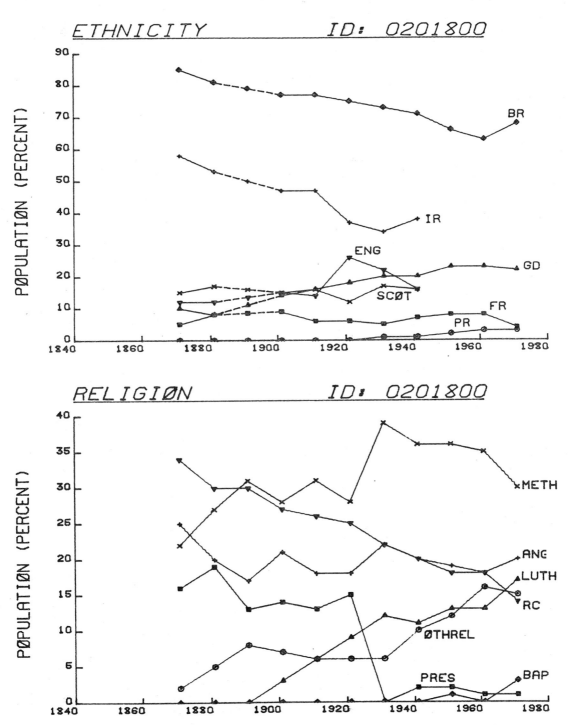

ID: 0201800 SUBFILES

a. <u>BANGOR, McCLURE, WICKLOW</u>

    AREA: 217.28 sq. miles

    1971 DENSITY:
       3.74 persons/sq. mile

    POPULATION:
       1881:   855
       1941: 1107
       1971:   812

b. <u>HERSCHEL, MONTEAGLE</u>

    AREA: 163.88 sq. miles

    1971 DENSITY:
       9.95 persons/sq. mile

    POPULATION:
       1881: 1072
       1941: 1757
       1971: 1630

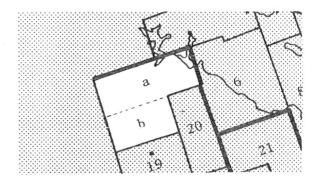

ID: 0201800 SUBFILES cont'd

ETHNICITY

PLACE	YEAR	ENG	SCOT	IR	FR	GD	PR
Bangor, McClure, Wicklow	1881	143	188	391	65	50	0
Bangor, McClure, Wicklow	1941	151	174	341	79	334	22
Bangor	1941	73	18	90	41	139	13
McClure	1941	40	88	108	11	44	8
Wicklow	1941	38	68	143	27	151	1
Herschel, Monteagle	1881	80	137	631	92	112	0
Herschel, Monteagle	1941	311	290	754	122	247	19
Herschel	1941	164	126	272	29	36	15
Monteagle	1941	147	164	482	93	211	4

RELIGION

PLACE	YEAR	ANG	RC	PRES	METH/UC	BAP	LUTH
Bangor, McClure, Wicklow	1881	199	132	193	314		
Bangor, McClure, Wicklow	1941	280	235	49	271		242
Bangor	1941	144	77	1	32		107
McClure	1941	68	66	33	117		15
Wicklow	1941	68	92	15	122		120
Herschel, Monteagle	1881	189	449	164	200		
Herschel, Monteagle	1941	298	347	2	772		86
Herschel	1941	144	184	0	246		8
Monteagle	1941	154	163	2	526		78

ID: 0201999   <u>DUNGANNON, FARADAY</u>

AREA: 180.65 sq. miles

1971 DENSITY:
   24.44 persons/sq. mile

TYPE:
   Combined

POPULATION:
   1871:   446
   1881:   970
   1941:   2745
   1971:   4416

CHANGES: 1871 created;
   1911 Bancroft incorporated.

SUBFILES:
   a. Dungannon
   b. Faraday (Rural)
   c. Bancroft

NOTES:

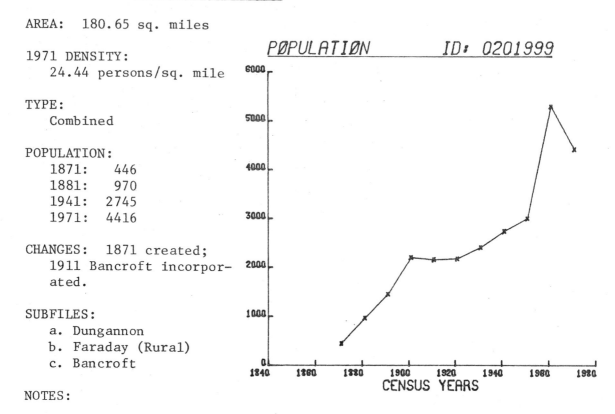

There are discussions of the settlement of the Bancroft area and its
economy in the nineteenth century in 115 (Burns, 1961) and 59 (Langman
1971), which contain a case study of Bancroft.

Dungannon and Faraday have both had an English plurality since 1881,
longer than any other group in the Valley area. The two townships
lie about 60 miles northwest of Belleville by Highway 62.

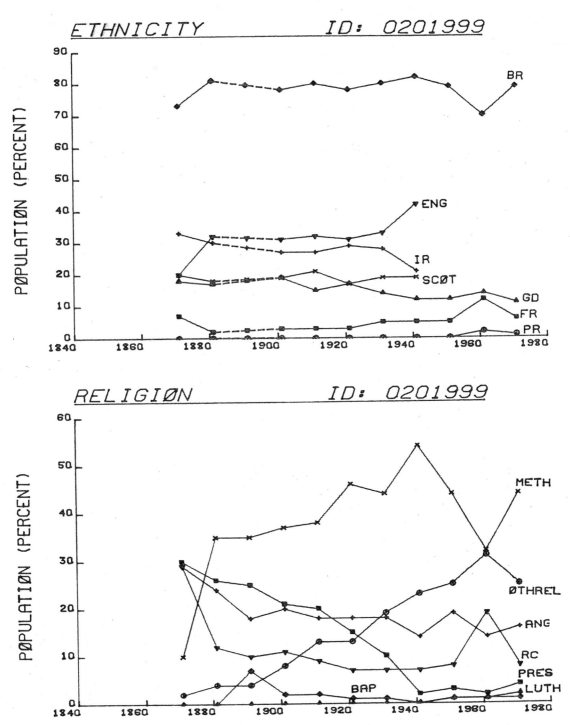

72

ID: 0201999 SUBFILES

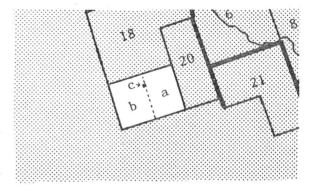

a. DUNGANNON

AREA: 87.69 sq. miles

1971 DENSITY:
   10.06 persons/sq. mile

POPULATION:
   1881: 578
   1941: 790
   1971: 882

CHANGES: 1961 part annexed to Bancroft village.

b. FARADAY (RURAL)

AREA: 85.50 sq. miles

1971 DENSITY:
   14.71 persons/sq. mile

POPULATION:
   1881: 392
   1941: 861
   1971: 1258

CHANGES: 1911 Bancroft incorporated; 1961 parts annexed to
   Bancroft village.

c. BANCROFT

AREA: 7.48 sq. miles

1971 DENSITY:
   304.28 persons/sq. mile

POPULATION:
   1911: 625
   1941: 1094
   1971: 2276

CHANGES: 1911 incorporated; 1961 annexed parts of Faraday and
   Dungannon.

ID: 0201999   SUBFILES   cont'd

ETHNICITY

PLACE	YEAR	ENG	SCOT	IR	FR	GD	PR
Dungannon	1881	155	142	190	7	84	0
Dungannon	1941	320	219	142	45	62	0
Faraday	1881	158	37	105	10	82	0
Faraday (Rural)	1941	422	118	126	35	154	5
Bancroft	1911	216	101	175	18	89	0
Bancroft	1941	412	180	303	46	125	1

RELIGION

PLACE	YEAR	ANG	RC	PRES	METH/UC	BAP	LUTH
Dungannon	1881	128	84	168	183		
Dungannon	1941	71	28	8	452		
Faraday	1881	105	30	82	153		
Faraday (Rural)	1941	107	35	43	561		
Bancroft	1911	142	56	117	217	26	
Bancroft	1941	198	116	12	457	10	

ID: 0202000 <u>CARLOW, MAYO</u>

AREA: 151.80 sq. miles

1971 DENSITY:
  4.74 persons/sq. mile

TYPE:
  Rural

POPULATION:
  1871: 285
  1881: 935
  1941: 1076
  1971: 720

CHANGES: None.

SUBFILES:
  a. Carlow
  b. Mayo

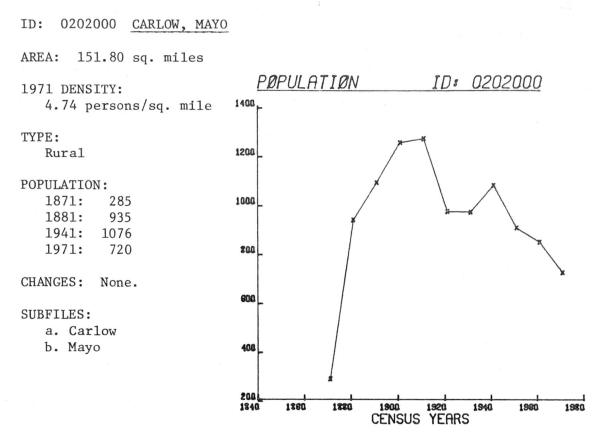

PØPULATIØN   *ID: 0202000*

CENSUS YEARS

NOTES:

None of the sources listed in the Bibliography deals specifically
with Carlow and Mayo.

75

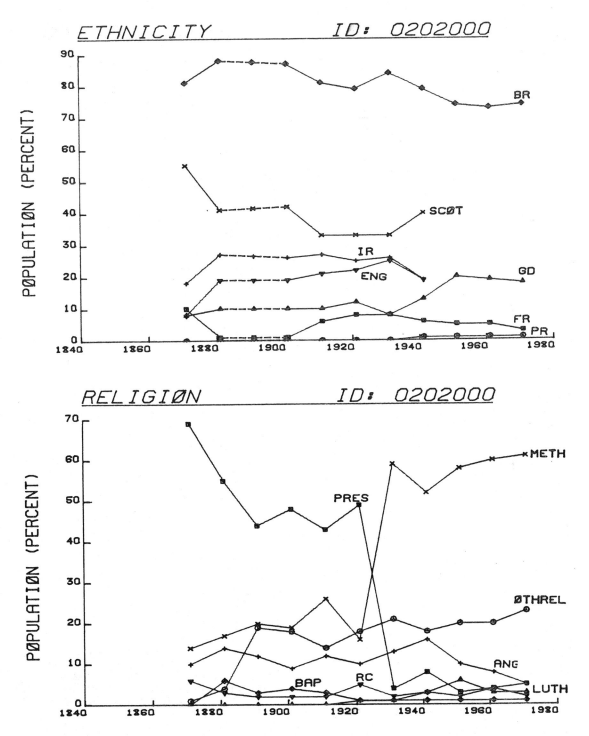

ID: 0202000   SUBFILES

a. <u>CARLOW</u>

   AREA: 74.38 sq. miles

   1971 DENSITY:
      4.81 persons/sq. mile

   POPULATION:
      1901: 655
      1941: 550
      1971: 358

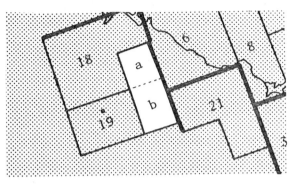

b. <u>MAYO</u>

   AREA: 77.42 sq. miles

   1971 DENSITY:
      4.68 persons/sq. mile

   POPULATION:
      1901: 597
      1941: 526
      1971: 362

ID: 0202000 SUBFILES cont'd

ETHNICITY

PLACE	YEAR	ENG	SCOT	IR	FR	GD	PR
Carlow	1901	79	330	189	2	43	0
Carlow	1941	48	241	135	46	68	12
Mayo	1901	163	192	141	14	87	0
Mayo	1941	161	193	68	23	74	2

RELIGION

PLACE	YEAR	ANG	RC	PRES	METH/UC	BAP	LUTH
Carlow	1901	49	12	356	119	25	
Carlow	1941	68	26	77	269	2	29
Mayo	1901	86	1	232	136	13	
Mayo	1941	100	7	7	290	4	

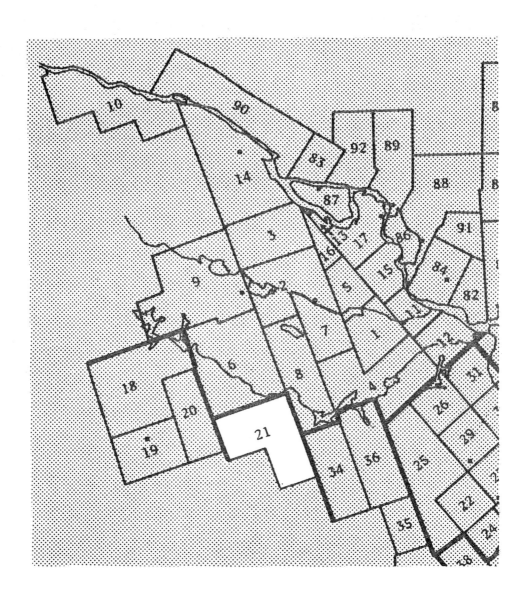

LENNOX AND ADDINGTON COUNTY (03)

Integral Unit   021

A small number of works listed in the bibliography deal with Lennox and Addington: 101 (Belden, 1878), 127 (Cooper, 1856), 155 (Herrington, 1913), and 159 (Lennox and Addington County Council, 1964). As can be seen, only the last of these is at all recent, and all deal predominantly with the southern townships that do not fall within the study area. Some information about the economy of the region can be derived from 28 (Dean, 1969).

The one IU included in the study forms only a small part of the whole county (population 684 out of the county's 28,359).

ID: 0302100   ABINGER, ASHBY, DENBIGH

AREA: 244.29 sq. miles

1971 DENSITY:
   2.80 persons/sq. mile

TYPE:
   Rural

POPULATION:
   1861:   195
   1881:   621
   1941:   837
   1971:   684

CHANGES: 1861 created.

SUBFILES: None

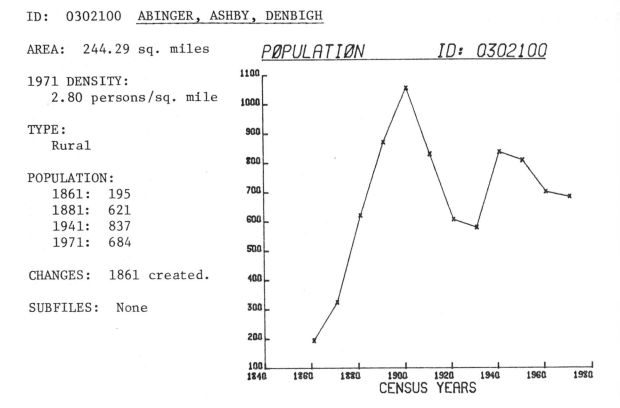

POPULATION   ID: 0302100

CENSUS YEARS

NOTES:

A passage quoted in 155 (Herrington, 1913), pp. 339 f. from land
agent in 1856 shows something of the optimism involved in the building of the Addington Road.

In reality, the poor soils made farming extremely difficult and rural
poverty has persisted.

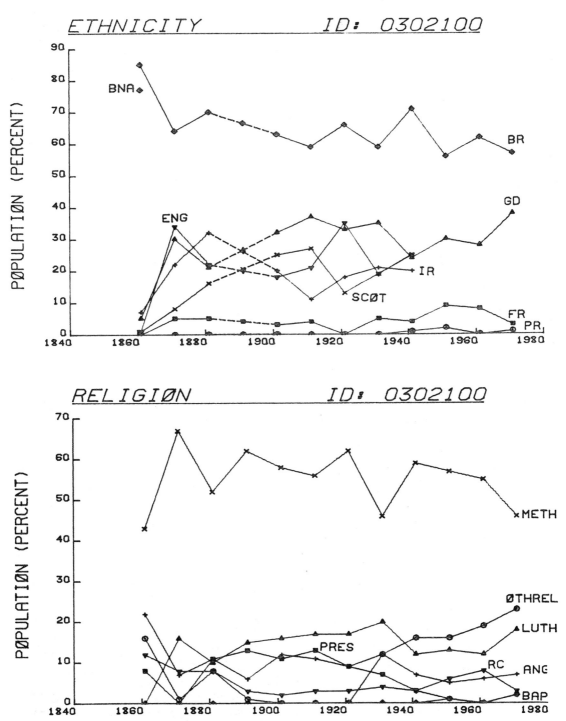

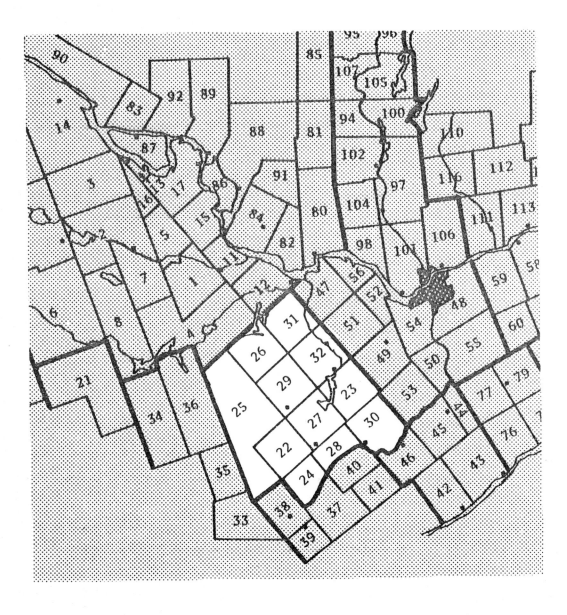

Integral Units   022 - 032

The treatment of the towns, villages and townships of Lanark by historians has been uneven in that some parts have an extensive bibliography whereas others have little or none. There are a large number of works, however, which treat aspects of the whole county.

The early history is dealt with in 174 (McGill, 1969), 195 (Shortt, 1967), 261 (Playter, 1923), and 283 (Lindsay, 1972). The Beckwith Settlement is treated especially in 165 (Kidd, 1943), and the Lanark Settlement in 174 (McGill, 1969), 23 (Cowan, 1961: p.23) and 156 (Haydon, 1925: p.120). McGiffen, 1963 (173: pp.23-38) deals with the Southern Irish immigration to Ramsay Township.

Economic activity is mentioned in 86 (Smith, 1851: pp.312,317, 350), and the impact of the Rideau Canal is discussed in George, 1972 (277). Relevant data on immigration and ethnicity are given in 23 (Cowan, 1961: pp.288,294) and 238 (Hunter, 1901).

Sim, 1963 (196) is particularly useful on factors leading to out-migration since 1851 (see especially p.29). Macleod 1972 (68) gives figures for population increase since 1951.

Other works relevant to the history of Lanark County include 66 (Macdonald, 1939), 103 (Belden, 1880), 154 (Haydon, 1925), 160 (Jamieson, 1974), 177 (MacNaughton, 1950), 206 (Thompson, 1970), 261 (Playter, 1923), 275 (Dawes, 1968), and 283 (Lindsay, 1972).

Considerable census information on Lanark County is available in tables, maps, and analyses at the census division level. County totals for 1971: population 42,259; area 1,182.94 sq. miles; density 35.72 persons/sq. mile.

84

ID: 0402200 BATHURST

AREA: 97.08 sq. miles

1971 DENSITY:
   21.34 persons/sq. mile

TYPE:
   Rural

POPULATION:
   1851: 2868
   1881: 2960
   1941: 1763
   1971: 2072

CHANGES: None.

SUBFILES: None

NOTES:

PØPULATIØN   ID: 0402200

CENSUS YEARS

Aspects of the early settlement of Bathurst are discussed in 283
(Lindsay, 1972).

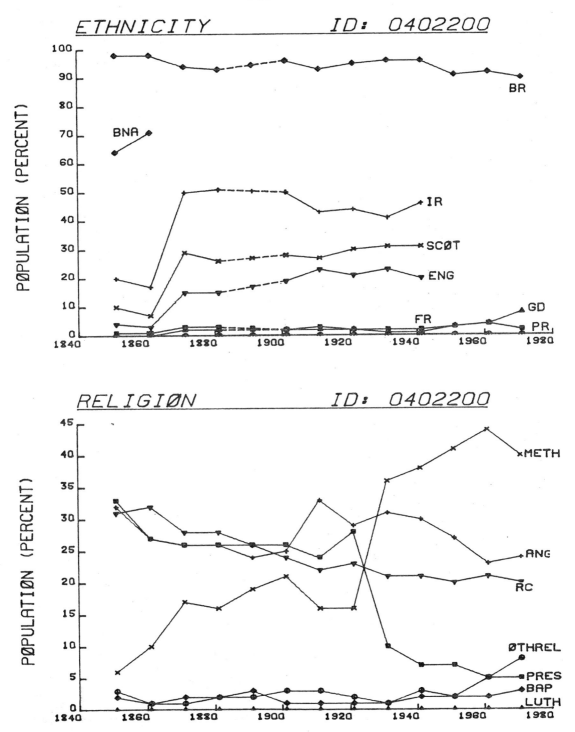

ID: 0402399 BECKWITH

AREA: 96.55 sq. miles

1971 DENSITY:
  69.73 persons/sq. mile

TYPE:
  Combined

POPULATION:
  1851: 2540
  1881: 3903
  1941: 5459
  1971: 6732

CHANGES: 1871 Carleton
  Place incorporated;
  1961 annexed part of
  Ramsay (0403299)

SUBFILES:
  a. Beckwith (Rural)
  b. Carleton Place

NOTES:

The fairly extensive bibliography relating to Beckwith Township and
Carleton Place includes: 105 (Bennett, 1973), 112 (Brown, 1963), 113
(Brown, 1973), 165 (Kidd, 1943), and 250 (MacKay, 1954).

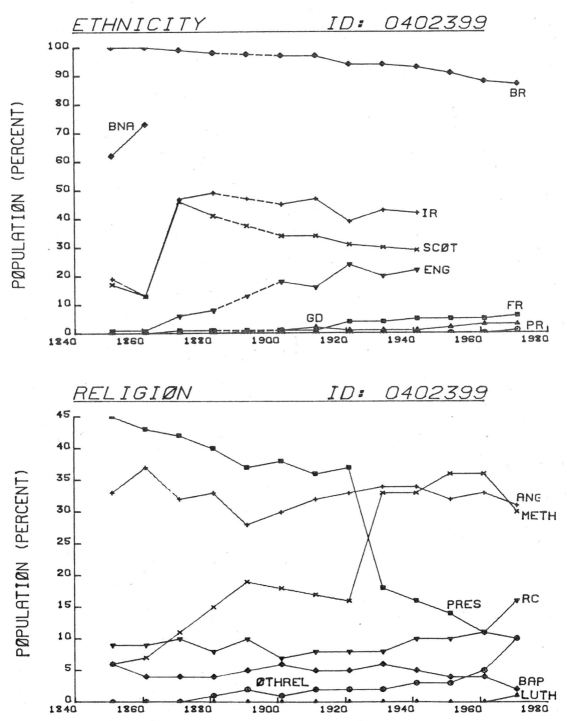

ETHNICITY   ID: 0402399

RELIGION   ID: 0402399

ID: 0402399 SUBFILES

a. BECKWITH (RURAL)

AREA: 94.59 sq. miles

1971 DENSITY:
    18.10 persons/sq. mile

POPULATION:
    1881: 1928
    1941: 1154
    1971: 1712

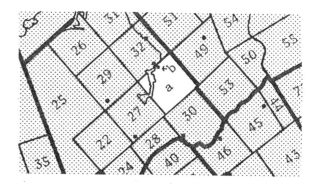

CHANGES: 1871 Carleton Place incorporated.

b. CARLETON PLACE

AREA: 1.96 sq. miles

1971 DENSITY:
    2561.22 persons/sq. mile

POPULATION:
    1881: 1975
    1941: 4305
    1971: 5020

CHANGES: 1871 incorporated; 1961 annexed part of Ramsay
    (0403299).

89

ID: 0402399 SUBFILES cont'd

ETHNICITY

PLACE	YEAR	ENG	SCOT	IR	FR	GD	PR
Beckwith (Rural)	1881	88	861	966	0	0	0
Beckwith (Rural)	1941	119	407	583	13	22	0
Carleton Place	1881	224	747	933	41	11	0
Carleton Place	1941	1079	1172	1694	237	47	11

RELIGION

PLACE	YEAR	ANG	RC	PRES	METH/UC	BAP	LUTH
Beckwith (Rural)	1881	654	119	846	216	87	
Beckwith (Rural)	1941	379	75	147	459	62	
Carleton Place	1881	617	197	712	357	54	
Carleton Place	1941	1455	446	726	1351	195	

ID: 0402400 BURGESS NORTH

AREA: 58.30 sq. miles

1971 DENSITY:
   9.30 persons/sq. mile

TYPE:
   Rural

POPULATION:
   1851: 1110
   1881: 1287
   1941:   563
   1971:   542

CHANGES: None

SUBFILES: None

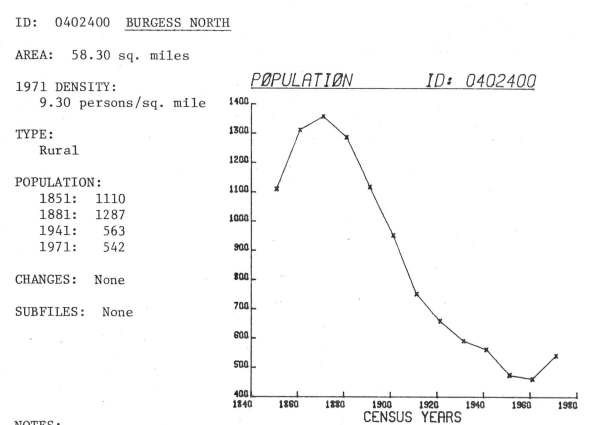

POPULATION   ID: 0402400

CENSUS YEARS

NOTES:

None of the sources examined deals specifically with Burgess North.

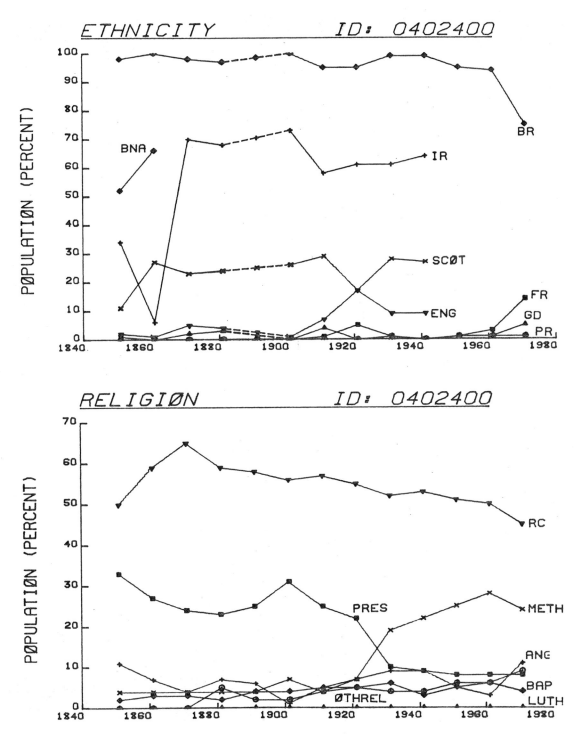

ID: 0402500 <u>DALHOUSIE, LAVANT, SHERBROOKE NORTH, SHERBROOKE SOUTH</u>

AREA: 271.17 sq. miles

1971 DENSITY:
   5.35 persons/sq. mile

TYPE:
   Rural

POPULATION:
   1851: 2405
   1881: 3476
   1941: 2224
   1971: 1450

CHANGES: None.

SUBFILES:
   a. Dalhousie, Lavant,
      Sherbrooke North
   b. Sherbrooke South

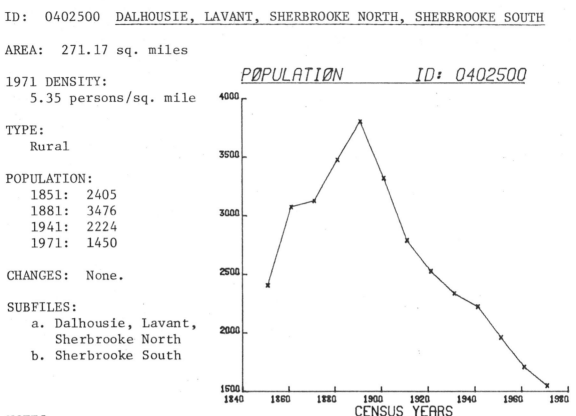

POPULATION   ID: 0402500

NOTES:

None of the sources examined deals specifically with this area. If
the figures for 1941 are to be trusted (and they have been double-
checked), the large increase in the English group takes place in
Sherbrooke South, an area of relatively strong English settlement
over the years. See Subfiles. The population graph above contains
an error. The 1971 population should be shown as 1450 not 1550.

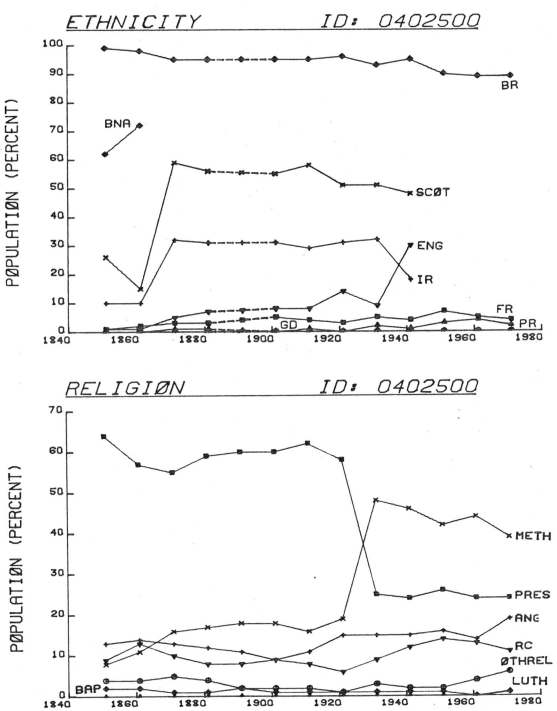

ETHNICITY   ID: 0402500

RELIGION   ID: 0402500

ID: 0402500   SUBFILES

a. <u>DALHOUSIE, LAVANT, SHERBROOKE NORTH</u>

   AREA: 212.46 sq. miles

   1971 DENSITY:
     8.53 persons/sq. mile

   POPULATION:
     1881: 2398
     1941: 1564
     1971:   968

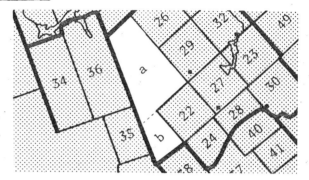

b. <u>SHERBROOKE SOUTH</u>

   AREA: 58.71 sq. miles

   1971 DENSITY:
     8.21 persons/sq. mile

   POPULATION:
     1881: 948
     1901: 924
     1941: 660
     1971: 482

ID: 0402500 SUBFILES cont'd

ETHNICITY

PLACE	YEAR	ENG	SCOT	IR	FR	GD	PR
Dalhousie, Lavant, Sherbrooke North	1881	93	1828	481	82	18	13
Dalhousie, Lavant, Sherbrooke North	1941	89	1004	363	83	14	0
Dalhousie	1911	10	962	220	31	2	0
Dalhousie	1941	33	654	177	40	3	0
Lavant	1911	24	312	123	50	6	0
Lavant	1941	27	175	112	33	5	0
Sherbrooke North	1911	4	214	46	8	4	0
Sherbrooke North	1941	29	175	74	10	6	0
Sherbrooke South	1881	167	111	613	14	33	4
Sherbrooke South	1911	184	137	407	9	4	0
Sherbrooke South	1941	569	53	30	8	0	0

RELIGION

PLACE	YEAR	ANG	RC	PRES	METH/UC	BAP	LUTH
Dalhousie, Lavant, Sherbrooke North	1881	100	178	1976	180	12	
Dalhousie, Lavant, Sherbrooke North	1941	83	229	527	690	14	
Dalhousie	1911	21	123	1036	6	12	
Dalhousie	1941	49	152	286	410	12	
Lavant	1911	36	55	341	83		14
Lavant	1941	3	52	17	264		1
Sherbrooke North	1911	20	1	244	5		
Sherbrooke North	1941	31	25	224	16	1	
Sherbrooke South	1881	316	83	104	406	23	
Sherbrooke South	1911	231	34	98	357	22	
Sherbrooke South	1941	256	28	9	333	1	

ID: 0402600   DARLING

AREA: 98.32 sq. miles

1971 DENSITY:
    2.75 persons/sq. mile

TYPE:
    Rural

POPULATION:
    1851:   670
    1881:   767
    1941:   452
    1971:   270

CHANGES: None

SUBFILES: None

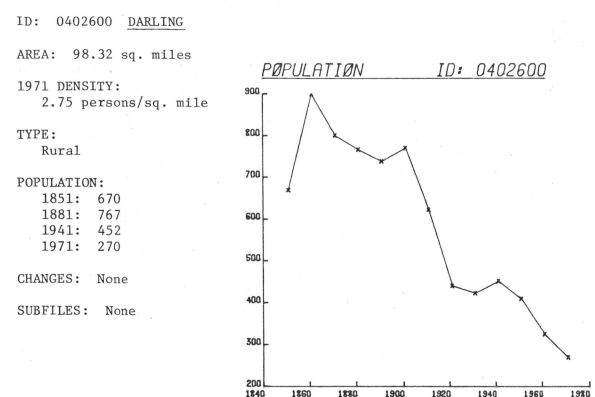

NOTES:

None of the sources examined deals specifically with Darling.

The Religion graph shows a particularly clear example of the success of the union of Methodist and Presbyterian into the United Church in 1931.

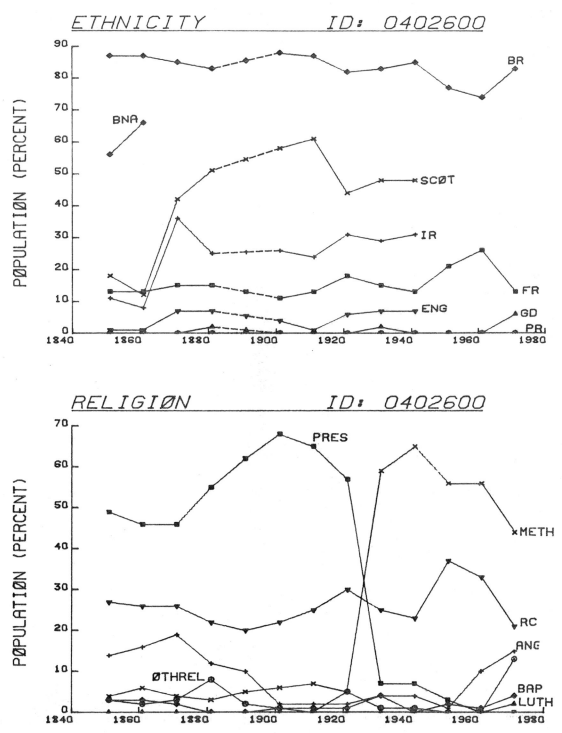

ID: 0402799 <u>DRUMMOND</u>

AREA: 96.46 sq. miles

1971 DENSITY:
  74.39 persons/sq. mile

TYPE:
  Combined

POPULATION:
  1851: 4564
  1881: 4845
  1941: 5881
  1971: 7176

CHANGES: 1971 annexed part
  of Elmsley North
  (0402800).

SUBFILES:
  a. Drummond (Rural)
  b. Perth

NOTES:

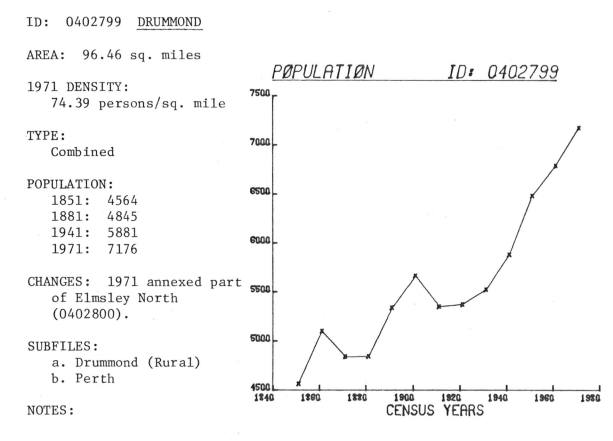

POPULATION   ID: 0402799

CENSUS YEARS

The following works deal with aspects of the history of Drummond
Township and Perth: 174 (McGill, 1969), 195 (Shortt, 1967), 199
(Smith, 1901), 242 (Kinlock, 1969), 261 (Playter, 1923), 272
(Buckley, 1968), and 283 (Lindsay, 1972).

Further information is available in the works discussed earlier which
deal with the County as a whole.

As the Subfiles show, most of the recent population growth has taken
place in the town of Perth.

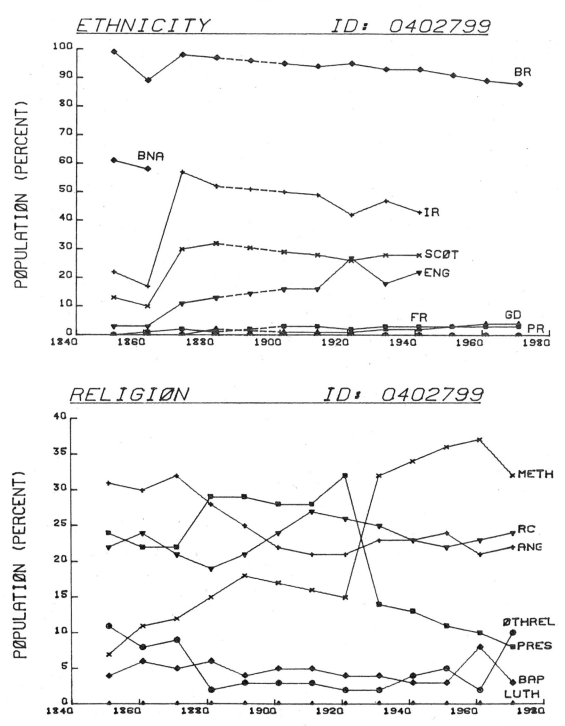

ID: 0402799 SUBFILES

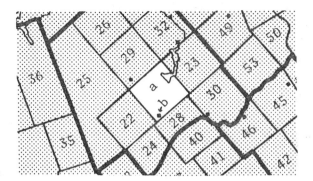

a. DRUMMOND (RURAL)

   AREA: 94.30 sq. miles

   1971 DENSITY:
      17.38 persons/sq. mile

   POPULATION:
      1851: 2648
      1881: 2378
      1941: 1423
      1971: 1639

   CHANGES: 1961 part annexed to Perth.

b. PERTH

   AREA: 2.16 sq. miles

   1971 DENSITY:
      2563.43 persons/sq. mile

   POPULATION:
      1851: 1916
      1881: 2467
      1941: 4458
      1971: 5537

   CHANGES: 1961 annexed part of Drummond (Rural); 1971 annexed part
      of Elmsley North (0402800).

ID: 0402799 SUBFILES cont'd

ETHNICITY

PLACE	YEAR	ENG	SCOT	IR	FR	GD	PR
Drummond (Rural)	1881	194	733	1401	9	32	0
Drummond (Rural)	1941	186	504	686	15	26	0
Perth	1881	458	799	1096	62	47	0
Perth	1941	1099	1129	1871	177	72	9

RELIGION

PLACE	YEAR	ANG	RC	PRES	METH/UC	BAP	LUTH
Drummond (Rural)	1881	702	382	690	400	159	
Drummond (Rural)	1941	326	216	85	694	56	
Perth	1881	671	520	725	343	133	
Perth	1941	1026	1138	653	1308	136	

ID: 0402800 ELMSLEY NORTH

AREA: 50.08 sq. miles

1971 DENSITY:
   31.31 persons/sq. mile

TYPE:
   Rural

POPULATION:
   1851: 2031
   1881: 1319
   1941:   725
   1971: 1568

CHANGES: 1971 part annexed
   to Perth in Drummond
   (0402799).

SUBFILES: None

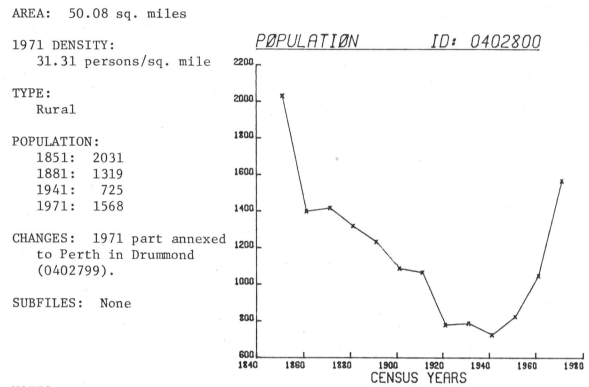

POPULATION   ID: 0402800

CENSUS YEARS

NOTES:

None of the sources examined deals particularly with Elmsley North.

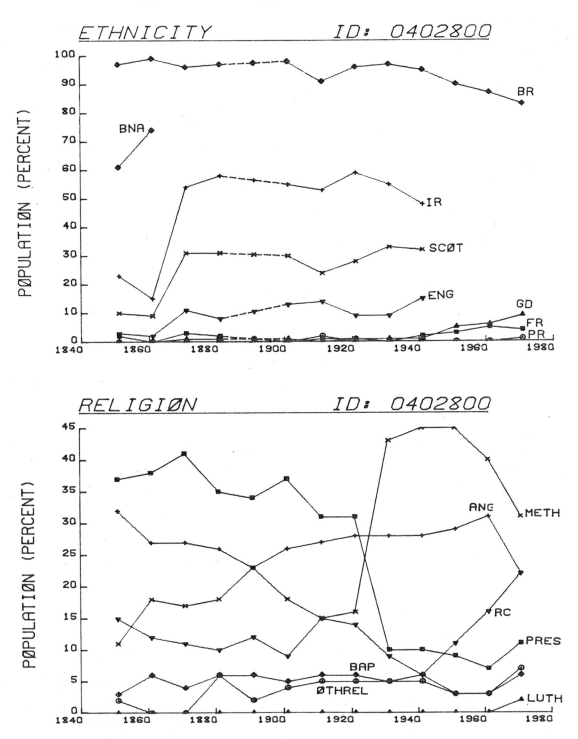

ID: 0402999   LANARK

AREA: 100.31 sq. miles

1971 DENSITY:
  16.33 persons/sq. mile

TYPE:
  Combined

POPULATION:
  1851:   2649
  1881:   2781
  1941:   1880
  1971:   1638

CHANGES: 1871 Lanark
  (Urban) incorporated.

SUBFILES:
  a. Lanark (Rural)
  b. Lanark (Urban)

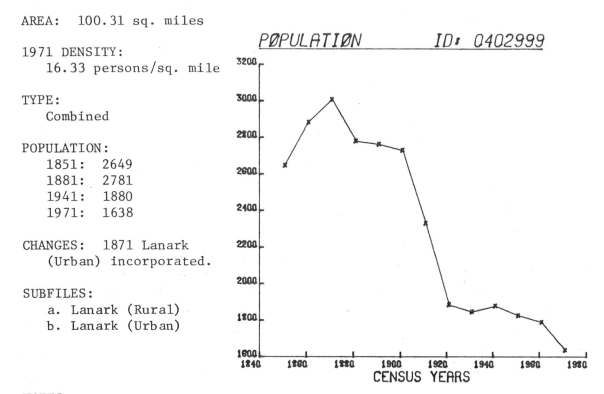

NOTES:

The following works deal with Lanark Village and Township: 23 (Cowan, 1961: p. 64), 154 (Haydon, 1925), 160 (Jamieson, 1974), 206 (Thompson, 1970), 261 (Playter, 1923).

Further information is available in the works noted earlier which deal with Lanark County as a whole.

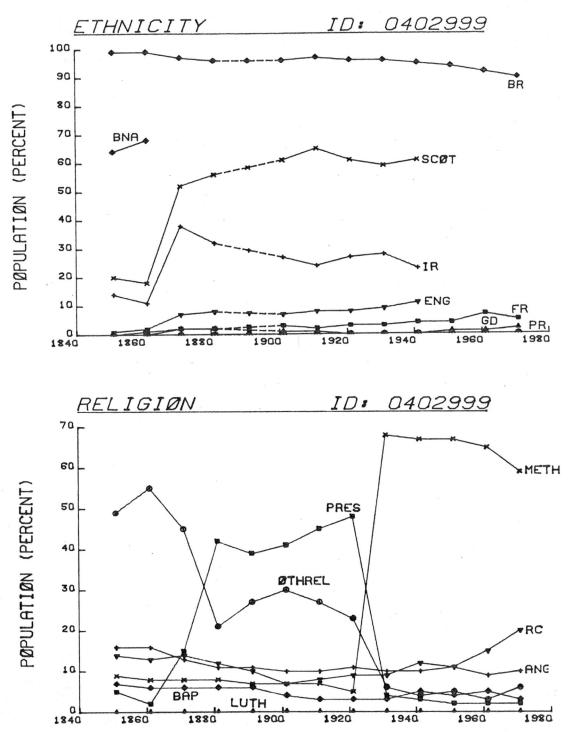

ID: 0402999   SUBFILES

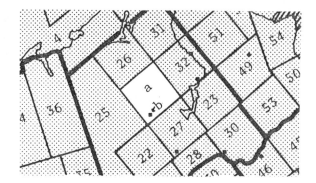

a. LANARK (RURAL)

   AREA: 98.38 sq. miles

   1971 DENSITY:
      7.90 persons/sq. mile

   POPULATION:
      1881: 2029
      1941: 1217
      1971:   777

   CHANGES: 1871 Lanark (Urban) incorporated; 1971 part annexed to
    Lanark (Urban).

b. LANARK (URBAN)

   AREA: 1.93 sq. miles

   1971 DENSITY:
      446.11 persons/sq. mile

   POPULATION:
      1881: 752
      1941: 663
      1971: 861

   CHANGES: 1871 incorporated; 1971 annexed part of Lanark (Rural).

ID: 0402999 SUBFILES cont'd

ETHNICITY

PLACE	YEAR	ENG	SCOT	IR	FR	GD	PR
Lanark (Rural)	1881	163	1124	701	3	37	0
Lanark (Rural)	1941	107	792	284	28	3	0
Lanark (Urban)	1881	73	427	191	43	18	0
Lanark (Urban)	1941	99	357	147	55	3	1

RELIGION

PLACE	YEAR	ANG	RC	PRES	METH/UC	BAP	LUTH
Lanark (Rural)	1881	222	255	815	205	149	
Lanark (Rural)	1941	114	130	43	818	53	
Lanark (Urban)	1881	81	78	366	10	7	
Lanark (Urban)	1941	68	91	22	434	39	

ID: 0403099 <u>MONTAGUE</u>

AREA: 112.57 sq. miles

1971 DENSITY:
124.76 persons/sq. mile

TYPE:
Combined

POPULATION:
1851: 3356
1881: 4770
1941: 8706
1971: 14044

CHANGES: 1861 Smiths Falls
incorporated; 1961
annexed part of Elmsley
South (0604000).

SUBFILES:
a. Montague (Rural)
b. Smiths Falls

NOTES:

PØPULATIØN *ID: 0403099*

CENSUS YEARS

A geography thesis which offers a useful analysis of the development
of Smiths Falls is 282 (Laughton, 1970). Further detail is available
in: 200 (Smiths Falls, 1957) and 201 (Smiths Falls University
Women's Club, 1967). Considerable census information on Montague is
available in the tables dealing with the Census Agglomeration of
Smiths Falls.

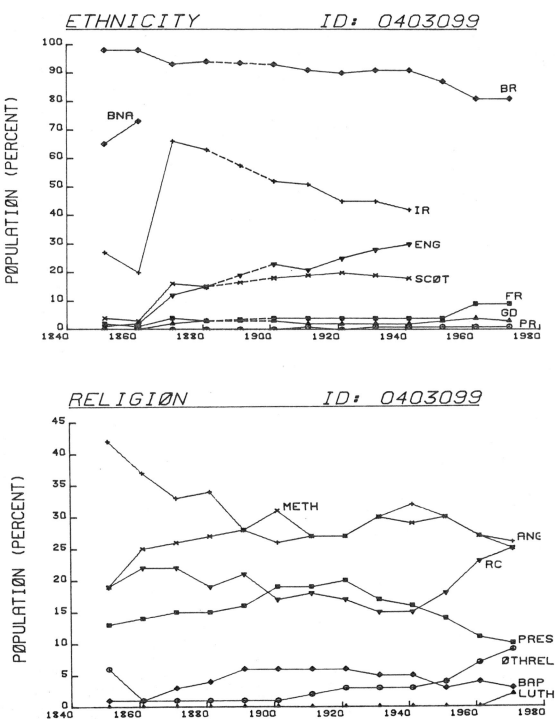

ID: 0403099 SUBFILES

a. <u>MONTAGUE (RURAL)</u>

AREA: 109.97 sq. miles

1971 DENSITY:
  40.55 persons/sq. mile

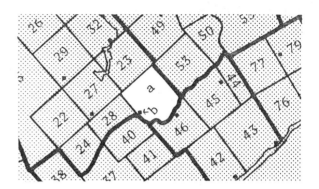

POPULATION:
  1881: 2683
  1941: 1547
  1971: 4459

CHANGES: 1861 Smiths Falls incorporated; 1961 and 1971 parts
annexed to Smiths Falls.

b. <u>SMITHS FALLS</u>

AREA: 2.60 sq. miles

1971 DENSITY:
  3686.54 persons/sq. mile

POPULATION:
  1881: 2087
  1941: 7159
  1971: 9585

CHANGES: 1861 incorporated; 1961 annexed part of Elmsley South
(0604000); 1961 and 1971 annexed parts of Montague (Rural).

ID: 0403099 SUBFILES cont'd

ETHNICITY

PLACE	YEAR	ENG	SCOT	IR	FR	GD	PR
Montague (Rural)	1881	248	317	2022	30	64	0
Montague (Rural)	1941	316	282	856	30	13	13
Smiths Falls	1881	458	422	1003	114	75	0
Smiths Falls	1941	2335	1324	2798	276	140	38

RELIGION

PLACE	YEAR	ANG	RC	PRES	METH/UC	BAP	LUTH
Montague (Rural)	1881	248	317	302	847	60	
Montague (Rural)	1941	604	222	128	500	52	
Smiths Falls	1881	701	394	416	435	110	
Smiths Falls	1941	2162	1120	1249	2014	376	

ID: 0403100 PAKENHAM

AREA: 99.61 sq. miles

1971 DENSITY:
  11.61 persons/sq. mile

TYPE:
  Rural

POPULATION:
  1851: 1868
  1881: 2284
  1941: 1277
  1971: 1156

CHANGES: None

SUBFILES: None

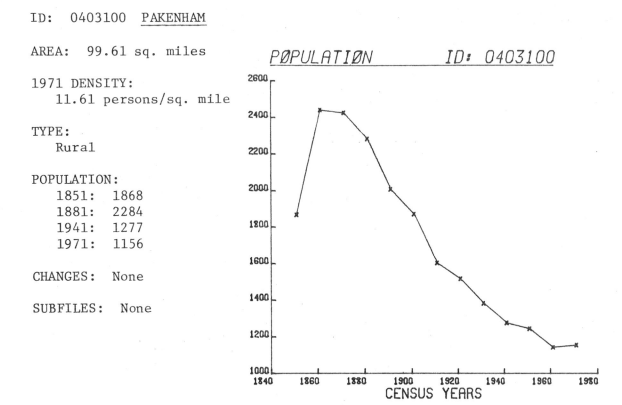

NOTES:

The unincorporated village of Pakenham (1971 population: 371) is the subject of a major, two-volume monograph, 173 (McGiffin, 1963, 1967).

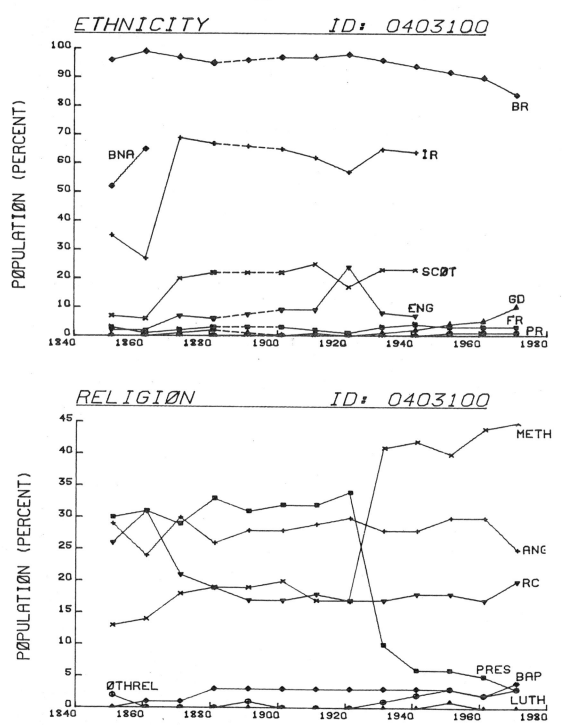

ETHNICITY   ID: 0403100

RELIGIØN   ID: 0403100

ID: 0403299   RAMSAY

AREA: 102.49 sq. miles

1971 DENSITY:
   54.75 persons/sq. mile

TYPE:
   Combined

POPULATION:
   1851:   3256
   1881:   5583
   1941:   4213
   1971:   5611

CHANGES: 1871 Almonte
   incorporated; 1961 part
   annexed to Carleton
   Place in Beckwith
   (0402399).

SUBFILES:
   a.   Ramsay (Rural)
   b.   Almonte

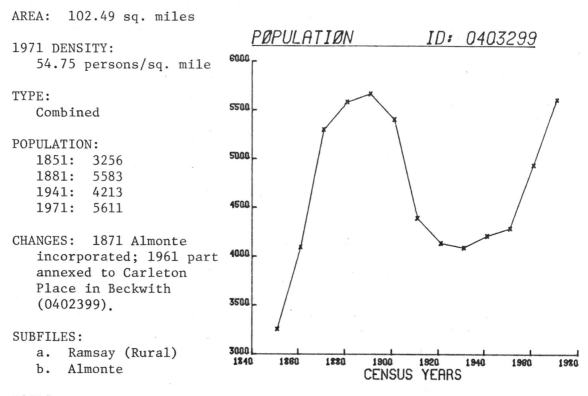

POPULATION   ID: 0403299

CENSUS YEARS

NOTES:

Although no source deals specifically with Ramsay or Almonte, 173
(McGiffin, 1962), pp. 23-38 gives details relating to the southern
Irish settlement in the area in 1823.

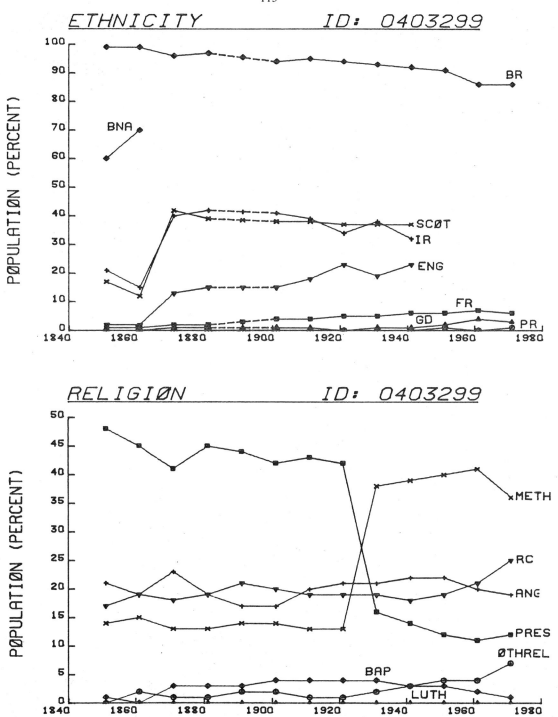

ID: 0403299 SUBFILES

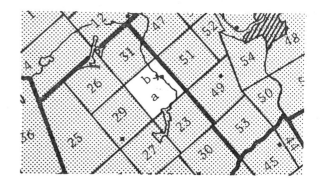

a. RAMSAY (RURAL)

   AREA: 100.81 sq. miles

   1971 DENSITY:
      19.0 persons/sq. mile

   POPULATION:
      1881: 2899
      1941: 1670
      1971: 1915

   CHANGES: 1871 Almonte incorporated; 1961 part annexed to Carleton
   Place in Beckwith (0402399); 1971 part annexed to Almonte.

b. ALMONTE

   AREA: 1.68 sq. miles

   1971 DENSITY:
      2200.0 persons/sq. mile

   POPULATION:
      1881: 2684
      1941: 2543
      1971: 3696

   CHANGES: 1871 incorporated; 1971 annexed part of Ramsay (Rural).

ID: 0403299 SUBFILES cont'd

ETHNICITY

PLACE	YEAR	ENG	SCOT	IR	FR	GD	PR
Ramsay (Rural)	1881	384	1238	1222	25	26	0
Ramsay (Rural)	1941	246	763	597	50	9	0
Almonte	1881	457	963	1142	92	24	0
Almonte	1941	712	775	770	202	37	1

RELIGION

PLACE	YEAR	ANG	RC	PRES	METH/UC	BAP	LUTH
Ramsay (Rural)	1881	609	325	1556	337	43	
Ramsay (Rural)	1941	434	155	277	694	43	
Almonte	1881	454	722	937	402	148	
Almonte	1941	511	609	306	965	90	

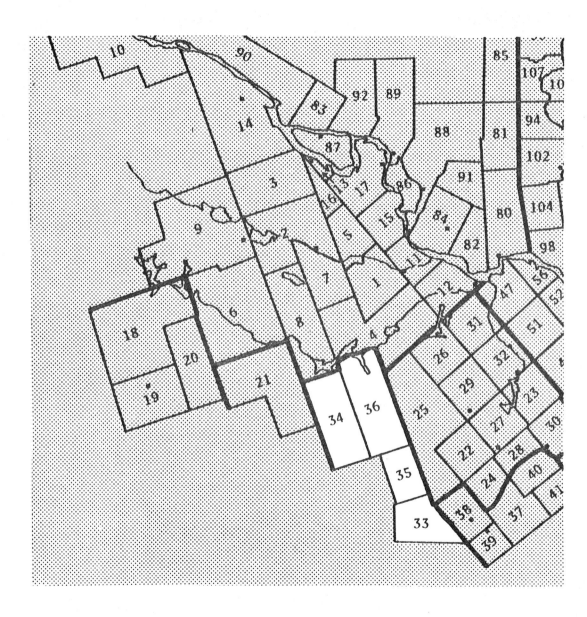

FRONTENAC COUNTY (05)

Integral Units   033 - 036

There are no good sources which deal extensively with those upper townships of Frontenac County which fall within the study area. The statistical material dealing with the County as a whole is not useful in a study restricted to these sparsely populated townships. There appear to be few local histories, no specialized studies, and no thesis dealing with the area. Apart from the works mentioned within in relation to Bedford and to Clarendon and Miller, it is necessary to mention only 28 (Dean, 1969), 101 (Belden, 1878) and 127 (Cooper, 1856).

The four IU's of the study area had a combined population of 2,722 in 1971, a combined area of 563.67 sq. miles, and a population density of 4.83. County wide totals for 1971: population 101,692; area 1,474.81 sq. miles; density 68.95 persons/sq. mile.

ID: 0503300 <u>BEDFORD</u>

AREA: 116.22 sq. miles

1971 DENSITY:
 6.44 persons/sq. mile

TYPE:
 Rural

POPULATION:
 1861: 1691
 1881: 2019
 1941: 975
 1971: 749

CHANGES: 1861 created.

SUBFILES: None

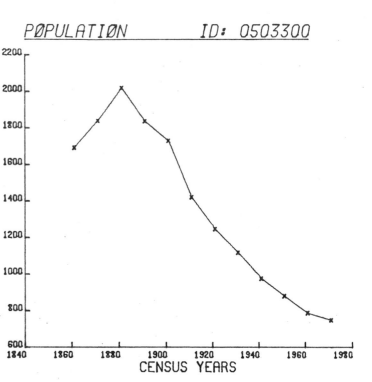

PØPULATIØN   ID: 0503300

CENSUS YEARS

NOTES:

Bedford Township adjoins the Rideau Canal and includes the once
thriving community of Bedford Mills where the water from Devil's
Lake falls 30 feet to Loon Lake. Aspects of the history of the
community and its economic base are mentioned in: 11b (Brown,
1978), pp. 27f.; 77 (Paterson, 1921), p. 60; 260b (Patterson, 1977);
263b (Robertson, 1969); and 277 (George, 1972), <u>passim</u>.

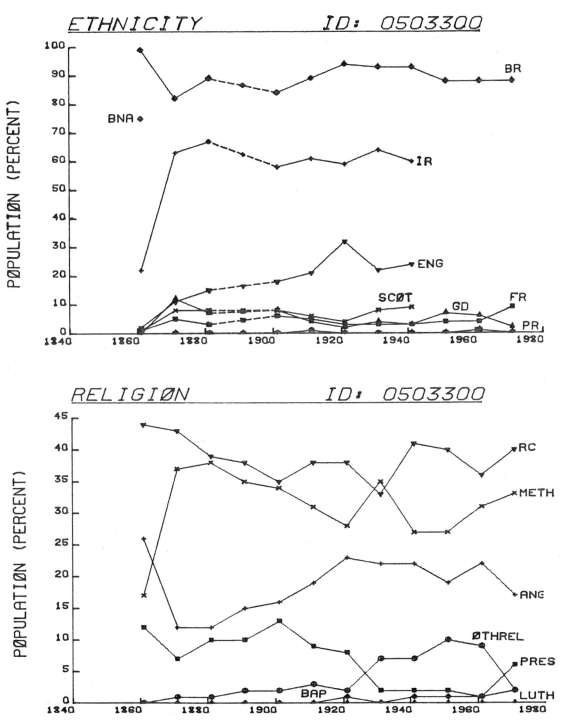

ID: 0503400 CLARENDON, MILLER

AREA: 169.85 sq. miles

1971 DENSITY:
  2.71 persons/sq. mile

TYPE:
  Rural

POPULATION:
  1871: 408
  1881: 685
  1941: 615
  1971: 461

CHANGES: 1871 created.

SUBFILES: None

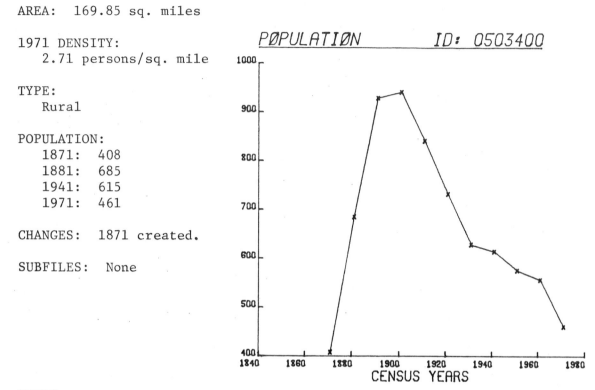

POPULATION   ID: 0503400

CENSUS YEARS

NOTES:

The combined townships of Clarendon and Miller are the subject of a
monograph, 96c (Armstrong, 1976).

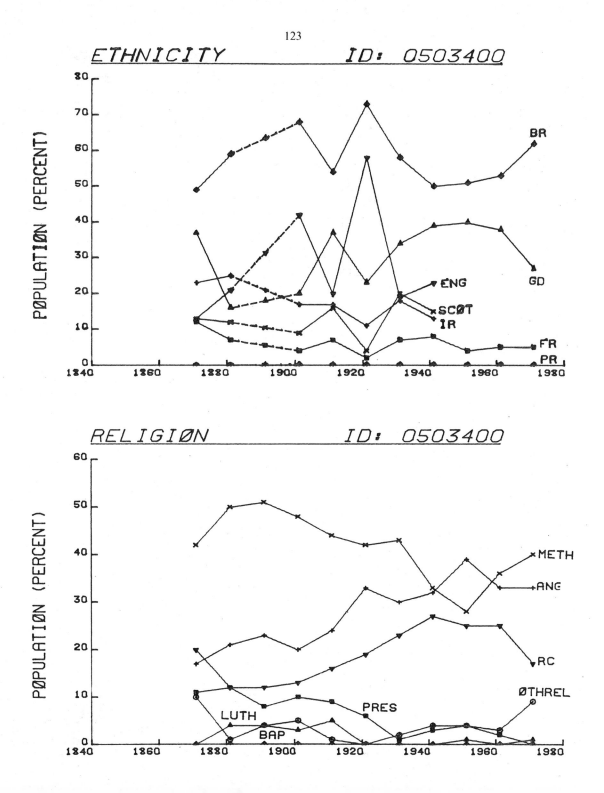

ETHNICITY   ID: 0503400

RELIGION   ID: 0503400

ID: 0503500 OSO

AREA: 72.23 sq. miles

1971 DENSITY:
  16.67 persons/sq. mile

TYPE:
  Rural

POPULATION:
  1861:   349
  1881:   959
  1941: 1099
  1971: 1204

CHANGES: 1861 created.

SUBFILES: None

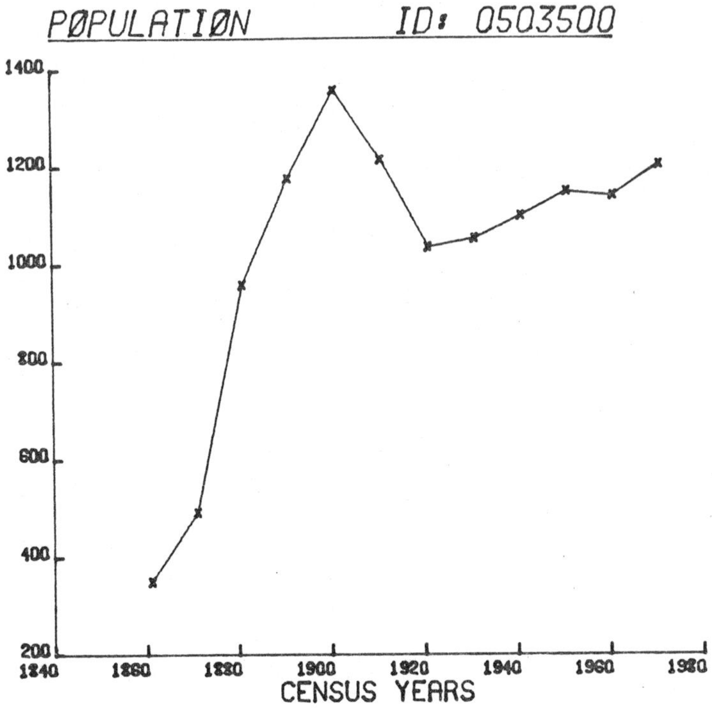

NOTES:

PØPULATIØN   ID: 0503500

CENSUS YEARS

Item 134 (E.O.D.C., 1971), p. 96, gives figures on employment in this area. The unincorporated village of Sharbot Lake (1971 population 461) is the largest community in the township.

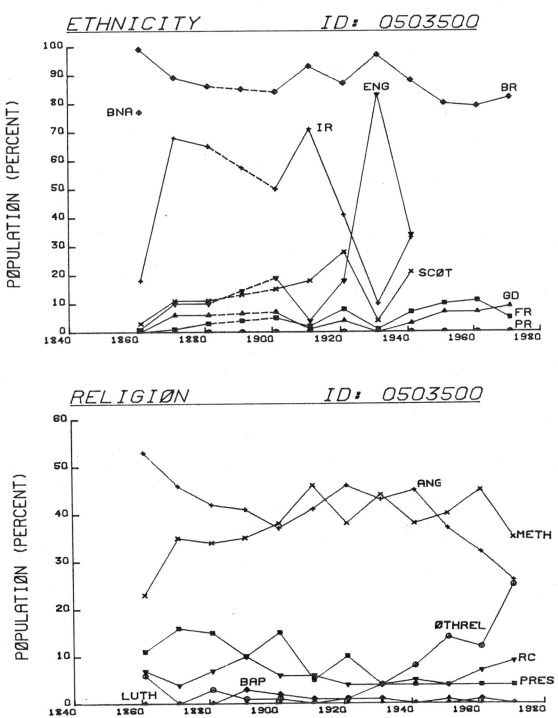

ETHNICITY   ID: 0503500

RELIGIØN   ID: 0503500

ID: 0503600 PALMERSTON, CANONTO NORTH, CANONTO SOUTH

AREA: 205.37 sq. miles

1971 DENSITY:
1.50 persons/sq. mile

TYPE:
Rural

POPULATION:
1871: 546
1881: 1005
1941: 695
1971: 308

CHANGES: 1871 created.

SUBFILES: None

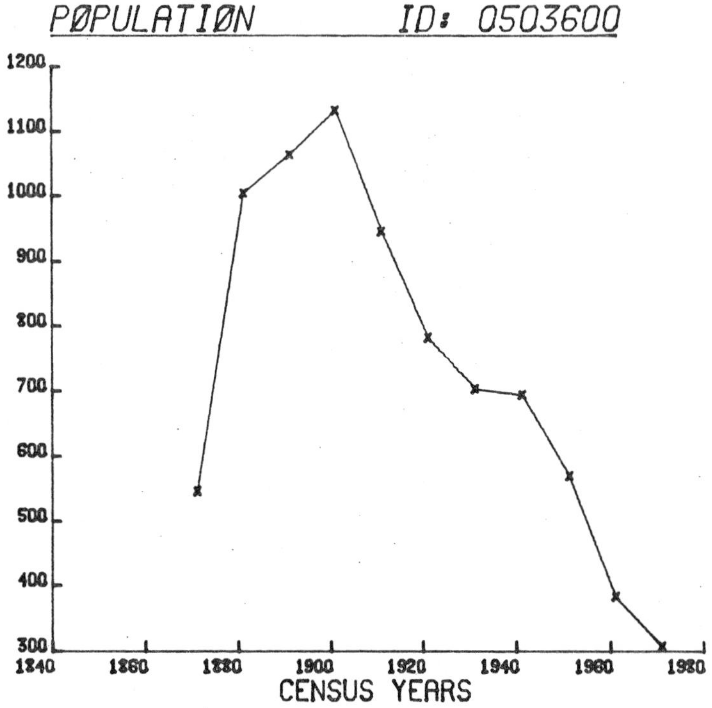

POPULATION   ID: 0503600

CENSUS YEARS

NOTES:

None of the sources examined deals specifically with this area.

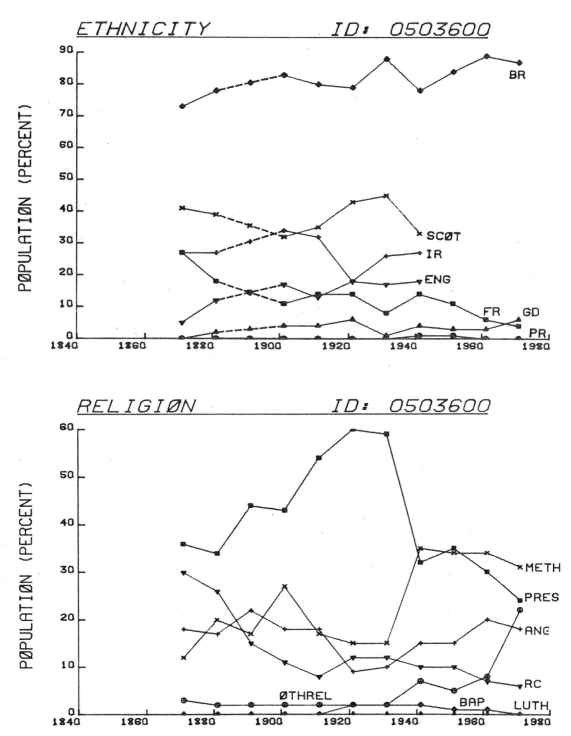

ETHNICITY   ID: 0503600

RELIGIØN   ID: 0503600

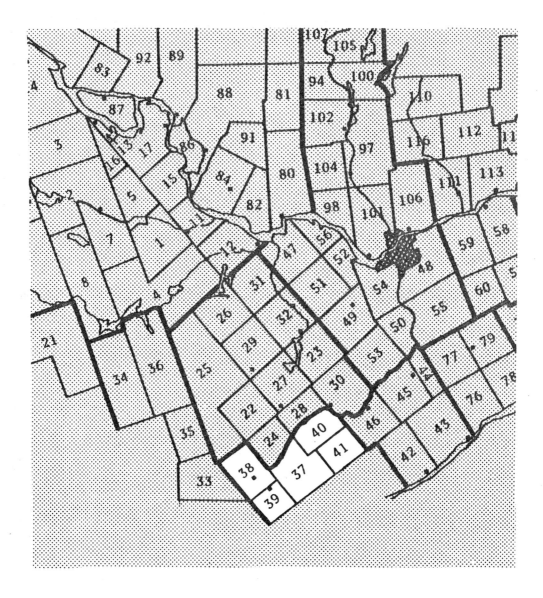

The early settlement of the area is discussed in 175 (McKenzie, 1967), 84 (Shortt and Doughty, 1914) and 277 (George, 1972).

The distribution of the population in the area before 1851 is discussed in 87 (Smyth, 1977), 238 (Hunter, 1901) and 277 (George, 1972). The subsequent growth of the population is discussed in 68 (Macleod, 1972), and 175 (McKenzie, 1967). 275 (Dawes, 1968), includes a map of population change between 1931 and 1961 (Map 11). The major history of the area is 175 (McKenzie, 1967). Among the earlier works are 167 (Leavitt, 1879), 202 (Stevens, 1961) and 249 (McDougall, 1910).

Information on earlier economic activity, especially dairying and crops, is given in 86 (Smith, 1851); much information about subsequent economic activity is given in 175 (McKenzie, 1967). A map in 286 (MacKay, 1949) shows the soil types in the region: large parts of Leeds dominated by the Canadian Shield; Grenville mostly till plain.

The five IU's of the study area had a combined population of 8,390 in 1971, a combined area of 371.41 sq. miles, and a population density of 22.59. County wide totals for 1971: population 50,093; area 847.33 sq. miles; density 59.12 persons/sq. mile.

ID: 0603700   BASTARD, BURGESS SOUTH

AREA: 102.90 sq. miles

1971 DENSITY:
    22.21 persons/sq. mile

TYPE:
    Rural

POPULATION:
    1851:   3724
    1881:   3500
    1941:   2334
    1971:   2285

CHANGES: None

SUBFILES: None

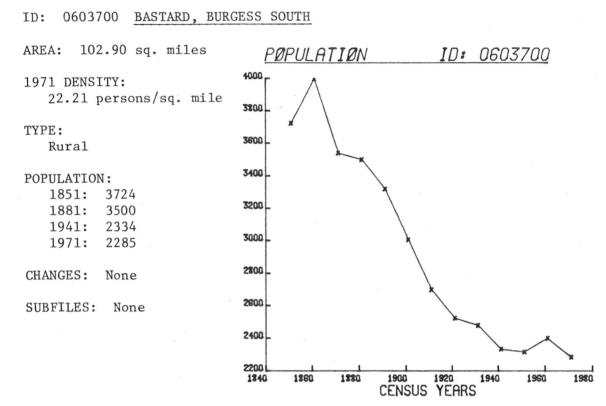

POPULATION   ID: 0603700

CENSUS YEARS

NOTES:

None of the sources consulted deals specifically with this area.
Bastard Township contains 2 unincorporated villages of some size:
Delta (1971 population 465) and Portland (1971 population 253).

131

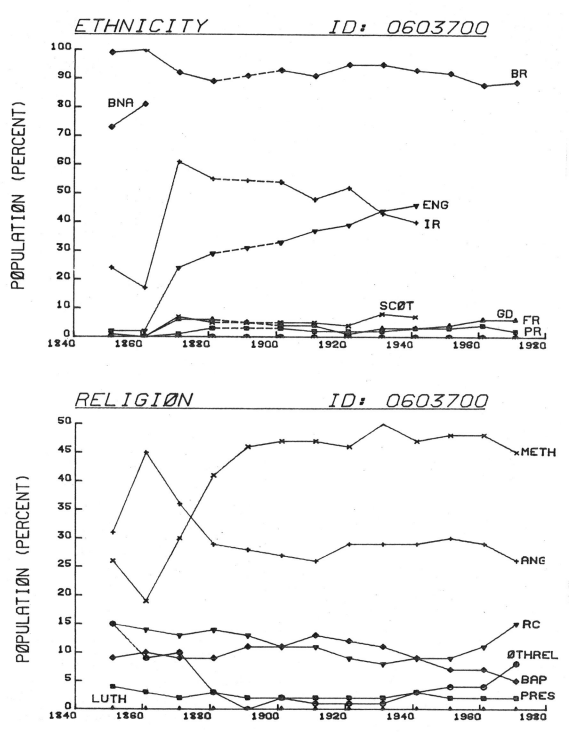

ID: 0603899   CROSBY NORTH

AREA: 74.01 sq. miles

1971 DENSITY:
    16.74 persons/sq. mile

TYPE:
    Combined

POPULATION:
    1851:   1785
    1881:   1999
    1941:   1527
    1971:   1239

CHANGES: 1911 Westport
    incorporated.

SUBFILES:
    a. Crosby North (Rural)
    b. Westport

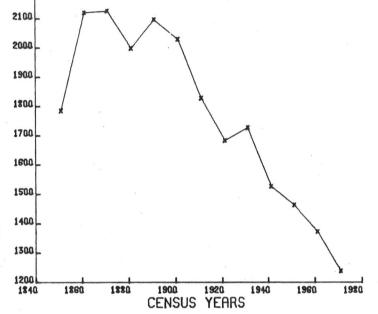

POPULATION   ID: 0603899

CENSUS YEARS

NOTES:

None of the sources consulted deals specifically with this area.

133

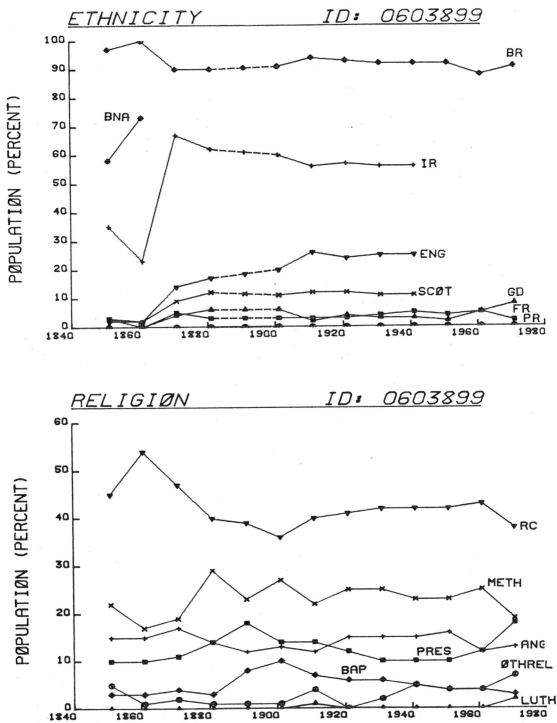

ID: 0603899 SUBFILES

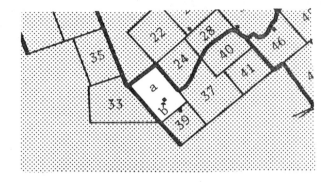

a. CROSBY NORTH (RURAL)

AREA: 73.28 sq. miles

1971 DENSITY:
8.71 persons/sq. mile

POPULATION:
1911: 1025
1941:   801
1971:   638

CHANGES: 1911 Westport incorporated.

b. WESTPORT

AREA: 0.73 sq. miles

1971 DENSITY:
823.29 persons/sq. mile

POPULATION:
1911: 803
1941: 726
1971: 601

CHANGES: 1911 incorporated.

ID: 0603899 SUBFILES cont'd

ETHNICITY

PLACE	YEAR	ENG	SCOT	IR	FR	GD	PR
Crosby North (Rural)	1911	265	86	642	26	5	0
Crosby North (Rural)	1941	207	67	465	39	22	0
Westport	1911	217	137	376	29	36	0
Westport	1941	174	98	395	32	20	0

RELIGION

PLACE	YEAR	ANG	RC	PRES	METH/UC	BAP	LUTH
Crosby North (Rural)	1911	165	413	101	286	60	
Crosby North (Rural)	1941	147	345	57	195	44	
Westport	1911	56	317	154	112	71	25
Westport	1941	88	303	95	153	30	0

ID: 0603999   CROSBY SOUTH

AREA: 69.05 sq. miles

1971 DENSITY:
   24.52 persons/sq. mile

TYPE:
   Combined

POPULATION:
   1851:   1578
   1881:   2386
   1941:   1821
   1971:   1693

CHANGES: 1881 Newboro
   incorporated.

SUBFILES:
   a. Crosby South (Rural)
   b. Newboro

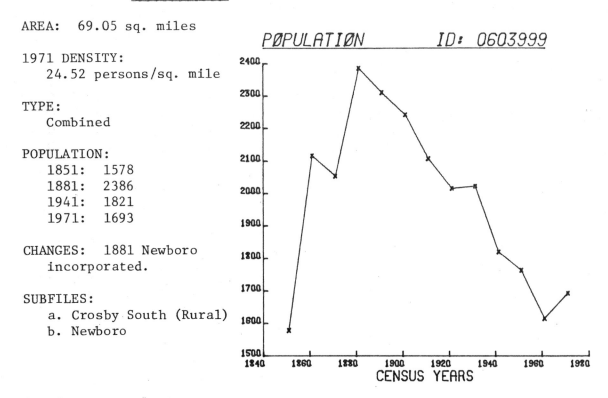

POPULATION   ID: 0603999

CENSUS YEARS

NOTES:

None of the sources consulted deals specifically with this area.   The
unincorporated village of Elgin had a population of 322 in 1971.

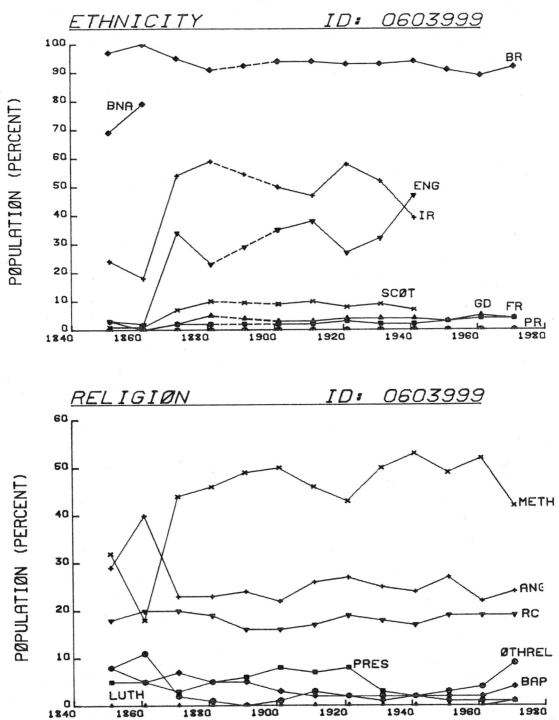

ID: 0603999 SUBFILES

a. <u>CROSBY SOUTH (RURAL)</u>

   AREA: 67.54 sq. miles

   1971 DENSITY:
      20.68 persons/sq. mile

   POPULATION:
      1881: 1968
      1941: 1489
      1971: 1397

   CHANGES: 1881 Newboro incorporated.

b. <u>NEWBORO</u>

   AREA: 1.51 sq. miles

   1971 DENSITY:
      196.03 persons/sq. mile

   POPULATION:
      1881: 418
      1941: 332
      1971: 296

   CHANGES: 1881 incorporated.

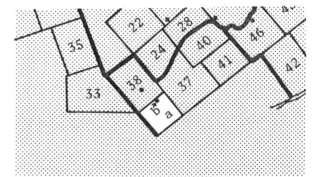

ID: 0603999 SUBFILES cont'd

ETHNICITY

PLACE	YEAR	ENG	SCOT	IR	FR	GD	PR
Crosby South (Rural)	1881	465	204	1106	54	109	0
Crosby South (Rural)	1941	663	86	637	39	52	0
Newboro	1881	74	32	302	1	9	0
Newboro	1941	199	41	77	2	13	0

RELIGION

PLACE	YEAR	ANG	RC	PRES	METH/UC	BAP	LUTH
Crosby South (Rural)	1881	436	367	73	967	109	
Crosby South (Rural)	1941	331	297	22	781	25	
Newboro	1881	124	89	53	141	10	
Newboro	1941	110	18	21	177	3	

ID: 0604000 ELMSLEY SOUTH

AREA: 38.00 sq. miles

1971 DENSITY:
  38.03 persons/sq. mile

TYPE:
  Rural

POPULATION:
  1851: 1442
  1881: 1121
  1941: 645
  1971: 1445

CHANGES: 1961 part annexed
  to Smiths Falls (in
  0403099).

SUBFILES: None

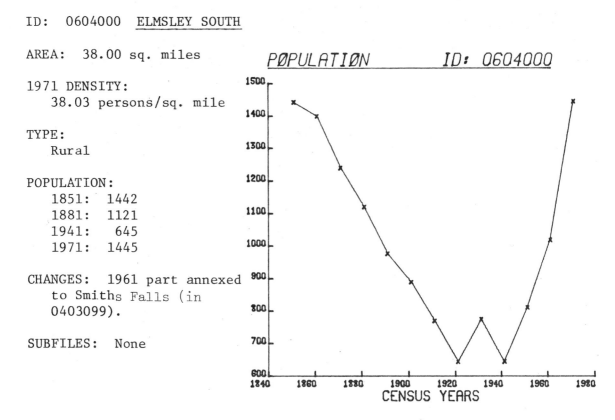

POPULATION   ID: 0604000

CENSUS YEARS

NOTES:

None of the sources consulted deals specifically with Elmsley South.
The growth in population since 1941 is due to its proximity to
neighbouring Smiths Falls.

141

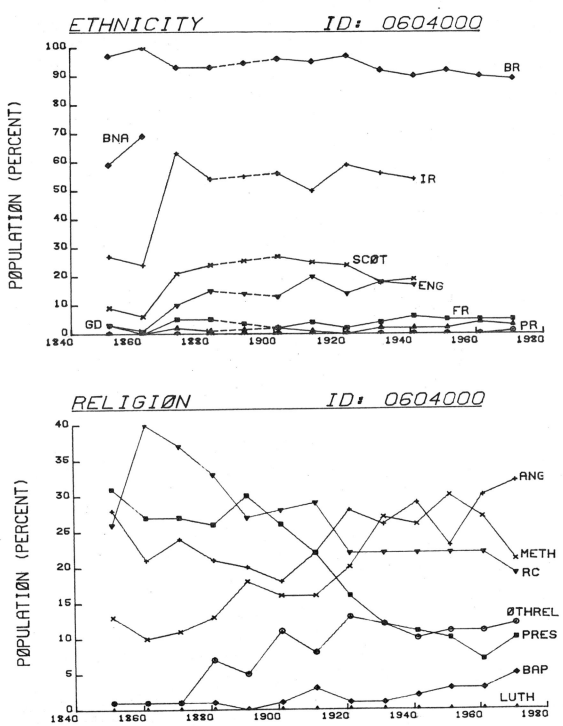

ID: 0604100 <u>KITLEY</u>

AREA: 87.45 sq. miles

1971 DENSITY:
  19.76 persons/sq mile

TYPE:
  Rural

POPULATION:
  1851: 3525
  1881: 2593
  1941: 1445
  1971: 1728

CHANGES: None

SUBFILES: None

PØPULATIØN   ID: 0604100

CENSUS YEARS

NOTES:

The original settlement of the area and its subsequent history are discussed in 175 (McKenzie, 1967) and 171 (Lockwood, 1974). Early economic activities are mentioned in 86 (Smith, 1851). Two unincorporated villages in Kitley are Toledo (1971 population 179) and Frankville (1971 population 143).

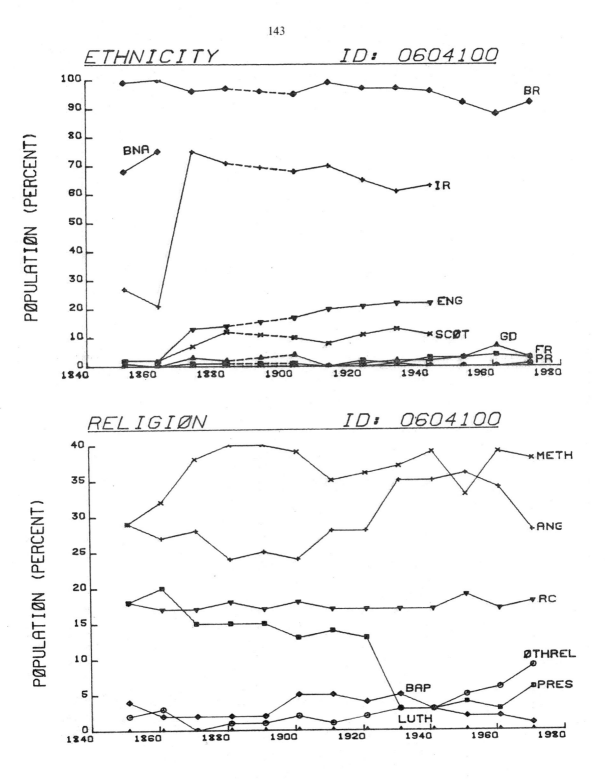

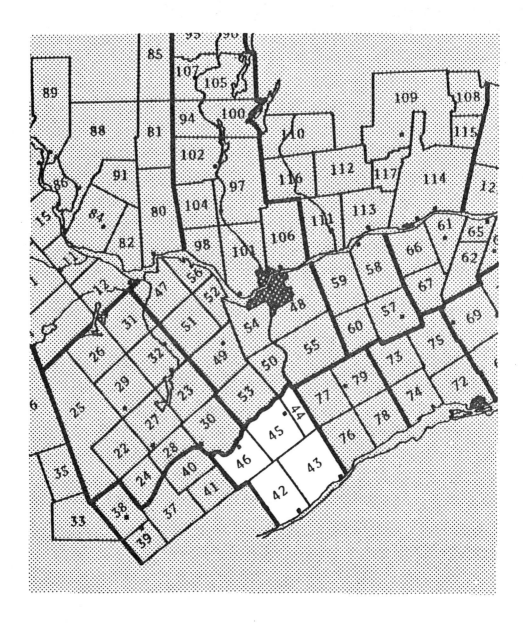

GRENVILLE COUNTY (07)

Integral Units   042 - 046

     With only a few exceptions, the works mentioned in the head-
note to 06, Leeds County (p.129), deal just as extensively with
Grenville County. Beyond these there are two studies which deal
with the early settlement of Grenville County: 219 (Burritt, 1901)
and 220 (Burritt, 1901).

     Considerable census information on Grenville County is avail-
able in tables, maps, and analyses at the census division level.
County totals for 1971:   population 24,316; area 461.59 sq. miles;
density 52.68 persons/sq. mile.

ID: 0704299   AUGUSTA

AREA: 123.10 sq. miles

1971 DENSITY:
   86.96 persons/sq. mile

TYPE:
   Combined

POPULATION:
   1851: 7310
   1881: 8095
   1941: 6000
   1971: 10705

CHANGES: 1961 annexed part
   of Edwardsburgh
   (0704399).

SUBFILES:
   a. Augusta (Rural)
   b. Prescott

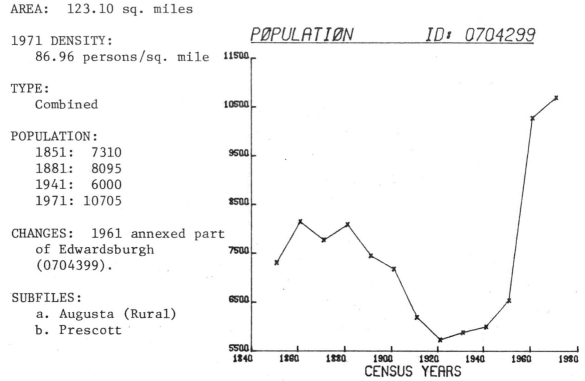

POPULATION   ID: 0704299

CENSUS YEARS

NOTES:

English immigration into Augusta is mentioned in 238 (Hunter, 1901).
Prescott is the subject of a monograph, 183 (Morris, 1967).

The 1971 census lists 7 unincorporated places of 50 persons and
over in Augusta, the largest being the village of Maitland (population
670) on the St. Lawrence River.

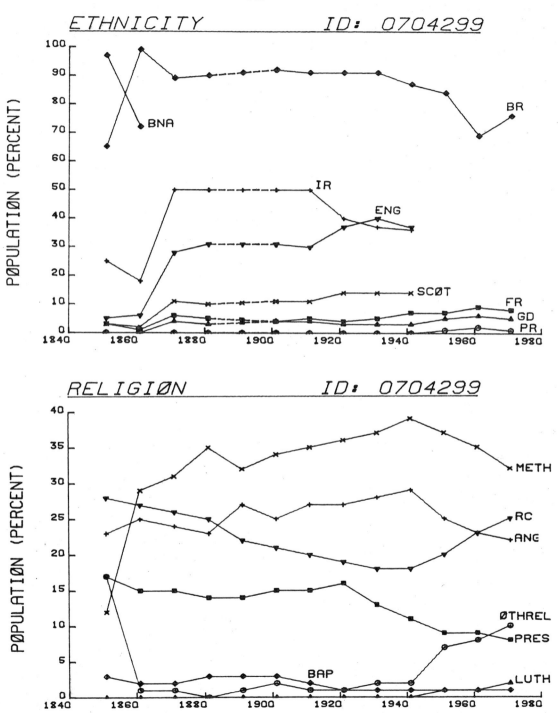

ID: 0704299   SUBFILES

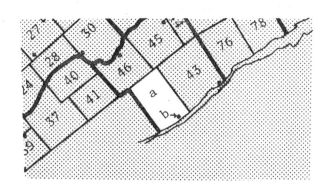

a. <u>AUGUSTA (RURAL)</u>

AREA: 121.54 sq. miles

1971 DENSITY:
  45.58 persons/sq. mile

POPULATION:
  1851: 5154
  1881: 5096
  1941: 2777
  1971: 5540

CHANGES: 1961 part annexed to Prescott.

b. <u>PRESCOTT</u>

AREA: 1.56 sq. miles

1971 DENSITY:
  3310.90 persons/sq. mile

POPULATION:
  1851: 2156
  1881: 2999
  1941: 3223
  1971: 5165

CHANGES: 1961 annexed parts of Augusta (Rural) and Edwardsburgh (0704399).

ID: 0704299 SUBFILES cont'd

ETHNICITY

PLACE	YEAR	ENG	SCOT	IR	FR	GD	PR
Augusta (Rural)	1881	1630	484	2680	115	147	1
Augusta (Rural)	1941	1049	370	1118	106	89	5
Prescott	1881	876	299	1351	317	133	0
Prescott	1941	1171	462	1068	307	118	5

RELIGION

PLACE	YEAR	ANG	RC	PRES	METH/UC	BAP	LUTH
Augusta (Rural)	1881	1168	786	742	2184	204	
Augusta (Rural)	1941	843	254	254	1322	30	
Prescott	1881	714	1203	387	663	16	
Prescott	1941	885	845	418	995	9	

ID: 0704399   EDWARDSBURGH

AREA: 119.97 sq. miles

1971 DENSITY:
   48.17 persons/sq. mile

TYPE:
   Combined

POPULATION:
   1851:   4779
   1881:   5431
   1941:   4280
   1971:   5779

CHANGES: 1891 Cardinal
   incorporated; 1961 part
   annexed to Prescott (in
   0704299).

SUBFILES:
   a. Edwardsburgh (Rural)
   b. Cardinal

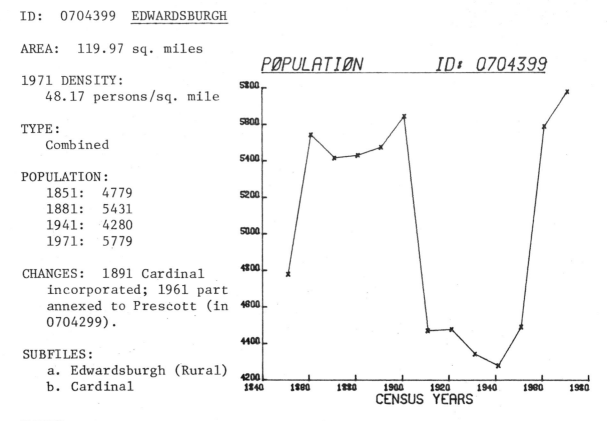

NOTES:

185 (Municipality of Cardinal, 1967) deals specifically with Cardinal.
Sawmilling in the township before 1851, and other economic activities,
are discussed in 86 (Smith, 1851).   The settlement history and the
decline of the population after 1900 are discussed in 175 (McKenzie,
1967).   Unincorporated villages of some note are Johnstown (1971
population 414) and Spencerville (1971 population 386).

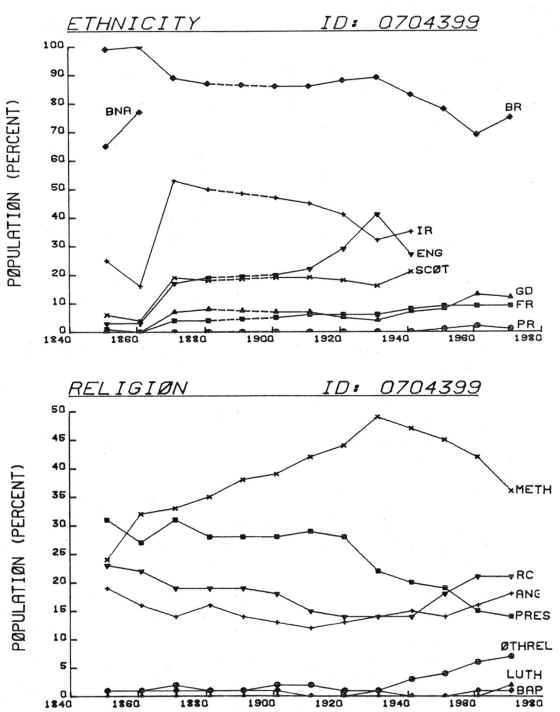

ID: 0704399   SUBFILES

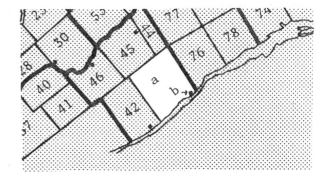

a. EDWARDSBURGH (RURAL)

    AREA: 119.06 sq. miles

    1971 DENSITY:
        32.87 persons/sq. mile

    POPULATION:
        1901:   4268
        1941:   2635
        1971:   3914

    CHANGES: 1891 Cardinal incorporated;   1961 part annexed to
        Prescott (in 0704299); 1971 part annexed to Cardinal.

b. CARDINAL

    AREA: 0.91 sq. miles

    1971 DENSITY:
        2049.45 persons/sq. mile

    POPULATION:
        1901:   1378
        1941:   1645
        1971:   1865

    CHANGES: 1891 incorporated; 1971 annexed part of Edwardsburgh
        (Rural).

ID: 0704399 SUBFILES cont'd

ETHNICITY

PLACE		YEAR	ENG	SCOT	IR	FR	GD	PR
Edwardsburgh	(Rural)	1901	859	824	2123	152	271	0
Edwardsburgh	(Rural)	1941	633	571	1075	164	137	6
Cardinal		1901	251	248	558	151	148	0
Cardinal		1941	530	310	442	189	151	5

RELIGION

PLACE		YEAR	ANG	RC	PRES	METH/UC	BAP	LUTH
Edwardsburgh	(Rural)	1901	456	656	1266	1768	40	
Edwardsburgh	(Rural)	1941	354	299	512	1373	12	
Cardinal		1901	277	333	319	424		
Cardinal		1941	276	313	360	654		

ID: 0704400 <u>GOWER SOUTH</u>

AREA: 34.29 sq. miles

1971 DENSITY:
  21.73 persons/sq. mile

TYPE:
  Rural

POPULATION:
  1851:   863
  1881: 1022
  1941:   668
  1971:   745

CHANGES: None

SUBFILES: None

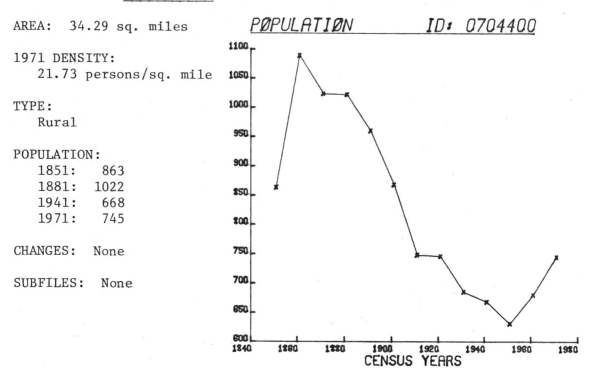

PØPULATIØN   *ID: 0704400*

CENSUS YEARS

NOTES:

None of the sources consulted deals specifically with Gower South.

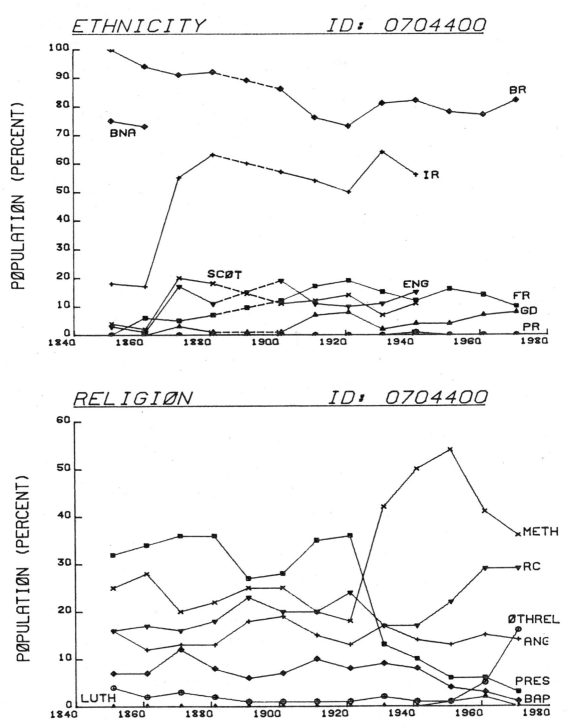

ETHNICITY   ID: 0704400

RELIGION   ID: 0704400

ID: 0704599 OXFORD (-ON-RIDEAU)

AREA: 101.10 sq. miles

1971 DENSITY:
   49.70 persons/sq. mile

TYPE:
   Combined

POPULATION:
   1851: 4496
   1881: 4973
   1941: 3215
   1971: 5025

CHANGES: 1861 Kemptville
   incorporated.

SUBFILES:
   a. Oxford (Rural)
   b. Kemptville

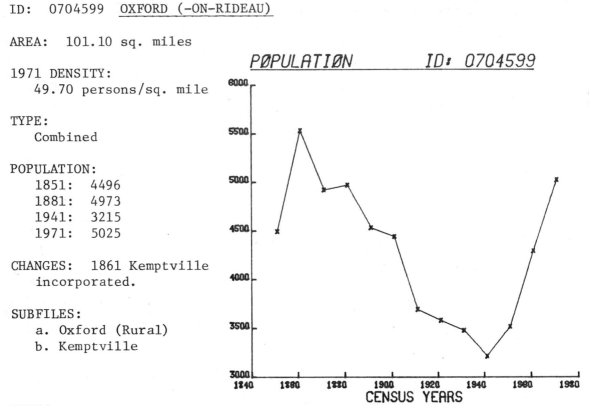

NOTES:

Kemptville is the subject of a monograph, 162 (Kemptville Centennial
Committee, 1967). Early economic activity in the village is detailed
in 86 (Smith, 1851). The history of Burritt's Rapids, on the border
with Marlborough Township (0805300) in Carleton County, is treated in
180 (Martyn, 1976). The largest unincorporated village is Oxford
Mills (1971 population 175).

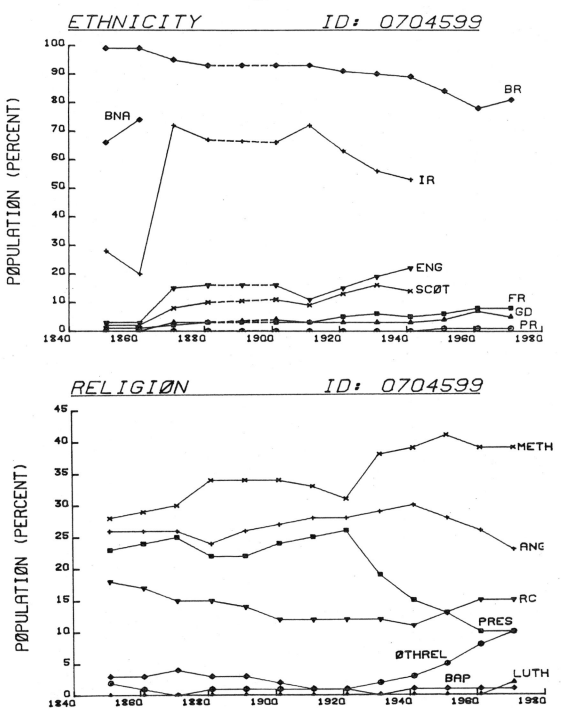

ID: 0704599   SUBFILES

a. OXFORD (RURAL)

   AREA: 100.42 sq. miles

   1971 DENSITY:
      26.01 persons/sq. mile

   POPULATION:
      1881:   3785
      1941:   1983
      1971:   2612

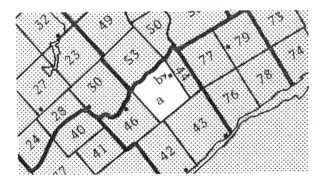

   CHANGES: 1861 Kemptville incorporated.

b. KEMPTVILLE

   AREA: 0.68 sq. miles

   1971 DENSITY:
      3548.53 persons/sq. mile

   POPULATION:
      1881:   1188
      1941:   1232
      1971:   2413

   CHANGES: 1861 incorporated.

ID: 0704599 SUBFILES cont'd

ETHNICITY

PLACE	YEAR	ENG	SCOT	IR	FR	GD	PR
Oxford (Rural)	1881	512	295	2795	79	91	0
Oxford (Rural)	1941	409	241	1160	82	51	8
Kemptville	1881	260	196	560	88	80	0
Kemptville	1941	309	213	530	93	51	0

RELIGION

PLACE	YEAR	ANG	RC	PRES	METH/UC	BAP	LUTH
Oxford (Rural)	1881	809	587	878	1371	123	
Oxford (Rural)	1941	572	247	286	814	21	
Kemptville	1881	403	175	226	334	41	
Kemptville	1941	397	119	199	430	27	

ID: 0704699   <u>WOLFORD</u>

AREA: 83.13 sq. miles

1971 DENSITY:
   24.80 persons/sq. mile

TYPE:
   Combined

POPULATION:
   1851:   3259
   1881:   3220
   1941:   1826
   1971:   2062

CHANGES: 1861 Merrickville
   incorporated.

SUBFILES:
   a. Wolford (Rural)
   b. Merrickville

PØPULATIØN   ID: 0704699

CENSUS YEARS

NOTES:

Merrickville is the subject of a monograph, 180 (Martyn, 1976). The
unincorporated village of Jasper, located on the border with Kitley
Township in Leeds County, had a population of 275 in 1971.

161

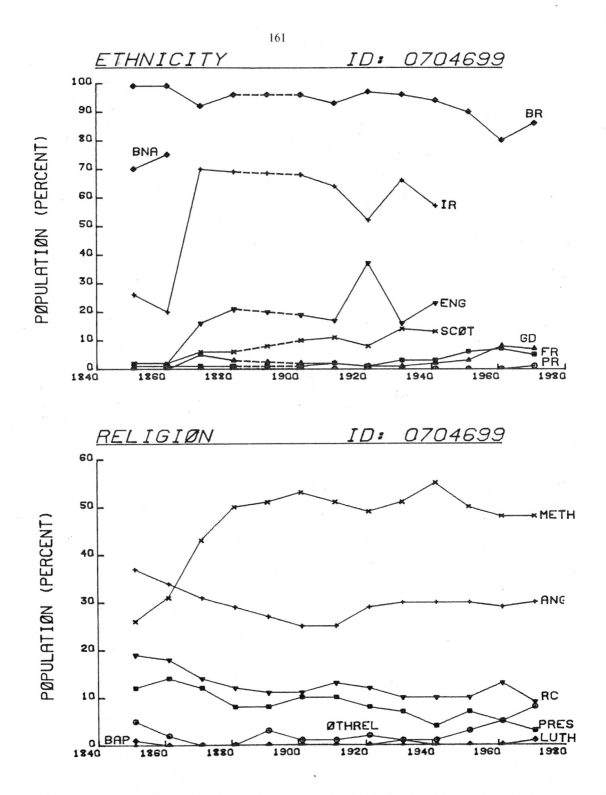

ID: 0704699 SUBFILES

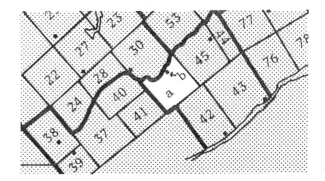

a. WOLFORD (RURAL)

AREA: 81.54 sq. miles

1971 DENSITY:
13.88 persons/sq. mile

POPULATION:
1881: 2401
1941: 1032
1971: 1132

CHANGES: 1861 Merrickville incorporated.

b. MERRICKVILLE

AREA: 1.59 sq. miles

1971 DENSITY:
584.91 persons/sq. mile

POPULATION:
1881: 819
1941: 794
1971: 930

CHANGES: 1861 incorporated.

ID: 0704699 SUBFILES cont'd

ETHNICITY

PLACE	YEAR	ENG	SCOT	IR	FR	GD	PR
Wolford (Rural)	1881	527	116	1666	4	88	0
Wolford (Rural)	1941	201	185	616	16	14	0
Merrickville	1881	145	82	553	22	16	0
Merrickville	1941	228	61	426	45	20	0

RELIGION

PLACE	YEAR	ANG	RC	PRES	METH/UC	BAP	LUTH
Wolford (Rural)	1881	652	188	205	1349	6	
Wolford (Rural)	1941	279	60	45	634	3	
Merrickville	1881	277	199	63	261	9	
Merrickville	1941	272	114	30	374	1	

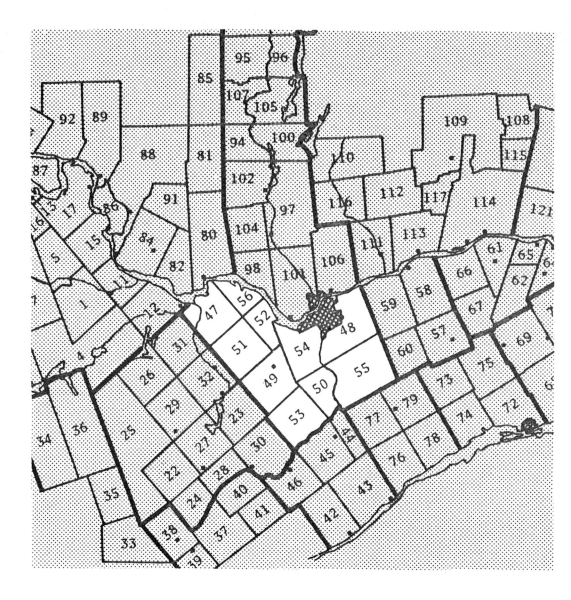

CARLETON COUNTY (08)

Integral Units   047 - 056

As Carleton County is defined for the purposes of this study, the City of Ottawa (including the village of Rockcliffe Park and the City of Vanier) is excluded from the County. So is Cumberland Township, which is treated as part of Russell County.

Even with these exclusions, Carleton County has a rich bibliography. It is the subject of two monographs: 107 (Bond, 1968) and 208 (Walker and Walker, 1968). The latter emphasizes settlement and economic development in each township. Earlier works include 99 and 100 (Belden, 1879) and 262 (Read, 1911). Figures for immigrants between 1833 and 1844 are given in 23 (Cowan, 1961), p.294. The demographic importance of Ottawa to the region is brought out in 275 (Dawes, 1961: Map 11) and 68 (Macleod, 1972). A map of land types in the region is given in 286 (MacKay, 1949).

In spite of the boundary changes and excluded areas, the considerable census information available at the county level may still be of interest and can be found at the census division level for The Regional Municipality of Ottawa-Carleton. Other valuable information is available for parts of the county in tables dealing with the Census Metropolitan Area of Ottawa-Hull. The 1971 totals for Carleton County were: population 135,681; area 898.28 sq. miles; density 151.05 persons/sq. mile. The totals for the Regional Municipality of Ottawa-Carleton (including Cumberland, City of Ottawa, etc.) were: population 471,931; area 1,064.50 sq. miles; density 443.34 persons/sq. mile.

ID: 0804700 FITZROY

AREA: 99.03 sq. miles

1971 DENSITY:
  23.80 persons/sq. mile

TYPE:
  Rural

POPULATION:
  1851: 2807
  1881: 3378
  1941: 2225
  1971: 2357

CHANGES: None

SUBFILES: None

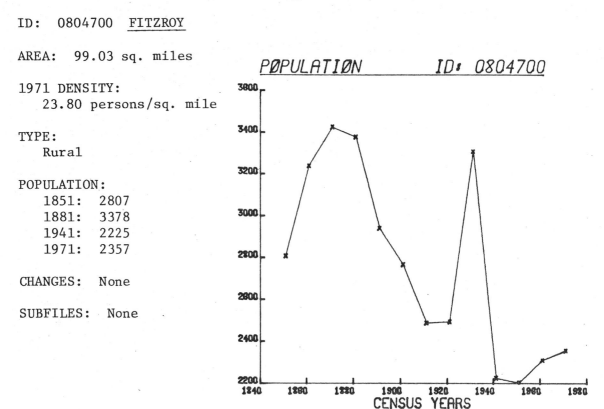

POPULATION   ID: 0804700

NOTES:

Walker, 1968 (item 208) includes a discussion of Fitzroy. Since 1976,
together with Huntley (0805100) and Torbolton (0805600), Fitzroy forms
part of the new township of West Carleton. In 1971 the unincorporated
village of Fitzroy Harbour had a population of 317 and that of Kinburn
was 180.

167

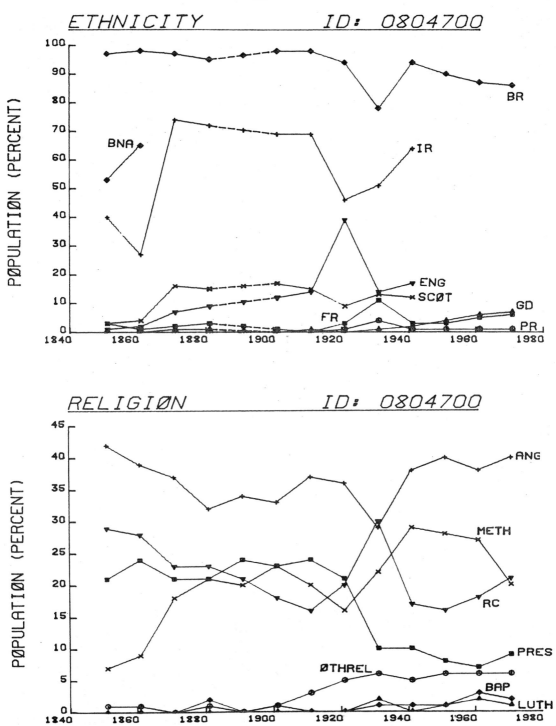

ID: 0804800   <u>GLOUCESTER</u>

AREA: 114.05 sq. miles

1971 DENSITY:
  325.69 persons/sq. mile

TYPE:
  Rural

POPULATION:
  1851:   3005
  1881:   6254
  1941:   9871
  1971: 37145

CHANGES: 1951 part annexed
  to City of Ottawa.

SUBFILES: None

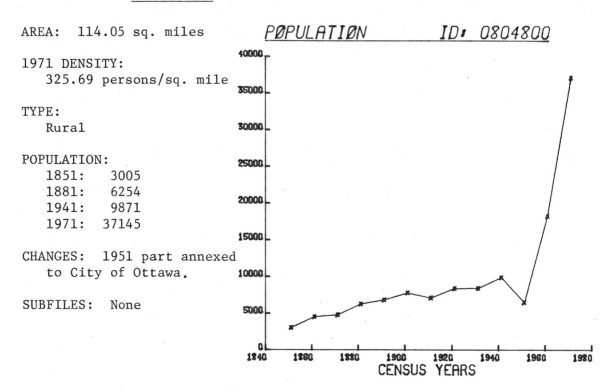

POPULATION   ID: 0804800

CENSUS YEARS

NOTES:

George, 1972 (item 277) gives information on early stages of population growth after 1830 as a result of the completion of the Rideau
Canal. The township of Gloucester has long contained urban components
and its marked population growth since 1951 more than matches that of
neighbouring Ottawa. Considerable census information is available in
tables dealing with the Census Metropolitan Area of Ottawa-Hull. In
1976, more than 2/3 of the township area is listed as Rural fringe;
the remainder is part of the Urbanized Core. 1976 Census Tract Nos.
120.01-127. In 1976 a small part was annexed to the new township of
Rideau (see 0805300). The township contains a long list of unincorporated places, some of them recent subdivisions. Among the most
important such places in 1971 were: Blackburn Hamlet (population
3841) Orleans (population 2810), Hillside Gardens (population 416),
South Gloucester (population 270), and Carlsbad Springs (population
226).

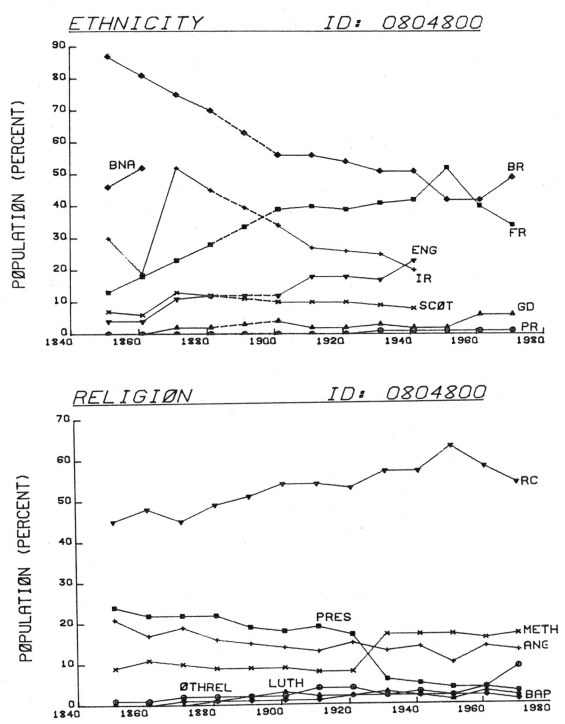

ID: 0804999   <u>GOULBOURN</u>

AREA: 108.04 sq. miles

1971 DENSITY:
  87.53 persons/sq. mile

TYPE:
  Combined

POPULATION:
  1851: 2959
  1881: 3820
  1941: 2350
  1971: 9457

CHANGES: 1961 Stittsville
  incorporated.

SUBFILES:
  a. Goulbourn (Rural)
  b. Richmond
  c. Stittsville

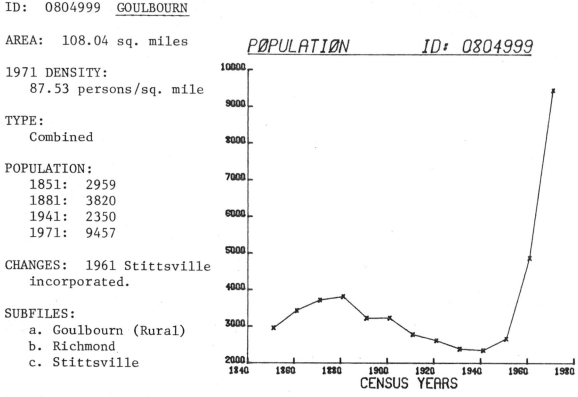

PØPULATIØN   *ID: 0804999*

CENSUS YEARS

NOTES:

Early population growth in the township is documented in 277 (George, 1972). Richmond is the subject of a monograph, 144 (Graham, 1968) and is treated as well in Walker, 1968 (item 208). Stittsville is also the subject of a monograph, 203 (Stittsville Women's Institute, 1963). Recent population growth since 1951 is due to proximity to the City of Ottawa. Considerable census information is available in tables dealing with the Census Metropolitan Area of Ottawa-Hull, Urban and Rural Fringe. 1976 Census Tract Numbers 150-151. Glen Cairn, an unincorporated suburban community, had grown rapidly to a population of 2448 by 1971.

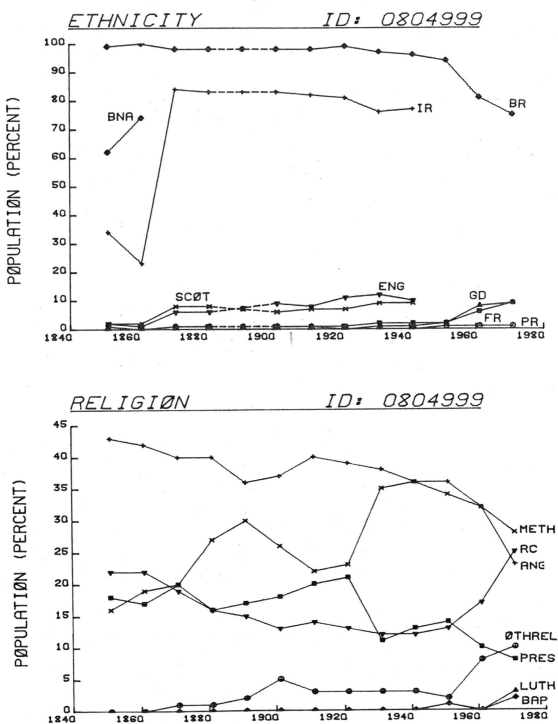

ID: 0804999 SUBFILES

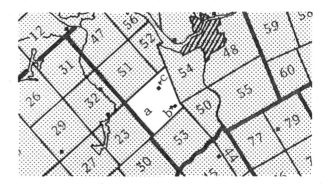

a. GOULBOURN (RURAL)

   AREA: 104.33 sq. miles

   1971 DENSITY:
      51.19 persons/sq. mile

   POPULATION:
      1881: 3381
      1941: 1893
      1971: 5341

   CHANGES: 1961 Stittsville incorporated.

b. RICHMOND

   AREA: 2.34 sq. miles

   1971 DENSITY:
      906.84 persons/sq. mile

   POPULATION:
      1881:   439
      1941:   457
      1971: 2122

   CHANGES: None

c. STITTSVILLE

   AREA: 1.37 sq. miles

   1971 DENSITY:
      1455.47 persons/sq. mile

   POPULATION:
      1971: 1994

   CHANGES: 1961 incorporated.

ID: 0804999 SUBFILES cont'd

ETHNICITY

PLACE	YEAR	ENG	SCOT	IR	FR	GD	PR
Goulbourn (Rural)	1881	178	248	2881	16	48	8
Goulbourn (Rural)	1941	155	143	1514	35	23	3
Goulbourn (Rural)	1971	(British)	4095		450	480	35
Richmond	1881	59	57	305	15	3	0
Richmond	1941	83	64	287	20	2	0
Richmond	1971	(British)	1555		210	240	15
Stittsville	1971	(British)	1465		160	90	10

RELIGION

PLACE	YEAR	ANG	RC	PRES	METH/UC	BAP	LUTH
Goulbourn (Rural)	1881	1339	534	536	938		
Goulbourn (Rural)	1941	672	247	217	712		
Goulbourn (Rural)	1971	1145	1500	395	1435	65	215
Richmond	1881	197	85	75	81		
Richmond	1941	170	45	83	128		
Richmond	1971	535	560	180	640	40	50
Stittsville	1971	530	300	185	560	120	65

ID: 0805000 <u>GOWER NORTH</u>

AREA: 55.88 sq. miles

1971 DENSITY:
  66.68 persons/sq. mile

TYPE:
  Rural

POPULATION:
  1851: 1777
  1881: 2481
  1941: 1777
  1971: 3726

CHANGES: None

SUBFILES: None

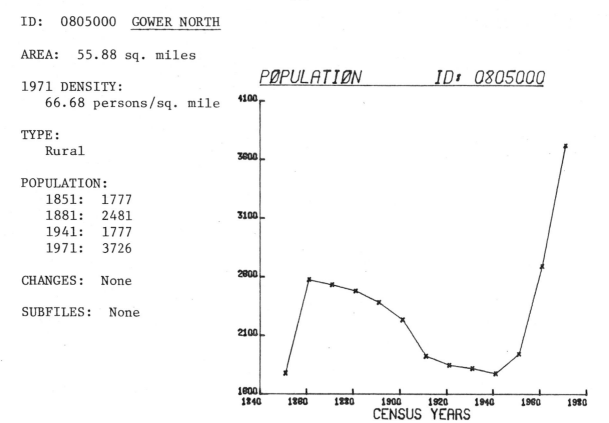

POPULATION   ID: 0805000

CENSUS YEARS

NOTES:

In addition to discussion in 208 (Walker, 1968), Gower North is
treated extensively in 70 (Lindsay, 1972). Since 1976 Gower North
forms part of the new township of Rideau (see 0805300) and is listed
as part of both Urban and Rural Fringe of the Census Metropolitan
Area of Ottawa. In 1976 a small part of Osgoode Township (0805500)
was annexed. In 1971 the township had three notable unincorporated
villages: Manotick (population 476), North Gower (population 363),
and Kars (population 183).

175

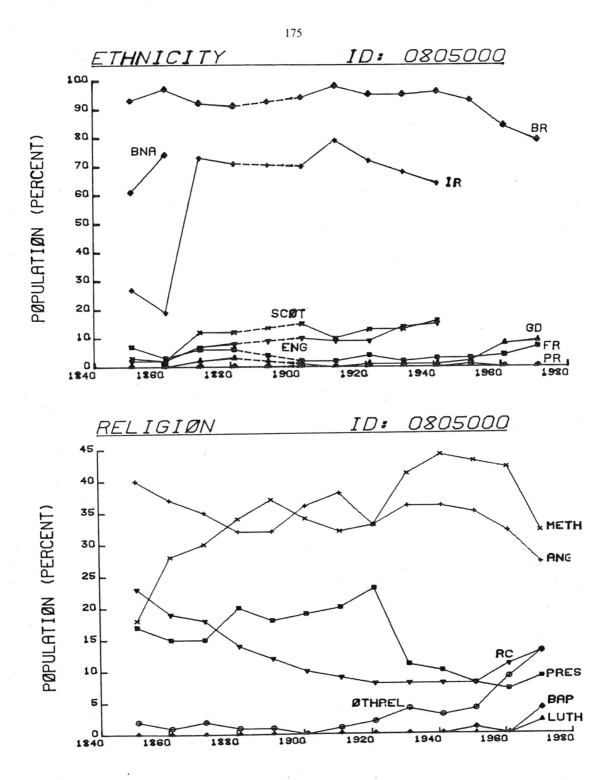

ID 0805100 <u>HUNTLEY</u>

AREA: 99.31 sq. miles

1971 DENSITY:
  22.94 persons/sq. mile

TYPE:
  Rural

POPULATION:
  1851: 2519
  1881: 2534
  1941: 1512
  1971: 2278

CHANGES: None

SUBFILES: None

NOTES:

In addition to discussion in 208 (Walker, 1968), Huntley is the subject of a monograph, 96 (Argue et al., 1974). Since 1976 Huntley
forms part of the new township of West Carleton (see 0804700). The
largest community, the unincorporated village of Carp, had a population of 516 in 1971. Note the very high percentage of Irish in the
ethnicity graph.

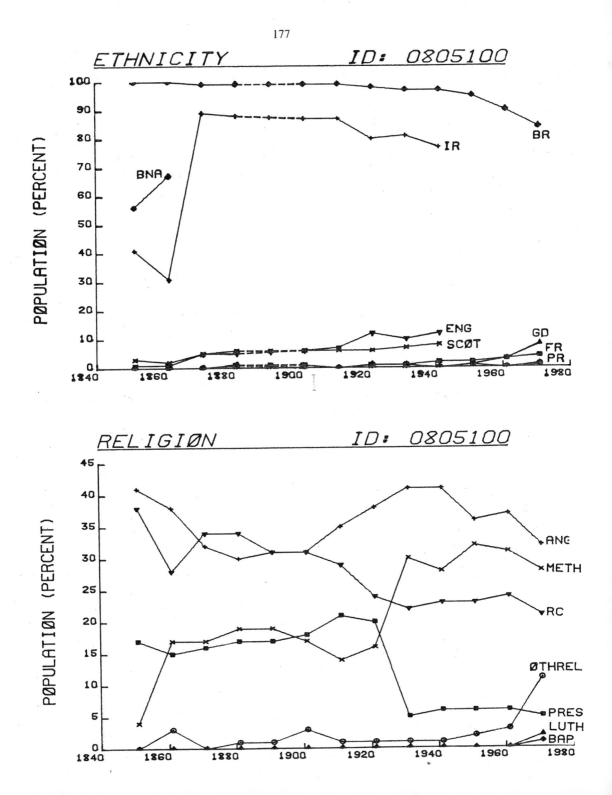

ID: 0805200 <u>MARCH</u>

AREA: 45.27 sq. miles

1971 DENSITY:
   128.61 persons/sq. mile

TYPE:
   Rural

POPULATION:
   1851: 1125
   1881: 1318
   1941:   829
   1971: 5822

CHANGES: None

SUBFILES: None

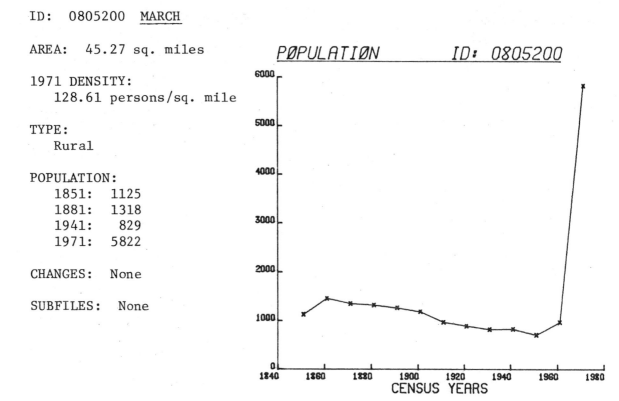

NOTES:

March is the subject of a monograph, 116 (Burns et al., 1972). There
has been sharp population growth in March since 1961 due to its
proximity to the City of Ottawa. Considerable census information is
available in tables dealing with the Census Metropolitan Area of
Ottawa-Hull, Urban and Rural Fringe. The centre of growth in the
township, the unincorporated suburban community of Kanata, had a
population of 4635 in 1971.

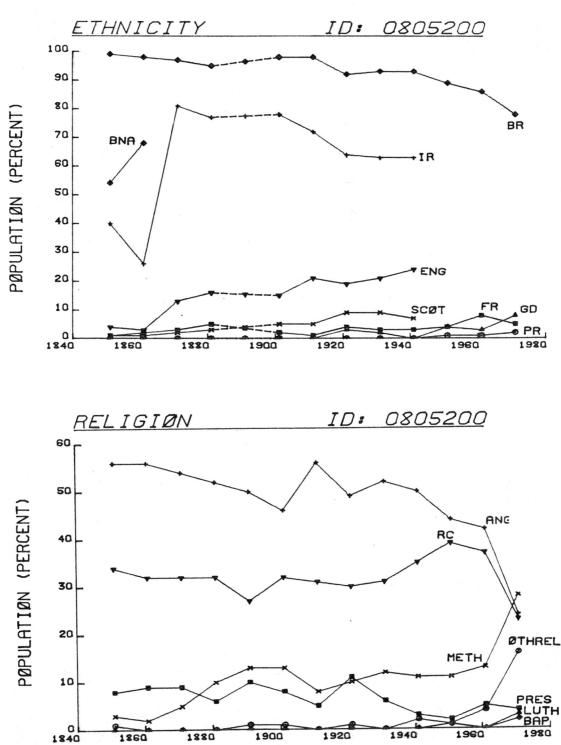

ID: 0805300 MARLBOROUGH

AREA: 101.13 sq. miles

1971 DENSITY:
  11.54 persons/sq. mile

TYPE:
  Rural

POPULATION:
  1851: 2053
  1881: 2090
  1941:   886
  1971: 1167

CHANGES: None

SUBFILES: None

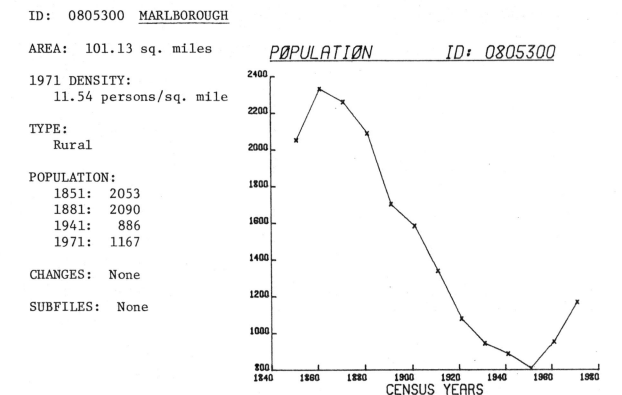

POPULATION   ID: 0805300

CENSUS YEARS

NOTES:

The history of Burritt's Rapids (now listed by the census as part of
Oxford township (0704599) in Grenville County) is treated in 180
(Martyn, 1976). In addition figures on early population growth for
Marlborough are given in 277 (George, 1972). Since 1976 Marlborough
forms, together with Gower North (0805000) and small parts of
Gloucester (0804800), Nepean (0805400), and Osgoode (0805500) the
new township of Rideau, which is listed as part of Urban and Rural
Fringe of the Census Metropolitan Area of Ottawa-Hull.

181

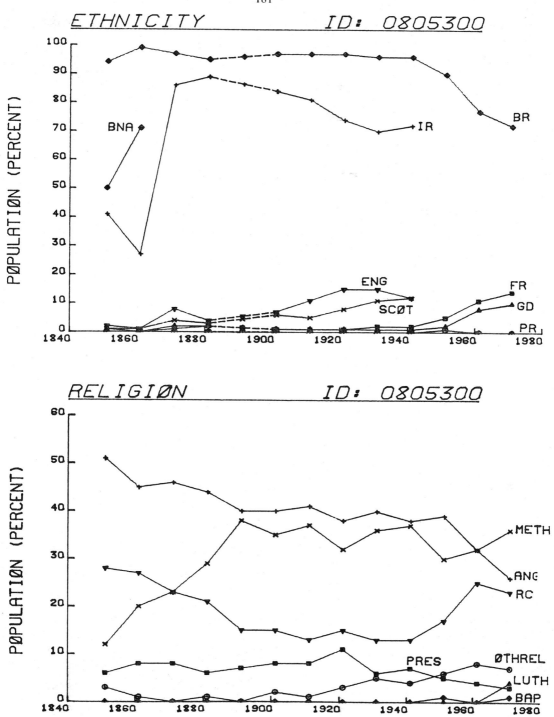

ID: 0805400 <u>NEPEAN</u>

AREA: 86.28 sq. miles

1971 DENSITY:
  748.79 persons/sq. mile

TYPE:
  Rural

POPULATION:
  1851: 3800
  1881: 8044
  1941: 13859
  1971: 64606

CHANGES: 1901 part annexed
  to City of Ottawa; 1951
  part annexed to City of
  Ottawa.

SUBFILES: None

POPULATION   ID: 0805400

CENSUS YEARS

NOTES:

In addition to treatments in 208 (Walker, 1968) and 277 (George, 1972)
the history of Nepean is the subject of a thesis, 280 (Heathcote,
1973). Nepean has long contained urban areas, which like those in
Gloucester and Cumberland are now among the fastest growing in the
Ottawa urban area. Considerable census information is available in
tables dealing with the Census Metropolitan Area of Ottawa-Hull. In
1976, 69 sq. mi. is listed as Rural Fringe; the remaining 17.3 sq. mi.
is part of the Urbanized Core. 1976 Census Tract Numbers 130-141.
Small part annexed to the new township of Rideau in 1976 (see 0805300).
The 1971 census lists two sizeable unincorporated places within Nepean:
Fallowfield (population 296) and Heart's Desire (population 235).
Nepean is unusual in that it is the only "core" Ottawa Valley township
to have an English plurality in 1941.

183

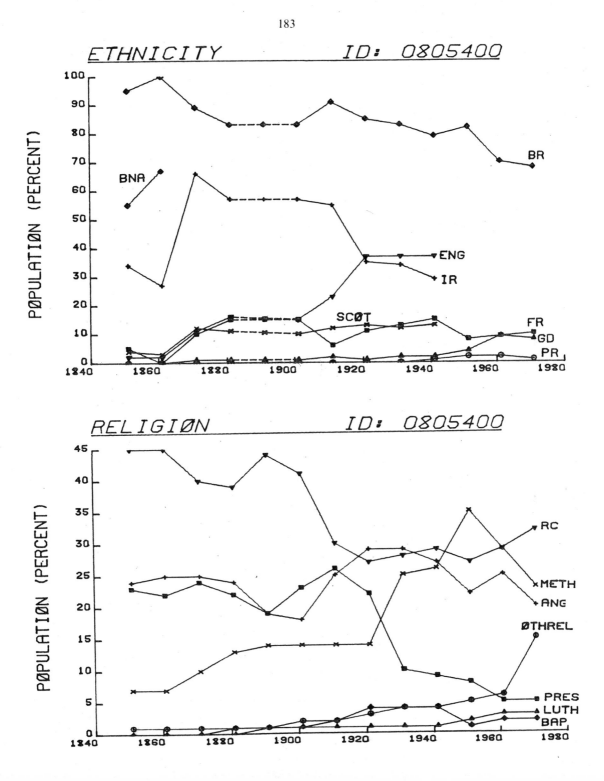

ID: 0805500 <u>OSGOODE</u>

AREA: 146.90 sq. miles

1971 DENSITY:
   52.80 persons/sq. mile

TYPE:
   Rural

POPULATION:
   1851: 3050
   1881: 4753
   1941: 4095
   1971: 7757

CHANGES: None

SUBFILES: None

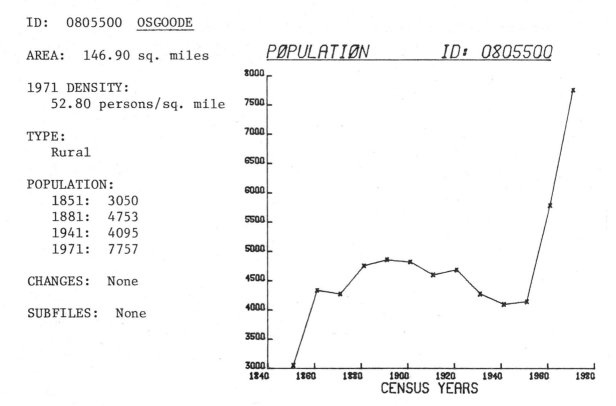

PØPULATIØN   *ID: 0805500*

CENSUS YEARS

NOTES:

Apart from 208 (Walker, 1968), none of the sources examined deals
specifically with Osgoode township. Since 1976 Osgoode is listed as
part of the Rural Fringe of the Census Metropolitan Area of Ottawa-
Hull. 1976 Census Tract Numbers 190-191. In 1976 a small part was
annexed to Rideau township (Gower North part) (see 0805300). The
1971 census gives a long list of unincorporated places for Osgoode
township. The most important are (with population figures): Osgoode
(823), Metcalfe (473), Green Acres (308), Vernon (237), Kenmore (220),
and Greely (193).

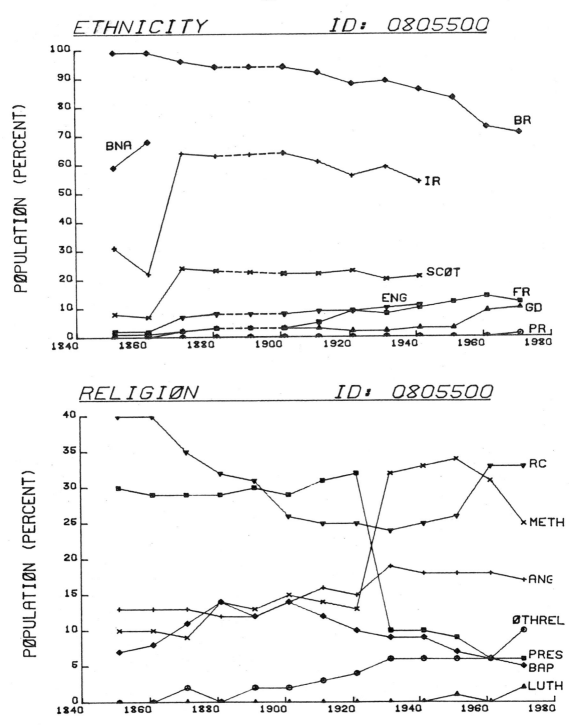

ID: 0805600 <u>TORBOLTON</u>

AREA: 42.39 sq. miles

1971 DENSITY:
  32.22 persons/sq. mile

TYPE:
  Rural

POPULATION:
  1851:   542
  1881:   1024
  1941:   719
  1971:   1366

CHANGES: None

SUBFILES: None

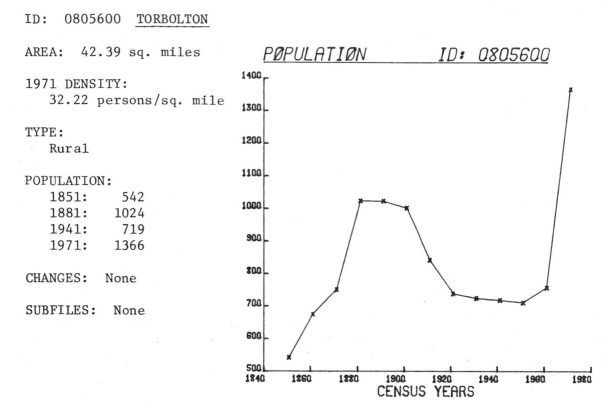

NOTES:

Since 1976 Torbolton forms part of the new township of West Carleton
(see 0804700). It is the subject of a monograph, 98 (Baskin and
Wilson, 1967). The 1971 population of the unincorporated community of
Constance Bay and Buckhams Bay was 532.

187

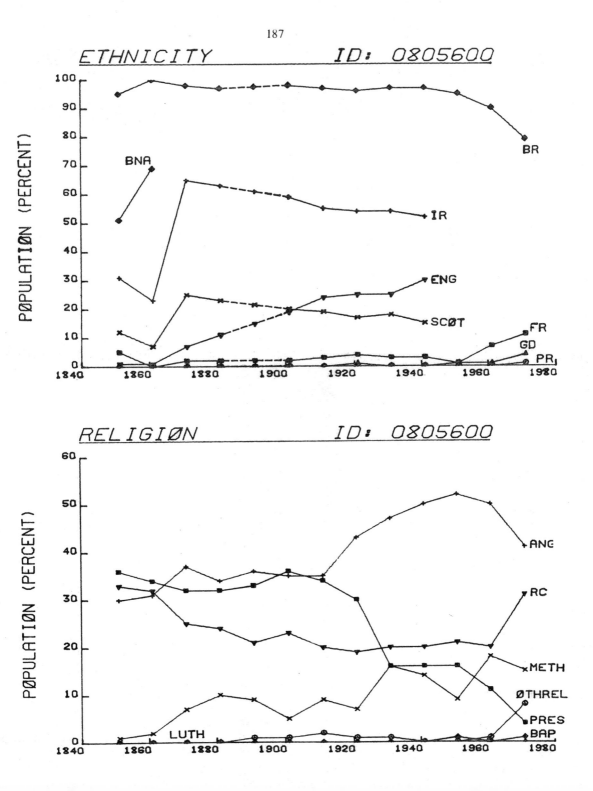

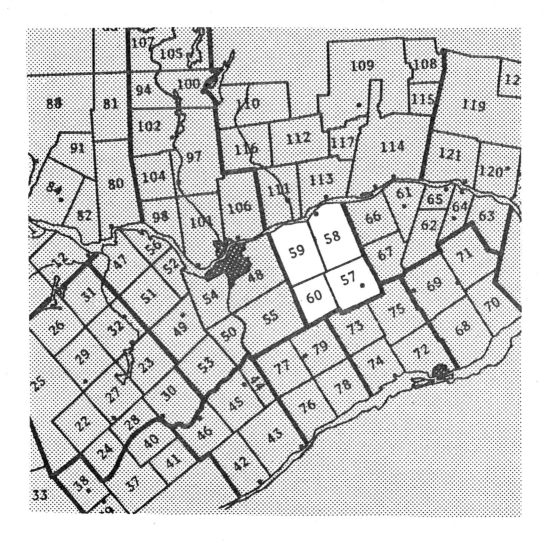

RUSSELL COUNTY (09)

Integral Units   057 - 060

Although there are few studies dealing with specific townships, towns or villages within the Prescott-Russell area, there is a major work dealing with the whole area, 109 (Brault, 1965), as well as two theses, 273 (Cartwright, 1973) and 290 (Ray, 1961), dealing with demographic changes. The French-Canadian population in the area is the subject of an article, 243b (Lapierre, 1977). The region features also in works of still wider scope, including 107 (Bond, 1968), 146 (Greening, 1961) and 168 (Legget, 1975). See also 68, 86, 275 and 286. Finally there is a bibliography of the two Counties, 2b (Emard, 1980).

The boundaries of Russell County in this study include Cumberland Township (now part of Ottawa-Carleton), which has been part of the County for most of its history. Early census tables for Russell County thus give considerable information at the census division level. The county totals for 1971 (including Cumberland) were: population 25,581; area 414.72 sq. miles; density 61.68 persons/sq. mile.

ID: 0905799 <u>CAMBRIDGE</u>

AREA: 100.49 sq. miles

1971 DENSITY:
  38.73 persons/sq. mile

TYPE:
  Combined

POPULATION:
  1851:   200
  1881: 1676
  1941: 3662
  1971: 3892

CHANGES: 1901 Casselman
  incorporated.

SUBFILES:
  a. Cambridge (Rural)
  b. Casselman

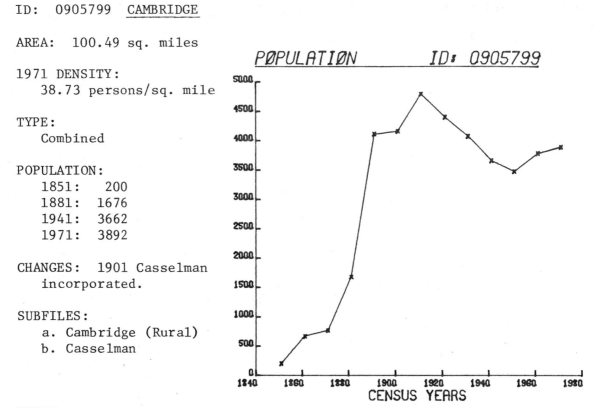

PØPULATIØN   ID: 0905799

CENSUS YEARS

NOTES:

None of the sources studied deals specifically with Cambridge. The
unincorporated villages of Limoges and St. Albert had populations of
355 and 239 respectively in 1971.

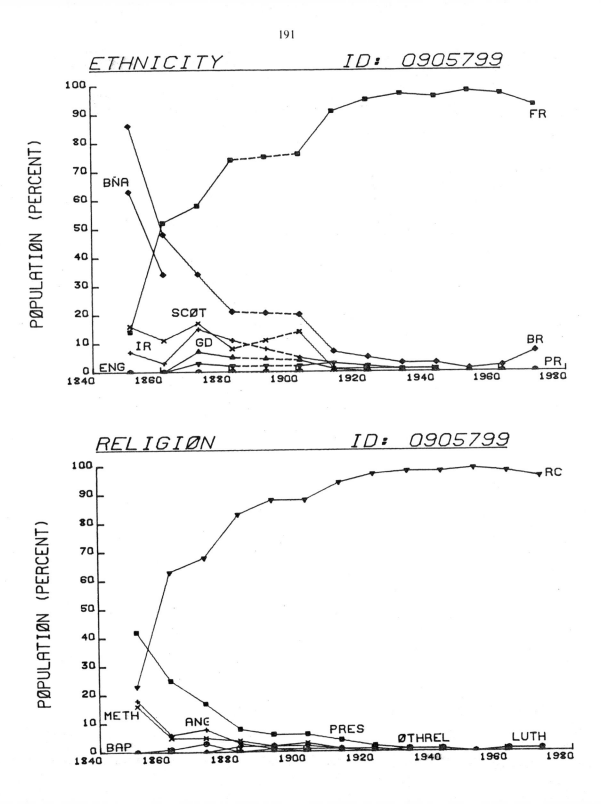

ID: 0905799   SUBFILES

a. <u>CAMBRIDGE (RURAL)</u>

   AREA: 98.72 sq. miles

   1971 DENSITY:
      25.88 persons/sq. mile

   POPULATION:
      1901:   3459
      1941:   2641
      1971:   2555

   CHANGES: 1901 Casselman incorporated.

b. <u>CASSELMAN</u>

   AREA: 1.77 sq. miles

   1971 DENSITY:
      755.37 persons/sq. mile

   POPULATION:
      1901:   707
      1941:   1021
      1971:   1337

   CHANGES: 1901 incorporated.

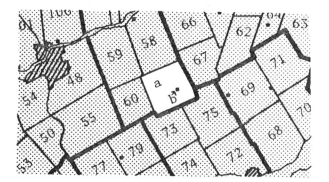

ID: 0905799 SUBFILES cont'd

ETHNICITY

PLACE		YEAR	ENG	SCOT	IR	FR	GD	PR
Cambridge	(Rural)	1901	41	524	163	2608	120	0
Cambridge	(Rural)	1941	28	25	37	2523	15	6
Casselman		1901	23	42	32	571	39	0
Casselman		1941	8	2	3	1008	0	0

RELIGION

PLACE		YEAR	ANG	RC	PRES	METH/UC	BAP	LUTH
Cambridge	(Rural)	1901	25	3093	195	91	49	
Cambridge	(Rural)	1941	15	2573	27	6	11	
Casselman		1901	14	583	70	15	17	
Casselman		1941	0	1002	2	1	0	

ID: 0905899 <u>CLARENCE</u>

AREA: 115.55 sq. miles

1971 DENSITY:
    71.29 persons/sq. mile

TYPE:
    Combined

POPULATION:
    1851:   508
    1881: 4411
    1941: 6670
    1971: 8238

CHANGES: 1891 Rockland
    incorporated.

SUBFILES:
    a. Clarence (Rural)
    b. Rockland

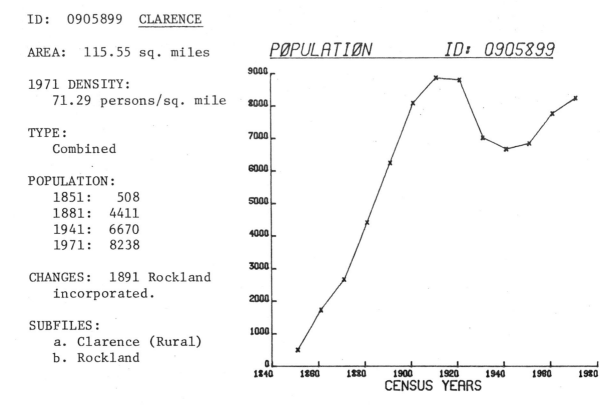

POPULATION   ID: 0905899

CENSUS YEARS

NOTES:

No source deals specifically with Clarence or Rockland. Since 1976
Clarence is listed as part of the Urban and Rural Fringe of the Census
Metropolitan Area of Ottawa-Hull.   In 1971 the unincorporated
communities had the following populations: Bourget (855), Clarence
Creek (411), Hammond (270), St. Pascal Baylon (185). The 1961 drop in
the French line of the Ethnicity Graph most probably does not
represent any actual change. In that year there was an unusually
high count (15 percent of the township) of those whose ethnicity was
"not stated" - Rockland (703), rest of Clarence (446).

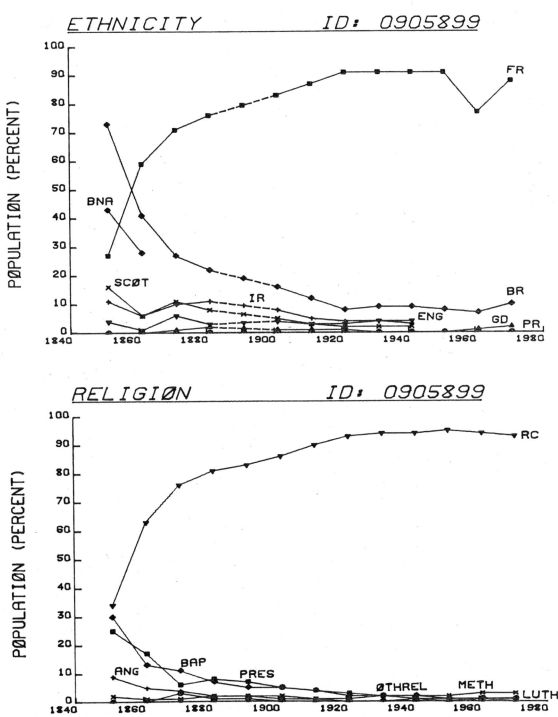

ETHNICITY   ID: 0905899

RELIGION   ID: 0905899

ID: 0905899 SUBFILES

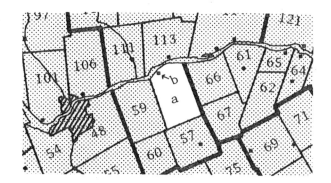

a. CLARENCE (RURAL)

AREA: 112.30 sq. miles

1971 DENSITY:
    40.86 persons/sq. mile

POPULATION:
    1901: 6085
    1941: 4630
    1971: 4589

CHANGES: 1891 Rockland incorporated; 1971 part annexed to Rock-
    land.

b. ROCKLAND

AREA: 3.25 sq. miles

1971 DENSITY:
    1122.77 persons/sq. mile

POPULATION:
    1901: 1998
    1941: 2040
    1971: 3649

CHANGES: 1891 incorporated; 1971 annexed part of Clarence (Rural).

ID: 0905899 SUBFILES cont'd

ETHNICITY

PLACE	YEAR	ENG	SCOT	IR	FR	GD	PR
Clarence (Rural)	1901	246	255	463	5085	29	0
Clarence (Rural)	1941	251	47	132	4193	6	0
Rockland	1901	71	126	147	1636	14	0
Rockland	1941	48	62	66	1849	1	1

RELIGION

PLACE	YEAR	ANG	RC	PRES	METH/UC	BAP	LUTH
Clarence (Rural)	1901	80	5283	282	144	280	
Clarence (Rural)	1941	30	4330	41	110	96	
Rockland	1901	35	1677	118	12	155	
Rockland	1941	9	1923	32	45	24	

ID: 0905900 CUMBERLAND

AREA: 121.89 sq. miles

1971 DENSITY:
   76.25 persons/sq. mile

TYPE:
   Rural

POPULATION:
   1851: 1659
   1881: 3535
   1941: 3847
   1971: 9294

CHANGES: Since 1971 listed
   in the Census as part of
   the Regional Municipality of Ottawa.

SUBFILES: None

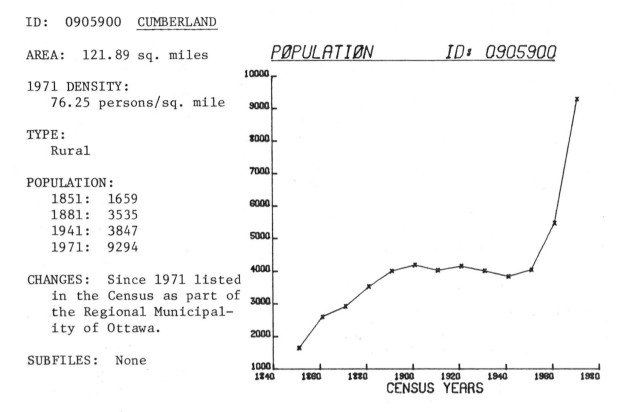

POPULATION   ID: 0905900

CENSUS YEARS

NOTES:

There are no historical works dealing with Cumberland specifically.
Cumberland has contained urban areas since 1971, when it was listed as
part of the Regional Municipality of Ottawa. Along with Gloucester,
it has one of the fastest growth rates in the Ottawa Area. Considerable census information is available in tables dealing with the
Census Metropolitan Area of Ottawa-Hull. In 1976, 2.9 sq. mi. were
listed as part of the Urbanized Core; the remaining 119.2 sq. mi. as
Rural Fringe. The 1971 census lists the following unincorporated
places (with their populations): Queenswood Heights (1980), Queenswood (757), Cumberland (581), Vars (395), Sarsfield (254), Navan (238).

199

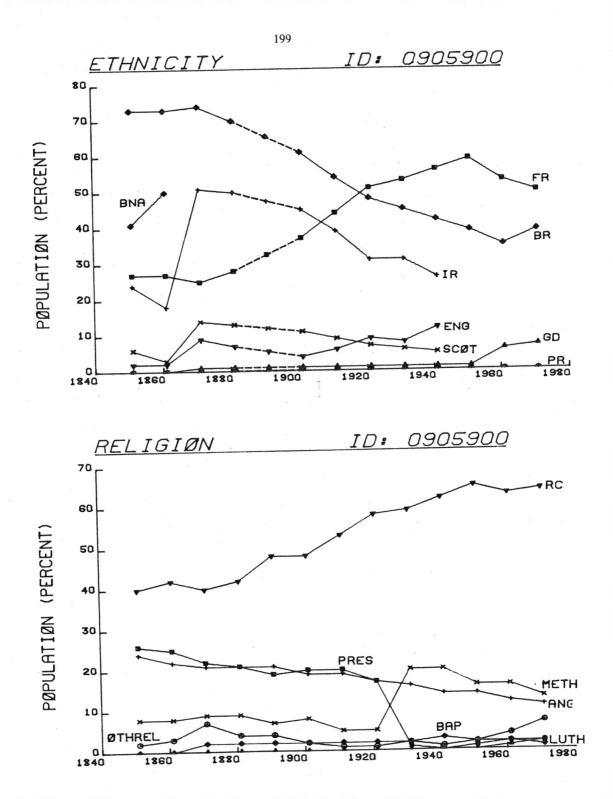

ID: 0906000   <u>RUSSELL</u>

AREA: 76.79 sq. miles

1971 DENSITY:
   54.13 persons/sq. mile

TYPE:
   Rural

POPULATION:
   1851:   503
   1881:   3458
   1941:   3269
   1971:   4157

CHANGES: None

SUBFILES: None

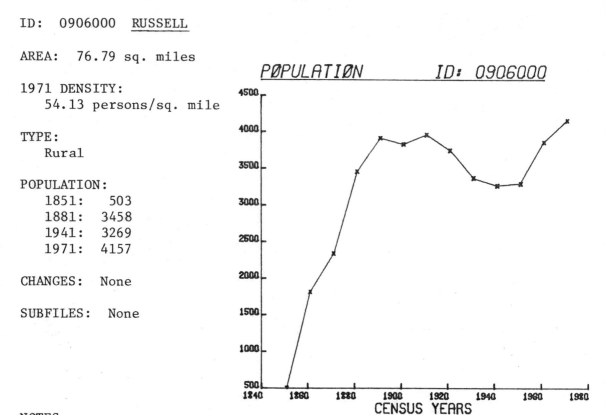

NOTES:

None of the sources examined deal specifically with Russell Township.
The township contains two important unincorporated villages: Embrum
(1971 population 1452) and Russell (1971 population 583).

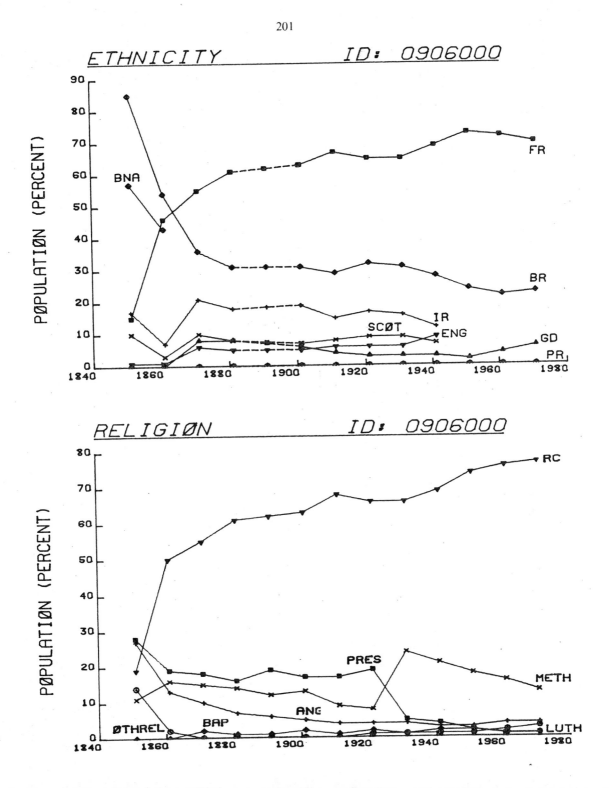

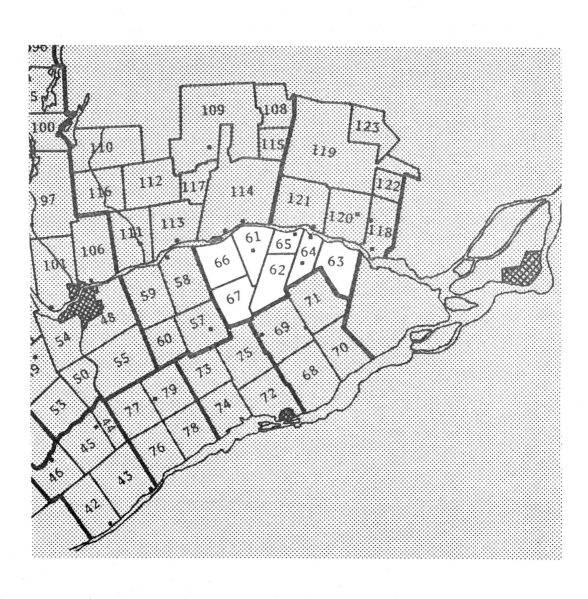

Integral Units   061 - 067

For general historical studies, see the introduction to 09 - Russell County. In addition to the works listed there, 205 (Thomas, 1896) deals with Prescott County together with Argenteuil - an exceptional leap across the River in the historiography of the Ottawa Valley.

Considerable census information on Prescott County is available in tables, maps, and analyses at the census division level. County totals for 1971: population 27,832; area 480.43 sq. miles; density 57.93 persons/sq. mile.

ID: 1006199   ALFRED

AREA: 71.25 sq. miles

1971 DENSITY:
   41.47 persons/sq. mile

TYPE:
   Combined

POPULATION:
   1851:   584
   1881:   3208
   1941:   2910
   1971:   2955

CHANGES: 1961 Alfred
   incorporated.

SUBFILES:
   a. Alfred (Rural)
   b. Alfred (Urban)

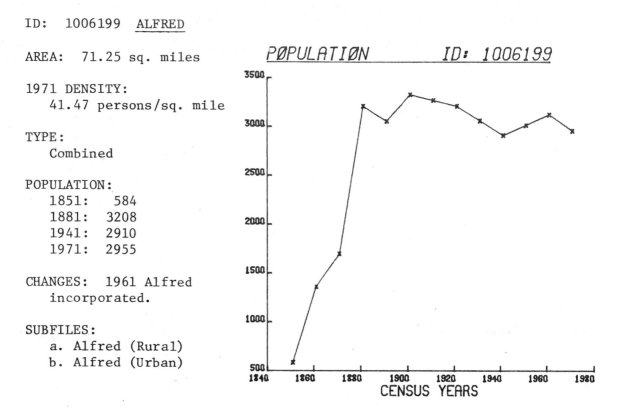

NOTES:

Brault, 1965 (item 109) is particularly detailed in his treatment of
Alfred. The unincorporated village of Lefaivre had a population of
214 in 1971.

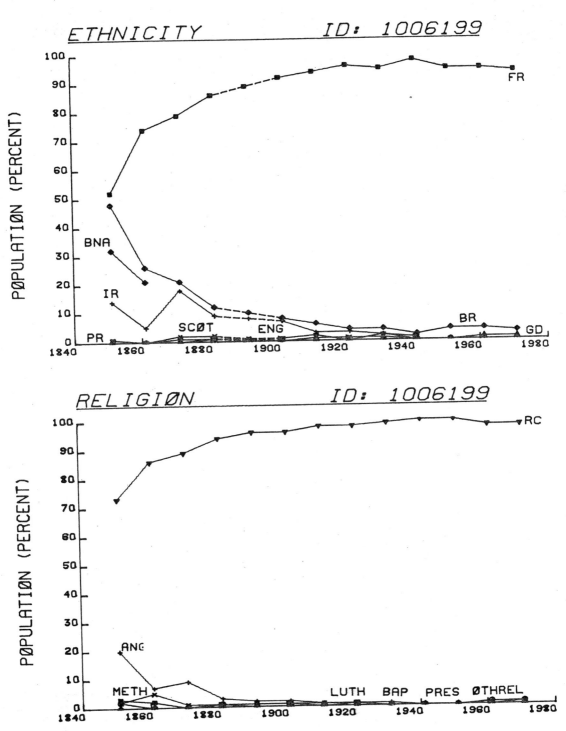

ETHNICITY   ID: 1006199

RELIGIØN   ID: 1006199

ID: 1006199   SUBFILES

a. ALFRED (RURAL)

   AREA: 70.38 sq. miles

   1971 DENSITY:
       24.51 persons/sq. mile

   POPULATION:
       1971: 1725

   CHANGES: 1961 Alfred
       (Urban) incorporated.

b. ALFRED (URBAN)

   AREA: 0.87 sq. miles

   1971 DENSITY:
       1413.79 persons/sq. mile

   POPULATION:
       1971: 1230

   CHANGES: 1961 incorporated.

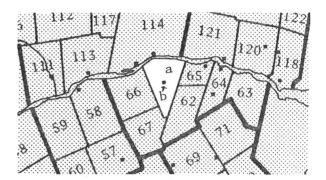

ID: 1006199 SUBFILES cont'd

ETHNICITY

PLACE	YEAR	ENG	SCOT	IR	FR	GD	PR
Alfred (Rural)	1971	(British)	70		1535	5	0
Alfred (Urban)	1971	(British)	30		1315	40	10

RELIGION

PLACE	YEAR	ANG	RC	PRES	METH/UC	BAP	LUTH
Alfred (Rural)	1971	20	1595	0	0	0	0
Alfred (Urban)	1971	0	1385	0	0	0	15

208

ID: 1006200   CALEDONIA

AREA: 72.90 sq. miles

1971 DENSITY:
    17.38 persons/sq. mile

TYPE:
    Rural

POPULATION:
    1851:   958
    1881:   1751
    1941:   1757
    1971:   1267

CHANGES: 1971 part annexed
    to St. Isidore de Pres-
    cott (in 1006799).

SUBFILES: None

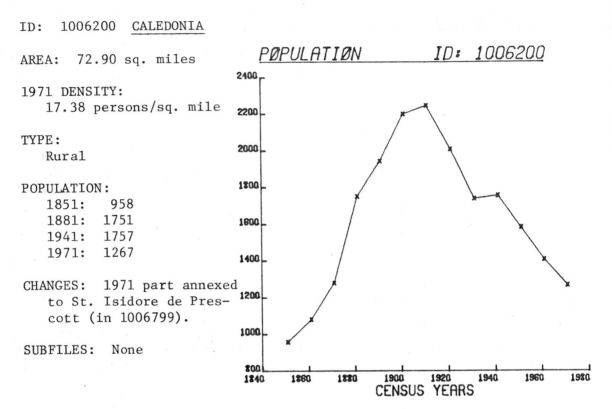

POPULATION   ID: 1006200

CENSUS YEARS

NOTES:

None of the sources examined deals specifically with Caledonia
Township.

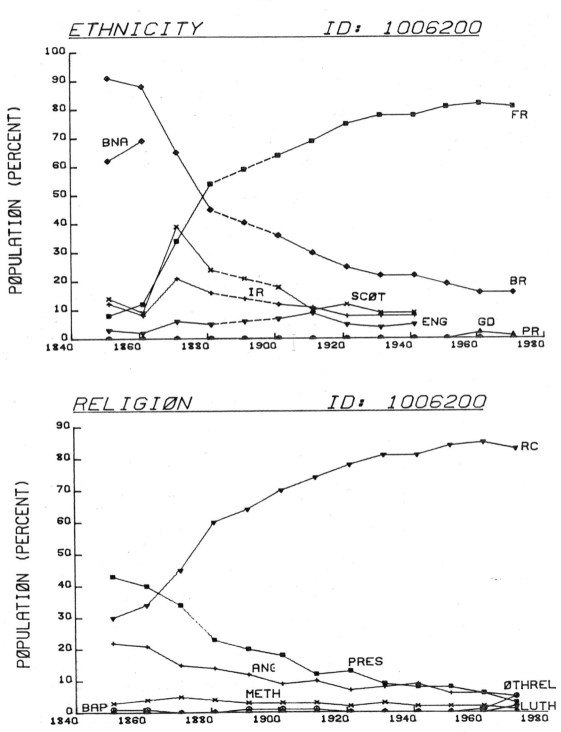

ID: 1006300   HAWKESBURY EAST

AREA: 92.47 sq. miles

1971 DENSITY:
   30.73 persons/sq. mile

TYPE:
   Rural

POPULATION:
   1851:   3029
   1881:   5082
   1941:   3465
   1971:   2842

CHANGES: None

SUBFILES: None

POPULATIØN   ID: 1006300

CENSUS YEARS

NOTES:

None of the sources examined deals specifically with Hawkesbury East.
In 1971 the unincorporated localities of St. Eugene and Chute-à-
Blondeau had populations of 512 and 420 respectively.

211

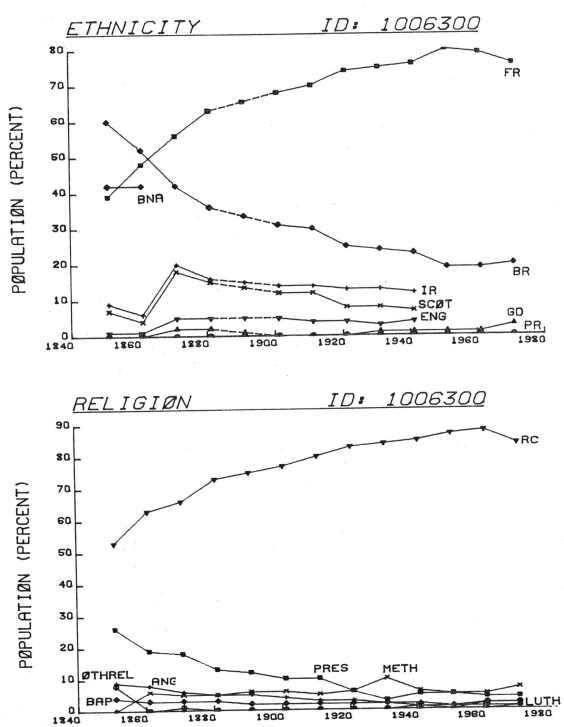

ID: 1006499 <u>HAWKESBURY WEST</u>

AREA: 50.27 sq. miles

1971 DENSITY:
  260.67 persons/sq. mile

TYPE:
  Combined

POPULATION:
  1851: 2665
  1881: 4280
  1941: 9224
  1971: 13104

CHANGES: 1861 Hawkesbury
  incorporated; 1901 Van-
  kleek Hill incorporated.

SUBFILES:
  a. Hawkesbury West
       (Rural)
  b. Hawkesbury
  c. Vankleek Hill

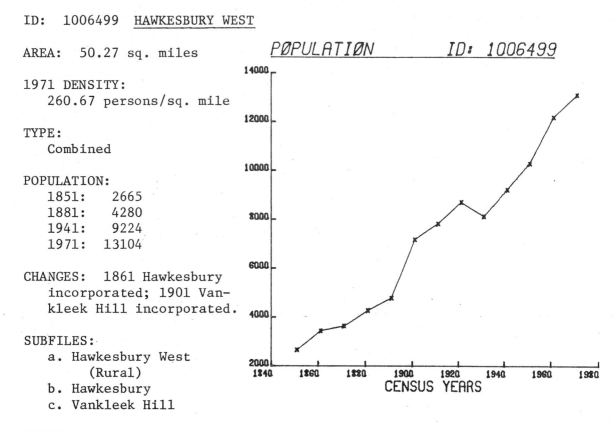

POPULATION   *ID: 1006499*

CENSUS YEARS

NOTES:

In addition to the historical treatment in 109 (Brault, 1965),
Hawkesbury is the subject of a monograph, 156 (Higginson and
Brock, 1961). See also 153 (Hawkesbury Chamber of Commerce,
1957). 175b (MacKinnon, 1972) is a local history of
Vankleek Hill. Considerable census information is available
in tables dealing with the Census Agglomeration of Hawkesbury
which is composed of the town of Hawkesbury and the village
of Grenville, Quebec.

213

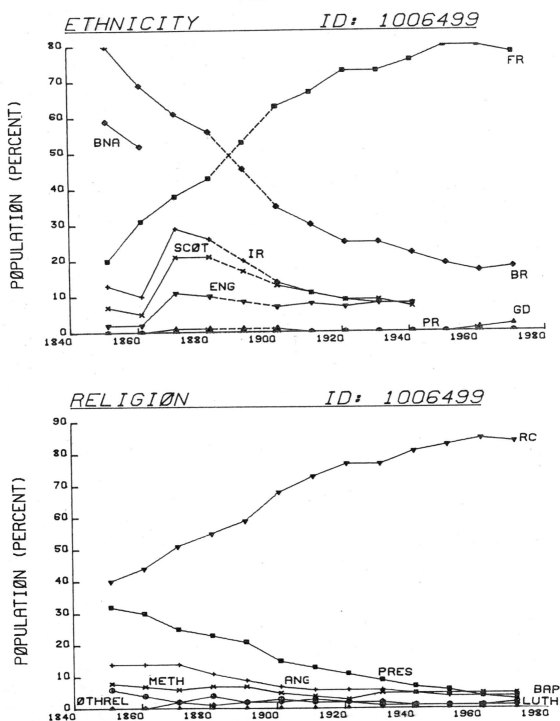

ID: 1006499   SUBFILES

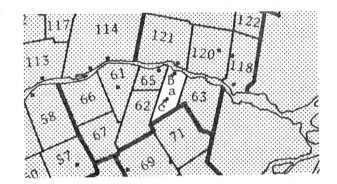

a. HAWKESBURY WEST (RURAL)

   AREA: 46.71 sq. miles

   1971 DENSITY:
      45.75 persons/sq. mile

   POPULATION:
      1881:   2360
      1941:   1526
      1971:   2137

   CHANGES: 1861 Hawkesbury incorporated; 1901 Vankleek Hill incorporated; 1971 part annexed to Hawkesbury.

b. HAWKESBURY

   AREA: 2.49 sq. miles

   1971 DENSITY:
      3725.30 persons/sq. mile

   POPULATION:
      1881:   1920
      1941:   4150
      1971:   9276

   CHANGES: 1861 incorporated; 1971 annexed part of Hawkesbury West
   (Rural).

c. VANKLEEK HILL

   AREA: 1.07 sq. miles

   1971 DENSITY:
      1580.37 persons/sq. mile

   POPULATION:
      1901:   1674
      1941:   1435
      1971:   1691

   CHANGES: 1901 incorporated.

ID: 1006499 SUBFILES cont'd

ETHNICITY

PLACE	YEAR	ENG	SCOT	IR	FR	GD	PR
Hawkesbury West (Rural)	1881	248	678	633	781	7	0
Hawkesbury West (Rural)	1941	246	182	247	842	0	0
Hawkesbury	1881	159	202	493	1046	17	0
Hawkesbury	1941	350	125	272	5396	3	19
Vankleek Hill	1901	150	443	317	716	21	0
Vankleek Hill	1941	115	319	185	798	3	2

RELIGION

PLACE	YEAR	ANG	RC	PRES	METH/UC	BAP	LUTH
Hawkesbury West (Rural)	1881	189	1101	671	261	30	
Hawkesbury West (Rural)	1941	155	940	289	113	15	
Hawkesbury	1881	264	1244	324	27		
Hawkesbury	1941	225	5659	174	123	7	
Vankleek Hill	1901	93	804	461	192	109	
Vankleek Hill	1941	80	878	212	197	56	

ID: 1006599 <u>LONGUEUIL</u>

AREA: 33.02 sq. miles

1971 DENSITY:
72.02 persons/sq. mile

TYPE:
Combined

POPULATION:
1851: 1406
1881: 2015
1941: 1869
1971: 2378

CHANGES: 1881 L'Orignal
incorporated.

SUBFILES:
a. Longueuil (Rural)
b. L'Orignal

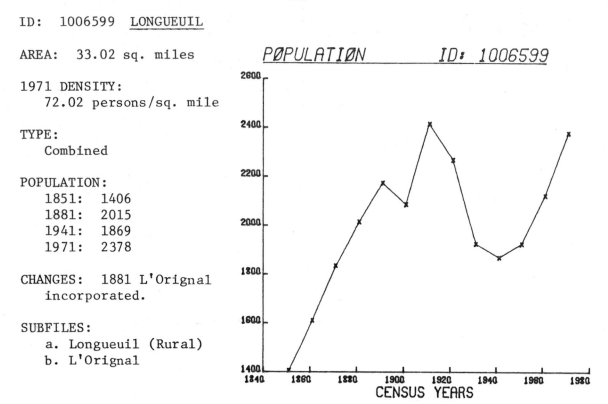

POPULATION   *ID: 1006599*

CENSUS YEARS

NOTES:

None of the sources examined deals specifically with Longueuil.

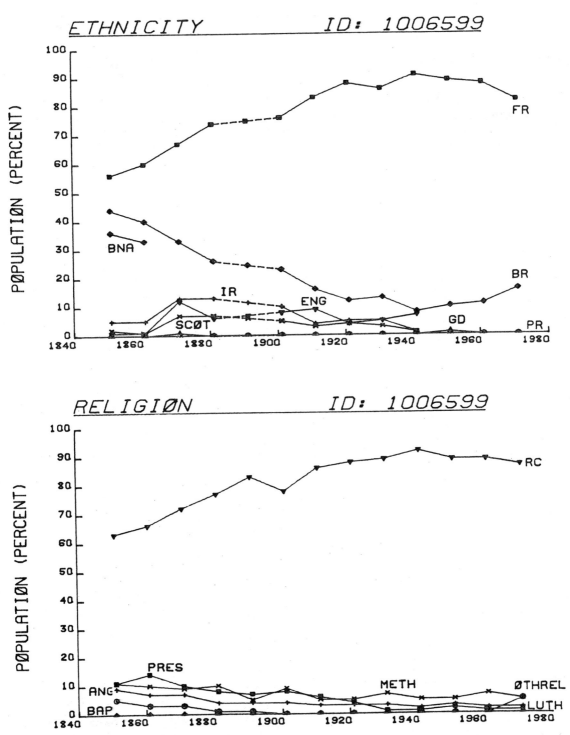

ID: 1006599   SUBFILES

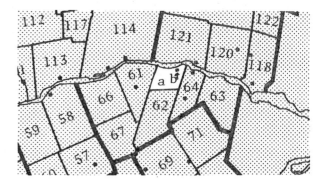

a. LONGUEUIL (RURAL)

   AREA: 30.75 sq. miles

   1971 DENSITY:
      31.64 persons/sq. mile

   POPULATION:
      1881:   1162
      1941:   751
      1971:   973

   CHANGES: 1881 L'Orignal
   incorporated.

b. L'ORIGNAL

   AREA: 2.27 sq. miles

   1971 DENSITY:
      618.94 persons/sq. mile

   POPULATION:
      1881:   853
      1941:   1118
      1971:   1405

   CHANGES: 1881 incorporated.

ID: 1006599   SUBFILES   cont'd

ETHNICITY

PLACE		YEAR	ENG	SCOT	IR	FR	GD	PR
Longueuil	(Rural)	1881	35	21	124	981	1	0
Longueuil	(Rural)	1941	68	12	11	660	0	0
L'Orignal		1881	79	123	136	513	2	0
L'Orignal		1941	63	2	2	1049	2	0

RELIGION

PLACE		YEAR	ANG	RC	PRES	METH/UC	BAP	LUTH
Longueuil	(Rural)	1881	27	967	31	133		
Longueuil	(Rural)	1941	25	661	6	59		
L'Orignal		1881	61	588	121	62		
L'Orignal		1941	19	1050	8	38		

ID: 1006699 <u>PLANTAGENET NORTH</u>

AREA: 80.99 sq. miles

1971 DENSITY:
   36.37 persons/sq. mile

TYPE:
   Combined

POPULATION:
   1851:   1202
   1881:   3997
   1941:   3257
   1971:   2946

CHANGES: 1971 Plantagenet
   incorporated.

SUBFILES:
   a. Plantagenet North
         (Rural)
   b. Plantagenet

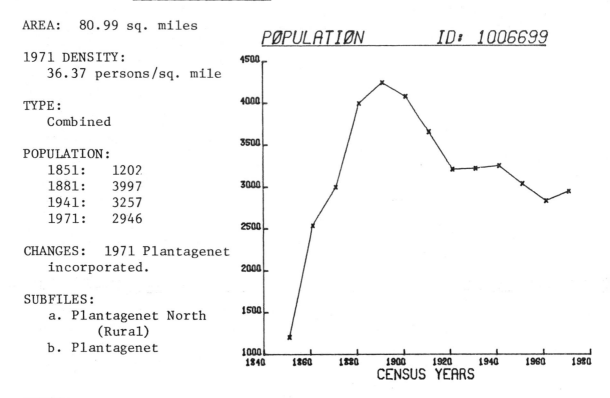

PØPULATIØN   ID: 1006699

CENSUS YEARS

NOTES:

None of the sources examined deals specifically with Plantagenet
North. The unincorporated village of Wendover situated on the
Ottawa River, had a population of 313 in 1971.

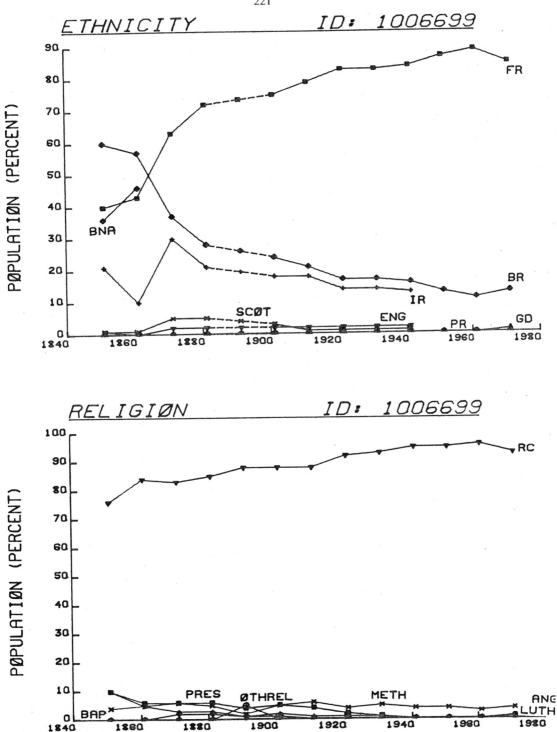

ETHNICITY   ID: 1006699

RELIGION   ID: 1006699

ID: 1006699   SUBFILES

a. <u>PLANTAGENET NORTH (RURAL)</u>

   AREA: 79.37 sq. miles

   1971 DENSITY:
     25.66 persons/sq. mile

   POPULATION:
     1971: 2037

   CHANGES: 1971 Planta-
     genet incorporated.

b. <u>PLANTAGENET</u>

   AREA: 1.62 sq. miles

   1971 DENSITY:
     561.11 persons/sq. mile

   POPULATION:
     1971: 909

   CHANGES: 1971 incorporated.

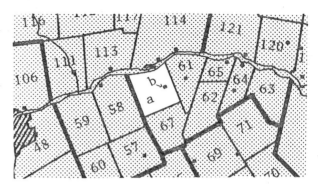

ID: 1006699   SUBFILES   cont'd

ETHNICITY

PLACE	YEAR	BRITISH	FR	GD	PR
Plantagenet North (Rural)	1971	265	1650	25	0
Plantagenet	1971	110	780	0	0

RELIGION

PLACE	YEAR	ANG	RC	PRES	METH/UC	BAP	LUTH
Plantagenet North (Rural)	1971	25	1810	10	100	0	5
Plantagenet	1971	10	870	0	10	0	0

ID: 1006799   PLANTAGENET SOUTH

AREA: 79.53 sq. miles

1971 DENSITY:
   29.42 persons/sq. mile

TYPE:
   Combined

POPULATION:
   1851:   643
   1881:   2524
   1941:   2799
   1971:   2340

CHANGES: 1971 St. Isidore
   de Prescott incorporated;
   annexed part of Caledonia
   (1006200).

SUBFILES:
   a. Plantagenet South
       (Rural)
   b. St. Isidore de
       Prescott

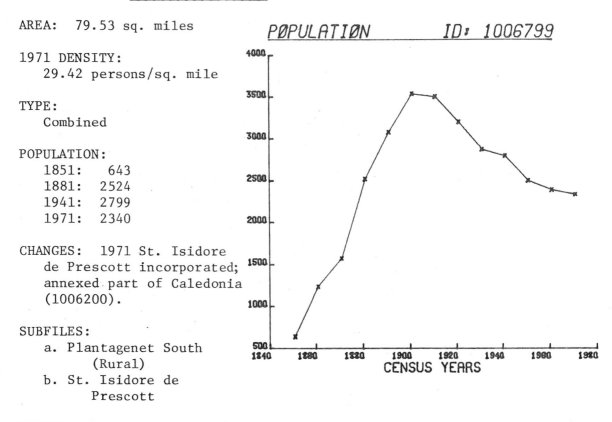

POPULATION   ID: 1006799

CENSUS YEARS

NOTES:

None of the sources examined deals specifically with Plantagenet South.
The unincorporated village of Fournier had a population of 252 in 1971.

225

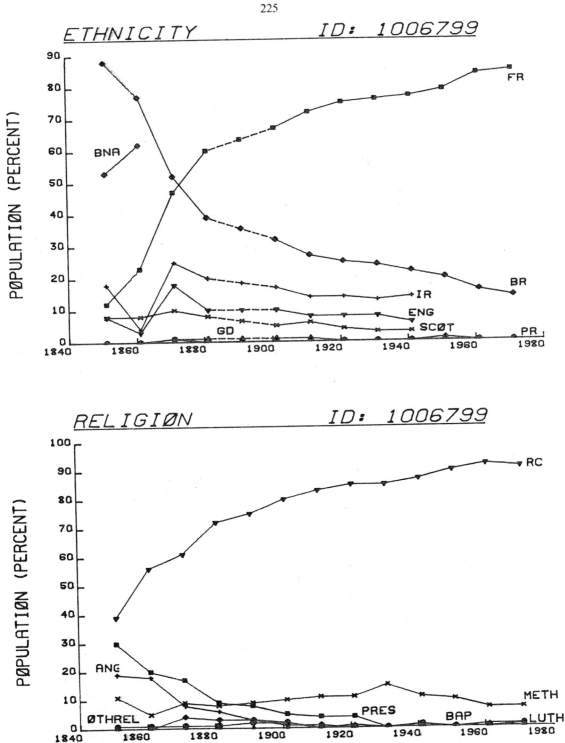

ID: 1006799 SUBFILES

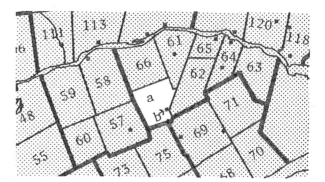

a. PLANTAGENET SOUTH (RURAL)

AREA: 79.05 sq. miles

1971 DENSITY:
21.82 persons/sq. mile

POPULATION:
1971: 1725

CHANGES: 1971 St.
Isidore de Prescott
incorporated.

b. ST. ISIDORE DE PRESCOTT

AREA: 0.48 sq. miles

1971 DENSITY:
1281.25 persons/sq. mile

POPULATION:
1971: 615

CHANGES: 1971 incorporated; annexed part of Caledonia (1006200).

ID: 1006799 SUBFILES cont'd

ETHNICITY

PLACE	YEAR	BRITISH	FR	GD	PR
Plantagenet South (Rural)	1971	305	1350	5	0
St. Isidore de Prescott	1971	10	630	0	0

RELIGION

PLACE	YEAR	ANG	RC	PRES	METH/UC	BAP	LUTH
Plantagenet South (Rural)	1971	20	1470	0	165	10	0
St. Isidore de Prescott	1971	0	635	0	0	0	0

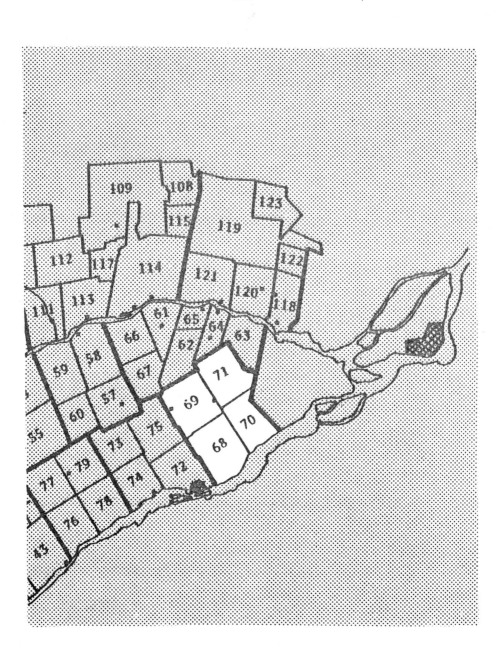

The historical bibliography of the United Counties of Stormont, Dundas and Glengarry is comparatively rich. In different ways the following works deal with aspects of the history of the whole area: 49 (Hill, 1972); 82 (Reid, 1977); 84 (Shortt and Doughty, 1914); 86 (Smith, 1851); 87 (Smyth, 1977); 104 (Belden, 1879); 150 (Harkness, 1946); 203b (Stormont, Dundas and Glengarry Historical Society, 1977); 287 (MacLeod, 1972) and 290 (Ray, 1961).

In addition to these more general works, an important local history is devoted entirely to Glengarry: 174b (McGillivray and Ross, 1979), and 281 (Hunter, 1968) gives information particularly about early settlement in Lancaster and Charlottenburgh. Early settlement is also the subject of 234 (Foran, 1917), 253b (MacLennan, 1883), 253c (MacNab, 1892), 254 (MacRae, 1959) and 260a (Murison, 1903-4). The Gaelic tradition of Glengarry is the subject of 233 (Dunn, 1962-3). See also 130 (Dumbrille, 1956), 131 (Dumbrille, 1954) and 172 (Macdonnell, 1893).

Considerable census information on Glengarry County is available in tables, maps, and analyses at the census division level. County totals for 1971: population 18,480; area 481.29 sq. miles; density 38.40 persons/sq. mile.

ID: 1106800 CHARLOTTENBURGH

AREA: 137.38 sq. miles

1971 DENSITY:
    37.87 persons/sq. mile

TYPE:
    Rural

POPULATION:
    1851: 5557
    1881: 6354
    1941: 4694
    1971: 5202

CHANGES: None.

SUBFILES: None

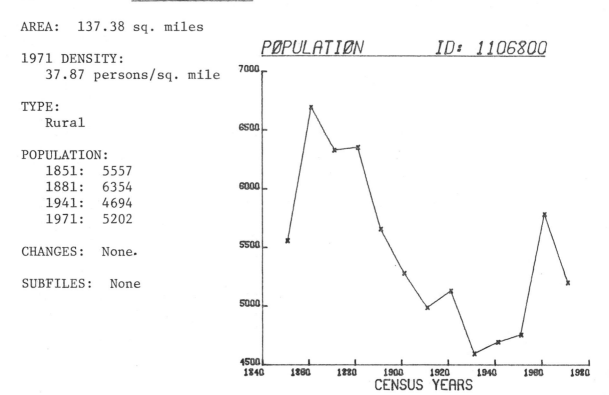

NOTES:

Apart from the works already mentioned, none of the sources listed in the bibliography deals specifically with Charlottenburgh.

The list of unincorporated places in Charlottenburgh includes 3 important villages (with 1971 populations): Glen Walter (656), Martintown (394), and Williamstown (312).

231

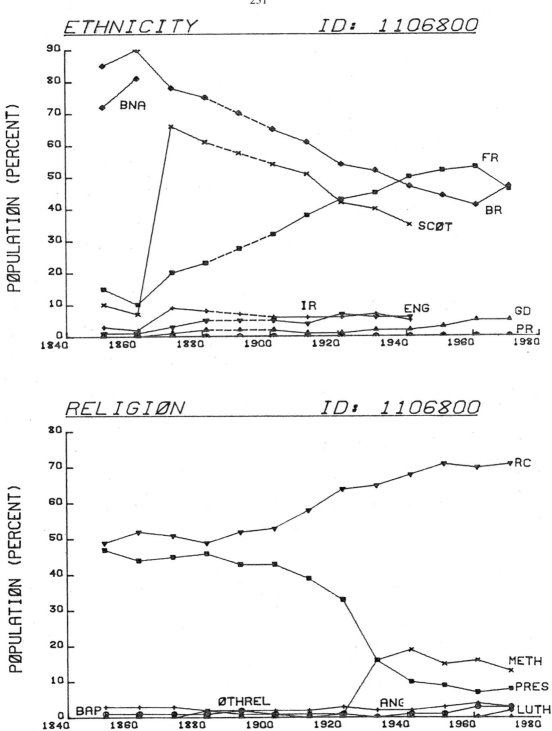

ID: 1106999 KENYON

AREA: 127.06 sq. miles

1971 DENSITY:
  26.92 persons/sq. mile

TYPE:
  Combined

POPULATION:
  1851: 3842
  1881: 5491
  1941: 4242
  1971: 3421

CHANGES: 1901 Maxville
  incorporated; 1961 part
  annexed to Alexandria
  (in 1107199).

SUBFILES:
  a. Kenyon (Rural)
  b. Maxville

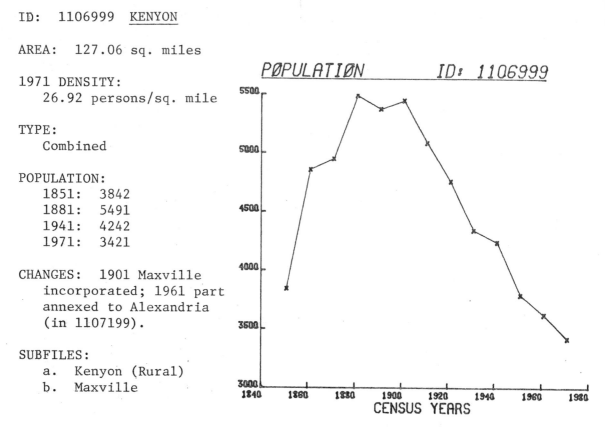

POPULATION   ID: 1106999

CENSUS YEARS

NOTES:

The historical sources for the early history of Kenyon are particularly rich. For the clearing of the land and the Highland settlements see 84 (Shortt and Doughty, 1914), 49 (Hill, 1972), 86 (Smith,
1851), and 290 (Ray, 1961). 87 (Smyth, 1977) and 238 (Hunter, 1901)
also give information on Irish settlements. Maxville is the subject
of a monograph, 181 (Maxville Women's Institute, 1967).

The unincorporated village of Apple Hill had a population of 318
in 1971.

233

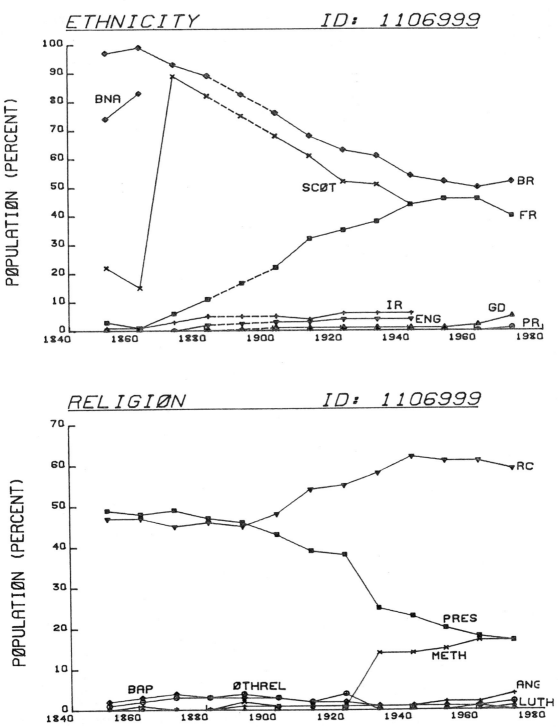

ETHNICITY   ID: 1106999

RELIGION   ID: 1106999

ID: 1106999   SUBFILES

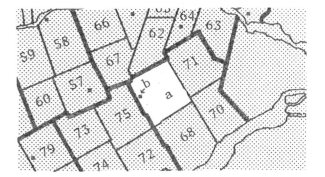

a. KENYON (RURAL)

   AREA: 126.08 sq. miles

   1971 DENSITY:
      10.42 persons/sq.mile

   POPULATION:
      1901: 4700
      1941: 3438
      1971: 2575

   CHANGES: 1901 Maxville
      incorporated; 1961
      part annexed to
      Alexandria (in
      1107199); 1971 part
      annexed to Maxville.

b. MAXVILLE

   AREA: 0.98 sq. miles

   1971 DENSITY:
      863.27 persons/sq.
      mile

   POPULATION:
      1901: 749
      1941: 804
      1971: 846

   CHANGES: 1901 incorporated; 1971 annexed
      part of Kenyon (Rural).

ID: 1106999   SUBFILES cont'd

ETHNICITY

PLACE	YEAR	ENG	SCOT	IR	FR	GD	PR
Kenyon (Rural)	1901	76	3342	207	1035	23	1
Kenyon (Rural)	1941	109	1569	176	1545	13	6
Maxville	1901	92	379	62	164	52	0
Maxville	1941	68	285	81	327	37	5

RELIGION

PLACE	YEAR	ANG	RC	PRES	METH/UC	BAP	LUTH
Kenyon (Rural)	1901	19	2421	2031	26	109	
Kenyon (Rural)	1941	15	2251	777	368	21	
Maxville	1901	37	207	330	48	54	
Maxville	1941	13	363	186	216	26	

ID: 1107099   <u>LANCASTER</u>

AREA: 96.96 sq. miles

1971 DENSITY:
    36.74 persons/sq. mile

TYPE:
    Combined

POPULATION:
    1851:   4023
    1881:   4851
    1941:   3827
    1971:   3562

CHANGES: 1891 Lancaster
    (Urban) incorporated.

SUBFILES:
    a. Lancaster (Rural)
    b. Lancaster (Urban)

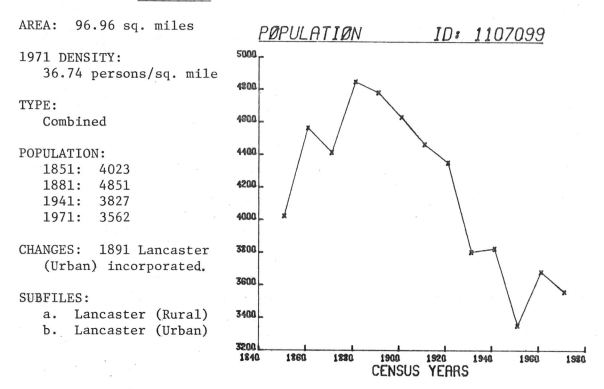

POPULATION   ID: 1107099

CENSUS YEARS

NOTES:

In addition to the more inclusive works already mentioned - note
especially 281 (Hunter, 1968), 215b (Blair, 1978) and 287b (McRae,
1977) deal specifically with Lancaster.

Unincorporated villages (with 1971 populations) include: Green
Valley (363), South Lancaster (264), and North Lancaster (155).

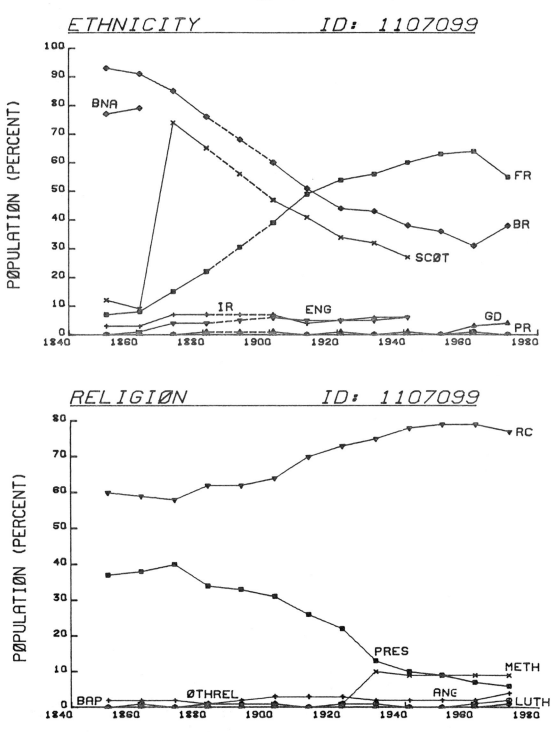

ID: 1107099   SUBFILES

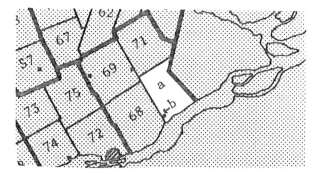

a. LANCASTER (RURAL)

   AREA: 96.71 sq. miles

   1971 DENSITY:
      30.45 persons/sq.
      mile

   POPULATION:
      1901: 4051
      1941: 3143
      1971: 2945

   CHANGES: 1891 Lancaster
   incorporated.

b. LANCASTER (URBAN)

   AREA: 0.25 sq. miles

   1971 DENSITY:
      2468.00 persons/sq.
      mile

   POPULATION:
      1901: 583
      1941: 684
      1971: 617

   CHANGES: 1891 incorporated.

ID: 1107099   SUBFILES   cont'd

ETHNICITY

PLACE		YEAR	ENG	SCOT	IR	FR	GD	PR
Lancaster	(Rural)	1901	227	1900	262	1607	44	0
Lancaster	(Rural)	1941	140	881	160	1911	26	1
Lancaster	(Urban)	1901	28	291	55	203	4	0
Lancaster	(Urban)	1941	72	149	61	388	6	1

RELIGION

PLACE		YEAR	ANG	RC	PRES	METH/UC	BAP	LUTH
Lancaster	(Rural)	1901	111	2692	1189	24	29	
Lancaster	(Rural)	1941	52	2491	314	278	4	
Lancaster	(Urban)	1901	24	263	267	28		
Lancaster	(Urban)	1941	23	501	81	69		

ID: 1107199   <u>LOCHIEL</u>

AREA: 119.89 sq. miles

1971 DENSITY:
  52.51 persons/sq. mile

TYPE:
  Combined

POPULATION:
  1851:   4174
  1881:   5525
  1941:   5969
  1971:   6295

CHANGES: 1891 Alexandria
  incorporated; 1961
  annexed part of Kenyon
  (1106999).

SUBFILES:
  a.   Lochiel (Rural)
  b.   Alexandria

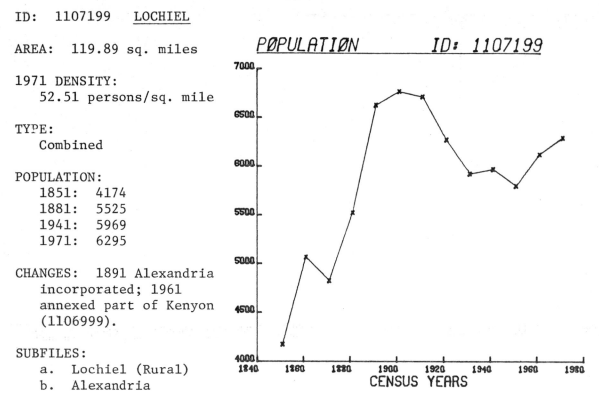

POPULATION   ID: 1107199

CENSUS YEARS

NOTES:

Information on early economic activities in Alexandria is available
in 86 (Smith, 1851); see also 187c (Ostrum, ms). 253c (MacNab, 1892)
deals with settlement.

Lochiel's unincorporated villages (with 1971 populations) include:
Glen Robertson (345) and Dalkeith (155).

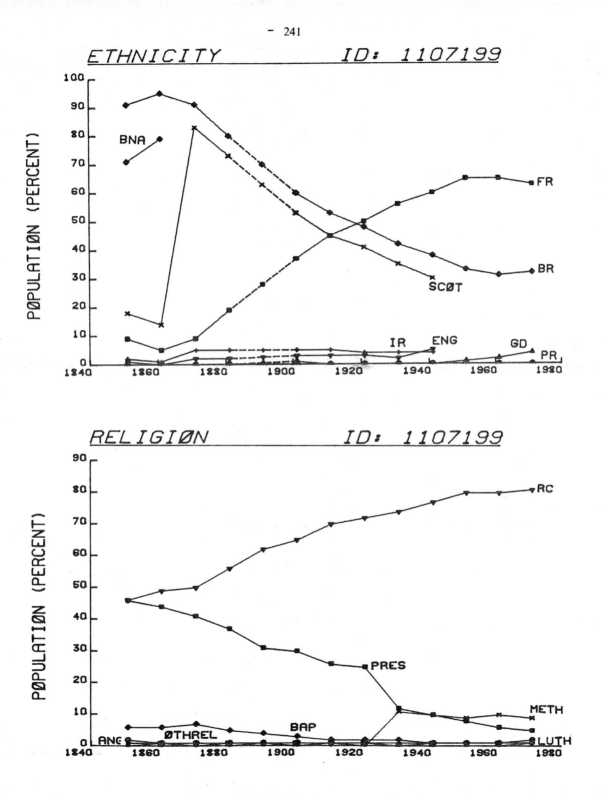

ID: 1107199   SUBFILES

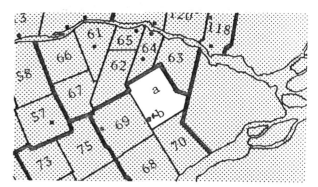

a. <u>LOCHIEL (RURAL)</u>

   AREA: 118.79 sq. miles

   1971 DENSITY:
      25.72 persons/sq.
      mile

   POPULATION:
      1901:   4857
      1941:   3794
      1971:   3055

   CHANGES: 1891
      Alexandria incorpora-
      ted.

b. <u>ALEXANDRIA</u>

   AREA: 1.1 sq. miles

   1971 DENSITY:
      2945.45 persons/sq.
      mile

   POPULATION:
      1901:   1911
      1941:   2175
      1971:   3240

   CHANGES: 1891 incorporated; 1961 annexed part of Kenyon
      (1106999).

ID: 1107199   SUBFILES   cont'd

ETHNICITY

PLACE	YEAR	ENG	SCOT	IR	FR	GD	PR
Lochiel (Rural)	1901	114	2735	213	1722	18	0
Lochiel (Rural)	1941	198	1320	136	2132	2	2
Alexandria	1901	57	845	127	805	19	0
Alexandria	1941	78	446	114	1461	11	1

RELIGION

PLACE	YEAR	ANG	RC	PRES	METH/UC	BAP	LUTH
Lochiel (Rural)	1901	10	2800	1741	45	216	
Lochiel (Rural)	1941	23	2661	513	498	82	
Alexandria	1901	20	1567	258	21		
Alexandria	1941	20	1936	72	111		

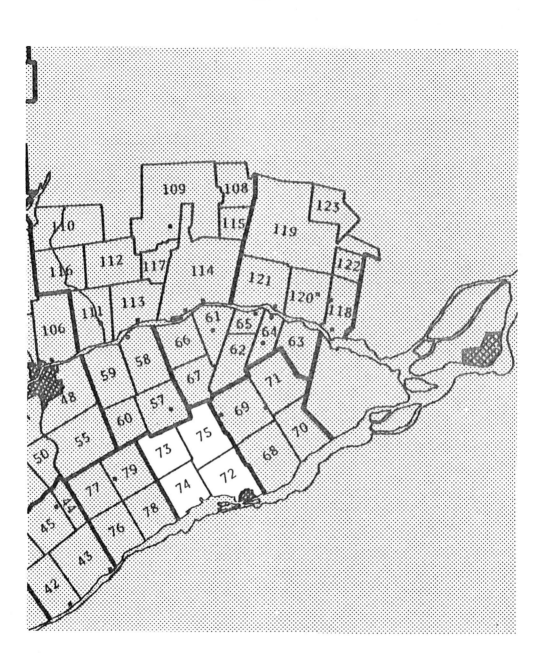

STORMONT COUNTY (12)

Integral Units 072 - 075

    Works which deal with Stormont County as one of the three
United Counties are listed in the headnote to 11 Glengarry County
(p.229). Information about early economic activity is available in
86 (Smith, 1851), and much detail is offered in 190 (Pringle, 1890).
The changing balance of the two official language groups in the area
since the first settlements is treated extensively in 273 (Cartwright,
1973).

    Considerable census information on Stormont County is available
in tables, maps, and analyses at the census division level. County
totals for 1971: population 61,302; area 400.28 sq. miles; density
153.15 persons/sq. mile. The Cornwall Island Indian Reserve (1971
population 644; area 3.45 sq. miles) has not been included in the
figures for IU 72.

ID: 1207299   CORNWALL

AREA: 104.64 sq. miles

1971 DENSITY:
   493.65 persons/sq. mile

TYPE:
   Combined

POPULATION:
   1851:   6353
   1881:   9904
   1941: 30151
   1971: 51656

CHANGES: None.

SUBFILES:
   a. Cornwall (Rural)
   b. Cornwall (Urban)

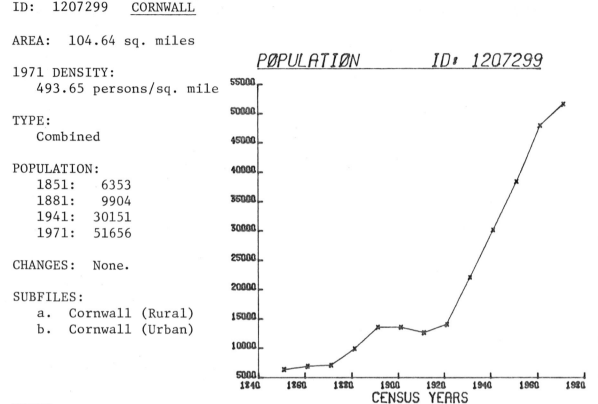

POPULATION   ID: 1207299

CENSUS YEARS

NOTES:

For the history of Cornwall, see especially Smith, 1851 (86) and
Pringle, 1890 (190).

Cornwall's unincorporated communities include: Long Sault (1971
population 965), St. Andrews West (1971 population 478), and Rosedale
Terrace (1971 population 219). The Cornwall Island Indian Reserve
(1971 population 644; area 3.45 sq.miles) has not been included in
the IU figures.

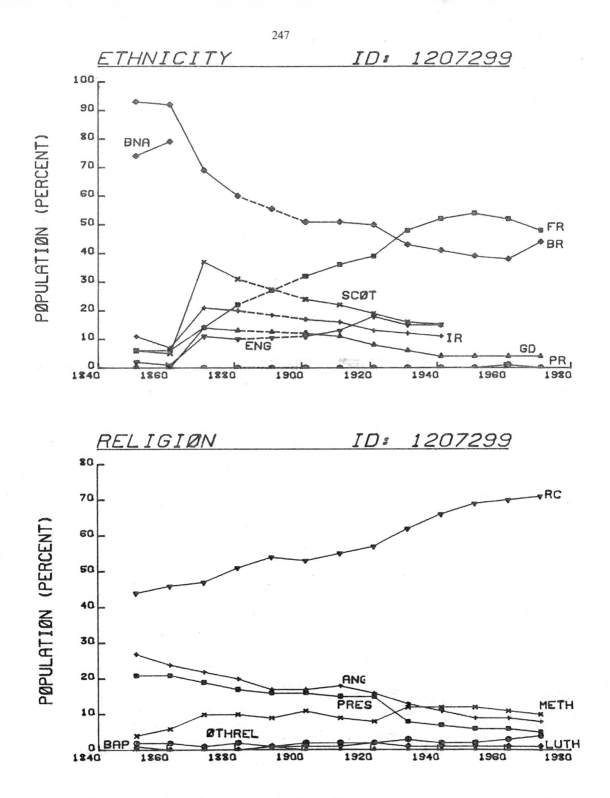

ID: 1207299   SUBFILES

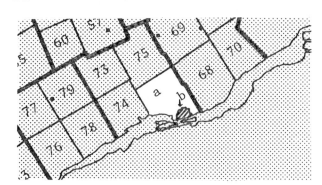

a. CORNWALL (RURAL)

AREA: 80.24 sq. miles

1971 DENSITY:
   56.58 persons/sq.
   mile

POPULATION:
   1851:   4707
   1881:   5436
   1941:   16034
   1971:   4540

CHANGES: 1951 & 1961
   parts annexed to
   Cornwall (Urban)

b. CORNWALL (URBAN)

AREA: 24.40 sq. miles

1971 DENSITY:
   1930.98 persons/sq.
   mile

POPULATION:
   1851:   1646
   1881:   4468
   1941:   14117
   1971:   47116

CHANGES: 1951 & 1961 parts of Cornwall (Rural) annexed.

ID: 1207299   SUBFILES   cont'd

ETHNICITY

PLACE		YEAR	ENG	SCOT	IR	FR	GD	PR
Cornwall	(Rural)	1881	445	1924	905	899	948	9
Cornwall	(Rural)	1941	1651	2086	1557	9702	759	16
Cornwall	(Urban)	1881	530	1109	1070	1323	363	14
Cornwall	(Urban)	1941	2829	2302	1860	5969	577	27

RELIGION

PLACE		YEAR	ANG	RC	PRES	METH/UC	BAP	LUTH
Cornwall	(Rural)	1881	1047	2730	835	686		15
Cornwall	(Rural)	1941	1516	11764	887	1633	104	14
Cornwall	(Urban)	1881	912	2290	861	339		
Cornwall	(Urban)	1941	1904	8229	1333	1943	279	

ID: 1207399   FINCH

AREA: 82.27 sq. miles

1971 DENSITY:
   32.70 persons/sq. mile

TYPE:
   Combined

POPULATION:
   1851: 1450
   1881: 3493
   1941: 3179
   1971: 2690

CHANGES: 1911 Finch
   (Urban) incorporated.

SUBFILES:
   a. Finch (Rural
   b. Finch (Urban)

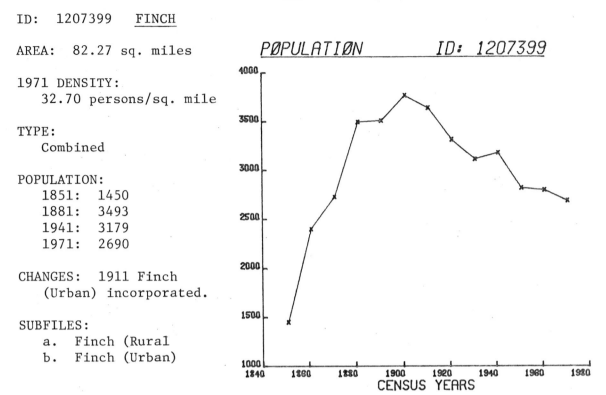

POPULATIØN   ID: 1207399

CENSUS YEARS

NOTES:

None of the works listed in the bibliography deals specifically with Finch.

The unincorporated village of Crysler had a population of 481 in 1971.

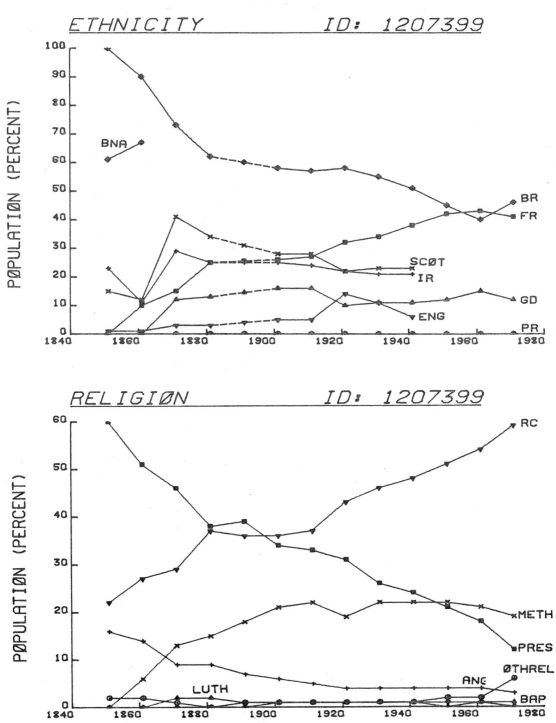

ETHNICITY   ID: 1207399

RELIGIØN   ID: 1207399

ID: 1207399   SUBFILES

a. FINCH (RURAL)

AREA: 81.30 sq. miles

1971 DENSITY:
    28.20 persons/sq. mile

POPULATION:
    1911: 3227
    1941: 2782
    1971: 2293

CHANGES: 1911 Finch
(Urban) incorporated.

b. FINCH (URBAN)

AREA: 0.97 sq. miles

1971 DENSITY:
    409.28 persons/sq.
    mile

POPULATION:
    1911: 411
    1941: 397
    1971: 397

CHANGES: 1911 incorporated

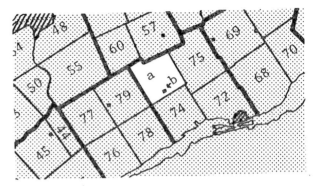

ID: 1207399   SUBFILES   cont'd

ETHNICITY

PLACE	YEAR	ENG	SCOT	IR	FR	GD	PR
Finch (Rural)	1911	141	815	801	965	504	0
Finch (Rural)	1941	130	586	586	1176	296	0
Finch (Urban)	1911	24	214	86	9	77	0
Finch (Urban)	1941	69	145	93	31	59	0

RELIGION

PLACE	YEAR	ANG	RC	PRES	METH/UC	BAP	LUTH
Finch (Rural)	1911	169	1343	961	688	21	24
Finch (Rural)	1941	104	1499	521	587	28	17
Finch (Urban)	1911	9	14	256	127		
Finch (Urban)	1941	14	35	243	98		

ID: 1207400   OSNABRUCK

AREA: 93.43 sq. miles

1971 DENSITY:
  36.09 persons/sq. mile

TYPE:
  Rural

POPULATION:
  1851: 4699
  1881: 5796
  1941: 3584
  1971: 3372

CHANGES: None

SUBFILES: None

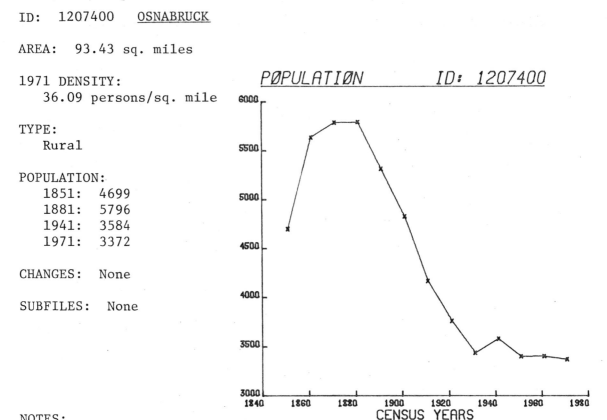

POPULATION   ID: 1207400

CENSUS YEARS

NOTES:

None of the works listed in the bibliography deals specifically with Osnabruck.

The largest centre in Osnabruck is the unincorporated village of Ingleside (1971 population 899) located on the St. Lawrence. The village of Newington in the northern part of the township away from the river, had a population of 265 in 1971.

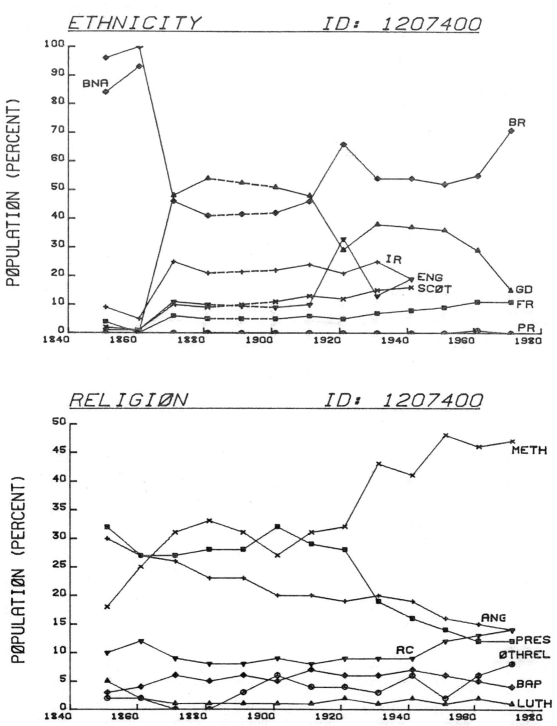

ID: 1207500   ROXBOROUGH

AREA: 116.49 sq. miles

1971 DENSITY:
  25.24 persons/sq. mile

TYPE:
  Rural

POPULATION:
  1851: 2141
  1881: 4005
  1941: 3541
  1971: 2940

CHANGES: None.

SUBFILES: None

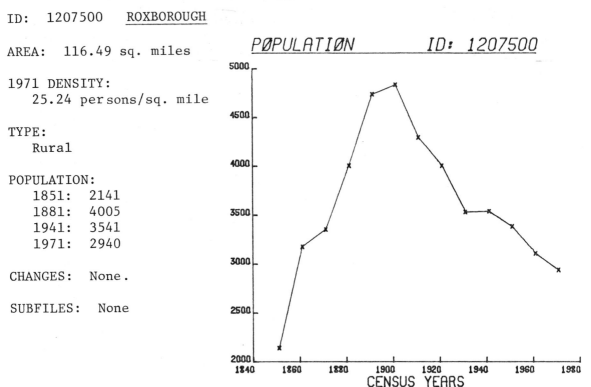

POPULATION   ID: 1207500

CENSUS YEARS

NOTES:

None of the works listed in the bibliography deals specifically with Roxborough.

The unincorporated village of Moose Creek had a population of 391 in 1971; that of Avonmore was 287.

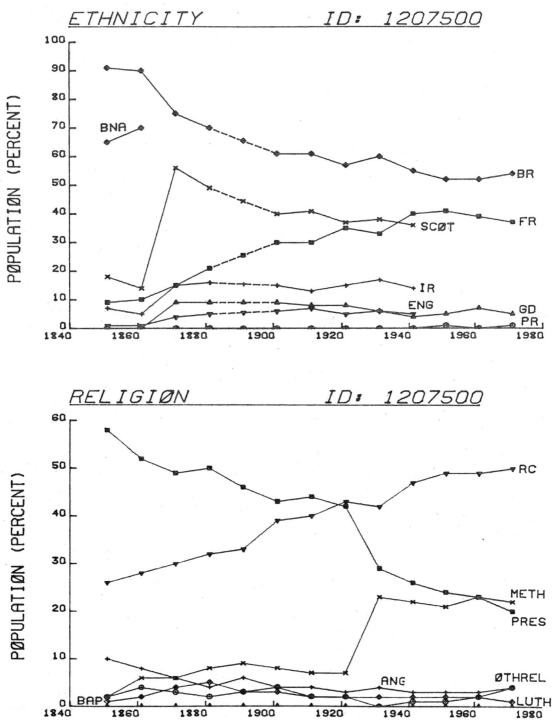

258

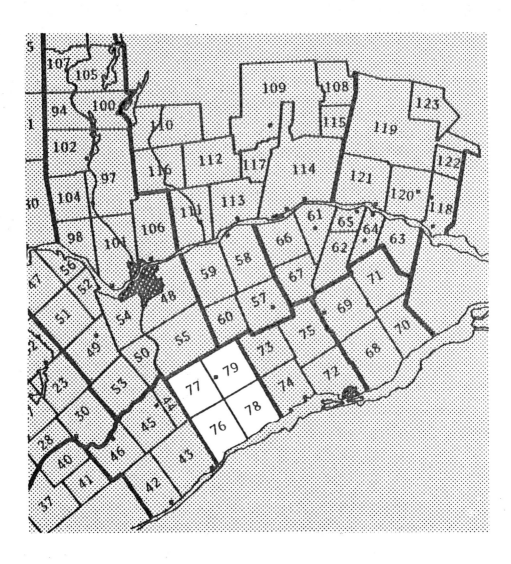

DUNDAS COUNTY (13)

Integral Units 076 - 079

For works which deal with Dundas County as one of the three
United Counties, see the headnote to 11 Glengarry County (p.229).
In addition to those more general works and the more specific works
listed within, two early monographs are devoted to Dundas County:
129 (Croil, 1861) and 119 (Carter, 1905).

Considerable census information on Dundas County is available
in tables, maps, and analyses at the census division level. County
totals for 1971: population 17,457; area 393.47 sq. miles; density
44.37 persons/sq. mile.

ID: 1307699   <u>MATILDA</u>

AREA: 102.75 sq. miles

1971 DENSITY:
   41.60 persons/sq. mile

TYPE:
   Combined

POPULATION:
   1851:   4198
   1881:   5693
   1941:   3847
   1971:   4274

CHANGES: 1861 Iroquois
   incorporated.

SUBFILES:
   a. Matilda (Rural)
   b. Iroquois

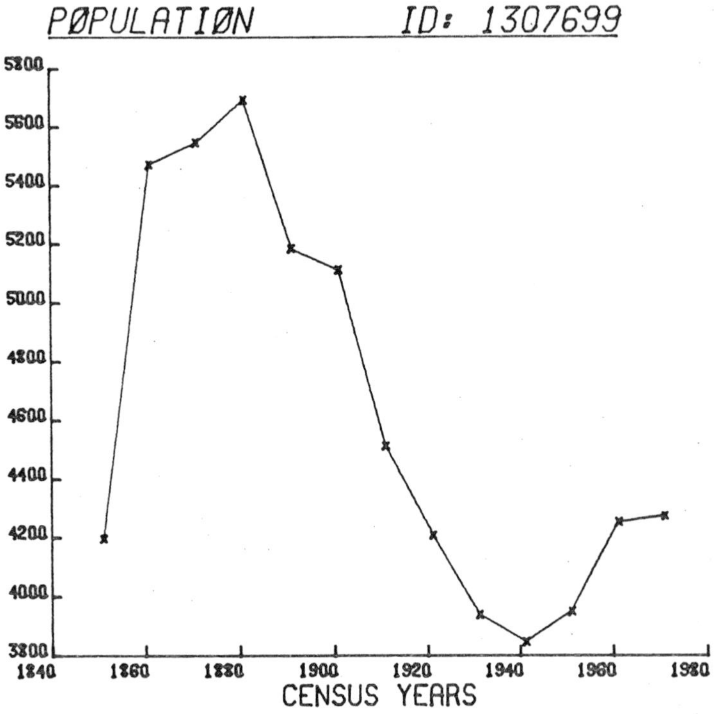

POPULATION   ID: 1307699

CENSUS YEARS

NOTES:

Early information on Iroquois is given in 86 (Smith, 1851) and 119
(Carter, 1905).

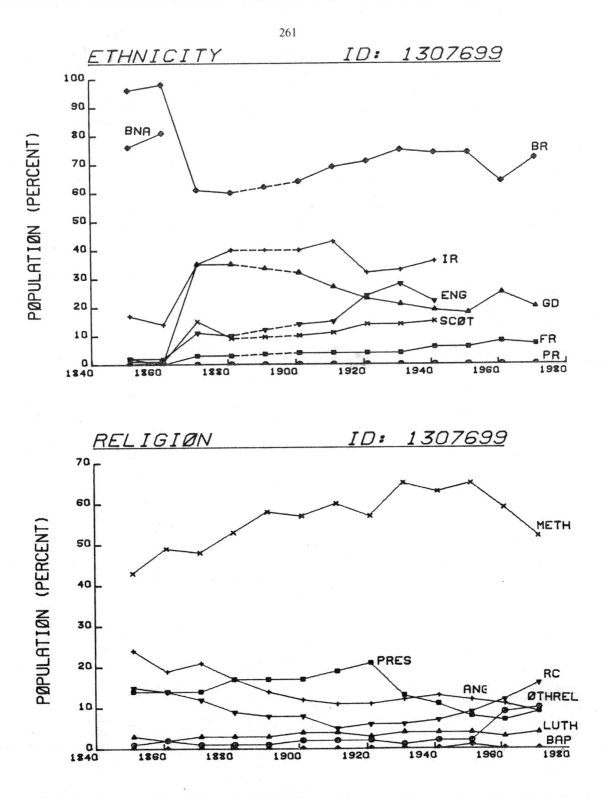

ETHNICITY   ID: 1307699

RELIGION   ID: 1307699

ID: 1307699 SUBFILES

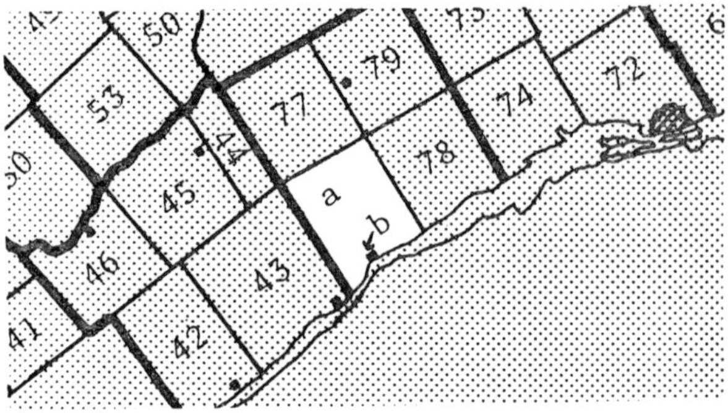

a. MATILDA (RURAL)

AREA: 100.76 sq. miles

1971 DENSITY:
   30.27 persons/sq. mile

POPULATION:
   1881: 4692
   1941: 2891
   1971: 3050

CHANGES: 1861 Iroquois incorporated.

b. IROQUOIS

AREA: 1.99 sq. miles

1971 DENSITY:
   615.08 persons/sq. mile

POPULATION:
   1881: 1001
   1941:   956
   1971: 1224

CHANGES: 1861 incorporated.

ID: 1307699 SUBFILES cont'd

ETHNICITY

PLACE	YEAR	ENG	SCOT	IR	FR	GD	PR
Matilda (Rural)	1881	415	345	2015	144	1673	0
Matilda (Rural)	1941	629	378	1142	168	565	0
Iroquois	1881	174	169	288	40	323	0
Iroquois	1941	233	200	256	74	180	0

RELIGION

PLACE	YEAR	ANG	RC	PRES	METH/UC	BAP	LUTH
Matilda (Rural)	1881	724	422	763	2558		185
Matilda (Rural)	1941	331	166	289	1927		139
Iroquois	1881	231	83	184	467		
Iroquois	1941	167	96	148	514		

ID: 1307700 MOUNTAIN

AREA: 96.17 sq. miles

1971 DENSITY:
  25.30 persons/sq. mile

TYPE:
  Rural

POPULATION:
  1851: 2764
  1881: 3719
  1941: 2685
  1971: 2433

CHANGES: None

SUBFILES: None

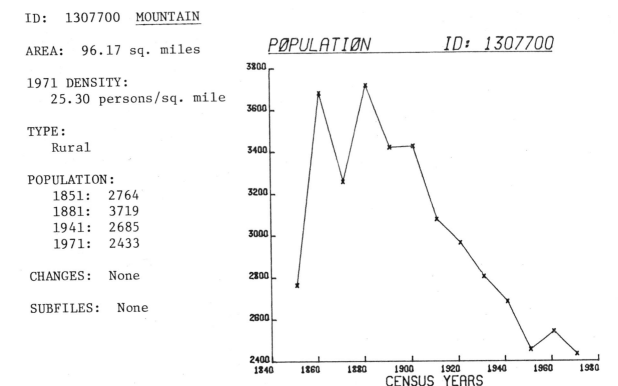

POPULATION   ID: 1307700

CENSUS YEARS

NOTES:

None of the sources listed in the bibliography deals particularly
with Mountain. The list of unincorporated villages includes (with
1971 populations): South Mountain (224) and Mountain (172).

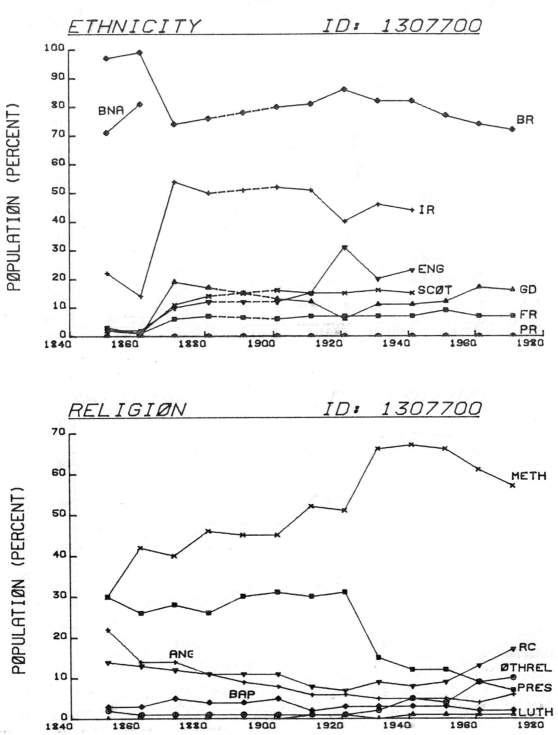

ETHNICITY   ID: 1307700

RELIGION   ID: 1307700

ID: 1307899 WILLIAMSBURGH

AREA: 97.65 sq. miles

1971 DENSITY:
  52.24 persons/sq. mile

TYPE:
  Combined

POPULATION:
  1851: 4284
  1881: 6390
  1941: 4572
  1971: 5101

CHANGES: 1861 Morrisburg
  incorporated.

SUBFILES:
  a. Williamsburgh (Rural)
  b. Morrisburg

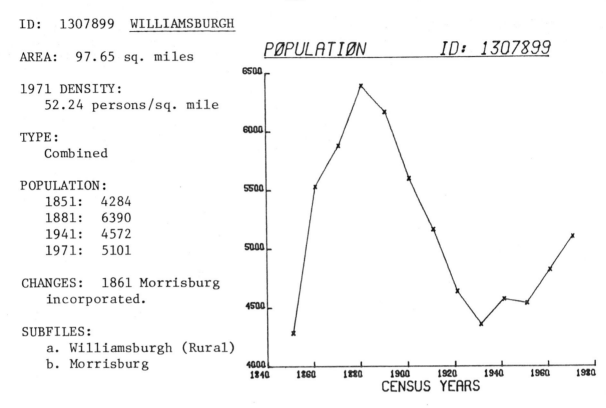

POPULATION   ID: 1307899

CENSUS YEARS

NOTES:

Early information on economic activity in Morrisburg is given in 86
(Smith, 1851). The town is also the subject of a monograph, 182
(Morgan, 1961). The village of Williamsburg (1971 population 398) was
the largest of the 9 unincorporated places listed in 1971.

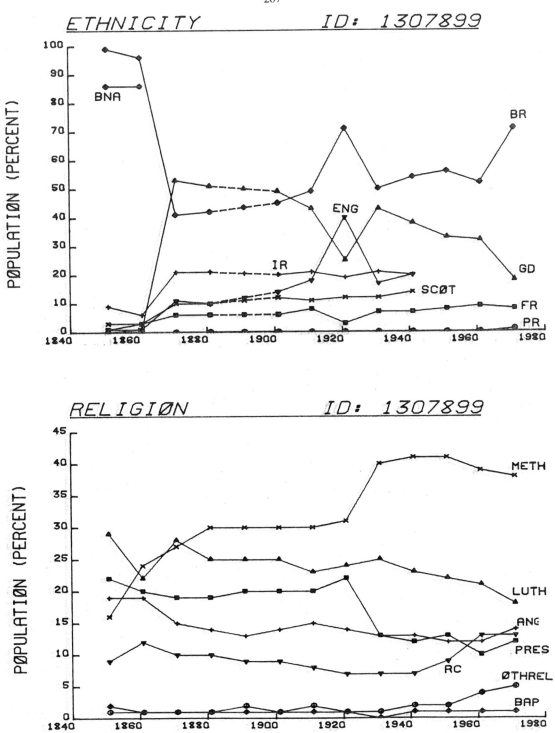

ETHNICITY   ID: 1307899

RELIGION   ID: 1307899

ID: 1307899 SUBFILES

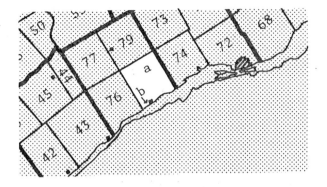

a. <u>WILLIAMSBURGH (RURAL)</u>

   AREA: 95.23 sq. miles

   1971 DENSITY:
      31.99 persons/sq. mile

   POPULATION:
      1881: 4671
      1941: 2997
      1971: 3046

   CHANGES: 1861 Morrisburg incorporated.

b. <u>MORRISBURG</u>

   AREA: 2.42 sq. miles

   1971 DENSITY:
      849.17 persons/sq. mile

   POPULATION:
      1881: 1719
      1941: 1575
      1971: 2055

   CHANGES: 1861 incorporated.

ID: 1307899 SUBFILES cont'd

ETHNICITY

PLACE	YEAR	ENG	SCOT	IR	FR	GD	PR
Williamsburgh (Rural)	1881	410	400	925	198	2735	0
Williamsburgh (Rural)	1941	549	366	599	141	1319	0
Morrisburg	1881	247	244	440	178	543	0
Morrisburg	1941	357	259	319	184	424	1

RELIGION

PLACE	YEAR	ANG	RC	PRES	METH/UC	BAP	LUTH
Williamsburgh (Rural)	1881	455	273	935	1459	34	1495
Williamsburgh (Rural)	1941	261	130	326	1358	30	857
Morrisburg	1881	417	356	303	452		123
Morrisburg	1941	352	212	230	534	14	197

ID: 1307999 <u>WINCHESTER</u>

AREA: 96.90 sq. miles

1971 DENSITY:
58.30 persons/sq. mile

TYPE:
Combined

POPULATION:
1851: 2565
1881: 4796
1941: 5106
1971: 5649

CHANGES: 1891 Chesterville
and Winchester (Urban)
incorporated.

SUBFILES:
a. Winchester (Rural)
b. Chesterville
c. Winchester (Urban)

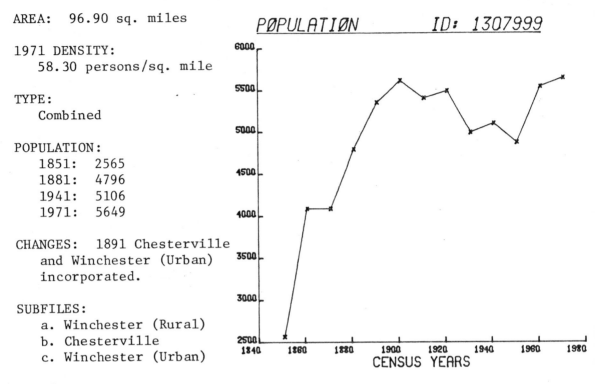

POPULATION   ID: 1307999

CENSUS YEARS

NOTES:

Chesterville is the subject of a monograph, 179 (Marcellus, 1971).
Information on early economic activity is available in 119 (Carter,
1905). The unincorporated village of Morewood had a population of
214 in 1971.

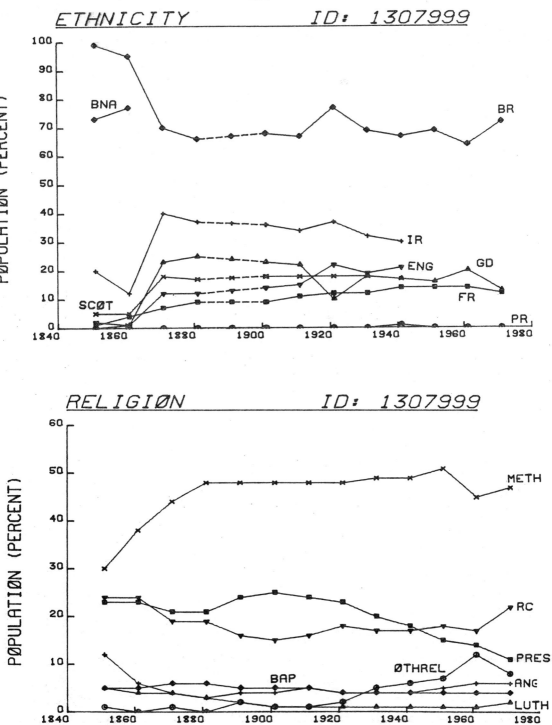

ID: 1307999 SUBFILES

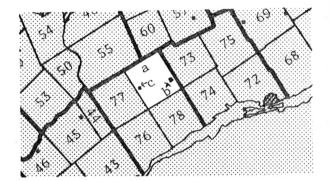

a. WINCHESTER (RURAL)

    AREA: 95.17 sq. miles

    1971 DENSITY:
       29.65 persons/sq. mile

    POPULATION:
       1901: 3585
       1941: 2990
       1971: 2822

    CHANGES: 1891 Chesterville and Winchester (Urban) incorporated;
    1971 parts annexed to Chesterville and Winchester (Urban).

b. CHESTERVILLE

    AREA: 0.77 sq. miles

    1971 DENSITY:
       1901:   932
       1941: 1067
       1971: 1252

    CHANGES: 1891 incorporated; 1971 annexed part of Winchester
    (Rural).

c. WINCHESTER (URBAN)

    AREA: 0.96 sq. miles

    1971 DENSITY:
       1640.62 persons/sq. mile

    POPULATION:
       1901: 1101
       1941: 1049
       1971: 1575

    CHANGES: 1891 incorporated; 1971 annexed part of Winchester
    (Rural).

ID: 1307999 SUBFILES cont'd

ETHNICITY

PLACE	YEAR	ENG	SCOT	IR	FR	GD	PR
Winchester (Rural)	1901	419	632	1362	346	824	0
Winchester (Rural)	1941	352	443	947	517	538	0
Chesterville	1901	101	109	346	75	298	0
Chesterville	1941	216	151	289	120	258	0
Winchester (Urban)	1901	253	284	302	92	160	0
Winchester (Urban)	1941	306	250	309	84	71	28

RELIGION

PLACE	YEAR	ANG	RC	PRES	METH/UC	BAP	LUTH
Winchester (Rural)	1901	120	566	932	1679	200	59
Winchester (Rural)	1941	74	636	483	1484	148	48
Chesterville	1901	50	252	144	470		
Chesterville	1941	83	236	218	495		
Winchester (Urban)	1901	70	36	351	559	73	
Winchester (Urban)	1941	56	18	213	527	80	

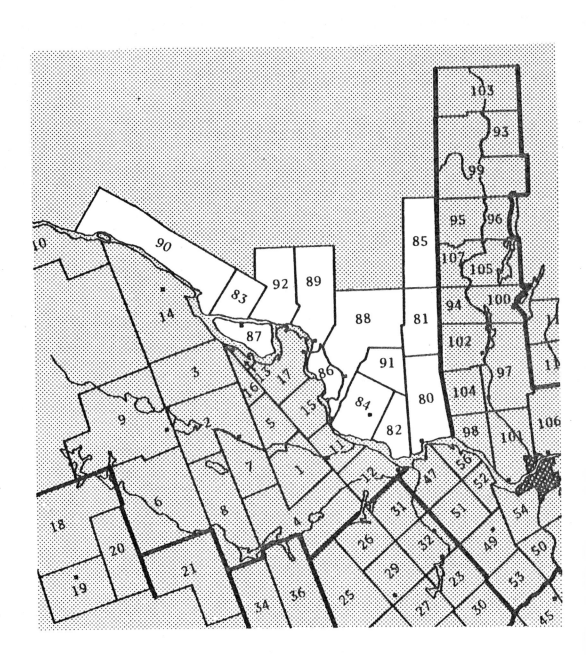

The historical bibliography of Pontiac County is very small.
The best single source is 106 (Blanchard, 1954). Items 276 (Fraser,
n.d.) and 286 (MacKay, 1949) add some details. There are few local
histories other than 111 (Bretzlaff et al. 1973) and 123 (Chapeau
Centennial, 1974), and the major sources have very little on the
forest industry in the County, despite its historical importance.

Although the northern areas of Pontiac County away from the
Ottawa River have not been included, almost all the population in the
county is located to the south and is covered by the study area. The
tables, maps, and analyses available in the census at the census
division level for Pontiac County are thus still well worth consult-
ing for comparative use with our figures. The unorganized territory
excluded from the study had a 1971 area of 7,964.21 sq. miles and a
population of only 54. The population on Indian Reserves (272 in
1971) has also been excluded from our figures. County wide totals
for 1971: population 19,570; area 9,848.33 sq. miles; density 1.99
persons/sq. mile. The study area of Pontiac County was 1,844.12
sq. miles and had a 1971 density of 10.21 persons/sq. mile.

ID: 1408099 ALDFIELD, ONSLOW, ONSLOW SOUTH

AREA: 177.74 sq. miles

1971 DENSITY:
  12.57 persons/sq. mile

TYPE:
  Combined

POPULATION:
  1851:   833
  1881:   2927
  1941:   2528
  1971:   2234

CHANGES: 1891 Quyon
  incorporated.

SUBFILES:
  a. Aldfield
  b. Onslow
  c. Onslow South (Rural)
  d. Quyon

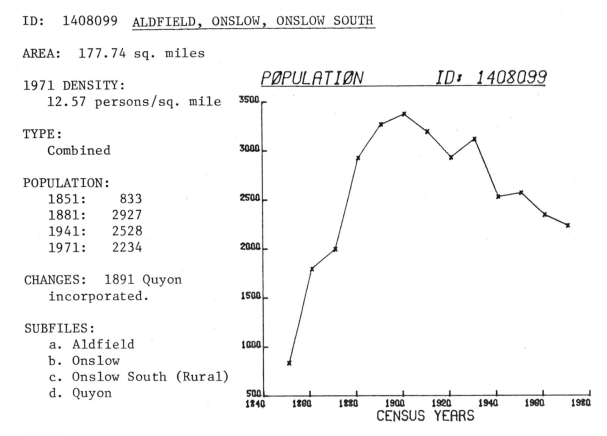

POPULATION   ID: 1408099

CENSUS YEARS

NOTES:

In 1976 Aldfield is part of LaPêche Village (see 1509799) which is
part of the Rural Fringe of the Census Metropolitan Area of Ottawa-
Hull. The remaining parts, together with Eardley (1509800), form the
new municipality of Pontiac. Because soils in this area are better
than in most of the county, it was settled earlier. The molybdenite
mine in Onslow Township is mentioned in 164 (Kennedy, 1970), p. 49. Iter
106 (Blanchard, 1954), p. 111 mentions the sawmills in Quyon.

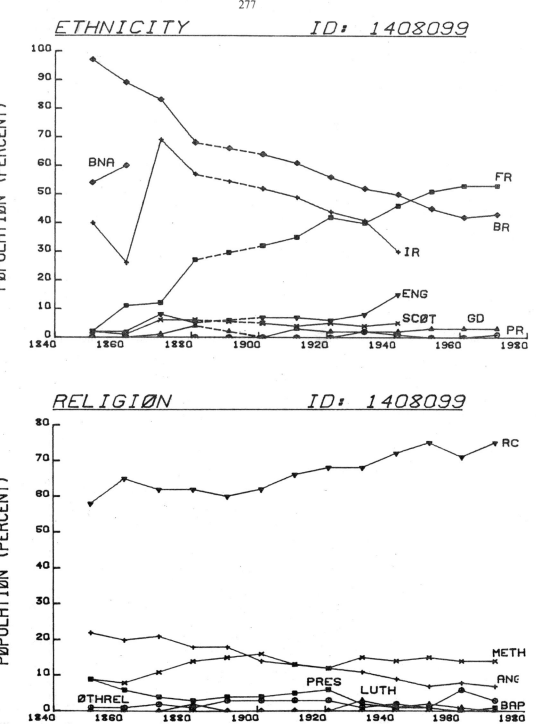

ETHNICITY   ID: 1408099

RELIGIØN   ID: 1408099

ID: 1408099 SUBFILES

a. ALDFIELD

   AREA: 77.43 sq. miles

   1971 DENSITY:
      7.05 persons/sq. mile

   POPULATION:
      1881: 682
      1901: 817
      1941: 676
      1971: 546

b. ONSLOW

   AREA: 60.38 sq. miles

   1971 DENSITY:
      3.59 persons/sq. mile

   POPULATION:
      1881: 913
      1901: 825
      1941: 445
      1971: 217

   CHANGES: Formerly called
      Onslow North.

c. ONSLOW SOUTH (RURAL)

   AREA: 37.17 sq. miles

   1971 DENSITY:
      15.93 persons/sq. mile

   POPULATION:
      1881: 922 (1332 including
                      Quyon)
      1901: 1050
      1941: 770
      1971: 592

   CHANGES: 1891 Quyon incorporated.

d. QUYON

   AREA: 2.76 sq. miles

   1971 DENSITY:
      318.48 persons/sq. mile

   POPULATION:
      1881: 410 (unincorporated)
      1901: 682
      1941: 637
      1971: 879

   CHANGES: 1891 incorporated.

ID: 1408099   SUBFILES cont'd

ETHNICITY

PLACE	YEAR	ENG	SCOT	IR	FR	GD	PR
Aldfield	1881	1	6	143	450	63	0
Aldfield	1901	37	1	136	553	84	0
Aldfield	1941	33	0	38	537	45	16
Onslow	1881	7	50	683	168	0	0
Onslow	1901	11	25	542	245	0	0
Onslow	1941	2	19	205	218	0	1
Onslow South (Rural)	1881	127	109	854	180	40	0
Onslow South (Rural)	1901	111	85	734	97	3	0
Onslow South (Rural)	1941	93	75	456	132	9	0
Quyon	1901	83	48	339	201	5	0
Quyon	1941	260	24	53	281	0	8

RELIGION

PLACE	YEAR	ANG	RC	PRES	METH/UC	BAP	LUTH
Aldfield	1881	16	613	5	4		45
Aldfield	1901	44	647	0	36		84
Aldfield	1941	9	618	1	7		34
Onslow	1881	113	609	13	178		
Onslow	1901	26	607	6	186		
Onslow	1941	5	356	2	43		
Onslow South (Rural)	1881	402	603	71	220		
Onslow South (Rural)	1901	218	392	107	256	14	
Onslow South (Rural)	1941	157	356	7	244	3	
Quyon	1901	138	439	31	73		
Quyon	1941	52	497	11	72		

ID: 1408100 ALLEYN, CAWOOD

AREA: 133.84 sq. miles

1971 DENSITY:
   1.26 persons/sq. mile

TYPE:
   Rural

POPULATION:
   1881: 330
   1941: 397
   1971: 168

CHANGES: 1881 created.

SUBFILES: None

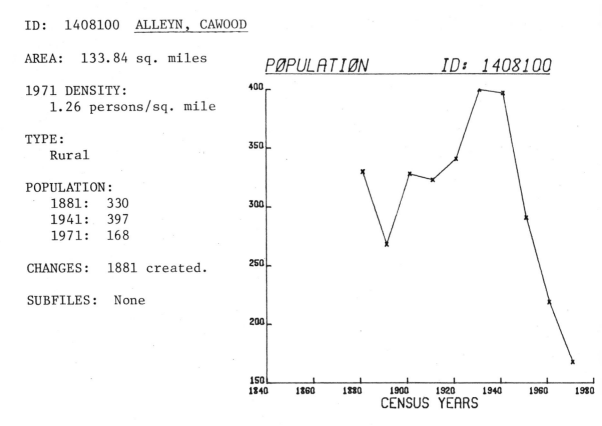

POPULATION   ID: 1408100

CENSUS YEARS

NOTES:

Most of the present population of these two townships is located in
the unincorporated village of Danford Lake (1971 population 128)
located in Alleyn. The unlikely looking shift in Irish and English
lines for 1911 in the Ethnicity graph has been double-checked. There
may be a census error. Compare the Religion graph as well for that
year.

281

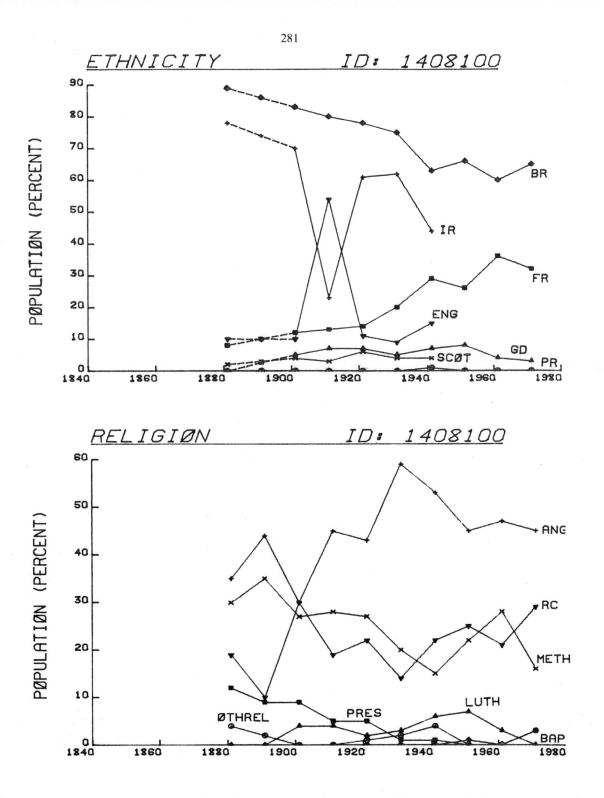

ID: 1408200 <u>BRISTOL</u>

AREA: 86.52 sq. miles

1971 DENSITY:
  11.78 persons/sq. mile

TYPE:
  Rural

POPULATION:
  1851: 1491
  1881: 2198
  1941: 1503
  1971: 1019

CHANGES: None.

SUBFILES: None

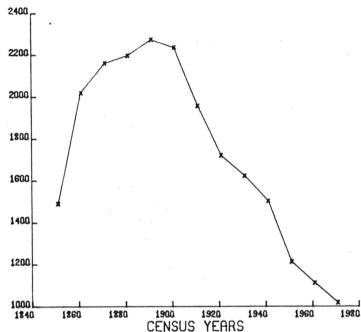

POPULATION   ID: 1408200

CENSUS YEARS

NOTES:

Bristol is an area of relatively good soil. Iron mining in the area is
mentioned in 164 (Kennedy, 1970), p. 48.

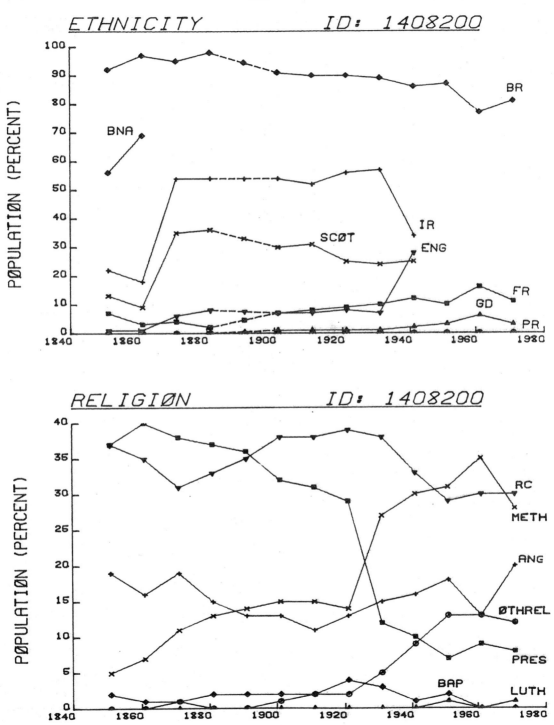

ETHNICITY   ID: 1408200

RELIGION   ID: 1408200

ID: 1408300   CHICHESTER

AREA: 87.15 sq. miles

1971 DENSITY:
   6.44 persons/sq. mile

TYPE:
   Rural

POPULATION:
   1851:   172
   1881:   702
   1941:   789
   1971:   561

CHANGES: None.

SUBFILES: None

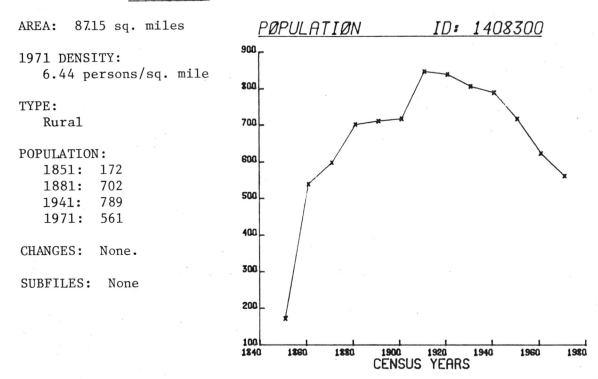

POPULATIØN   ID: 1408300

CENSUS YEARS

NOTES:

In the 1851 census there were 40 "Protestants" listed. These appear
in the Other Religions line of the Religion graph. If it is accurate,
the sharp reversal in the 1971 census of British and French, which
shows up in the Ethnicity graph, does not seem to be reflected in the
other two graphs.

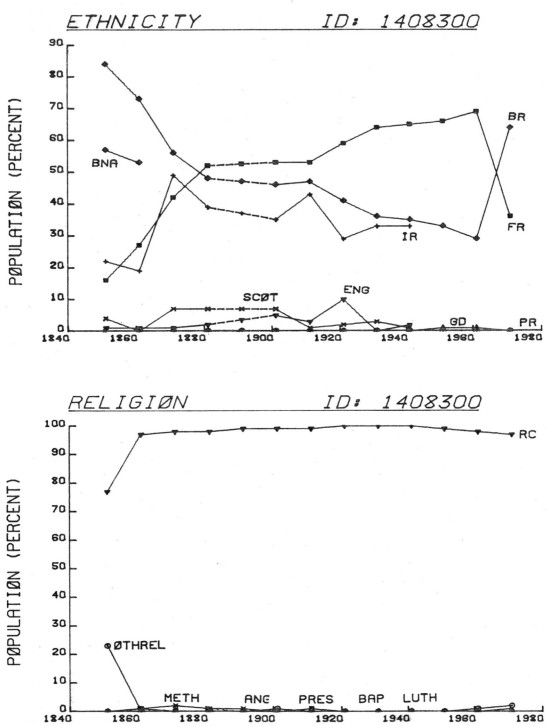

ID: 1408499 CLARENDON

AREA: 128.39 sq. miles

1971 DENSITY:
   26.39 persons/sq. mile

TYPE:
   Combined

POPULATION:
   1851: 1759
   1881: 2879
   1941: 2888
   1971: 3388

CHANGES: 1891 Shawville
   incorporated.

SUBFILES:
   a. Clarendon (Rural)
   b. Shawville

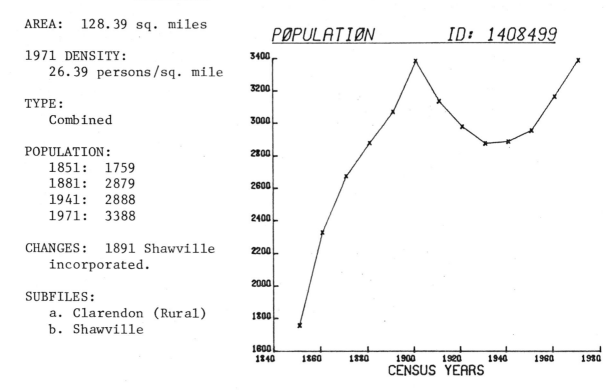

POPULATIØN   ID: 1408499

CENSUS YEARS

NOTES:

Like adjacent Bristol, Clarendon has relatively good soil for farming.
Shawville is the subject of one of Pontiac County's few local histories
III (Bretzlaff et al., 1973). Industry in the area is mentioned in
that work, and also in 276 (Fraser, n.d.), p. 107.

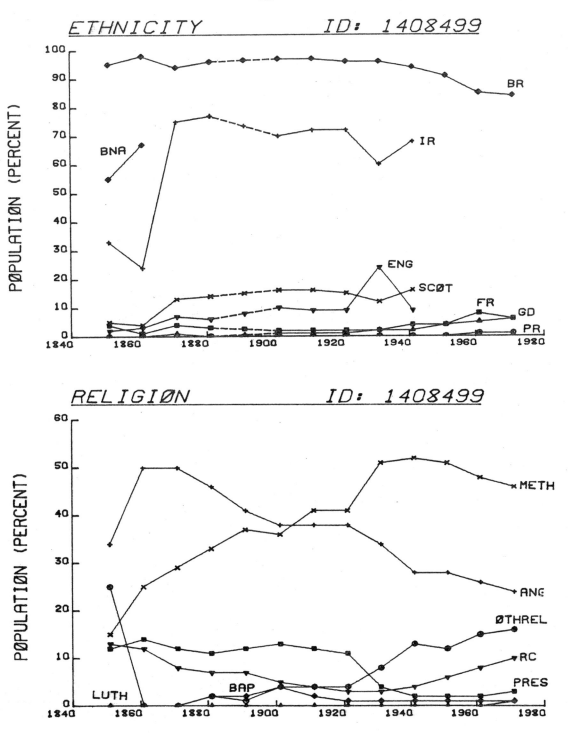

ID: 1408499   SUBFILES

a. <u>CLARENDON (RURAL)</u>

AREA: 126.36 sq. miles

1971 DENSITY:
   13.0 persons/sq. mile

POPULATION:
   1901:   2736
   1941:   1996
   1971:   1643

CHANGES: 1891 Shawville
incorporated.

b. <u>SHAWVILLE</u>

AREA: 2.03 sq. miles

1971 DENSITY:
   859.61 persons/sq. mile

POPULATION:
   1901:   648
   1941:   892
   1971:   1745

CHANGES: 1891 incorporated.

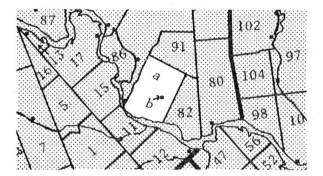

ID: 1408499 SUBFILES cont'd

ETHNICITY

PLACE		YEAR	ENG	SCOT	IR	FR	GD	PR
Clarendon	(Rural)	1901	254	423	1974	61	19	0
Clarendon	(Rural)	1941	171	314	1399	77	32	0
Shawville		1901	99	132	390	14	7	1
Shawville		1941	98	154	575	31	23	1

RELIGION

PLACE		YEAR	ANG	RC	PRES	METH/UC	BAP	LUTH
Clarendon	(Rural)	1901	1042	157	342	970	109	
Clarendon	(Rural)	1941	550	99	32	1081	12	
Shawville		1901	253	15	88	248	21	
Shawville		1941	256	25	28	407	18	

ID: 1408500 <u>DORION</u>

AREA: 158.74 sq. miles

1971 DENSITY:
   2.18 persons/sq. mile

TYPE:
   Rural

POPULATION:
   1911:   408
   1941:   554
   1971:   346

CHANGES: 1911 created.
   After 1931, the
   unincorporated township
   of Church is included in
   Dorion.

SUBFILES: None

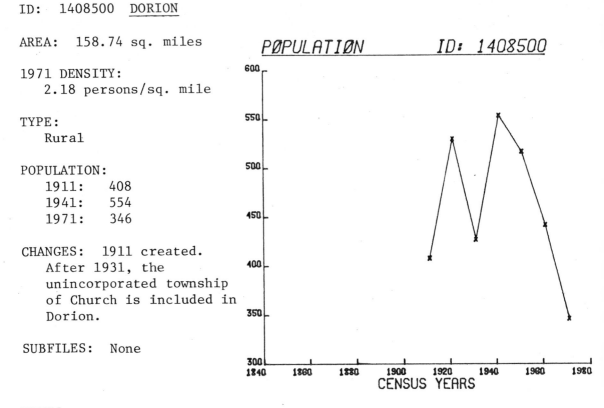

NOTES:

The largest community in this area is the unincorporated village of
Lac-Cayamant (1971 population 170), located in Dorion Township. The
soil in the area is poor.

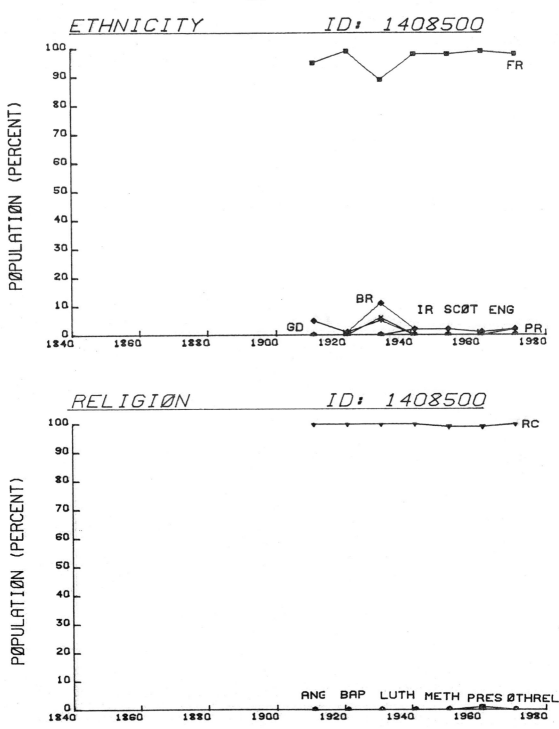

ID: 1408600 <u>GRAND-CALUMET</u>

AREA: 50.43 sq. miles

1971 DENSITY:
  20.46 persons/sq. mile

TYPE:
  Rural

POPULATION:
  1851:   783
  1881: 1269
  1941: 1244
  1971: 1032

CHANGES: None.

SUBFILES: None.

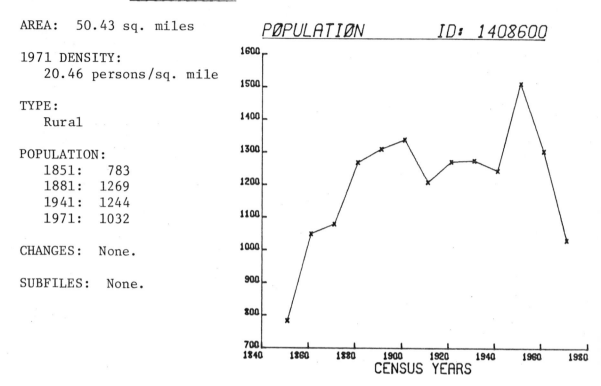

PØPULATIØN   ID: 1408600

CENSUS YEARS

NOTES:

The soil of the area is relatively good. Lead and zinc mining are
mentioned in 164 (Kennedy, 1970), p. 48 and 216 (Blanchard, 1954),
p. 117. The unincorporated village of Calumet Island had a
population of 215 in 1971.

293

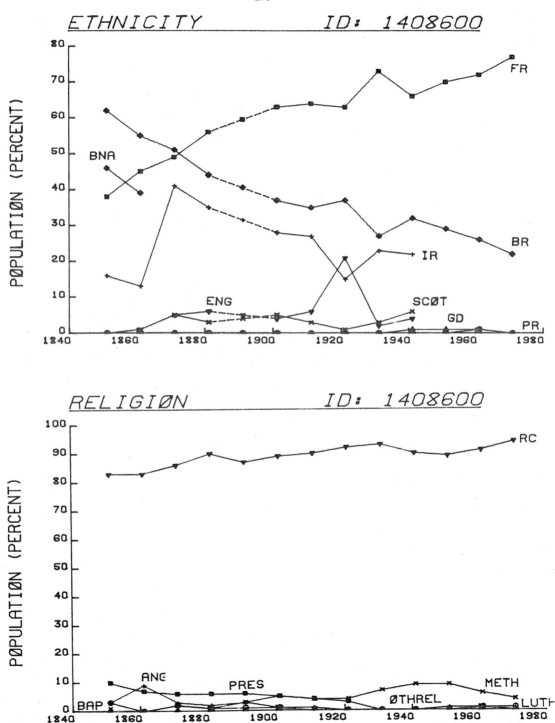

ID: 1408799 ISLE-DES-ALLUMETTES, ISLE-AUX-ALLUMETTES EAST

AREA: 73.44 sq. miles

1971 DENSITY:
   21.36 persons/sq. mile

TYPE:
   Combined

POPULATION:
   1851:   1025
   1881:   1715
   1941:   1822
   1971:   1569

CHANGES: Isle-des-
   Allumettes and Isle-aux-
   Allumettes East formerly
   known together as
   Allumettes.

SUBFILES:
   a. Isle-des-Allumettes
      Isle-aux-Allumettes
      East
   b. Chapeau

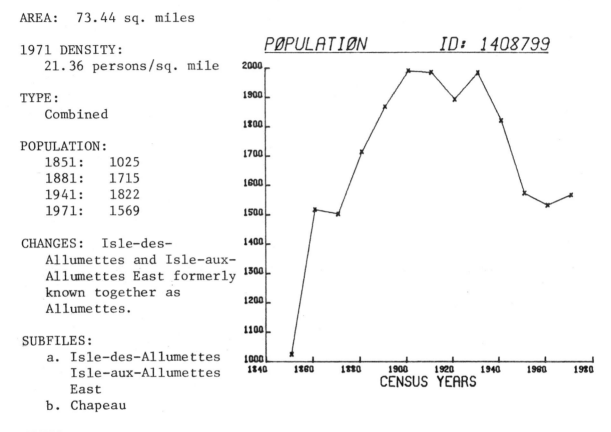

POPULATION   ID: 1408799

CENSUS YEARS

NOTES:

None of the sources examined deals specifically with Isle-des-Allumettes or Isle-aux-Allumettes East.

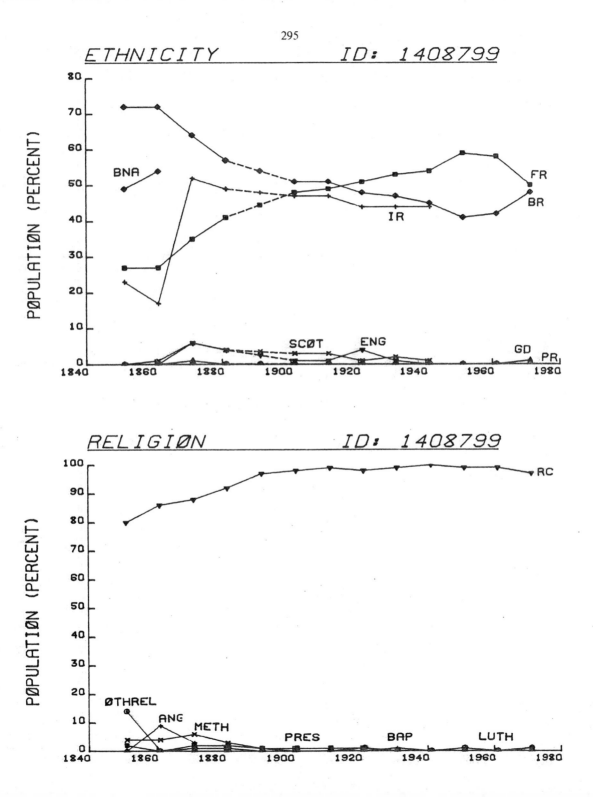

ID: 1408799 SUBFILES

a. ISLE-DES-ALLUMETTES (RURAL), ISLE-AUX-ALLUMETTES EAST

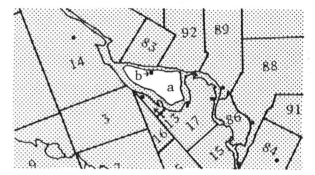

    AREA: 70.96 sq. miles

    1971 DENSITY:
      14.54 persons/sq. mile

    POPULATION:
      1901: 1761
      1941: 1351
      1971: 1032

    CHANGES: 1891 Chapeau
    incorporated.

b. CHAPEAU

    AREA: 2.48 sq. miles

    1971 DENSITY:
      216.53 persons/sq. mile

    POPULATION:
      1901: 230
      1941: 471
      1971: 537

    CHANGES: 1891 incorporated.

ID: 1408799 SUBFILES

ETHNICITY

PLACE	YEAR	ENG	SCOT	IR	FR	GD	PR
Isle-des-Allumettes (Rural)							
Isle-aux-Allumettes East	1901	25	47	838	837	1	0
Isle-des-Allumettes (Rural)							
Isle-aux-Allumettes East	1941	5	8	624	710	1	1
Chapeau	1901	2	9	90	127	0	0
Chapeau	1941	4	11	173	280	1	2

RELIGION

PLACE	YEAR	ANG	RC	PRES	METH/UC	BAP	LUTH
Isle-des-Allumettes (Rural)							
Isle-aux-Allumettes East	1901	6	1719	29	1		
Isle-des-Allumettes (Rural)							
Isle-aux-Allumettes East	1941	1	1349	0	1		
Chapeau	1901	0	229	0	1		
Chapeau	1941	0	470	1	0		

ID: 1408899 LITCHFIELD, CLAPHAM, LESLIE, HUDDERSFIELD

AREA: 264.72 sq. miles

1971 DENSITY:
  15.54 persons/sq. mile

TYPE:
  Combined

POPULATION:
  1851: 756
  1881: 3112
  1941: 3861
  1971: 4115

CHANGES: 1901 Portage-du-
  Fort and Bryson incor-
  porated. 1911 Campbell's
  Bay incorporated.

SUBFILES:
  a. Litchfield (Rural)
  b. Leslie, Clapham,
     Huddersfield
  c. Portage-du-Fort
  d. Bryson
  e. Campbell's Bay

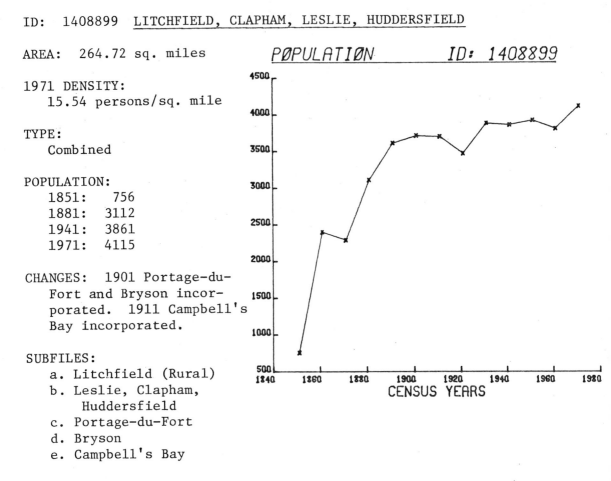

POPULATION   ID: 1408899

CENSUS YEARS

NOTES:

The Irish (and British groups generally) are mainly in Litchfield
Township; the French are the largest group in the other three. The
small Polish settlement (now much reduced) was mainly in Clapham; the
Germans mainly in Leslie. The pattern of French Canadian settlement
is discussed in 106 (Blanchard, 1954), pp. 91-92. Item 276 (Fraser,
n.d.), p. 164 mentions Bryson, and early sawmilling in Portage-du-
Fort is mentioned in 146 (Greening, 1961), p. 96. The important
unincorporated village of Otter Lake, located in Leslie
Township, had a population of 783 in 1971.

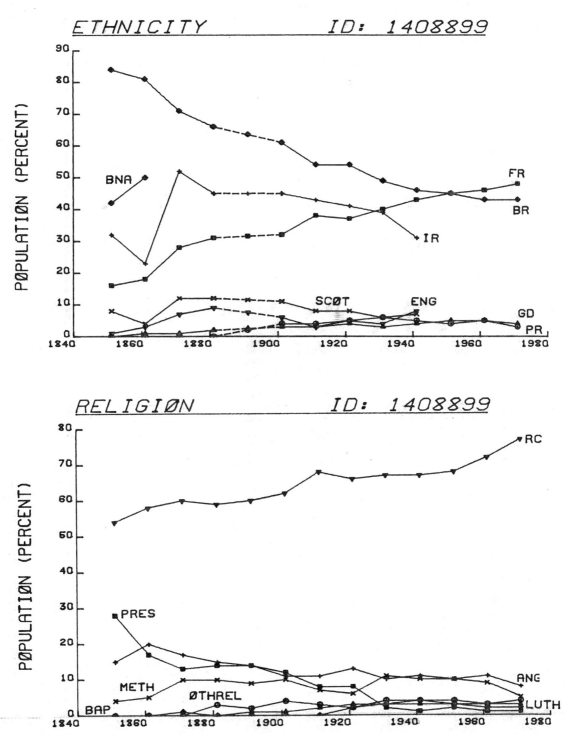

ID: 1408899   SUBFILES

a. <u>LITCHFIELD (RURAL)</u>

AREA: 69.10 sq. miles

1971 DENSITY:
   9.74 persons/sq. mile

POPULATION:
   1881: 1333 (2326
     including Portage-du-
     Fort and Bryson)
   1901: 1814
   1911: 1382
   1941: 1214
   1971:   673

CHANGES: 1901 Portage-du-Fort and Bryson incorporated.
           1911 Campbell's Bay incorporated.

b. <u>LESLIE, CLAPHAM, HUDDERSFIELD</u>

AREA: 191.59 sq. miles

1971 DENSITY:
   5.30 persons/sq. mile

POPULATION:
   1881:   786
   1901:   943
   1941: 1122
   1971: 1016

c. <u>PORTAGE-DU-FORT</u>

AREA: 1.64 sq. miles

1971 DENSITY:
   262.80 persons/sq. mile

POPULATION:
   1881:   564 (unincorporated)
   1901:   449
   1941:   361
   1971:   431

CHANGES: 1901 incorporated.

d. <u>BRYSON</u>

AREA: 1.20 sq. miles

1971 DENSITY:
   674.17 persons/sq. mile

POPULATION:
   1881:   429 (unincorporated)
   1901:   508
   1941:   264
   1971:   809

CHANGES: 1901 incorporated.

e. <u>CAMPBELL'S BAY</u>

AREA: 1.19 sq. miles

1971 DENSITY:
   996.64 persons/sq. mile

POPULATION:
   1911:   447
   1941:   900
   1971: 1186

CHANGES: 1911 incorporated.

ID: 1408899 SUBFILES cont'd

ETHNICITY

PLACE	YEAR	ENG	SCOT	IR	FR	GD	PR
Litchfield	1881	230	365	1187	497	18	0
Leslie, Clapham, Huddersfield	1881	41	12	204	456	56	0
Litchfield (Rural)	1901	90	198	1127	361	17	10
Litchfield (Rural)	1941	153	26	655	372	6	2
Leslie, Clapham, Huddersfield	1941	19	16	70	638	152	199
Portage-du-Fort	1901	53	95	186	113	2	0
Portage-du-Fort	1941	35	78	93	147	7	0
Bryson	1901	21	86	189	209	0	0
Bryson	1941	50	32	25	156	0	0
Campbell's Bay	1911	22	60	241	118	0	0
Campbell's Bay	1941	44	111	362	345	8	1

RELIGION

PLACE	YEAR	ANG	RC	PRES	METH/UC	BAP	LUTH
Litchfield	1881	293	1390	398	217		
Leslie, Clapham, Huddersfield	1881	163	433	34	80		
Litchfield (Rural)	1901	127	1188	270	199		
Litchfield (Rural)	1941	104	892	16	173	3	
Leslie, Clapham, Huddersfield	1941	118	769	8	4	109	109
Portage-du-Fort	1901	89	272	40	42		
Portage-du-Fort	1941	90	208	3	25	0	
Bryson	1901	71	262	91	75		
Bryson	1941	24	193	7	40	0	
Campbell's Bay	1911	68	239	70	57		
Campbell's Bay	1941	94	528	13	135	24	

ID: 1408999 <u>MANSFIELD, PONTEFRACT</u>

AREA: 163.80 sq. miles

1971 DENSITY:
    22.02 persons/sq. mile

TYPE:
    Combined

POPULATION:
    1851:   426
    1881:   1165
    1941:   2448
    1971:   3607

CHANGES: 1891 Fort-Coulonge
    incorporated.

SUBFILES:
    a. Mansfield (Rural)
         Pontefract
    b. Fort-Coulonge

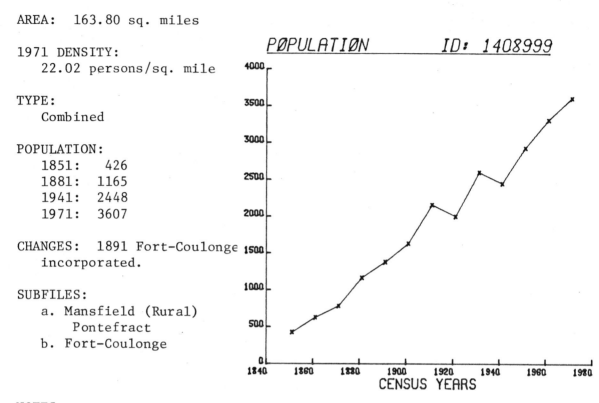

POPULATION   ID: 1408999

CENSUS YEARS

NOTES:

In this area the rocky uplands are close to the river and soils are
for the most part too poor for farming. Early settlement in Fort-
Coulonge is mentioned in 276 (Fraser, n.d.), p. 75 which also mentions
its importance for logging operations on the Coulonge River (p. 162).
The 1971 census lists two unincorporated places in Mansfield
Township: Fort-Coulonge-Nord-Est (population 586) and Davidson
(population 318).

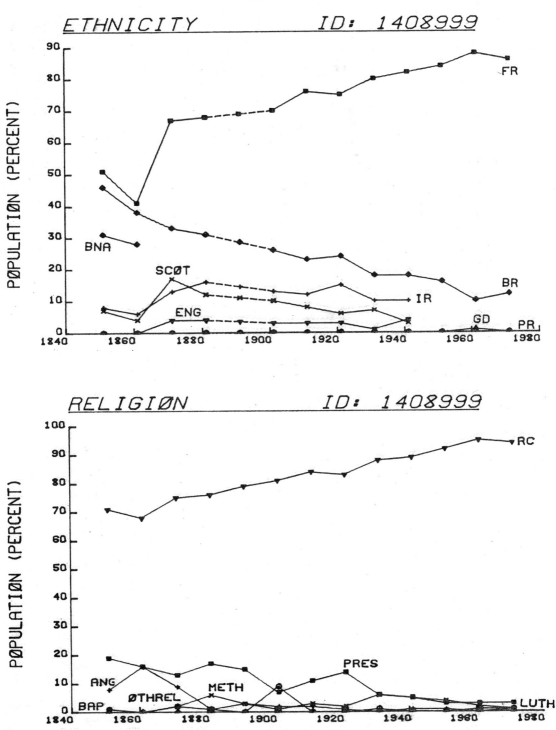

ETHNICITY   ID: 1408999

RELIGIØN   ID: 1408999

ID: 1408999 SUBFILES

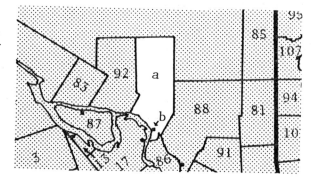

a. MANSFIELD (RURAL), PONTEFRACT

AREA: 162.47 sq. miles

1971 DENSITY:
11.2 persons/sq. mile

POPULATION:
1901: 1151
1941: 1376
1971: 1823

CHANGES: 1891 Fort-
Coulonge incorporated.

b. FORT-COULONGE

AREA: 1.33 sq. miles

1971 DENSITY:
1341.35 persons/sq. mile

POPULATION:
1901: 482
1941: 1072
1971: 1784

CHANGES: 1891 incorporated.

ID: 1408999 SUBFILES cont'd

ETHNICITY

PLACE	YEAR	ENG	SCOT	IR	FR	GD	PR
Mansfield (Rural), Pontefract	1901	13	81	120	935	0	0
Mansfield (Rural), Pontefract	1941	60	36	102	1173	1	0
Fort-Coulonge	1901	41	75	88	204	4	4
Fort-Coulonge	1941	47	45	140	829	2	1

RELIGION

PLACE	YEAR	ANG	RC	PRES	METH/UC	BAP	LUTH
Mansfield (Rural), Pontefract	1901	6	985	20	4		
Mansfield (Rural), Pontefract	1941	5	1220	76	74		
Fort-Coulonge	1901	26	338	93	20		
Fort-Coulonge	1941	11	952	47	57		

306

ID: 1409000 SHEEN, ABERDEEN, ESHER, MALAKOFF, RAPIDES-DES-JOACHIMS

AREA: 316.58 sq. miles

1971 DENSITY:
 1.34 persons/sq. mile

TYPE:
 Rural

POPULATION:
 1851:   230
 1881:   823
 1941:   537
 1971:   423

CHANGES: 1961 Rapides-des-
 Joachims created out of
 Aberdeen.

SUBFILES:
 a. Sheen, Aberdeen
    Esher, Malakoff
 b. Rapides-des-Joachims

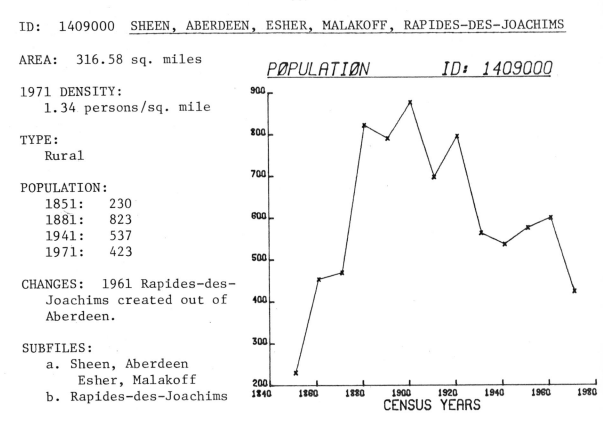

POPULATION   ID: 1409000

CENSUS YEARS

NOTES:

In the 1851 census there were 73 "Protestants" listed. These appear
in the Other Religions line of the Religion graph. In 1971 the
unincorporated village of Rapides-des-Joachims had a population of 120.
No historical information about this area could be gleaned from the
sources listed in the Bibliography.

307

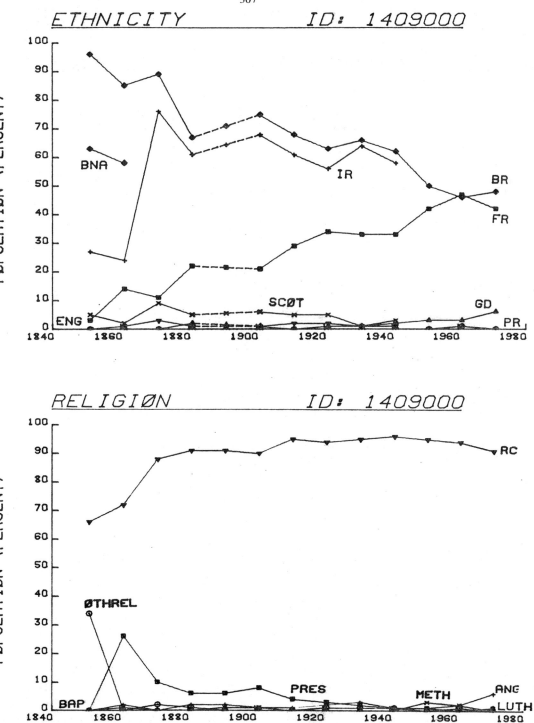

ID: 1409000 SUBFILES

a. SHEEN, ABERDEEN, ESHER, MALAKOFF

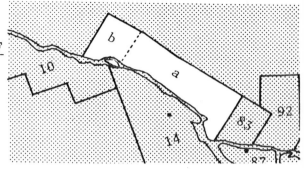

   AREA: 220.47 sq. miles

   1971 DENSITY:
      0.89 persons/sq. mile

   POPULATION:
      1971: 197

   CHANGES: 1961 Rapides-des-
      Joachims created out of
      Aberdeen.

b. RAPIDES-DES-JOACHIMS

   AREA: 96.11 sq. miles

   1971 DENSITY:
      2.35 persons/sq. mile

   POPULATION:
      1971: 226

   CHANGES: 1961 created out of Aberdeen.

ID: 1409000 SUBFILES cont'd

ETHNICITY

PLACE	YEAR	ENG	SCOT	IR	FR	GD	PR
Aberdeen, Malakoff	1901	2	34	104	108	5	0
Aberdeen, Malakoff	1921	3	19	30	108	1	
Sheen, Esher	1901	11	18	488	74	0	0
Sheen, Esher	1921	13	21	414	161	5	2
Sheen, Aberdeen, Esher, Malakoff	1971	(British) 95			30	10	0
Rapides-des Joachims	1971	(British) 70			115	10	0

RELIGION

PLACE	YEAR	ANG	RC	PRES	METH/UC	BAP	LUTH
Aberdeen, Malakoff	1901	5	223	52	6		
Aberdeen, Malakoff	1921	0	169	10	0		
Sheen, Esher	1901	6	567	17	1		
Sheen, Esher	1921	13	581	14	3		
Sheen, Aberdeen, Esher, Malakoff	1971	0	140	0	0		5
Rapides-des-Joachims	1971	20	175	5	0		

ID: 1409100   THORNE

AREA: 68.47 sq. miles

1971 DENSITY:
    4.25 persons/sq. mile

TYPE:
    Rural

POPULATION:
    1861:   450
    1881:   876
    1941:   580
    1971:   291

CHANGES: 1861 created.

SUBFILES: None

PØPULATIØN   ID: 1409100

CENSUS YEARS

NOTES:

Thorne is remarkable on the Quebec side of the river for its relatively high proportion of descendents of German settlers.

311

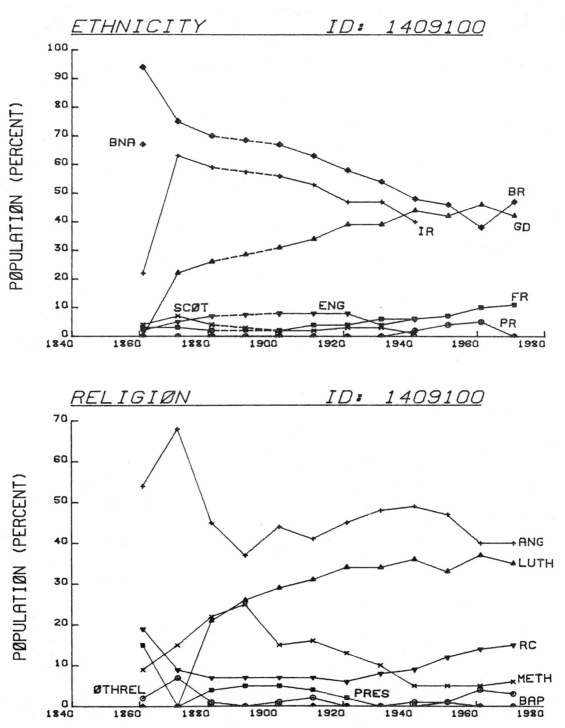

ID: 1409200 <u>WALTHAM, BRYSON</u>

AREA: 174.30 sq. miles

1971 DENSITY:
   2.82 persons/sq. mile

TYPE:
   Rural

POPULATION:
   1851:   186
   1881:   393
   1941:   386
   1971:   491

CHANGES: None.

SUBFILES: None

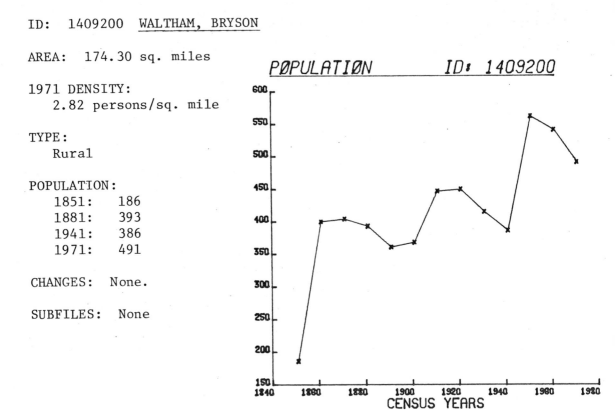

POPULATION   ID: 1409200

CENSUS YEARS

NOTES:

Most of the population in this area is located in the unincorporated village of Waltham Station (1971 population 378) in Waltham Township, which is at the end of Pontiac County's only railway. The Black River, which drains most of the area, has been of some importance in the logging industry.

313

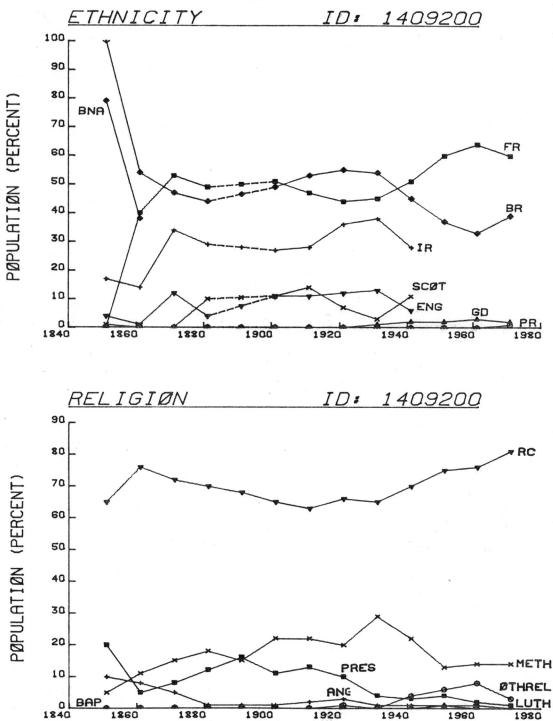

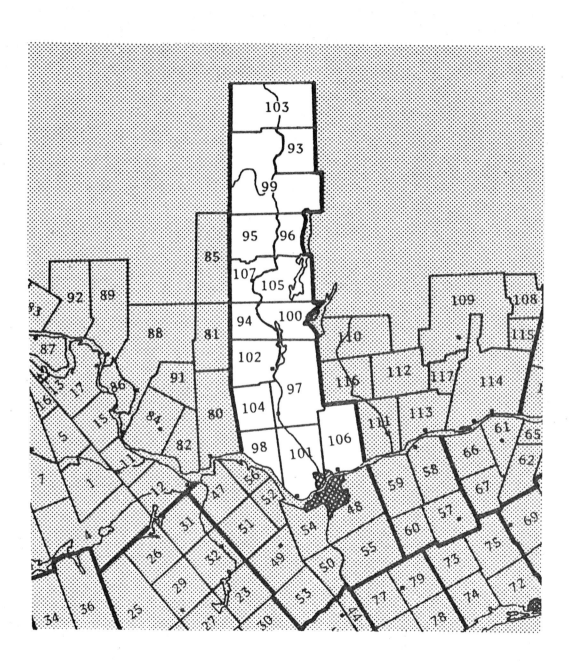

Since the City of Hull is located in these counties, the published historical studies of this area are fairly numerous. One work
studies the area as part of a wider region composed of Hull, Labelle
and Papineau Counties: 166 (Lajoie, 1968). The best single source
is 106 (Blanchard, 1954), which can be supplemented by 203 (Taché et
al, 1938), 286 (MacKay, 1949), 45 (Hamelin and Roby, 1971), 146
(Greening, 1961), and 169 (Legget, 1975), all of which are also concerned with a wider area. Hull itself is the subject of a number of
studies, including especially 109b (Brault, 1950), 192b (Rossignol et
al, 1975) and 233b (Elliot, 1979). Among the many works dealing with
Philemon Wright's role in the settlement of Hull, see 243c (Latchford,
1922). A series of sophisticated studies by Helen E. Parsons deal
with land use in the Gatineau Valley: 260c (Parsons, 1977), 260d
(Parsons, 1975) and 289b (Parsons, 1976).

Current census treatment of the two counties and of the assignment of the city of Hull differ considerably from earlier census
years. For details, see below, Notes to IU 101, p.336 and IU 106,
p.350. In spite of our combination of the two counties, the considerable census information available on each of the two may still be of
interest. In addition to the tables, maps, and analyses at the census
division level, there are also important sources on the county parts
listed in materials dealing with The Census Metropolitan Area of
Ottawa-Hull.

Unorganized territories in the north of Gatineau County (1971
area 248.46 sq. miles; population 8) and the Maniwaki Indian Reserve
in IU 99 (1971 area 69.70 sq. miles; population 768) have not been
included in our figures. The Gatineau-Hull study area totals for
1971: population 164,899; area 1,676.54 sq. miles; density 98.36
persons/sq. mile.

ID: 1509300   AUMOND

AREA: 83.06 sq. miles

1971 DENSITY:
   7.28 persons/sq. mile

TYPE:
   Rural

POPULATION:
   1861: 131
   1881: 421
   1941: 944
   1971: 605

CHANGES: 1861 created.

SUBFILES: None

PØPULATIØN   ID: 1509300

CENSUS YEARS

NOTES:

None of the works listed in the bibliography deals specifically with Aumond.

The unincorporated village of Ste-Famille-D'Aumond had a population of 213 in 1971.

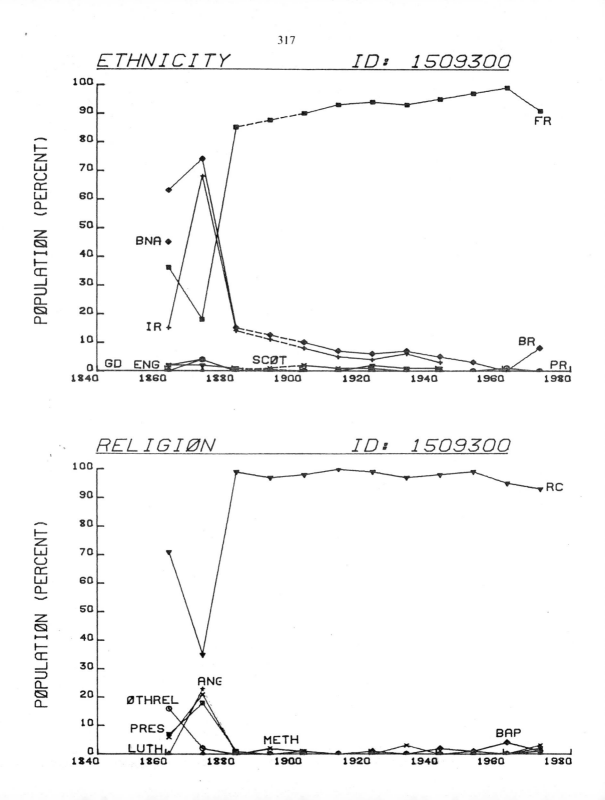

ID: 1509400   <u>AYLWIN</u>

AREA: 67.76 sq. miles

1971 DENSITY:
  9.14 persons/sq. mile

TYPE:
  Rural

POPULATION:
    1861: 350
    1881: 625
    1941: 828
    1971: 619

CHANGES: 1861 created.

SUBFILES: None

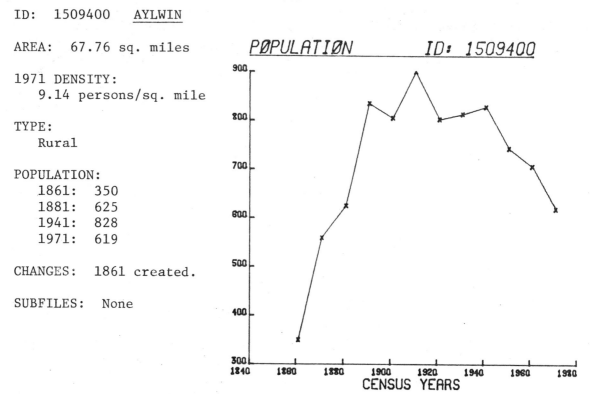

NOTES:

Aylwin is dealt with in the books listed in the bibliography only in discussions of a wider area, e.g. 159b (Houde, 1970) and 289b (Parson, 1976).

The unincorporated village of Kazabazua had a population of 238 in 1971.

319

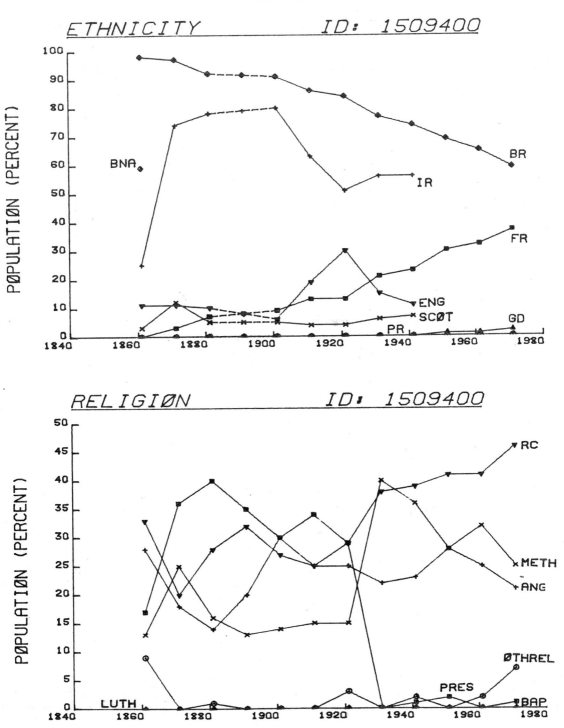

ETHNICITY   ID: 1509400

RELIGION   ID: 1509400

ID: 1509500   BOUCHETTE, BLUE SEA, MESSINE

AREA: 88.39 sq. miles

1971 DENSITY:
   24.37 persons/sq. mile

TYPE:
   Rural

POPULATION:
   1861:   400
   1881:   902
   1941:   2157
   1971:   2154

CHANGES: 1861 created.

SUBFILES: None

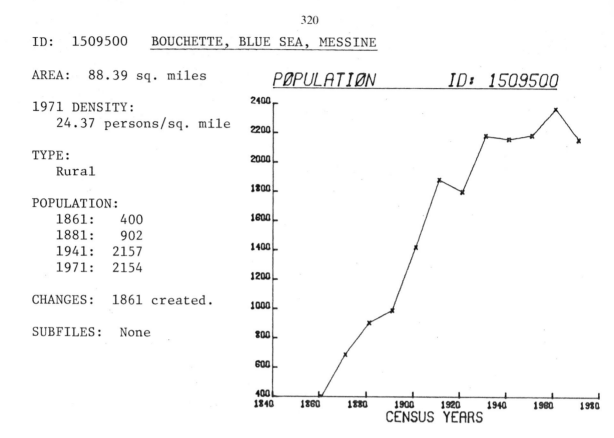

POPULATION   ID: 1509500

CENSUS YEARS

NOTES:

The early development of the Bouchette-Blue Sea area as a summer cottage area is suggested in 156b (Up the Gatineau, 1975), p.8.

The census subdivisions together form the township of Bouchette. In 1971 this area had the following major unincorporated places (with populations): Bouchette (406), Blue Sea Lake (343), and Messines (297).

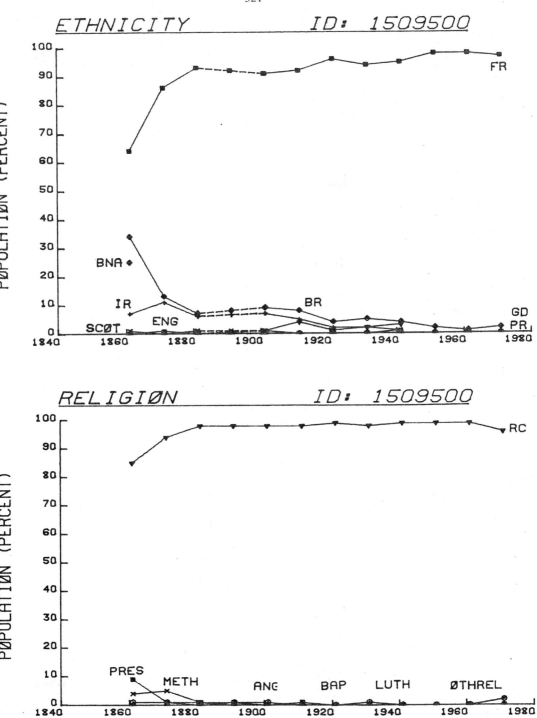

ID: 1509600   CAMERON, STE.-THÉRÈSE-DE-LA-GATINEAU

AREA: 52.46 sq. miles

1971 DENSITY:
   14.30 persons/sq. mile

TYPE:
   Rural

POPULATION:
   1861:   237
   1881:   448
   1941:   840
   1971:   750

CHANGES: 1861 created;
   formerly was just
   Cameron; 1961 annexed
   part of Northfield
   (1510500).

SUBFILES: None

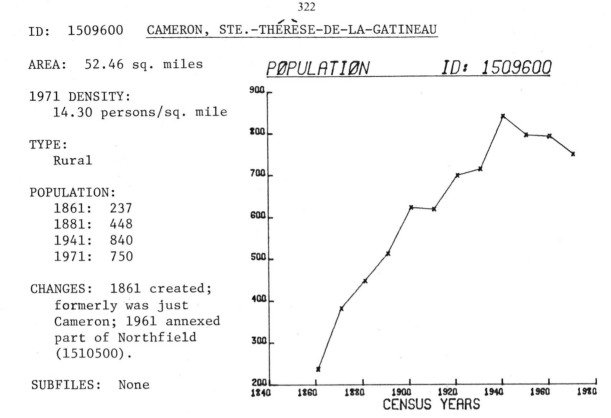

POPULATION   ID: 1509600

CENSUS YEARS

NOTES:

None of the works listed in the bibliography deals specifically with this area.

The census subdivisions together form the township of Cameron. In 1971 the unincorporated village of Ste-Thérèse-de-Gatineau had a population of 275.

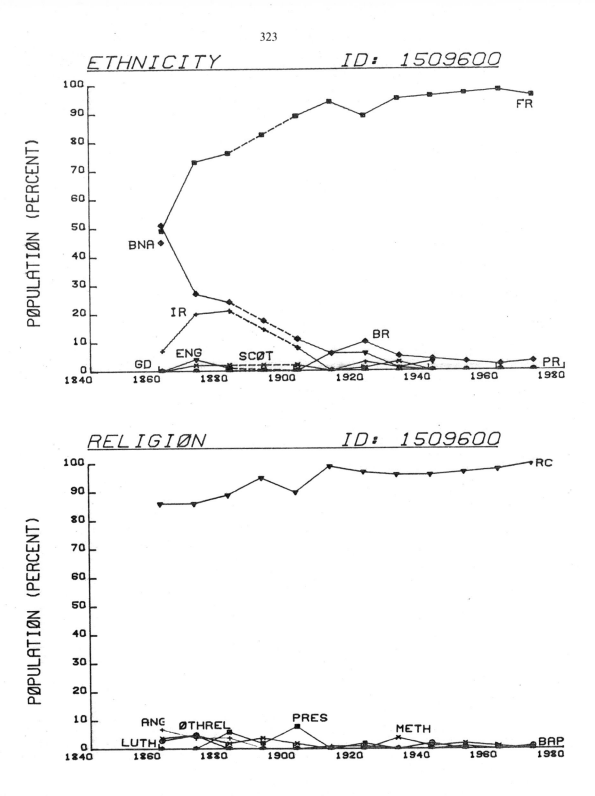

ID: 1509799   DENHOLM, WAKEFIELD, WAKEFIELD EAST

AREA: 181.42 sq. miles

1971 DENSITY:
   12.77 persons/sq. mile

TYPE:
   Combined

POPULATION:
   1851:   588
   1881:   1609
   1941:   1972
   1971:   2316

CHANGES: 1921 Wakefield
   (Urban) incorporated.
   Wakefield (formerly
   Wakefield West) and
   Wakefield East formerly
   combined as Wakefield.

SUBFILES:
   a. Denholm
   b. Wakefield (Rural),
       Wakefield East
   c. Wakefield (Urban)

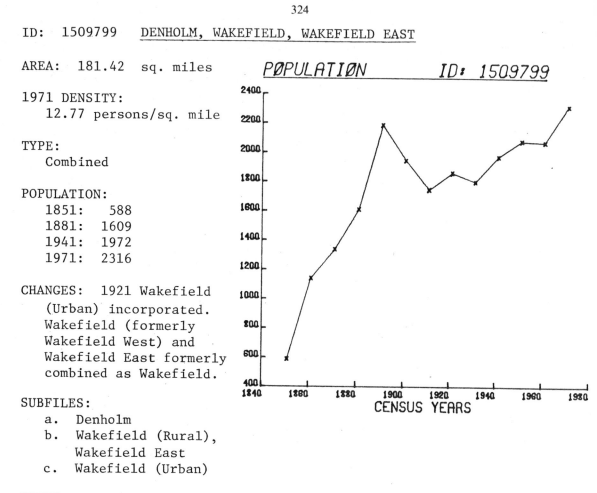

POPULATION   ID: 1509799

CENSUS YEARS

NOTES:

The most important work dealing with this area is 141 (N. and S. Geggie, 1974). Mining activity in the area is mentioned in 106 (Blanchard, 1954), p. 117.

In 1976 Wakefield and Wakefield Village, together with Masham North and Ste-Cécile-de-Masham (in 1510400) and Aldfield (in 1408099) form La Pêche Village; Wakefield East is part of Val-des-Monts Village (see 1611600). Both new areas are part of the Rural Fringe of the Census Metropolitan Area of Ottawa-Hull.

In 1971 the unincorporated village of St-Pierre-de-Wakefield, located in Wakefield East, had a population of 203.

325

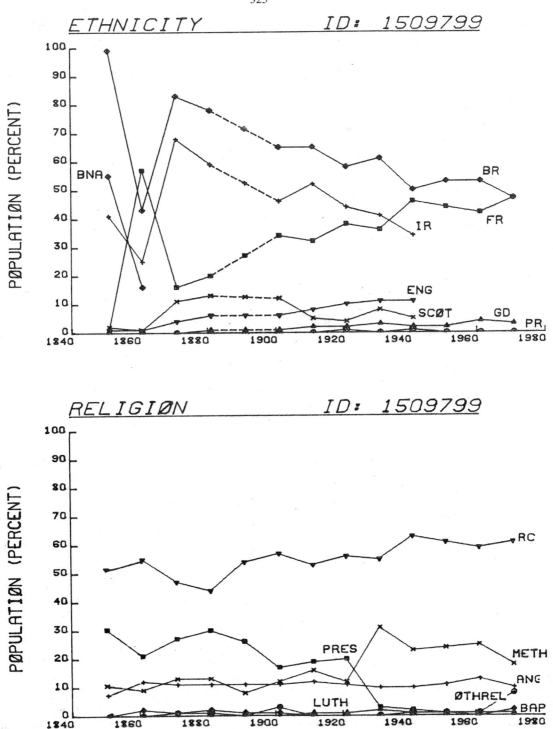

ID: 1509799   SUBFILES

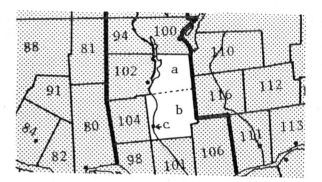

a. <u>DENHOLM</u>

AREA: 74.0 sq. miles

1971 DENSITY:
   2.78 persons/sq. mile

POPULATION:
   1881: 244
   1921: 319
   1941: 351
   1971: 206

b. <u>WAKEFIELD (RURAL), WAKEFIELD EAST</u>

AREA: 107.08 sq. miles

1971 DENSITY: 16.67 persons/sq. mile

POPULATION:
   1881: 1365
   1921: 1270
   1941: 1346
   1971: 1785

CHANGES: 1921 Wakefield East created; Wakefield (Urban) incorporated.

c. <u>WAKEFIELD (URBAN)</u>

AREA: 0.34 sq. miles

1971 DENSITY: 955.88 persons/sq. mile

POPULATION:
   1921: 271
   1941: 275
   1971: 325

CHANGES: 1921 incorporated.

ID: 1509799   SUBFILES   cont'd

ETHNICITY

PLACE	YEAR	ENG	SCOT	IR	FR	GD	PR
Denholm	1881	0	59	136	41	8	0
Wakefield, Wakefield E.	1881	102	145	813	275	4	0
Denholm	1941	31	18	64	205	32	1
Wakefield (Rural), Wakefield East	1941	111	53	486	669	12	11
Wakefield (Urban)	1941	80	33	119	40	2	0

RELIGION

PLACE	YEAR	ANG	RC	PRES	METH/UC	BAP	LUTH
Denholm	1881	14	87	122	21		
Wakefield, Wakefield E.	1881	156	625	354	187	27	
Denholm	1941	33	249	0	52		17
Wakefield (Rural), Wakefield East	1941	116	944	18	255	2	1
Wakefield (Urban)	1941	56	46	15	154		

I.D. 1509800   EARDLEY

AREA: 72.23 sq. miles

1971 DENSITY:
16.92 persons/sq. mile

TYPE:
Rural

POPULATION:
1851:   688
1881: 1475
1941: 1084
1971: 1222

CHANGES: None.

SUBFILES: None

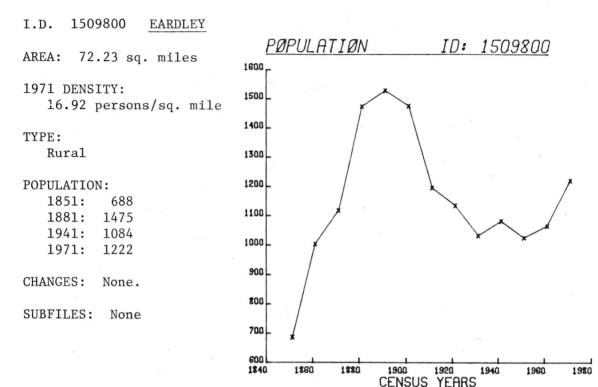

POPULATION   ID: 1509800

CENSUS YEARS

NOTES:

Early settlement in Eardley and the importance of agriculture in the area are mentioned in bibliography 106 (Blanchard, 1954), pp. 69, 133. The importance of the forest industry to the area is mentioned in 159b (Houde, 1970), p. 70.

In 1976 Eardley forms part of the new municipality of Pontiac (see 1408099).

329

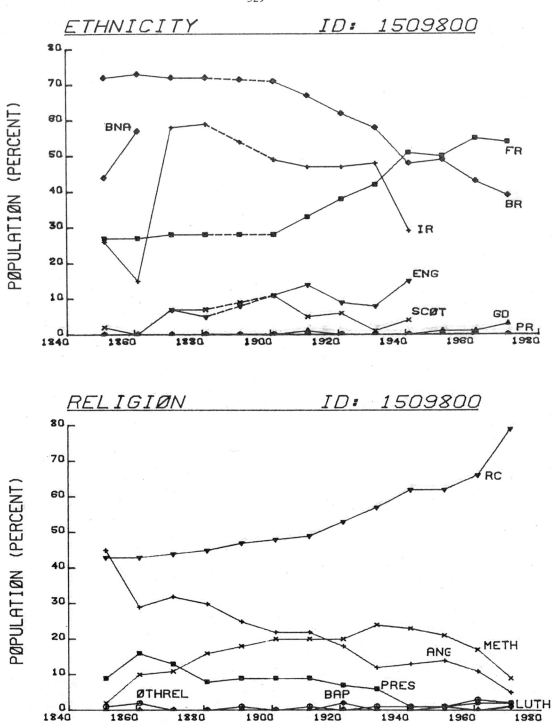

ID: 1509999   BOIS-FRANC, EGAN SOUTH, MONTCERF, DELÉAGE

AREA: 212.13 sq. miles

1971 DENSITY:
   44.46 persons/sq. mile

TYPE:
   Combined

POPULATION:
   1861:   573
   1881:   1342
   1941:   5344
   1971:   9431

CHANGES: 1861 created;
   1921 Maniwaki Indian
   Reserves henceforth
   excluded (see RES, subfile map); 1931 Maniwaki
   incorporated. Prior to
   1931 Deléage was called
   Kensington; the other
   areas Egan and Maniwaki.

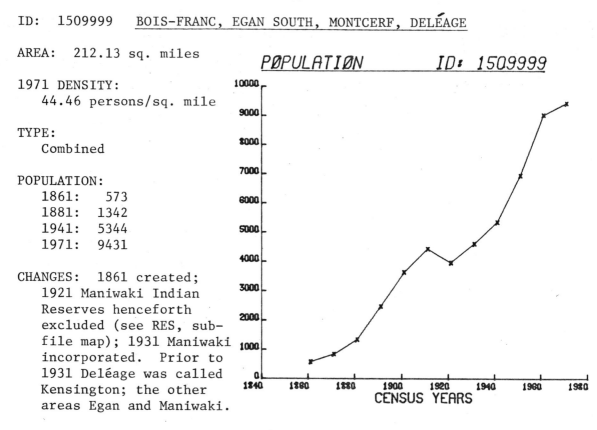

POPULATION   ID: 1509999

CENSUS YEARS

SUBFILES:
   a. Bois Franc, Egan South (Rural), Montcerf;
   b. Deléage;
   c. Maniwaki

NOTES:

The importance of the forest industry to this area is indicated in 53
(Hughson and Bond, 1965), p. 82.   106 (Blanchard, 1954), pp. 127, 151,
points out the partial dependence of agriculture on forestry.

The 1971 population of the excluded (RES) area was 763 of whom 630 are
listed as Native Indian; 675 are listed as Roman Catholic; 35% listed
English as mother tongue, 16% French, and 50% other language.
(Figures are approximate due to 1/3 sample and random rounding.)   In
1971 the area had two important unincorporated places (with populations): Maniwaki-Nord-Est (354) located in Deléage, and Montcerf
(362) in Montcerf census subdivision.

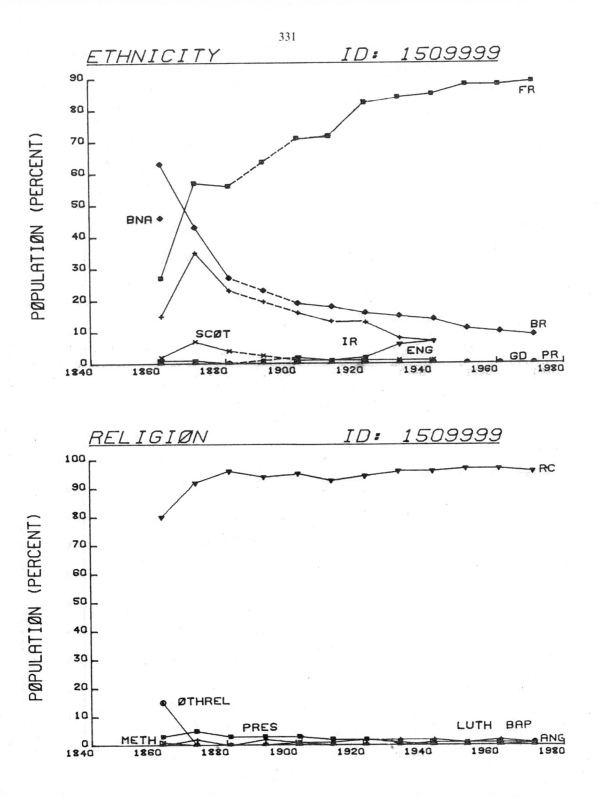

ID: 1509999   SUBFILES

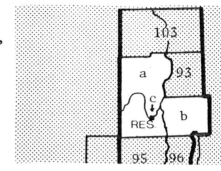

a. BOISFRANC, EGAN SOUTH (RURAL),
   MONTCERF

   AREA: 113.78 sq. miles

   1971 DENSITY:
      12.77 persons/sq. mile

   POPULATION:
      1861:   362
      1881:   1113
      1941:   2040
      1971:   1453

CHANGES: 1921 Maniwaki Indian Reserves (RES) excluded; 1931
   Maniwaki incorporated; 1961 & 1971 parts annexed to Maniwaki.
   These areas formerly called Egan & Maniwaki.

b. DELÉAGE

   AREA: 96.31 sq. miles

   1971 DENSITY: 13.38 persons/
      sq. mile

   POPULATION:
      1861:   211
      1881:   229
      1941:   984
      1971:   1289

   CHANGES: Formerly (pre-1931)
   called Kensington.

c. MANIWAKI

   AREA: 2.04 sq. miles

   1971 DENSITY: 3278.92
      persons/sq. mile

   POPULATION:
      1941:   2320
      1971:   6689

   CHANGES: 1931 incorporated;
   1961 & 1971 annexed parts
   of Egan South (Rural).

ID: 1509999   SUBFILES   cont'd

ETHNICITY

PLACE	YEAR	ENG	SCOT	IR	FR	GD	PR
Bois Franc, Egan South, Montcerf	1901	59	39	436	2190	1	0
Deléage	1901	14	9	134	374	0	0
Bois Franc, Egan South (Rural), Montcerf	1941	121	16	154	1746	0	0
Deléage	1941	160	1	7	792	1	0
Maniwaki	1941	78	26	204	1981	1	0

RELIGION

PLACE	YEAR	ANG	RC	PRES	METH/UC	BAP	LUTH
Bois Franc, Egan South, Montcerf	1901	26	2966	82	26		
Deléage	1901	12	485	27	0		
Bois Franc, Egan South (Rural), Montcerf	1941	1	2013	1	23		
Deléage	1941	65	899	12	8		
Maniwaki	1941	42	2208	9	44	12	

ID: 1510000   <u>HINCKS</u>

AREA: 81.52 sq. miles

1971 DENSITY:
    4.62 persons/sq. mile

TYPE:
    Rural

POPULATION:
    1861:   262
    1881:   495
    1941:   733
    1971:   377

CHANGES: 1861 created.

SUBFILES: None

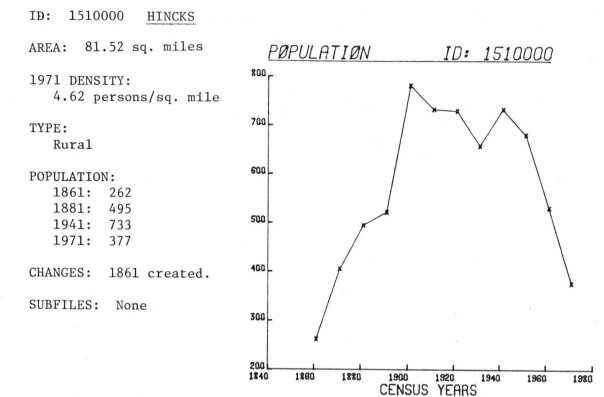

NOTES:

None of the works listed in the bibliography deals specifically with Hincks.

In 1976 name changed to Lac-Sainte-Marie.

335

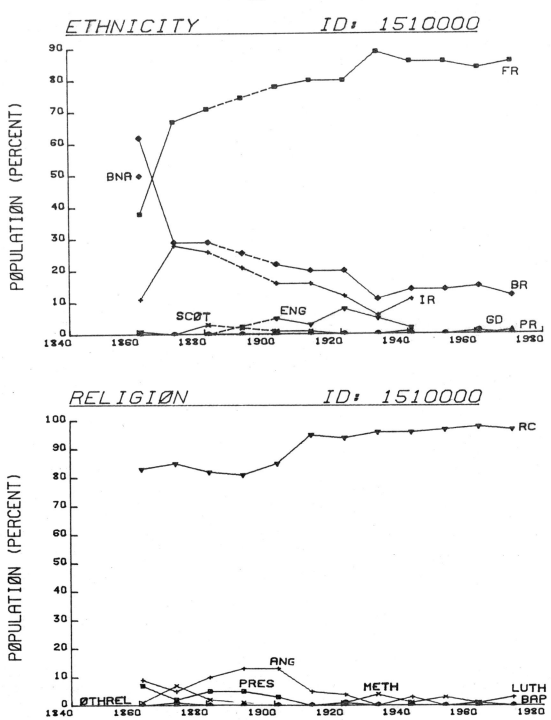

ID: 1510199   HULL WEST, LUCERNE, TOURAINE

AREA: 136.72 sq. miles

1971 DENSITY;
  686.10 persons/sq. mile

TYPE:
  Combined

POPULATION
  1851:   3980
  1881: 12814
  1941: 40709
  1971: 93804

CHANGES: 1881 Hull incorporated; 1921 Deschênes
  incorporated. Lucerne
  formerly called Hull
  South; Touraine formerly
  called Hull East. The
  whole area formerly
  called Hull Township.

SUBFILES:
  a. Hull West, Lucerne
      Touraine (Rural)
  b. Aylmer
  c. Hull
  d. Deschênes

NOTES:

  See pages 338-339.

POPULATION   ID: 1510199

CENSUS YEARS

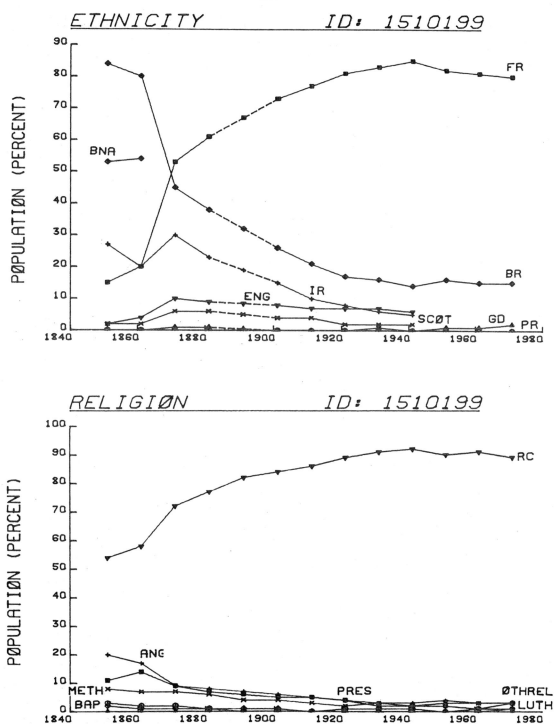

ID: 1510199   <u>HULL WEST, LUCERNE, TOURAINE</u>   cont'd

NOTES:

Among the works listed in the bibliography dealing with this area,
see especially 109b (Brault, 1950, 136b (Evans, 1978), 159b (Houde,
1970), 192b (Rossignol et al, 1975), 211b (Wesche and Kugler-Gagnon,
1978), 233b (Elliot, 1979), and 243c (Latchford, 1922).

The city of Hull has been kept in this, its traditional area, in
spite of later census assignment to the County of Hull, formerly
known as the Township of Templeton (1510699). Considerable census
information on this area is available in tables dealing with the
Census Metropolitan Area of Ottawa-Hull, 1976 Census Tract Numbers
800, 810-11, 820-22, 840-41. In 1976 Touraine forms part of Gatineau
City in Hull County (see 1510699); Lucerne, Aylmer and Deschênes form
the new City of Aylmer.

ID: 1510199 <u>HULL WEST, LUCERNE, TOURAINE</u>   cont'd

NOTES: cont'd

The 1971 census lists a large number of unincorporated places in
this area, many of them recent subdivisions. The major ones (with
populations) are the following – in Hull West: Chelsea (562),
Farm Point (290), Old Chelsea (269), Cascades (237), and Glen
Eagle (192); in Lucerne: Glenwood Domaine (3997), Lakeview
Terrace (1170), Champlain Park (634), Connaught Gardens (507),
and Boulevard Gamelin Subdivision (198); in Touraine: Riviera
(6427), Limbour (573), and Riviera-Sud (551).

ID: 1510199   SUBFILES

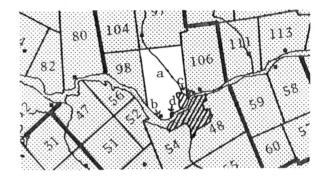

a. <u>HULL WEST, LUCERNE,</u>
   <u>TOURAINE, (RURAL)</u>

   AREA: 123.90 sq. miles

   1971 DENSITY: 171.27
     persons/sq. mile

   POPULATION: 1851:   2811
                 1881:   4162
                 1941:   4363
                 1971: 21220

   CHANGES: 1881 Hull incorporated; 1921 Deschênes incorporated; 1961
     & 1971 part annexed to Hull.

b. <u>AYLMER</u>

   AREA: 2.24 sq. miles

   1971 DENSITY: 3213.39 persons/sq. mile

   POPULATION: 1851:   1169
                 1881:   1762
                 1941:   3115
                 1971:   7198

c. <u>HULL</u>

   AREA: 10.30 sq. miles

   1971 DENSITY: 6172.82
     persons/sq. mile

   POPULATION: 1881:   6890
                 1941: 32947
                 1971: 63580

   CHANGES: 1881 incorporated;
     1961 & 1971 incorporated
     parts of Hull West, Lucerne,
     Touraine, (Rural).

d. <u>DESCHENES</u>

   AREA: 0.28 sq. miles

   1971 DENSITY: 6450.0
     persons/sq. mile

   POPULATION: 1921:   321
                 1941:   284
                 1971: 1806

   CHANGES: 1921 incorporated.

ID: 1510199   SUBFILES   cont'd

ETHNICITY

PLACE	YEAR	BNA	ENG	SCOT	IR	FR	GD	PR
Hull West, Lucerne, Touraine, (Rural)	1851	1649	67	53	770	244	1	0
Hull West, Lucerne, Touraine, (Rural)	1881		648	402	2123	922	19	7
Hull West, Lucerne, Touraine, (Rural)	1941		777	391	1205	1860	69	3
Aylmer	1851	467	26	36	292	344	0	0
Aylmer	1881		261	90	429	959	20	0
Aylmer	1941		671	116	777	2114	9	4
Hull	1881		258	259	371	5933	49	0
Hull	1941		1097	341	668	30541	31	34
Deschênes	1941		64	0	2	213	0	0

RELIGION

PLACE	YEAR	ANG	RC	PRES	METH/UC	BAP	LUTH
Hull West, Lucerne, Touraine, (Rural)	1851	597	1375	375	253	98	
Hull West, Lucerne, Touraine, (Rural)	1881	539	2363	602	516	80	
Hull West, Lucerne, Touraine, (Rural)	1941	549	2701	246	719	19	
Aylmer	1851	212	794	70	70		
Aylmer	1881	243	1269	125	110	13	
Aylmer	1941	376	2427	130	165	7	
Hull	1881	263	6234	155	118	79	
Hull	1941	377	31921	350	111	48	
Deschênes	1941	41	229	1	6	3	

ID: 1510200   <u>LOW</u>

AREA: 100.37 sq. miles

1971 DENSITY:
  9.83 persons/sq. mile

TYPE:
  Rural

POPULATION:
  1851:   272
  1881: 1230
  1941: 1307
  1971:   987

CHANGES: None.

SUBFILES: None

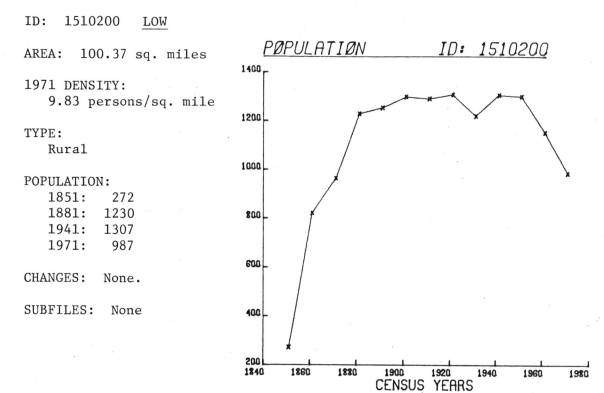

PØPULATIØN   *ID: 1510200*

CENSUS YEARS

NOTES:

None of the works listed in the bibliography deals specifically with Low.

In 1971 the unincorporated village of Low had a population of 371.

The unlikely looking ethnic figures for 1861 have been double checked; there may of course be a census error for that year.

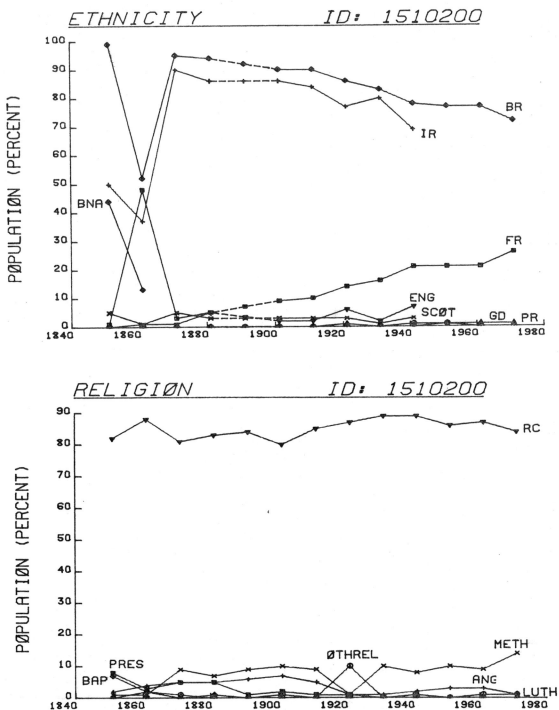

ID: 1510300 LYTTON, SICOTTE

AREA: 221.80 sq. miles

1971 DENSITY:
6.17 persons/sq. mile

TYPE:
Rural

POPULATION:
1891: 359
1941: 1074
1971: 1369

CHANGES: 1891 created;
1961 annexed "unor-
ganized" parts of the
county. ("Baskatong")
See notes below.

SUBFILES: None

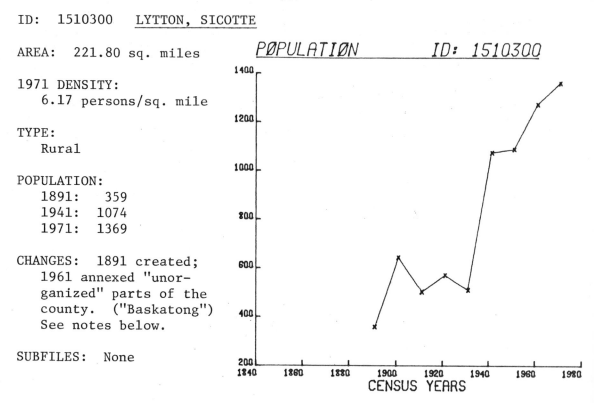

POPULATION   ID: 1510300

CENSUS YEARS

NOTES:

None of the works listed in the bibliography deals specifically with
this area.

There are some difficulties in establishing the boundaries and population covered by this unit over time. The present area (221.80 sq.
miles) includes the Baskatong Reservoir region though our base map
does not show this extension to the north-eastern boundary line. Our
figures include the following census listings: 1891-1901 Sicotte,
Lytton, and Baskatong (area 168,355 acres or c.263 sq. miles); 1911-
21 Lytton and Sicotte (the separate entry for Baskatong was not included by us); 1931 Lytton only; 1941-71 Lytton and Sicotte; 1961-71
the borders of Sicotte were extended to include at least part (?) of
the old Baskatong (see CHANGES, above.)

In 1976 the name of Sicotte was changed to Grand Remous.

In 1971 the unincorporated village of Grand-Remous, located in
Sicotte, had a population of 333.

345

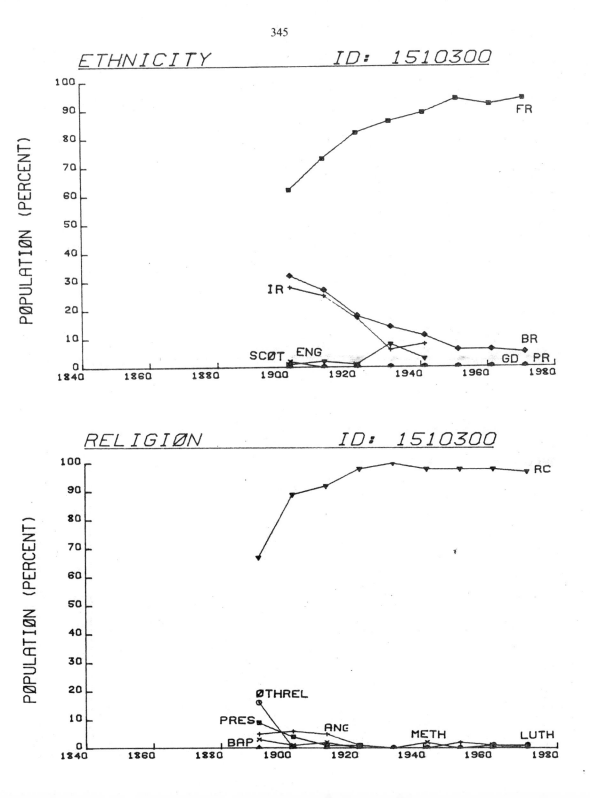

ID: 1510400 MASHAM NORTH, STE.-CÉCILE-DE-MASHAM

AREA: 97.06 sq. miles

1971 DENSITY:
  25.32 persons/sq. mile

TYPE:
  Rural

POPULATION:
  1851:   998
  1881: 1881
  1941: 1962
  1971: 2458

CHANGES: Formerly called
  just Masham; Sté-Cecile-
  de-Masham formerly called
  Masham South.

SUBFILES: None

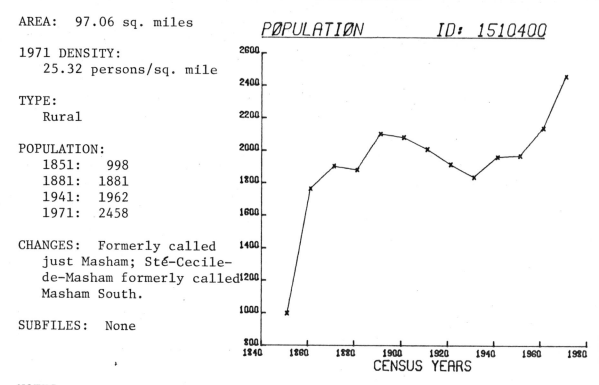

POPULATION   ID: 1510400

CENSUS YEARS

NOTES:

141 (N. and S.Geggie, 1974) deals extensively with this area.

In 1976 these areas are part of LaPêche Village, part of the Rural
Fringe of the Census Metropolitan Area of Ottawa-Hull.

In 1971 the unincorporated village of Ste-Cécile-de-Masham had a
population of 308.

The census ethnicity figures for 1861 have been doublechecked but are
suspect given the lack of a corresponding shift in religion figures
for that year. For example, the 1861 Census lists 1394 "Natives of
Canada-French" but only 948 Roman Catholics. In all other census
years the number of Catholics in this area is equal to or greater
than the number of French.

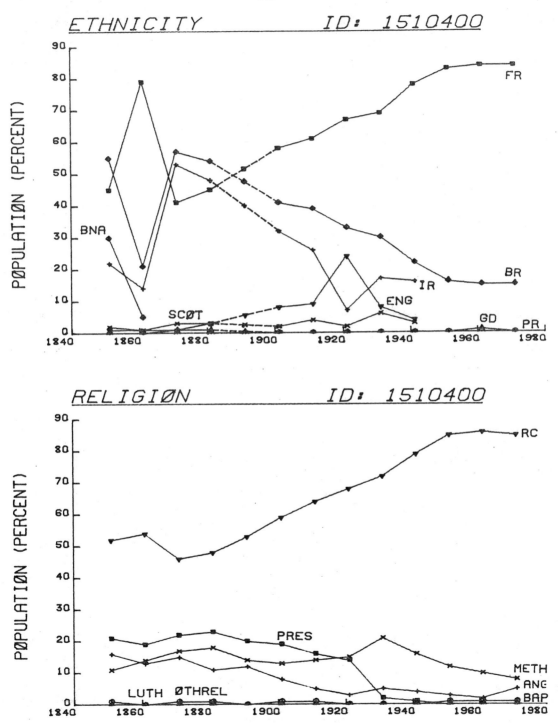

ID: 1510500   <u>NORTHFIELD</u>

AREA: 86.82 sq. miles

1971 DENSITY:
   5.70 persons/sq. mile

TYPE:
   Rural

POPULATION:
   1861:   206
   1881:   413
   1941:   753
   1971:   495

CHANGES: 1861 created;
   1961 part annexed to
   Cameron (1509600).

SUBFILES: None

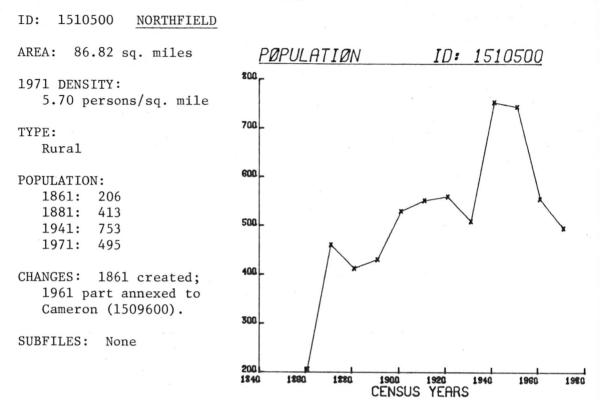

POPULATION   ID: 1510500

CENSUS YEARS

NOTES:

None of the works listed in the bibliography deals specifically with
Northfield.

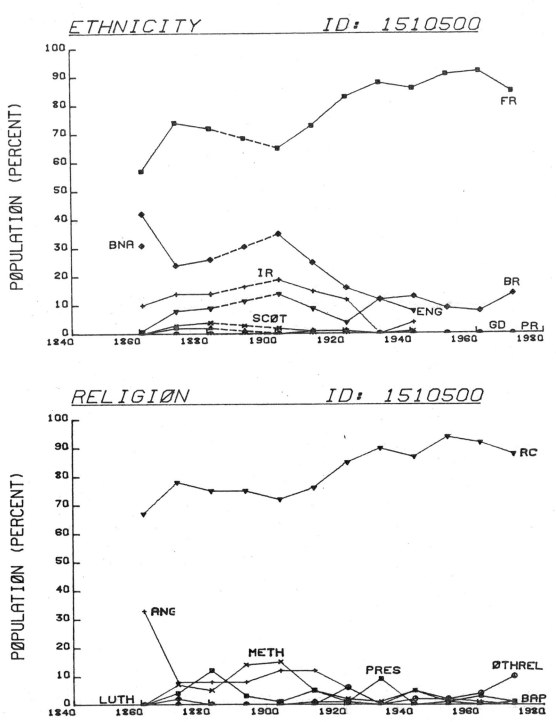

ID: 1510699   <u>TEMPLETON</u>
<u>EAST, TEMPLETON EAST-</u>
<u>PART EAST, TEMPLETON</u>
<u>WEST, PERKINS</u>

AREA: 132.21 sq. miles

1971 DENSITY:
     350.70 persons/sq. mile

TYPE:
     Combined

POPULATION:
     1851:   1711
     1881:   3607
     1941:   8487
     1971:   46366

CHANGES: 1881 Pointe-
     Gatineau incorporated;
     1921 Templeton incor-
     porated; 1941 Gatineau
     incorporated. Perkins
     formerly called Temple-
     ton North. (See also
     Notes below).

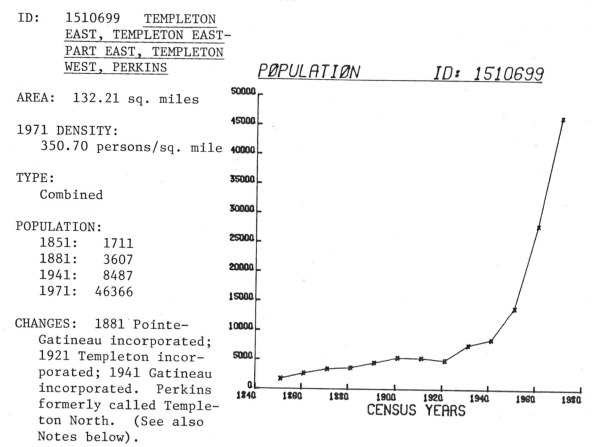

POPULATION   ID: 1510699

CENSUS YEARS

SUBFILES:
     a. Templeton East (Rural), Templeton East-Part East, Templeton
         West (Rural), Perkins
     b. Pointe-Gatineau; c. Templeton; d. Gatineau

NOTES:

     See page 352.

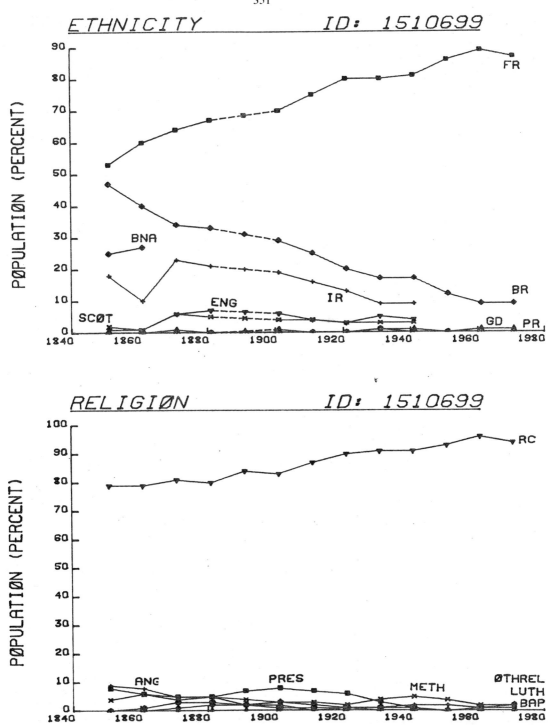

ID: 1510699 <u>TEMPLETON</u> cont'd
<u>EAST, TEMPLETON EAST-</u>
<u>PART EAST, TEMPLETON</u>
<u>WEST, PERKINS</u>

NOTES:

Settlement and early economic activity in this area are mentioned in
106 (Blanchard, 1954), pp. 65,79,80 and 45 (Hamelin and Roby, 1971),
p. 256. See also 109b (Brault, 1950) and 159b (Houde, 1970).

This whole area, formerly Templeton Township, is called Hull County
in the 1971 Census where it includes the city of Hull (in our
1510199). Considerable census information is available in tables
dealing with the Census Metropolitan Area of Ottawa-Hull, Urbanized
Core & Rural Fringe. 1976 Census Tract Numbers 600-2,610-13, 620,
630. In 1976 Perkins is part of Val-des-Monts Village (see 1611600);
the remaining parts, together with Touraine (in 1510199), form the new
city of Gatineau. In 1971 the unincorporated village of Perkins had
a population of 619.

ID: 1510699   SUBFILES

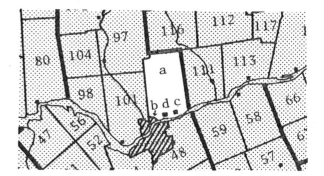

a. TEMPLETON EAST (RURAL),
   TEMPLETON EAST, PART EAST,
   TEMPLETON WEST (RURAL),
   PERKINS

AREA: 118.36 sq. miles

1971 DENSITY: 39.89
      persons/sq. mile

POPULATION: 1881:   2147
              1941:   2486
              1971:   4721

CHANGES: 1881 Point-Gatineau incorporated; 1921 Templeton incorporated; 1941 Gatineau incorporated; 1961 & 1971 parts annexed
   to Gatineau; 1971 part annexed to Pointe-Gatineau. In 1971 the
   area was called Hull County and included the city of Hull (in
                                                        (1510199).

b. POINTE-GATINEAU

AREA: 3.44 sq. miles

1971 DENSITY: 4546.51 persons/sq. mile

POPULATION: 1881:   1460
              1941:   2230
              1971: 15640

CHANGES: 1881 incorporated; 1971 annexed part Templeton West
   (Rural).

c. TEMPLETON

   AREA: 2.86 sq. miles

   1971 DENSITY: 1288.11 persons/
      sq. mile

   POPULATION: 1921:   428
                 1941:   822
                 1971: 3684

d. GATINEAU

   AREA: 7.55 sq. miles

   1971 DENSITY: 2956.42
      persons/sq. mile

   POPULATION: 1941:   2822
                 1971: 22321

   CHANGES: 1941 incorporated;
      1961 & 1971 annexed parts of
      Templeton West (Rural).

ID: 1510699   SUBFILES   cont'd

ETHNICITY

PLACE	YEAR	ENG	SCOT	IR	FR	GD	PR
Templeton East (Rural), Templeton East, Part East, Templeton West (Rural), Perkins	1881	236	167	685	1046	6	0
Templeton East (Rural), Templeton East, Part East, Templeton West (Rural), Perkins	1941	114	73	489	1790	6	10
Pointe-Gatineau	1881	13	2	88	1353	2	0
Pointe-Gatineau	1941	5	27	25	2159	1	4
Templeton	1941	83	73	47	717	29	0
Gatineau	1941	140	116	214	2170	23	18

RELIGION

PLACE	YEAR	ANG	RC	PRES	METH/UC	BAP	LUTH
Templeton East (Rural), Templeton East, Part East, Templeton West (Rural), Perkins	1881	146	1376	170	157	81	
Templeton East (Rural), Templeton East, Part East, Templeton West (Rural), Perkins	1941	85	2151	43	175	13	9
Pointe-Gatineau	1881	30	1406	3	20		
Pointe-Gatineau	1941	2	2221	0	3		
Templeton	1941	15	799	26	75	18	
Gatineau	1941	93	2511	5	168	5	10

356

ID: 1510799   WRIGHT

AREA: 62.59 sq. miles

1971 DENSITY:
  31.09 persons/sq. mile

TYPE:
  Combined

POPULATION:
  1861:   508
  1881: 1119
  1941: 2131
  1971: 1946

CHANGES: 1861 created;
  called Wabasse and
  Wright; 1911 Gracefield
  incorporated.

SUBFILES:
  a. Wright (Rural)
  b. Gracefield

NOTES:

None of the works listed in the bibliography deals specifically with
Wright.

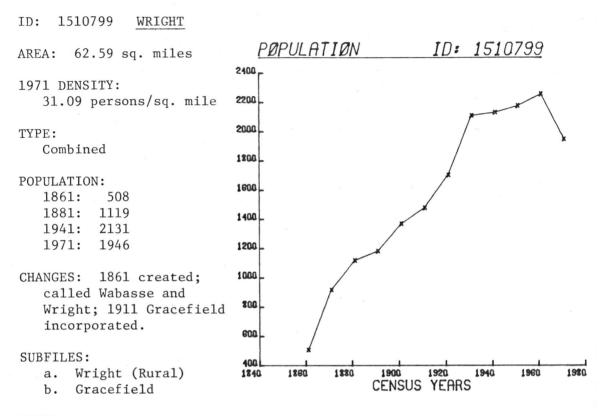

POPULATION   ID: 1510799

CENSUS YEARS

357

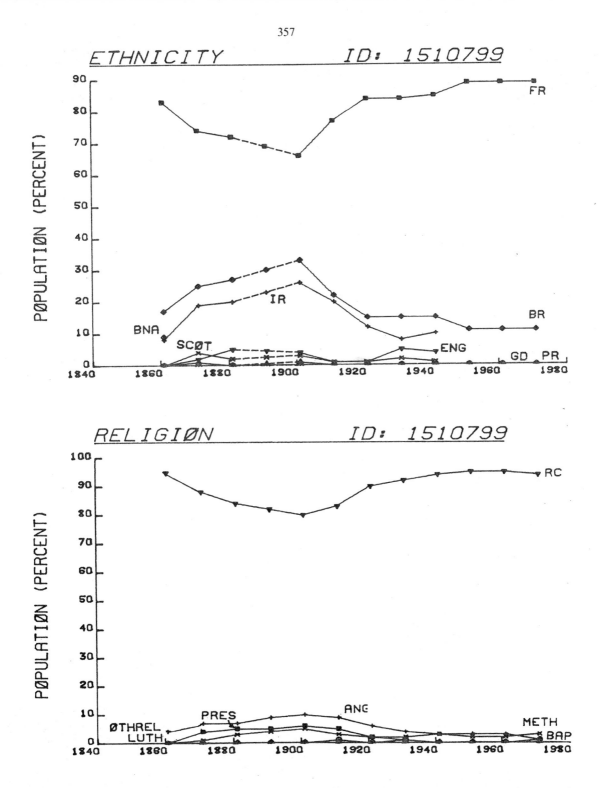

ID: 1510799   SUBFILES

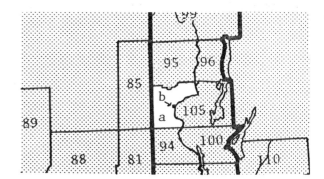

a. <u>WRIGHT (RURAL)</u>

    AREA: 61.42 sq. miles

    1971 DENSITY: 14.60
      persons/sq. mile

    POPULATION:
      1911: 1180
      1941: 1594
      1971:   897

    CHANGES: 1911 Grace-
      field incorporated;
      1971 part annexed to
      Gracefield.

b. <u>GRACEFIELD</u>

    AREA: 1.17 sq. miles

    1971 DENSITY: 896.58
      persons/sq. mile

    POPULATION:
      1911:   300
      1941:   537
      1971: 1049

    CHANGES: 1911 incorporated; 1971 annexed part of Wright (Rural).

ID: 1510799   SUBFILES   cont'd

ETHNICITY

PLACE	YEAR	ENG	SCOT	IR	FR	GD	PR
Wright (Rural)	1911	11	16	275	878	0	0
Wright (Rural)	1941	70	25	196	1300	3	0
Gracefield	1911	9	0	22	259	0	1
Gracefield	1941	11	6	11	507	0	0

RELIGION

PLACE	YEAR	ANG	RC	PRES	METH/UC	BAP	LUTH
Wright (Rural)	1911	133	939	68	39		
Wright (Rural)	1941	70	1471	1	52		
Gracefield	1911	2	288	0	0		
Gracefield	1941	0	533	0	2		

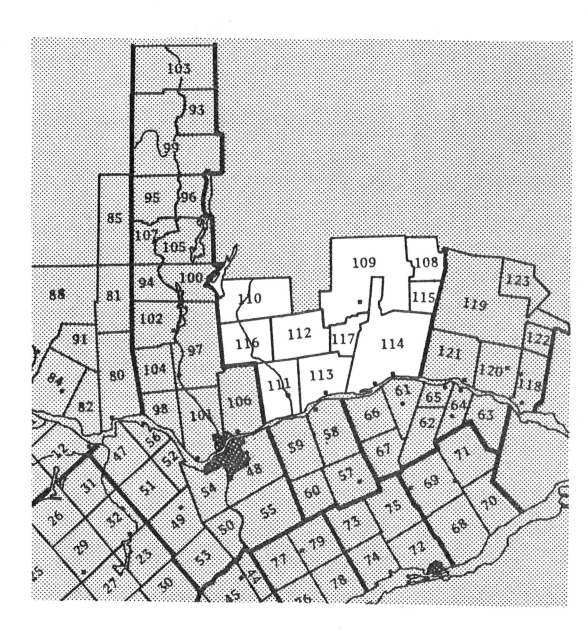

Perhaps the most important of the works dealing with Papineau
County are those which deal with West Quebec or larger areas, listed
in the headnote to 15 Gatineau and Hull Counties (p.313), and especially 106 (Blanchard, 1954). See also 166 (Lajoie, 1968). In
addition, Papineau is the subject of a thesis, 294 (Turay, 1969);
MacKay's thesis (286: MacKay, 1949) is again a valuable source. Some
supplementary information about early Scottish settlement can be
derived from 49 (Hill, 1972) and 82 (Reid, 1977). Some intimations
of the importance of the forest industry are suggested in 176
(Maclaren, 1973).

Considerable census information on Papineau County is available
in tables, maps, and analyses at the census division level. County
totals for 1971: population 31,793; area 1,384.33 sq. miles; density
22.97 persons/sq. mile. Uninhabited unorganized parts in the north
of the county (1971 area 132.46 sq. miles) have not been included; as
a result, the 1971 density of the study area was 25.40 persons/sq.
mile.

ID: 1610800 <u>AMHERST</u>

AREA: 61.71 sq. miles

1971 DENSITY:
   9.14 persons/sq. mile

TYPE:
   Rural

POPULATION:
   1891: 388
   1941: 1086
   1971: 564

CHANGES: 1891 created;
   1951 part annexed to
   Addington...Lac-Simon
   (1610999); 1971 part
   annexed to Ponsonby
   (1611500).

SUBFILES: None

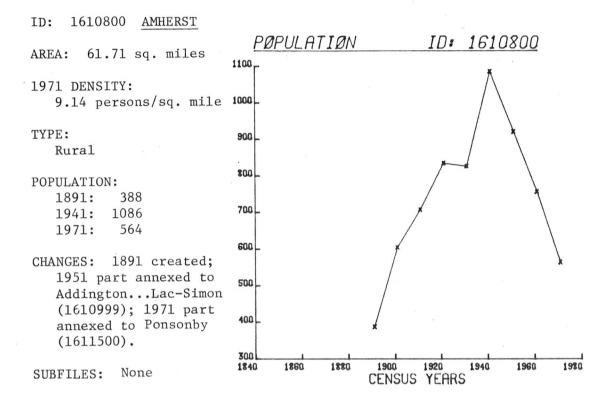

NOTES:

None of the works cited in the bibliography deals specifically
with Amherst.

The unincorporated locality of Lac-Rémi had a population of
336 in 1971.

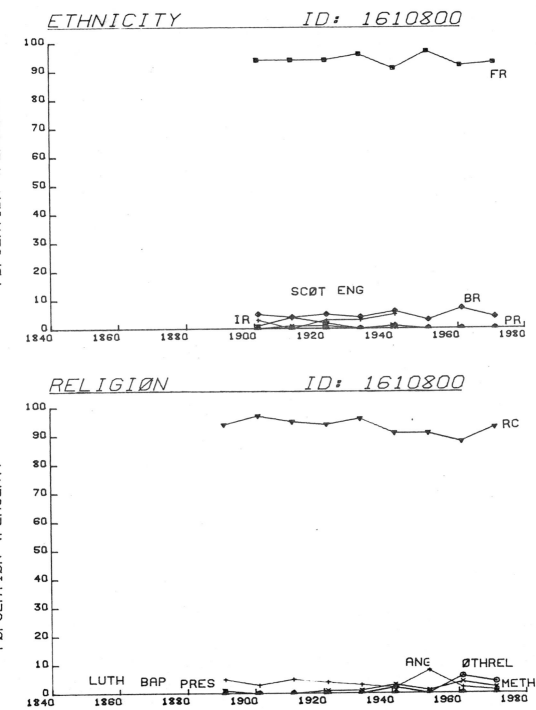

ID: 1610999 ADDINGTON,
SUFFOLK, MONTPELLIER,
DUHAMEL, LAC-DES-
PLAGES, NAMUR, LAC-
SIMON

AREA: 255.42 sq. miles

1971 DENSITY:
11.31 persons/sq. mile

TYPE:
Combined

POPULATION:
1861:   562
1881:   1634
1941:   3285
1971:   2889

CHANGES: 1861 created;
included Wells and
Villeneuve; 1911
Chénéville incorpor-
ated; 1951 annexed
part of Amherst
(1610800). Earlier

POPULATION   ID: 1610999

CENSUS YEARS

names/divisions for these areas include, in addition to Suffolk
and Addington, Hartwell and Preston. Lac-Simon was formerly
Chénéville and before that Hartwell.

SUBFILES:
a. Addington, Suffolk, Montpellier, Duhamel, Lac-des-Plages,
   Namur, Lac-Simon (Rural)
b. Chénéville

NOTES:

French Canadian migration into this area is discussed in 106
(Blanchard, 1954). In 1971 there were a number of important unincorporated places (with populations): Namur (337), St-Emile-de- Suffolk
(312), Montpellier (293), and Duhamel (167). Each of these places
is located in the subdivision of the same name i.e. Namur in
Namur, etc.

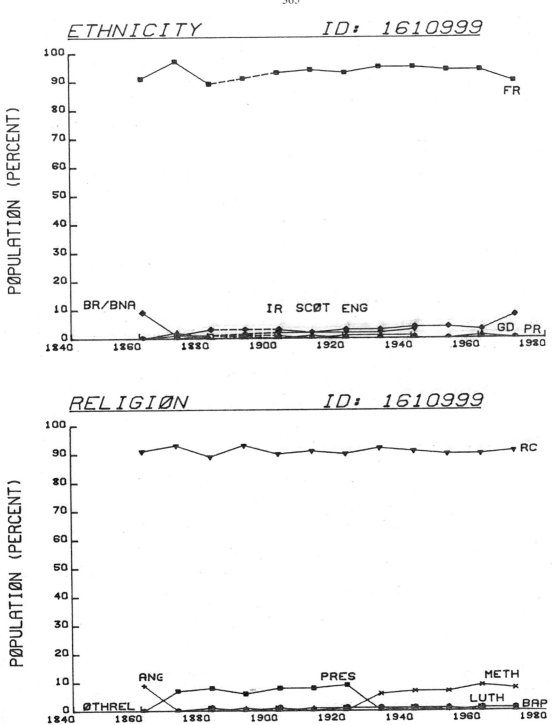

ETHNICITY   ID: 1610999

RELIGION   ID: 1610999

ID: 1610999 SUBFILES

a. ADDINGTON, SUFFOLK,
   MONTPELLIER, DUHAMEL,
   LAC-DES-PLAGES, NAMUR,
   LAC-SIMON (RURAL)

   AREA: 251.06 sq. miles

   1971 DENSITY:
      8.65 persons/sq. mile

   POPULATION:
      1911: 2578
      1941: 2696
      1971: 2171

CHANGES: 1861 included Wells (Labelle County) and Villeneuve (now called Val-des-Bois) in (1611000); 1911 Chénéville incorporated; 1951 annexed part of Amherst (1610800).

b. CHÉNÉVILLE

   AREA: 4.36 sq. miles

   1971 DENSITY:
      164.48 persons/sq. mile

   POPULATION:
      1911: 505
      1941: 589
      1971: 718

CHANGES: 1911 incorporated.

ID: 1610999 SUBFILES cont'd

ETHNICITY

PLACE	YEAR	ENG	SCOT	IR	FR	GD	PR
Addington...Lac-Simon (Rural)	1911	58	6	4	2422	1	0
Addington...Lac-Simon (Rural)	1941	94	12	10	2546	2	0
Chénéville	1911	3	0	0	473	18	0
Chénéville	1941	7	0	8	567	1	0

RELIGION

PLACE	YEAR	ANG	RC	PRES	METH/UC	BAP	LUTH
Addington...Lac-Simon (Rural)	1911	14	2314	288	0	9	
Addington...Lac-Simon (Rural)	1941	6	2402	17	233	14	
Chénéville	1911	3	497	4	0		
Chénéville	1941	1	588	0	0		

ID: 1611000 BOWMAN, VAL-
     DES-BOIS

AREA: 135.27 sq. miles

1971 DENSITY:
   6.15 persons/sq. mile

TYPE:
   Rural

POPULATION:
   1861:   232
   1881:   520
   1941:   732
   1971:   832

CHANGES: 1861 created;
   Bowman only; Val-des-
   Bois included in
   (1610999); 1871 also
   includes Bigelow
   (Labelle County). Val-
   des-Bois formerly
   called Villeneuve.

SUBFILES: None

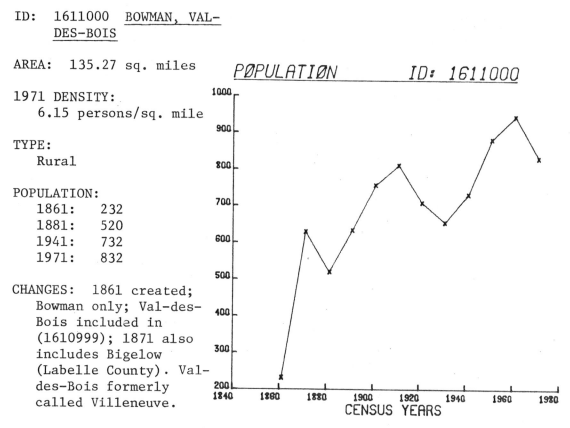

POPULATIØN   ID: 1611000

CENSUS YEARS

NOTES:

None of the works listed in the bibliography deals specifically
with this area.

In 1971 the unincorporated village of Val-des-Bois had a
population of 302.

369

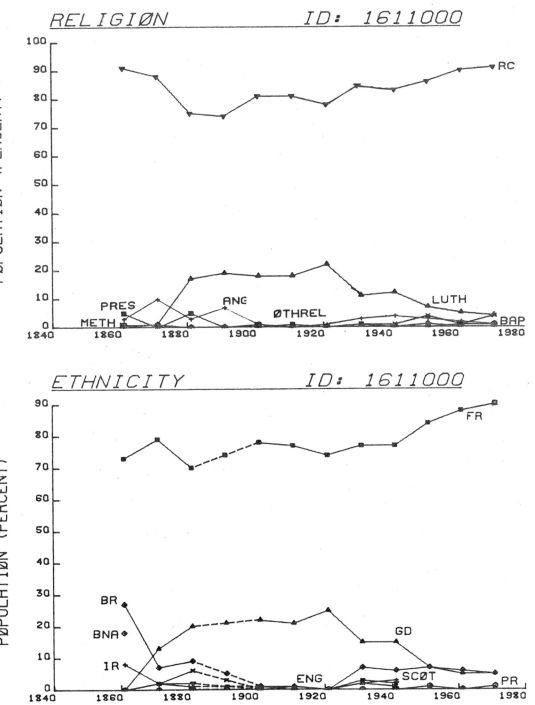

ID: 1611199 <u>BUCKINGHAM</u>,
<u>BUCKINGHAM WEST</u>,
<u>BUCKINGHAM SOUTH-EAST</u>,
<u>L'ANGE-GARDIEN</u>

AREA: 111.04 sq. miles

1971 DENSITY: 110.23
persons/sq. mile

TYPE:
Combined

POPULATION:
   1851:   2204
   1881:   4910
   1941:   7693
   1971: 12240

CHANGES: 1861 Buckingham
(Urban) incorporated;
1901 Masson incorporated;
1921 Angers incorporated.

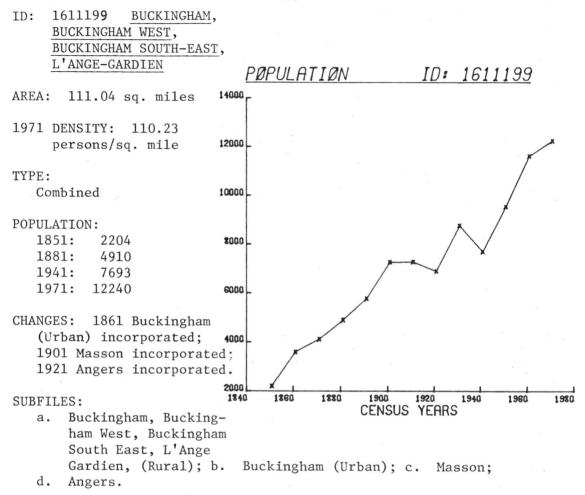

PØPULATIØN   ID: 1611199

CENSUS YEARS

SUBFILES:
  a. Buckingham, Bucking-
      ham West, Buckingham
      South East, L'Ange
      Gardien, (Rural); b. Buckingham (Urban); c. Masson;
  d. Angers.

NOTES:

Population figures from 1825-1851 are given in 187a (Taché et al., 1938) and 286 (MacKay, 1949). Some information about lumbering in the area is given in 278 (Gibson, 1967). A general outline of the history of Buckingham can be derived from 176 (Maclaren, 1973) and 286 (MacKay, 1949).

In 1976 all parts form together with Notre-Dame-de-la-Salette (in 1611600), the new city of Buckingham.

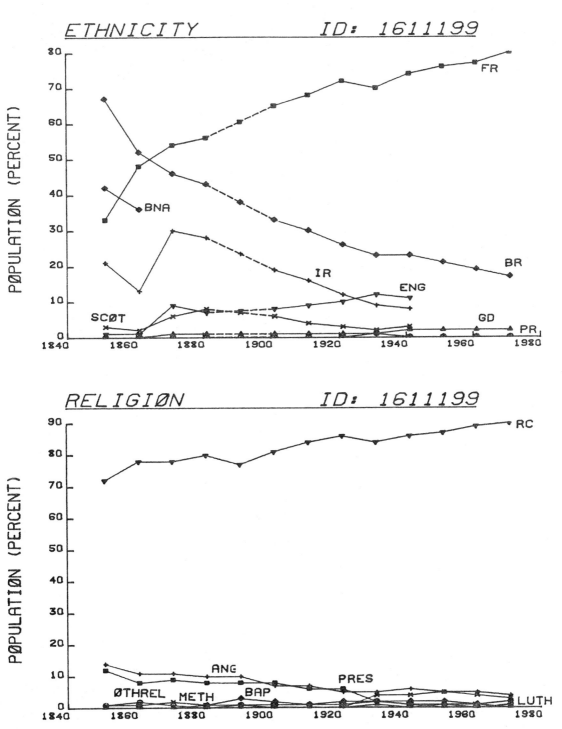

ID: 1611199   SUBFILES

a. <u>BUCKINGHAM, BUCKINGHAM WEST,
   BUCKINGHAM SOUTH-EAST,
   L'ANGE-GARDIEN (RURAL)</u>

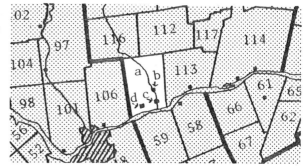

AREA: 95.18 sq. miles

1971 DENSITY: 18.06
   persons/sq. mile

POPULATION:
   1861: 2417
   1881: 3431
   1941: 1592
   1971: 1719

CHANGES: 1861 Buckingham (Urban) incorporated; 1901 Masson incorporated; 1921 Angers incorporated; 1941 part annexed to Angers;
   1961 & 1971 parts annexed to Buckingham (Urban).

b. <u>BUCKINGHAM (URBAN)</u>

AREA: 3.47 sq. miles

1971 DENSITY: 2104.90 persons/
   sq. mile

POPULATION: 1861: 1186
             1881: 1479
             1941: 4516
             1971: 7304

CHANGES: 1861 incorporated; 1961 &
   1971 annexed parts of Buckingham..
   L'Ange Gardien (Rural).

c. <u>MASSON</u>

AREA: 4.25 sq. miles

1971 DENSITY: 549 persons/sq. mile

POPULATION: 1901: 1012
             1941: 1226
             1971: 2336

CHANGES: 1901 incorporated.

d. <u>ANGERS</u>

AREA: 8.14 sq. miles

1971 DENSITY: 108.23
   persons/sq. mile

POPULATION: 1921: 284
             1941: 359
             1971: 881

CHANGES: 1921 incorpora-
   ted; 1941 annexed part
   of Buckingham..L'Ange
   Gardien (Rural).

ID: 1611199   SUBFILES   cont'd

ETHNICITY

PLACE	YEAR	ENG	SCOT	IR	FR	GD	PR
Buckingham, Buckingham West, Buckingham South-East, L'Ange-Gardien (Rural)	1881	278	253	993	1869	35	0
Buckingham, Buckingham West, Buckingham South-East, L'Ange-Gardien (Rural)	1941	174	45	299	1037	32	1
Buckingham (Urban)	1881	88	131	380	860	17	0
Buckingham (Urban)	1941	647	207	262	3255	92	11
Masson	1901	17	27	83	882	0	0
Masson	1941	45	11	59	1085	12	0
Angers	1921	0	0	8	272	0	0
Angers	1941	6	0	26	327	0	0

RELIGION

PLACE	YEAR	ANG	RC	PRES	METH/UC	BAP	LUTH
Buckingham, Buckingham West, Buckingham South-East, L'Ange-Gardien (Rural)	1881	377	2702	276	41	31	
Buckingham, Buckingham West, Buckingham South-East, L'Ange-Gardien (Rural)	1941	156	1322	33	37	35	
Buckingham (Urban)	1881	94	1229	116	5	29	
Buckingham (Urban)	1941	317	3777	62	243	82	
Masson	1901	23	946	35	2	5	
Masson	1941	23	1163	8	23	5	0
Angers	1921	0	263	17	0		
Angers	1941	0	356	0	3		

ID: 1611200   DERRY, MULGRAVE

AREA: 114.96 sq. miles

1971 DENSITY: 2.01 persons/
   sq. mile

TYPE:
   Rural

POPULATION:
   1851:   36
   1881:   537
   1941:   423
   1971:   231

CHANGES: None.

SUBFILES: None

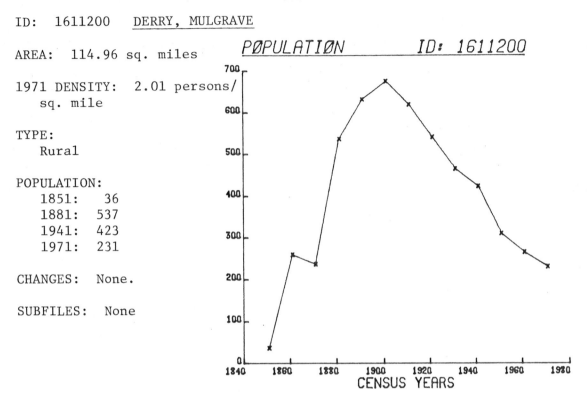

NOTES:

None of the works listed in the bibliography deals specifically with this area.

This area is noteworthy for the predominance of its German (and later British) groups in a region heavily French in the surrounding townships. Most of the Germans are in Mulgrave – 1911 Ethnicity: English 27, Irish 42, Scot. 33, French 90, German 268 (58.3%). The home language for all groups in 1971 was English.

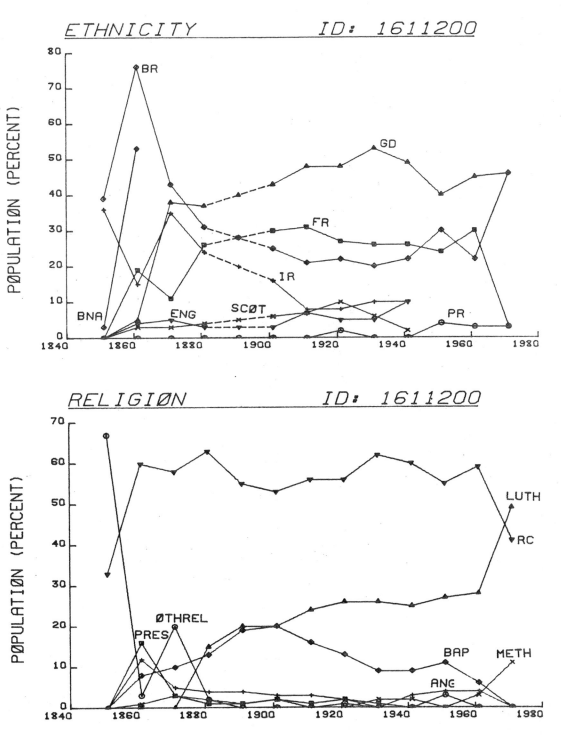

ID: 1611399 LOCHABER,
LOCHABER NORTH,
LOCHABER WEST, MAYO

AREA: 110.54 sq. miles

1971 DENSITY: 43.03
persons/sq. mile

TYPE:
Combined

POPULATION:
1851: 1307
1881: 2765
1941: 3014
1971: 4756

CHANGES: 1891 Thurso in-
corporated. Lochaber
area formerly called
Lochaber & Gore; Mayo
formerly called St.
Malachie.

SUBFILES:
a. Lochaber (Rural),
Lochaber North,
Lochaber West
b. Mayo; c. Thurso

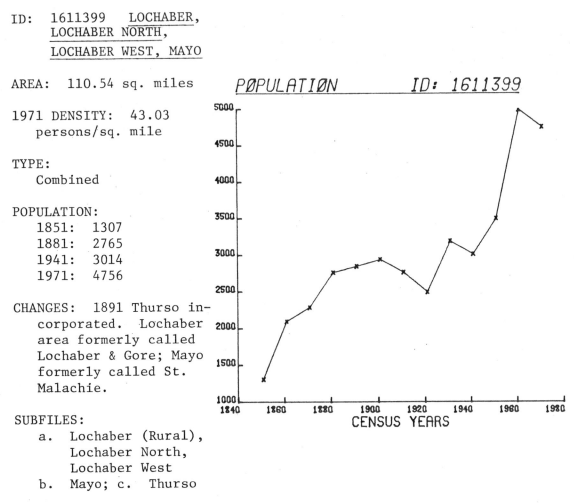

POPULATION   ID: 1611399

CENSUS YEARS

NOTES:

Pre-1851 population figures for Lochaber and Mayo are given in 187a
(Taché et al., 1938) and 286 (MacKay, 1949). The latter also gives
some more recent information about the economic history of Thurso.

377

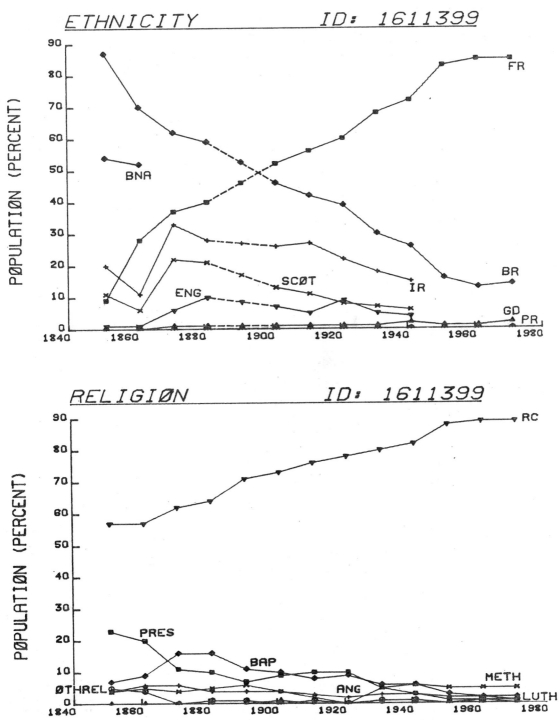

ETHNICITY   ID: 1611399

RELIGIØN   ID: 1611399

ID: 1611399   SUBFILES

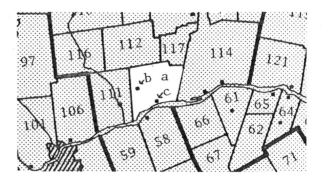

a. <u>LOCHABER (RURAL), LOCHABER
NORTH, LOCHABER WEST</u>

AREA: 80.92 sq. miles

1971 DENSITY: 17.03
persons/sq. mile

POPULATION:
1881: 2302
1941: 1488
1971: 1378

CHANGES: 1891 Thurso incorporated; parts of Lochaber and Lochaber
North, formerly called Gore of Lochaber.

b. <u>MAYO</u>

AREA: 28.06 sq. miles

1971 DENSITY: 5.67 persons/sq. mile

POPULATION: 1881:   463
1941:   231
1971:   159

CHANGES: Prior to 1954 called St. Malachie.

c. <u>THURSO</u>

AREA: 1.56 sq. miles

1971 DENSITY: 2063.46 persons/sq. mile

POPULATION: 1891:   578
1901:   525
1941: 1295
1971: 3219

CHANGES: 1891 incorporated.

ID: 1611399   SUBFILES   cont'd

ETHNICITY

PLACE	YEAR	ENG	SCOT	IR	FR	GD	PR
Lochaber (Rural), Lochaber North, Lochaber West	1881	253	587	351	1090	12	0
Lochaber (Rural), Lochaber North, Lochaber West	1901	162	306	369	1166	22	0
Lochaber (Rural), Lochaber North, Lochaber West	1941	81	122	227	1044	11	0
Mayo	1881	10	1	433	12	7	0
Mayo	1901	35	1	330	14	9	0
Mayo	1941	14	12	144	35	26	0
Thurso	1901	23	86	52	356	8	0
Thurso	1941	37	54	93	1099	10	0

RELIGION

PLACE	YEAR	ANG	RC	PRES	METH/UC	BAP	LUTH
Lochaber (Rural), Lochaber North, Lochaber West	1881	104	1330	288	139	422	
Lochaber (Rural), Lochaber North, Lochaber West	1901	77	1401	252	88	181	17
Lochaber (Rural), Lochaber North, Lochaber West	1941	58	1135	70	128	94	0
Mayo	1881	9	440	0	0	14	
Mayo	1901	9	376	0	0	4	
Mayo	1941	9	191	3	4	22	1
Thurso	1901	35	361	16	15	97	
Thurso	1941	18	1137	12	41	70	

ID: 1611499 [PETITE NATION] FASSETT, NOTRE-DAME-DE-BON-SECOURS NORTH, NOTRE-DAME-DE-LA PAIX, PLAISANCE, ST.-ANDRÉ AVELLIN, STE.-ANGELIQUE, VINOY

AREA: 261.51 sq. miles

1971 DENSITY:
30.13 persons/sq. mile

TYPE:
Combined

POPULATION:
1851: 3356
1881: 5864
1941: 8070
1971: 7879

CHANGES: 1861 Montebello incorporated; 1901 Papineauville incorporated; 1921 St.-André-Avellin incorporated.
This whole area formerly called Petite Nation; Fassett formerly called Notre-Dame-de-Bon-Secours.

SUBFILES:
a. [Petite Nation] (Rural)
b. Montebello
c. Papineauville
d. St.-André-Avellin (Urban)

NOTES:
See page 382.

POPULATION   ID: 1611499

CENSUS YEARS

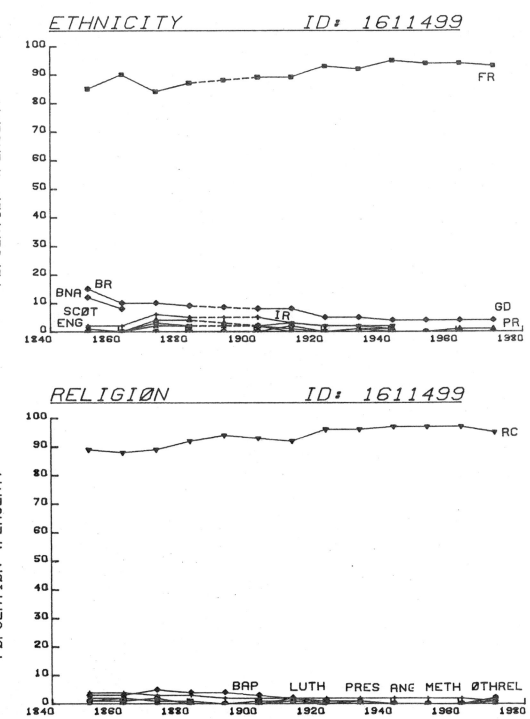

ID: 1611499 [PETITE NATION] FASSETT, NOTRE-DAME-DE-BON SECOURS
NORTH, NOTRE-DAME-DE-LA PAIX, PLAISANCE, ST.-ANDRÉ AVELLIN,
STE.-ANGELIQUE, VINOY   cont'd

NOTES:

Information on early Anglophone settlement and subsequent French
Canadian settlement in this area is given in 106 (Blanchard, 1954).
Pre-1851 population figures are given in 187a (Taché et al., 1938)
and 286 (MacKay, 1949). Lumbering in the area is discussed in 278
(Gibson, 1967).

In 1971 there were the following important unincorporated places
(with populations): Plaisance (651), Fassett (429), and Notre-Dame-
de-la-Paix (239). All are located in the subdivisions of the same
name.

ID: 1611499   SUBFILES

a. [PETITE NATION] (RURAL)

AREA: 254.76 sq. miles

1971 DENSITY:
16.18 persons/sq mile

POPULATION:
1881:   5267
1941:   5374
1971:   4122

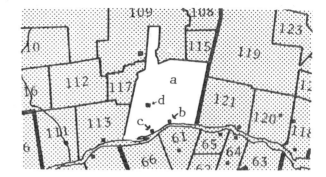

CHANGES: 1881 Montebello incorporated; 1901 Papineauville incorporated; 1921 St.-André-Avellin (Urban) incorporated; 1941 part
annexed to Montebello; 1951 part annexed to St.-André-Avellin
(Urban).

b. MONTEBELLO

AREA: 3.07 sq. miles

1971 DENSITY:
418.57 persons/sq. mile

POPULATION:
1881:   598
1941:   1266
1971:   1285

CHANGES: 1881 incorporated;
1941 annexed part of
[Petite Nation] (Rural).

c. PAPINEAUVILLE

AREA: 2.61 sq. miles

1971 DENSITY:
530.27 persons/sq. mile

POPULATION:
1901:   772
1941:   1023
1971:   1384

CHANGES: 1901 incorporated.

ID: 1611499   SUBFILES cont'd

d. ST-ANDRE-AVELLIN (URBAN)

AREA: 1.07 sq. miles

1971 DENSITY:
   1016.82 persons/sq. mile

POPULATION:
   1921:   446
   1941:   407
   1971:   1088

CHANGES: 1921 incorporated; 1951 annexed part of [Petite Nation]
(Rural) and part annexed by [Petite Nation] (Rural).

ETHNICITY

PLACE	YEAR	ENG	SCOT	IR	FR	GD	PR
[Petite Nation] (Rural)	1881	115	113	262	4529	201	0
[Petite Nation] (Rural)	1941	45	28	66	5180	1	0
Montebello	1881	15	19	13	545	5	0
Montebello	1941	86	26	15	1118	8	2
Papineauville	1901	25	19	23	659	17	0
Papineauville	1941	22	1	11	967	0	0
St-André-Avellin (Urban)	1921	1	0	0	445	0	0
St-André-Avellin (Urban)	1941	0	0	1	406	0	0

RELIGION

PLACE	YEAR	ANG	RC	PRES	METH/UC	BAP	LUTH
[Petite Nation] (Rural)	1881	140	4815	21	45	226	
[Petite Nation] (Rural)	1941	64	5263	18	4	29	0
Montebello	1881	11	555	9	16	5	
Montebello	1941	68	1163	15	7	4	4
Papineauville	1901	8	710	23	1	30	
Papineauville	1941	8	1009	0	0	6	
St-André-Avellin (Urban)	1921	0	446	0	0		
St-André-Avellin (Urban)	1941	0	407	0	0		

ID: 1611500   PONSONBY

AREA: 55.09 sq. miles

1971 DENSITY:
   3.52 persons/sq. mile

TYPE:
   Rural

POPULATION:
   1881:   310
   1941:   547
   1971:   194

CHANGES: 1881 created;
   1971 annexed part of
   Amherst (1610800).

SUBFILES:
   None

NOTES:

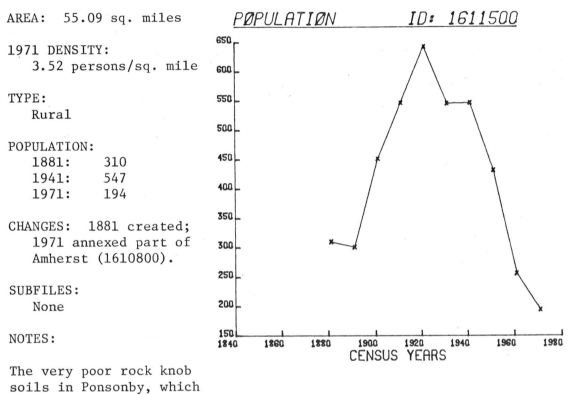

POPULATION   ID: 1611500

CENSUS YEARS

The very poor rock knob
soils in Ponsonby, which
account for the frequently
large farms, are mentioned in 278 (Gibson, 1967) and 294 (Turay,
1969).   See also 286 (MacKay, 1949).

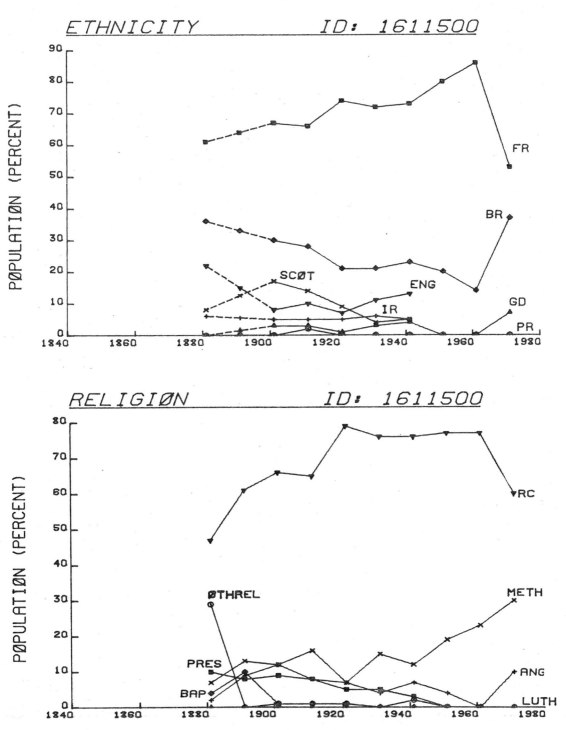

ETHNICITY   ID: 1611500

RELIGIØN   ID: 1611500

ID: 1611600 PORTLAND
WEST, NOTRE-DAME-DE-
LA-SALETTE

AREA: 95.62 sq. miles

1971 DENSITY:
    11.27 persons/sq. mile

TYPE:
    Rural

POPULATION:
    1851:   102
    1881:   672
    1941:   1295
    1971:   1078

CHANGES: Notre-Dame-de-
    la-Salette formerly
    called Portland
    East.

SUBFILES:
    None

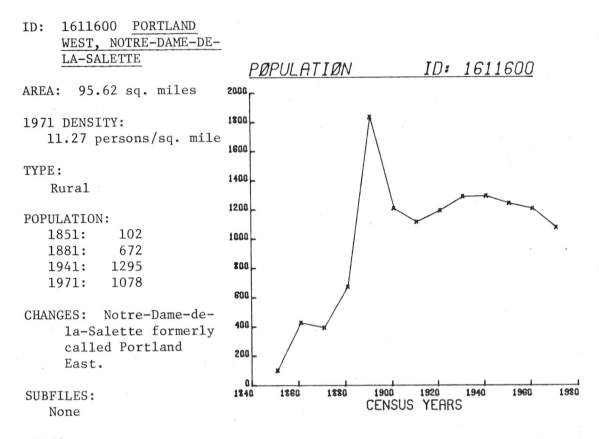

POPULATION   ID: 1611600

CENSUS YEARS

NOTES:

None of the works listed in the bibliography deal specifically with
this area.

In 1976 Portland West, together with Wakefield East (in 1509799) and
Perkins (in 1510699), form Val-de-Monts Village, part of the Rural
Fringe of the Census Metropolitan Area of Ottawa-Hull; Notre-Dame-
de-la Salette forms part of the new city of Buckingham (see
1611199).

In 1971 the unincorporated village of Notre-Dame-de-la-Salette,
located in the subdivision of the same name, had a population of
234.

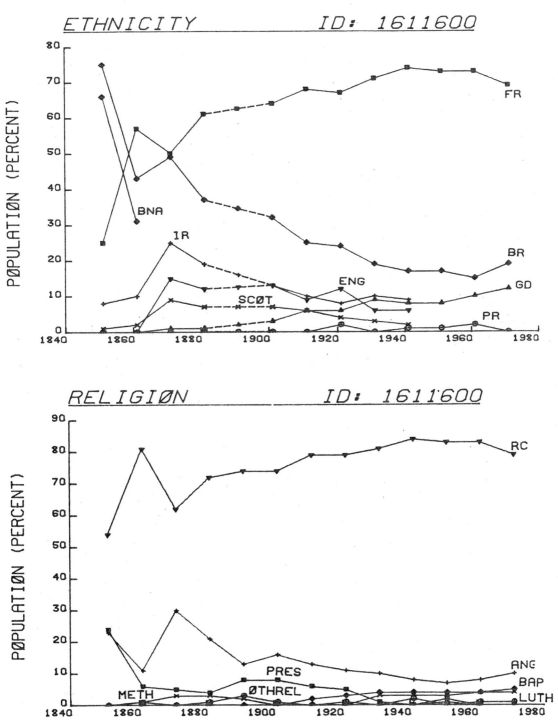

ETHNICITY   ID: 1611600

RELIGIØN   ID: 1611600

ID: 1611799   RIPON

AREA: 50.71 sq. miles

1971 DENSITY:
   22.28 persons/sq. mile

TYPE:
   Combined

POPULATION:
   1861:   609
   1881:   1602
   1941:   1404
   1971:   1130

CHANGES: 1861 created;
   1931 Ripon (Urban)
   incorporated.

SUBFILES:
   a. Ripon (Rural)
   b. Ripon (Urban)

NOTES:

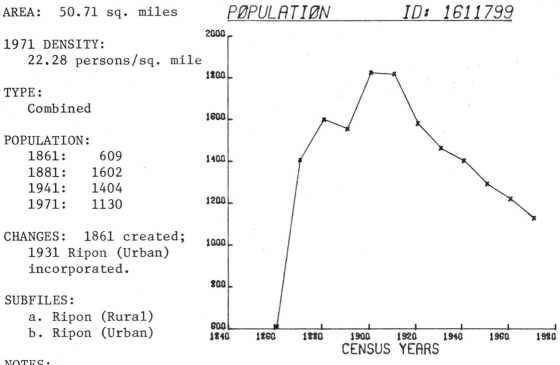

POPULATION   ID: 1611799

CENSUS YEARS

None of the works listed
in the bibliography deals specifically with this area.

Ripon has been close to 100% French since its creation in 1861.

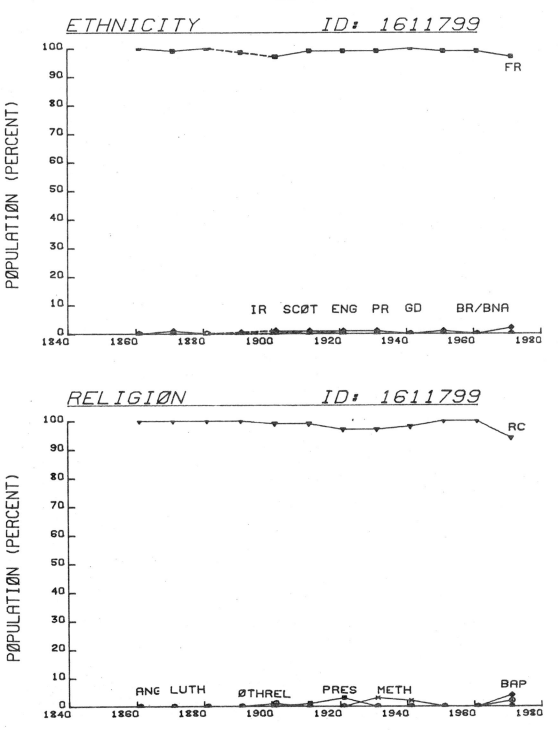

ID: 1611799 SUBFILES

a. RIPON (RURAL)

AREA: 49.13 sq. miles

1971 DENSITY:
    11.03 persons/sq. mile

POPULATION:
    1931:   1021
    1941:   957
    1971:   542

CHANGES: 1931 Ripon (Urban) incorporated.

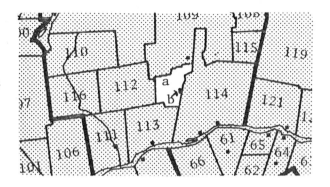

b. RIPON (URBAN)

AREA: 1.58 sq. miles

1971 DENSITY:
    372.15 persons/sq. mile

POPULATION:
    1931:   443
    1941:   447
    1971:   588

CHANGES: 1931 incorporated.

ID: 1611799 SUBFILES cont'd

ETHNICITY

PLACE	YEAR	ENG	SCOT	IR	FR	GD	PR
Ripon (Rural)	1931	6	0	5	1010	0	0
Ripon (Rural)	1941	0	0	0	957	0	0
Ripon (Urban)	1931	3	0	0	438	2	0
Ripon (Urban)	1941	0	0	0	447	0	0

RELIGION

PLACE	YEAR	ANG	RC	PRES	METH/UC	BAP	LUTH
Ripon (Rural)	1931	0	980	0	41	0	
Ripon (Rural)	1941	0	927	0	30	0	
Ripon (Urban)	1931	1	442	0	0		
Ripon (Urban)	1941	0	447	0	0		

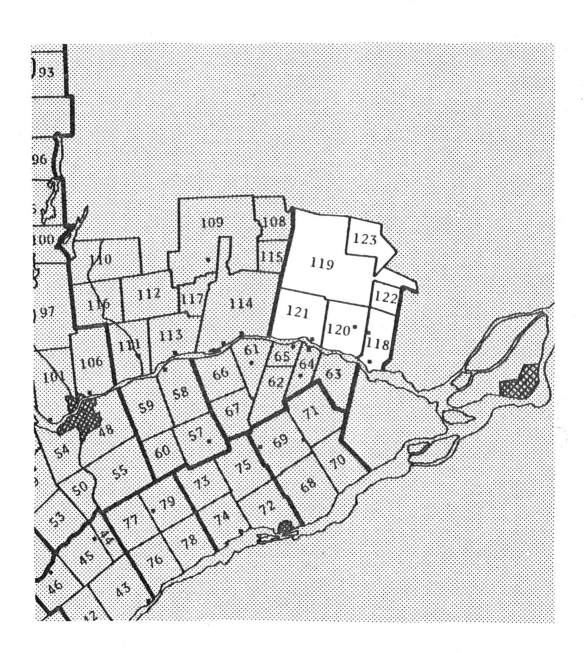

ARGENTEUIL COUNTY (17)

Integral Units   118 - 123

Apart from the few works (listed within) which deal with
specific areas in Argenteuil, most of the works dealing with this
area have a larger focus. Once again 106 (Blanchard, 1956) and 286
(MacKay, 1949) are important sources. Together with Prescott,
Argenteuil is the subject of an early monograph, 205 (Thomas, 1896),
and is itself the subject of an article, 236 (Greening, 1957). A
thesis, 278 (Gibson, 1967) is devoted to the settlement and abandonment of land in the Rouge Valley.

Considerable census information on Argenteuil County is available in tables, maps, and analyses at the census division level.
County totals for 1971: population 31,319; area 703.32 sq. miles;
density 44.54 persons/sq. mile.

ID: 1711899   ST-ANDRE-D'ARGENTEUIL

AREA: 47.82 sq. miles

1971 DENSITY:
   289.80 persons/sq. mile

TYPE:
   Combined

POPULATION:
   1851:   2326
   1881:   4400
   1941:   7943
   1971:   13858

CHANGES: Formerly called
   Argenteuil and formerl
   included St. Jerusalem
   d'Argenteuil; 1891
   Lachute incorporated;
   1961 part (Ayersville)
   annexed from Chatham
   (1712099); 1961 St.-
   André-Est incorporated;
   1971 part annexed to
   Ste-Scholastique City,
   Deux Montagnes County.

SUBFILES:
   a. St.-André-D'Argenteuil (Rural)
   b. Lachute
   c. St.-André-Est

NOTES:
   See page 398.

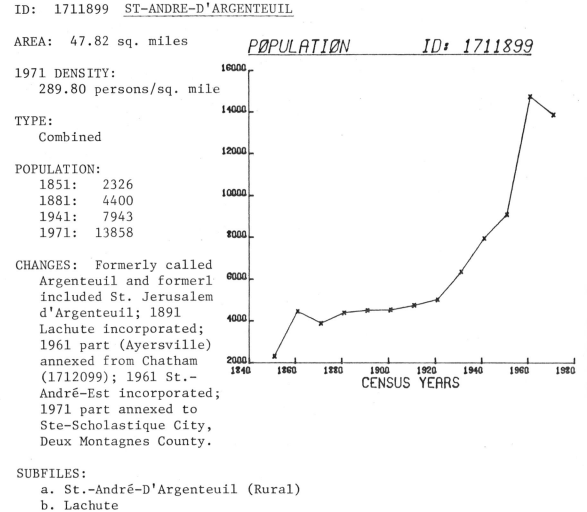

POPULATION   ID: 1711899

CENSUS YEARS

397

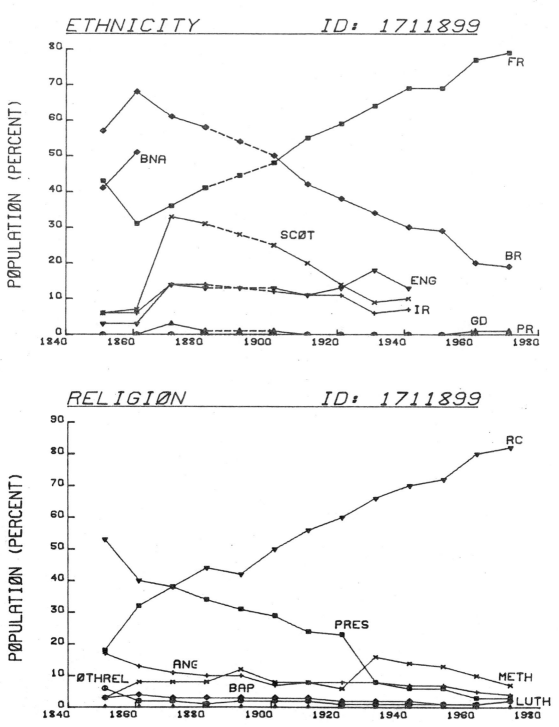

ID: 1711899   ST-ANDRE-D'ARGENTEUIL   cont'd

NOTES:

Some information on early Scottish settlement in this area is given
in 66 (Macdonald, 1939), and 106 (Blanchard, 1954) also discusses
Irish settlement. See also 278 (Gibson, 1967). Pre-1851 population figures for Argenteuil as a whole, Carillon, Lachute and
St. Andrews can be derived from 187a (Taché et al., 1938) and 286
(MacKay, 1969). 278 (Gibson, 1967) mentions the construction of
a grist mill in St. Andrews in 1800. The history of Lachute itself
is the subject of a monograph, 191 (Rigby, 1964). Some detail on
recent economic history is given in 295 (Zinman, 1976).

The large increase in population in recent years, and especially
between 1951 & 1961, occurred mostly in Lachute. The decrease
which shows up in 1971 may be partly due to the redrawing of area
boundaries.

Considerable census information is available in tables dealing with
the Census Agglomeration of Lachute which is composed of the city
of Lachute and the village of Brownsburg (in 1712099).

The 1971 boundary changes involving the annexation to Ste-
Scholastique City are not shown on our maps.

ID: 1711899   SUBFILES

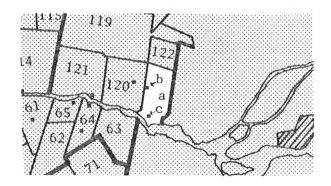

a   ST-ANDRÉ-D'ARGENTEUIL
    (RURAL)

    AREA: 29.16 sq. miles

    1971 DENSITY:
       28.94 persons/sq. mile

    POPULATION:
       1901:   2509
       1941:   2633
       1971:   844

    CHANGES: 1891 Lachute incorporated; 1961 St-André-Est incor-
       porated; 1971 part annexed to Lachute and part annexed to
       form Ste-Scholastique City, Deux Montagnes County (latter
       annexation not shown on maps).

b   LACHUTE

    AREA: 14.45 sq. miles

    1971 DENSITY:
       817.51 persons/sq. mile

    POPULATION:
       1901:   2022
       1941:   5310
       1971:   11813

    CHANGES: 1891 incorporated; 1961 annexed Ayersville from
       Chatham (1712099); 1971 annexed part of St-André d'Argenteuil
       (Rural); Lachute Town and Ayersville Village officially
       amalgamated as Lachute City.

ID: 1711899 SUBFILES cont'd

c <u>ST-ANDRÉ-EST</u>

  AREA: 4.21 sq. miles

  1971 DENSITY:
   285.27 persons/sq. mile

  POPULATION:
   1961:   1183
   1971:   1201

  CHANGES: 1961 incorporated; formerly called St. Andrews.

<u>ETHNICITY</u>

PLACE	YEAR	ENG	SCOT	IR	FR	GD	PR
St-André d'Argenteuil (Rural)	1901	328	726	290	1124	35	0
St-André d'Argenteuil (Rural)	1941	310	461	311	1536	3	0
Lachute	1901	252	421	238	1073	17	0
Lachute	1941	736	308	264	3919	10	1
St-André-Est	1971	(British) 255			950	15	0

<u>RELIGION</u>

PLACE	YEAR	ANG	RC	PRES	METH/UC	BAP	LUTH
St-André d'Argenteuil (Rural)	1901	188	1175	875	190	21	
St-André d'Argenteuil (Rural)	1941	215	1537	309	514	44	
Lachute	1901	126	1094	456	194	108	
Lachute	1941	360	3996	183	617	98	
St-André-Est	1971	80	1020	80	20	5	5

ID: 1711999 ARUNDEL,
HARRINGTON,
HUBERDEAU, LAC-DES-
SEIZE-ILES, MILLE-
ISLES, MONTCALM,
WENTWORTH, WENTWORTH
NORTH

AREA: 315.22 sq. miles

1971 DENSITY:
10.91 persons/sq. mile

TYPE:
Combined

POPULATION:
1851:   563
1881:   2501
1941:   3645
1971:   3440

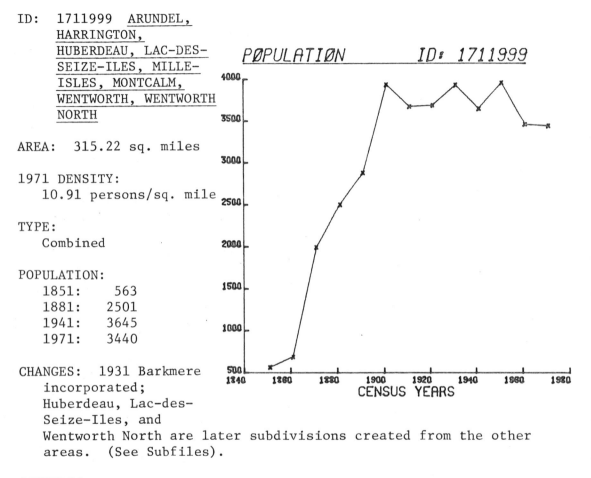

POPULATION   ID: 1711999
CENSUS YEARS

CHANGES: 1931 Barkmere
incorporated;
Huberdeau, Lac-des-
Seize-Iles, and
Wentworth North are later subdivisions created from the other
areas. (See Subfiles).

SUBFILES:
a. Arundel, Huberdeau (Rural)
b. Harrington, Montcalm, Wentworth and Wentworth North
c. Mille-Isles
d. Lac-des-Seize-Iles
e. Barkmere

NOTES:
See page 404.

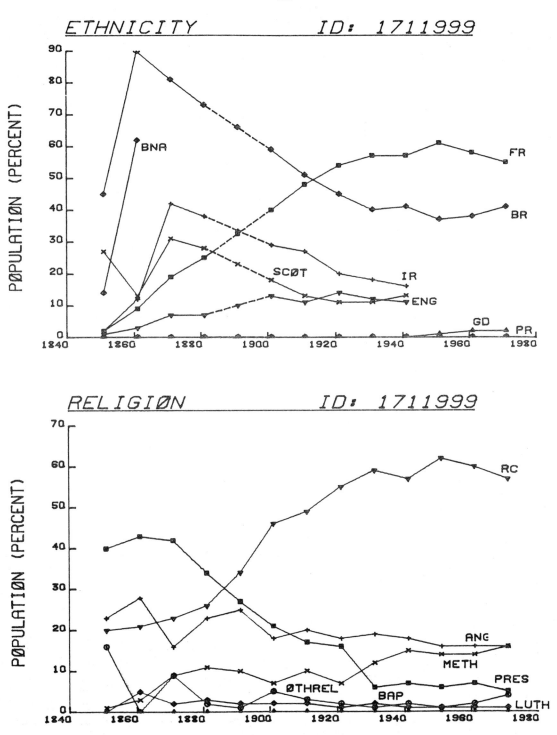

ID: 1711999 <u>ARUNDEL, HARRINGTON, HUBERDEAU, LAC-DES-</u>
      <u>SEIZE-ILES, MONTCALM, WENTWORTH, WENTWORTH NORTH</u>   cont'd

NOTES:

Some details of the early settlement of this area can be derived
from 106 (Blanchard, 1954), 187a (Taché et al., 1938), 278 (Gibson,
1967), and 286 (MacKay, 1949).

In 1971 the unincorporated village of Huberdeau, located in
Huberdeau subdivision, had a population of 505; Lac-des-Seize-Isles
village had a population of 181.

ID: 1711999 SUBFILES

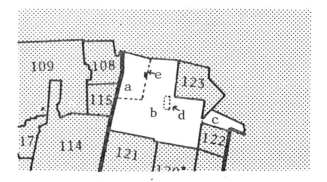

a. <u>ARUNDEL, HUBERDEAU</u>

   AREA: 46.96 sq. miles

   1971 DENSITY:
     28.26 persons/sq. mile

   POPULATION:
     1881:   606
     1941:   1617
     1971:   1327

   CHANGES: 1931 Huberdeau created.

b. <u>HARRINGTON, MONTCALM,</u>
   <u>WENTWORTH, WENTWORTH NORTH</u>

   AREA: 234.84 sq. miles

   1971 DENSITY:
     6.29 persons/sq. mile

   POPULATION:
     1881:   1328
     1941:   1483
     1971:   1478

   CHANGES: 1961 Wentworth
     North created.

c. <u>MILLE-ISLES</u>

   AREA: 23.16 sq. miles

   1971 DENSITY:
     15.98 persons/sq. mile

   POPULATION:
     1881:   567
     1941:   277
     1971:   370

d. <u>LAC-DES-SEIZE-ILES</u>

   AREA: 3.28 sq. miles

   1971 DENSITY:
     64.94 persons/sq. mile

   POPULATION:
     1921:   185
     1941:   228
     1971:   213

   CHANGES: 1921 created.

e. <u>BARKMERE</u>

   AREA: 6.98 sq. miles

   1971 DENSITY:
     7.45 persons/sq. mile

   POPULATION:
     1941:   40
     1971:   52

   CHANGES: 1931 incorporated.

ID: 1711999 SUBFILES cont'd

ETHNICITY

PLACE	YEAR	ENG	SCOT	IR	FR	GD	PR
Arundel & Huberdeau	1881	70	72	193	246	0	0
Arundel & Huberdeau (Rural)	1941	141	85	189	1181	4	0
Harrington, Montcalm, Wentworth, Wentworth North	1881	83	451	426	361	0	7
Harrington, Montcalm, Wentworth, Wentworth North	1941	213	363	221	645	13	0
Mille-Isles	1881	26	179	337	25	0	0
Mille-Isles	1941	33	26	184	31	0	0
Lac-des-Seize-Iles	1921	16	0	10	141	6	0
Lac-des-Seize-Iles	1941	19	8	3	187	0	0
Barkmere	1941	0	8	1	31	0	0

RELIGION

PLACE	YEAR	ANG	RC	PRES	METH/UC	BAP	LUTH
Arundel & Huberdeau	1881	102	225	110	114	13	
Arundel & Huberdeau (Rural)	1941	199	1152	37	192	4	
Harrington, Montcalm, Wentworth, Wentworth North	1881	259	360	498	106	63	
Harrington, Montcalm, Wentworth, Wentworth North	1941	347	634	134	301	38	
Mille-Isles	1881	220	72	213	62		
Mille-Isles	1941	108	45	87	37	0	
Lac-des-Seize-Iles	1921	12	163	0	5		
Lac-des-Seize-Iles	1941	18	198	3	8		
Barkmere	1941	0	32	0	8		

ID: 1712099 CHATHAM

AREA: 101.45 sq. miles

1971 DENSITY:
    68.83 persons/sq. mile

TYPE:
    Combined

POPULATION:
    1851:   3167
    1881:   3985
    1941:   6181
    1971:   6983

CHANGES: 1891 Carillon
    incorporated; 1941
    Brownsburg incor-
    porated; 1961 part
    (Ayersville) taken and
    added to Lachute
    (in 1711899).

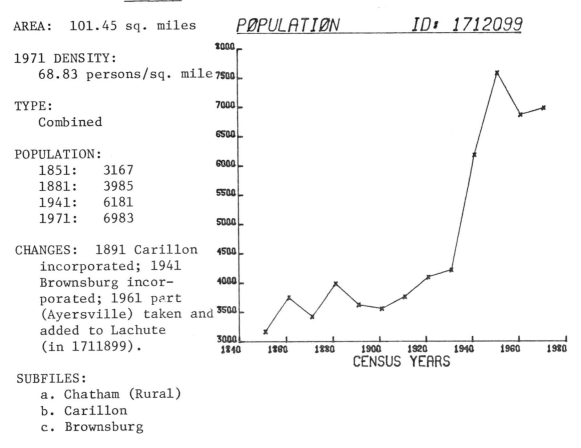

POPULATION   ID: 1712099

CENSUS YEARS

SUBFILES:
    a. Chatham (Rural)
    b. Carillon
    c. Brownsburg

NOTES:

Early Scottish settlement in Chatham is discussed in 66 (Macdonald,
1939). 187a (Taché et al., 1938) and 286 (MacKay, 1949) give
pre-1851 population figures. The latter also gives details on
more recent economic activities in Brownsburg.

Considerable census information on Brownsburg is available in tables
dealing with the Census Agglomeration of Lachute (in 1711899). In
the fairly long 1971 list of unincorporated places in Chatham, the
following stood out (with populations): Whissel Town (350),
Roussillon (288), and St-Philippe-D'Argenteuil (284).

409

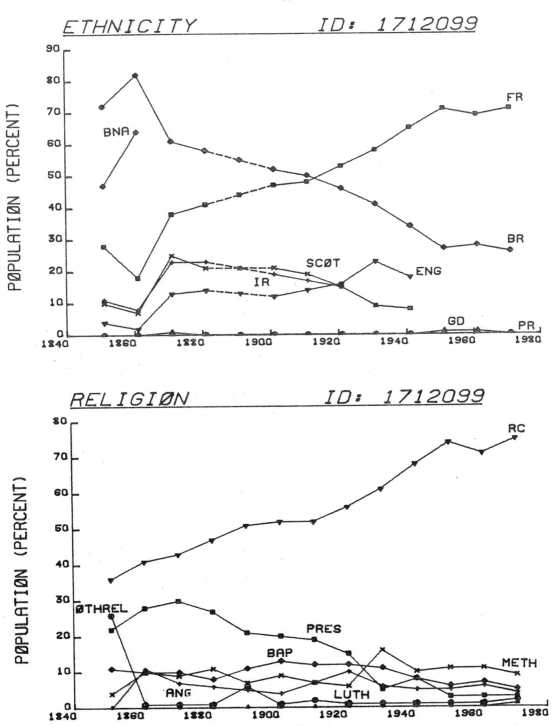

ID: 1712099 SUBFILES

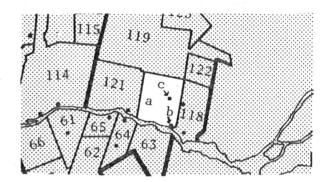

a. CHATHAM (RURAL)

AREA: 96.06 sq. miles

1971 DENSITY:
   32.08 persons/sq. mile

POPULATION:
   1901:   3327
   1941:   2836
   1971:   3082

CHANGES: 1891 Carillon incorporated; 1941 Brownsburg incorporated; 1961 part (Ayersville) added to Lachute (in 1711899).

b. CARILLON

AREA: 2.64 sq. miles

1971 DENSITY:
   159.09 persons/sq. mile

POPULATION:
   1901:   233
   1941:   240
   1971:   420

CHANGES: 1891 incorporated.

c. BROWNSBURG

AREA: 2.75 sq. miles

1971 DENSITY:
   1265.82 persons/sq. mile

POPULATION:
   1941:   3105
   1971:   3481

CHANGES: 1941 incorporated.

ID: 1712099 SUBFILES cont'd

ETHNICITY

PLACE	YEAR	ENG	SCOT	IR	FR	GD	PR
Chatham (Rural)	1901	409	744	665	1481	14	0
Chatham (Rural)	1941	375	262	317	1868	10	0
Carillon	1901	11	12	28	179	3	0
Carillon	1941	51	0	2	185	2	0
Brownsburg	1941	684	232	193	1959	1	1

RELIGION

PLACE	YEAR	ANG	RC	PRES	METH/UC	BAP	LUTH
Chatham (Rural)	1901	154	1646	686	335	461	
Chatham (Rural)	1941	77	1887	314	194	334	1
Carillon	1901	2	215	13	3		
Carillon	1941	9	190	37	3		
Brownsburg	1941	248	2104	143	413	180	9

ID: 1712199 <u>GRENVILLE</u>

AREA: 125.43 sq. miles

1971 DENSITY:
    32.94 persons/sq. mile

TYPE:
    Combined

POPULATION:
    1851:   1992
    1881:   2412
    1941:   3335
    1971:   4132

CHANGES: 1881 Grenville
    incorporated; 1921
    Calumet incorporated.

SUBFILES:
    a. Grenville (Rural)
    b. Grenville (Urban)
    c. Calumet

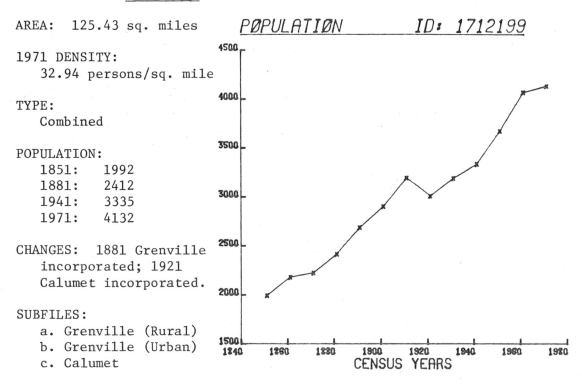

PØPULATIØN   *ID: 1712199*

CENSUS YEARS

NOTES:

Grenville is the subject of a monograph, 147 (Grenville Centennial Committee, 1976). Further information on the area can be derived from 66 (Macdonald, 1939), 106 (Blanchard, 1954), 187a (Taché et al., 1938), 278 (Gibson, 1967) and 286 (MacKay, 1949).

In 1971 the following important unincorporated places were found in Grenville (with populations): Kilmar (267), Pointe-au-Chêne (243), and Grenville Bay (230).

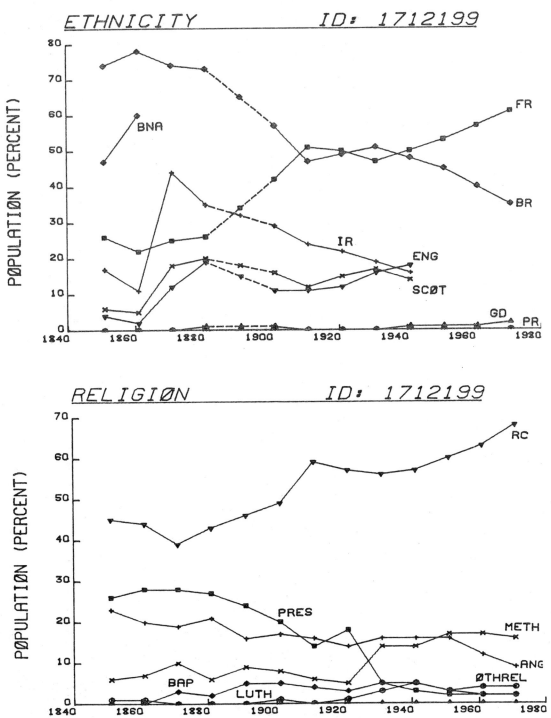

414

ID: 1712199   SUBFILES

a. GRENVILLE (RURAL)

AREA: 122.06 sq. miles

1971 DENSITY:
   15.34 persons/sq. mile

POPULATION:
   1881:   1844
   1941:   1893
   1971:   1873

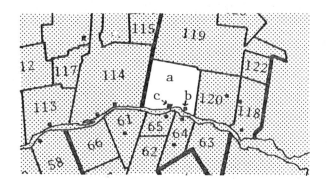

CHANGES: 1881 Grenville incorporated; 1911 population total
   taken from Vol. I, Table I of 1911 census; 1921 Calumet
   incorporated.

b. GRENVILLE (URBAN)

AREA: 1.23 sq. miles

1971 DENSITY:
   1215.45 persons/sq. mile

POPULATION:
   1881:   568
   1941:   737
   1971:   1495

CHANGES: 1881 incorporated;
   1911 population total taken
   from Vol. I, Table I of
   1911 census.

c. CALUMET

AREA: 2.14 sq. miles

1971 DENSITY:
   357.01 persons/sq. mile

POPULATION:
   1921:   682
   1941:   705
   1971:   764

CHANGES: 1921 incorporated.

ID: 1712199 SUBFILES cont'd

ETHNICITY

PLACE		YEAR	ENG	SCOT	IR	FR	GD	PR
Grenville	(Rural)	1881	340	410	656	438	0	0
Grenville	(Rural)	1941	453	334	411	633	16	3
Grenville	(Urban)	1881	115	71	179	189	13	0
Grenville	(Urban)	1941	62	73	55	541	0	1
Calumet		1921	73	48	68	490	2	0
Calumet		1941	94	49	70	487	2	0

RELIGION

PLACE		YEAR	ANG	RC	PRES	METH/UC	BAP	LUTH
Grenville	(Rural)	1881	404	758	549	99	34	
Grenville	(Rural)	1941	333	838	80	371	131	
Grenville	(Urban)	1881	102	286	101	54	24	
Grenville	(Urban)	1941	100	569	24	37	6	
Calumet		1921	80	519	22	46	4	
Calumet		1941	101	497	9	68	19	

ID: 1712200 <u>GORE</u>

AREA: 36.24 sq. miles

1971 DENSITY:
  7.09 persons/sq. mile

TYPE:
  Rural

POPULATION:
  1851:   996
  1881:   636
  1941:   266
  1971:   257

CHANGES: None.

SUBFILES: None

NOTES:

PØPULATIØN   ID: 1712200

CENSUS YEARS

The poor rock knob soils
of Gore, which account
for the extremely large
farms often found in the
area, are mentioned in 278 (Gibson, 1967) and 294 (Turay, 1969). See
also 286 (MacKay, 1949). The latter, together with 187a (Taché et
al., 1938), gives pre-1851 population figures.

Gore is noteworthy for its traditionally strong Irish predominance.

417

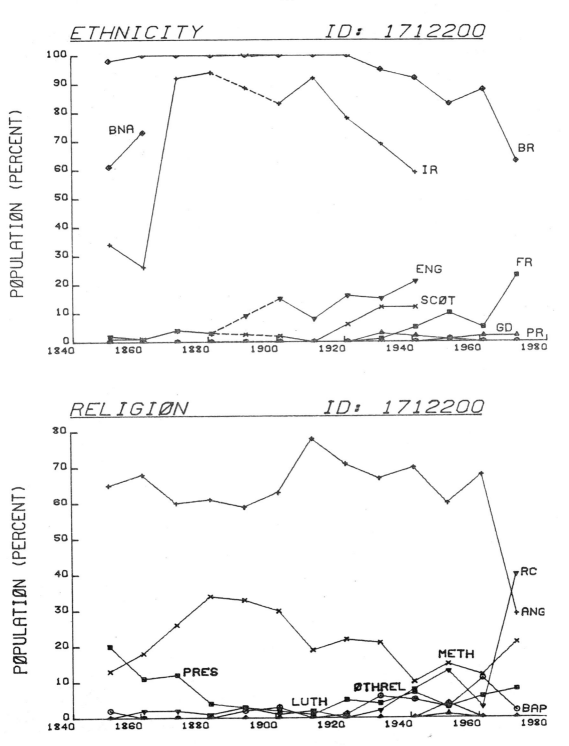

ID: 1712300   ST.-ADOLPHE-
      D'HOWARD, MORIN
      HEIGHTS

AREA: 77.16 sq. miles

1971 DENSITY:
   34.33 persons/sq. mile

TYPE:
   Rural

POPULATION:
   1861:   454
   1881:   1013
   1941:   1300
   1971:   2649

CHANGES: 1861 created.

SUBFILES:
   a. St.-Adolphe-D'Howard
   b. Morin Heights

NOTES:

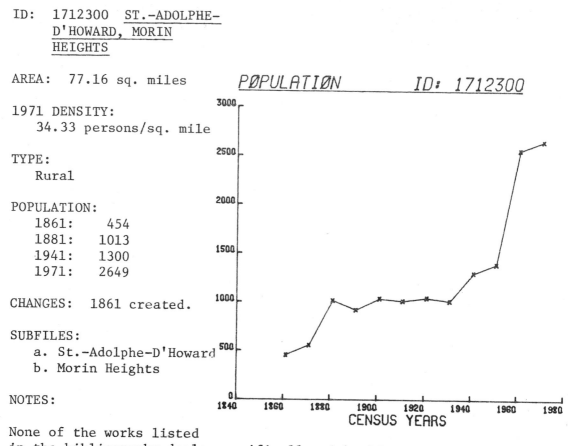

None of the works listed
in the bibliography deals specifically with this area.

In 1971 the unincorporated village of Morin Heights, located in the
subdivision of the same name, had a population of 710; the village
of St.-Adolphe-D'Howard had a population of 384.

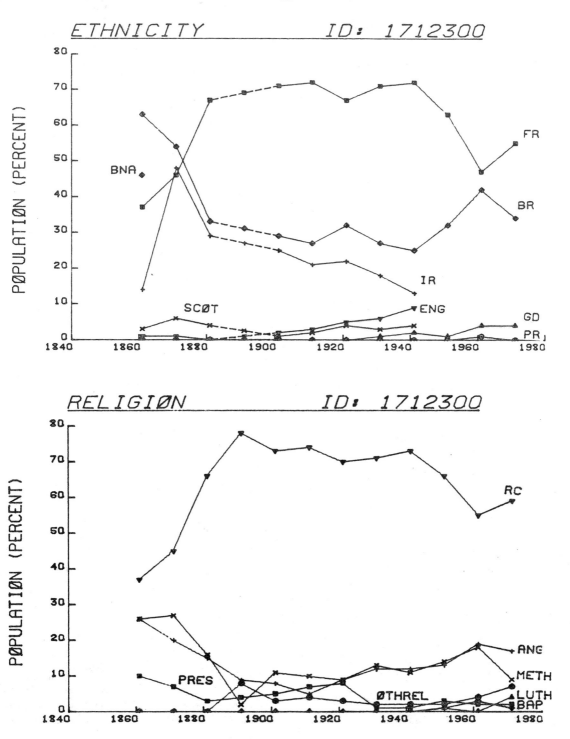

ID: 1712300 SUBFILES

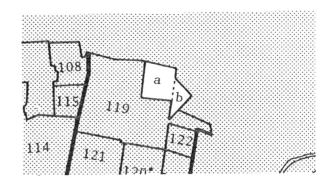

a. ST.ADOLPHE-D'HOWARD

   AREA: 55.76 sq. miles

   1971 DENSITY:
      23.91 persons/sq. mile

   POPULATION:
      1881:   455
      1941:   629
      1971:   1333

   CHANGES: Previously called Howard.

b. MORIN HEIGHTS

   AREA: 21.40 sq. miles

   1971 DENSITY:
      61.50 persons/sq. mile

   POPULATION:
      1881:   558
      1941:   671
      1971:   1316

   CHANGES: Previously called Morin South.

ID: 1712300   SUBFILES   cont'd

ETHNICITY

PLACE	YEAR	ENG	SCOT	IR	FR	GD	PR
St.-Adolphe-D'Howard	1881	0	0	25	428	0	0
St.-Adolphe-D'Howard	1941	21	1	2	593	2	1
Morin Heights	1881	3	39	267	249	0	0
Morin Heights	1941	94	47	161	343	20	0

RELIGION

PLACE	YEAR	ANG	RC	PRES	METH/UC	BAP	LUTH
St.-Adolphe-D'Howard	1881	23	423	9	0		
St.-Adolphe-D'Howard	1941	11	604	0	4		
Morin Heights	1881	125	250	0	23	160	
Morin Heights	1941	147	346	17	139		

GRAPHS

Graph 1: Population Ranges for Ottawa Valley Integral Units 1851-1971

This graph and the one that follows, "*British and French Ranges (By Percent) For Ottawa Valley Integral Units 1851-1971*," present historical overviews of all geographical areas (integral units) in the Ottawa Valley from 1851 to 1971. The "*Population Ranges*" graph shows the population distribution by IU *size category*: the lines on the graph represent seven categories—IU's with less than 500 population, 500-1249, 1250-2499, 2500-4999, 5000-9999, 10000-14999, and 15000 or more. The vertical axis of the graph gives the number of integral units in each of the size categories and the horizontal axis gives the census years from 1851 to 1971. The resulting graph reveals a considerable amount of information about the size and distribution of Valley population.

Reading down the graph along any one census year shows how many IU's there were in each size category—for example, in 1901 there were 25 IU's in the 500-1249 category. By following any one graph line, one can also trace the trend of particular size categories over time, for example, when and how fast the 10000-14999 category grew. Grouping several of the lines together can reveal other types of information. If we add together the yearly totals of all lines under 5000, and then calculate them as a percentage of the total number of IU's for each year, we find that the population of the vast majority of Valley IU's has always been below 5000, though the percentage is declining: 1851: 98%, 1911: 84%, 1971: 74%. Adding in the 5000-9999 line, we find that 89% of IU's had a population under 10,000 in 1971.

Taken as a whole, the graph also reflects historical population growth trends in the Valley. The period to about 1891 indicates widespread growth, shown by the fall in number of IU's below 1250, the increase above that, and the increase in absolute number of IU's. From the turn of the century to World War II, the general stability or peak and slow fall of groups below 10,000 reflects a net outmigration to major urban centres and presumably the city of Ottawa (which does not appear in the graph). Finally, the post-war period of urban spread is clearly seen in the combined fall of the three categories 500-4999, the sharp rise of the line 500 or less, and the rise of categories over 5000 and especially over 10,000.

This graph can also be used along with the information in the Main Files to see how typical any individual IU was in any census year or over time. For example, the population of Torbolton Township (0805600) was in the 500-1249 category from 1851 to 1961; only in 1971 did it move up to the next category. In contrast, neighbouring March Township (0805200) shifted between the 500-1249 and 1250-2499 lines until 1971 when it jumped to the 5000-9999 line. *Note*: It should be remembered that the absolute number of IU's in the Valley varies over time. (See Graph Note.)

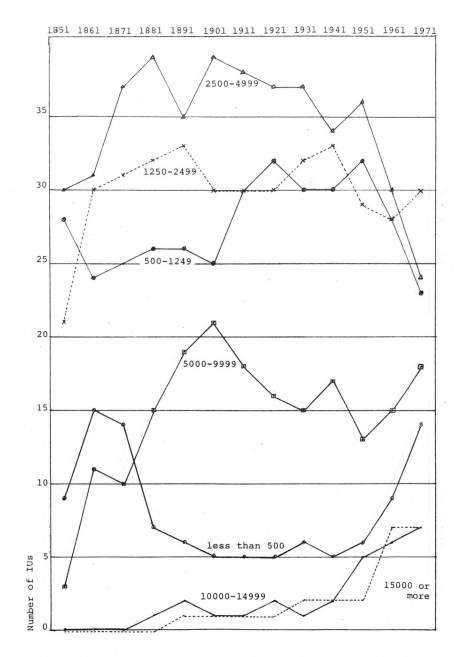

POPULATION RANGES FOR OTTAWA VALLEY INTEGRAL UNITS 1851-1971

Note: Number of IUs over time: 1851: 91, 1861: 111,

1871: 117, 1881: 120, 1891-1901: 122, 1911-1971: 123

Graph 2: British and French Ranges (By Percent) For Ottawa Valley Integral Units 1851-1971

This graph shows the relative positions of British and French ethnic groups in the Ottawa Valley over time. The lines on the graph represent six percentage categories: British under 30%, French under 30%, British 30% - 49%, French 30% - 49%, British over 50%, and French over 50%. The vertical axis of the graph gives the number of integral units (IU's) in each category and the horizontal axis give the census years from 1851 to 1971. The absence of ethnicity data for 1891 is indicated by a dotted line through that year for all graphs.

The most revealing lines in the graph are of course those indicating ethnic majorities (over 50%). These show the steady rise of majority French IU's until 1951 and the corresponding fall of majority British areas. The other lines, however, are also interesting. Though the number of places where the French are below 30% is still (in 1971) double that of the British category, the gap between the two lines has diminished in almost every census year since 1851. These lines too, then, indicate a rising and widespread French presence in the Valley and a corresponding decline in British dominance. Finally, the relative stability of moderate ethnic representation (i.e. 30% - 49%), is shown in the last 2 graph lines. Interestingly, the IU's in these two lines have been the least numerous since around the turn of the century and were very low before that. One can infer from this that the Valley has always had relatively few areas of British and French parity. The large percentage of absolute majority IU's of course also attests to this feature.

This graph can also be used in concert with the maps showing ethnic pluralities and ethnic group percentages for 1881, 1941, and 1971 (Maps 3 - 15). For example, the geographic distribution of the shift in number of majority areas mentioned above can be seen in the maps. The maps also show that the areas of dominance are heavily regional within the Valley and that the parity areas are geographically transitional.

It should be remembered when using this graph that the absolute number of IU's increases over time (see Graph Note). Furthermore, since German-Dutch and Polish-Russian ethnic groups are not included in the graph, British and French percentages do not necessarily total 100% for any IU in the graph. This also explains why the combined total of British and French majority IU's does not necessarily total the absolute number of IUs in any year.

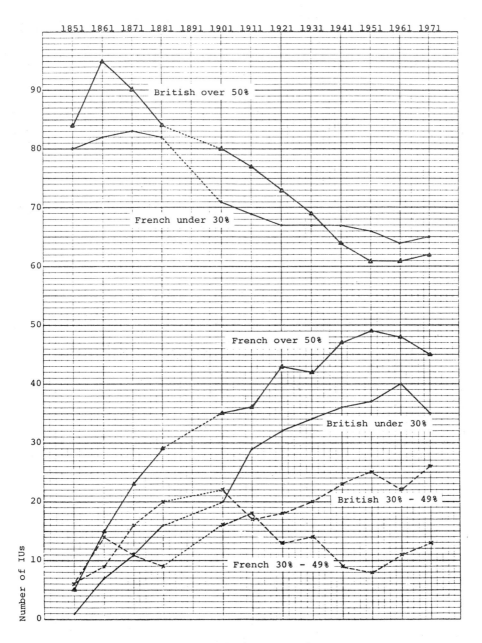

BRITISH AND FRENCH RANGES (BY PERCENT) FOR OTTAWA VALLEY

INTEGRAL UNITS 1851-1971

Note: Number of IUs over time: 1851: 91, 1861: 111,

1871: 117, 1881: 120, 1891-1901: 122, 1911-1971: 123

429

MAPS

INTRODUCTION

The 22 maps in this section show the distribution of various sorts of census information for the years 1881, 1941, 1971, and 1976 over the geographical area of the Ottawa Valley. Most of the maps present data from the census years 1881 (9 maps) and 1941 (9 maps). The predominance of these two dates here and indeed elsewhere in the book (for example, population figures in the Main Files and Ethnicity and Religion tables in the Subfiles), requires a brief explanation.

Since our aim throughout has been to provide information permitting historical comparisons, several different points in time needed to be chosen. Where possible, we tried to provide as many as four dates, usually the first (1851) and last (1971) census years, in addition to 1881 and 1941. For the maps and Subfiles, however, limitations of space, time and resources forced us to concentrate our efforts for the most part on only two different dates. The nature of the census data on the Ottawa Valley strongly recommended 1881 and 1941. Those two dates represent both the nineteenth and twentieth centuries and are sufficiently far apart to provide a perspective on a significant period of change. Moreover, by 1881, most of the major groups had arrived in the Ottawa Valley and had appeared in the census. Furthermore, most of the IU's themselves (120 out of 123) had been created and listed in the census. The only other nineteenth century date — 1871 — showed a much less complete picture, especially in the outlying areas. The years 1851, 1861, and 1891 were of course unsuitable for ethnicity maps since the presentation of the ethnic groups was not consistent with that of later censuses. As to 1941, again the choice was easy — it was the last date in which the census provided the breakdown of the British ethnic category into the component groups: English, Scottish, Irish. For these reasons, the maps and to some extent the Subfiles concentrate on these 2 census years. Those wishing to go beyond the picture presented in these maps can of course do their own analysis based on the IU graphs or can consult the full datafile by contacting us at Carleton University. (See Introduction, p. xxiii).

NOTES FOR THE MAPS

For the identification of the individual IU numbers shown in these maps, see Map 1, "The Ottawa Valley" and the adjoining list of names (above, pp. viii-ix). A complete list of names is found only in the Main File headings opposite the full ID Number.

MAP 2 Rural - Urban 1976

This map shows Rural and Urban distributions in 1976 according to census definitions of that year. Urban, for example, is defined basically as incorporated municipalities or other areas of more than 1000 inhabitants having a population density of at least 1000 people per square mile. (For a full definition of "urban" as well as "census metropolitan area" and "census agglomeration," see 1976 Census Catalogue No. 99-819 "EA Reference List: Components [Census Metropolitan Areas and Census Agglomerations]".) Map 2 thus shows all Valley IU's which have urban parts according to three categories: 1. Those IU's which contain urban areas which form part of the Census Metropolitan Area of Ottawa-Hull; 2. Those IU's containing urban areas which form part of the six Census agglomerations found in the Ottawa Valley, namely: Arnprior, Hawkesbury, Lachute, Pembroke, Petawawa, and Smiths Falls; 3. Those IU's containing other areas defined as urban.

Remaining IU's in the Valley are shown as "Rural," including those IU's containing *only* rural parts of the Census Metropolitan Area of Ottawa-Hull. The fact that these latter IU's are included within the CMA of Ottawa-Hull is of course significant and should be kept in mind in analyzing rural IU's in the Valley. Note also that the classification of some IU's as "Urban" does not imply that the entire IU is urban; most, if not all urban IU's still have rural parts.

MAPS 3 to 15 Ethnicity

These 13 maps draw on census ethnic data and were created by mapping geographical distributions (i.e. ID numbers) provided by computer analysis of the datafile. The following features were selected: ethnic pluralities for each IU for 1881, 1941, and 1971; distribution by percentage categories of English, Scottish, Irish (1881 and 1941), British (1971), and French (1881, 1941, and 1971). Each of these maps considered individually thus reveals the distribution and relative status of the numerically dominant Ottawa Valley ethnic groups. Taken together, the maps reveal the relative changes over time.

MAPS 16 to 23 Religion

These eight maps present census information on the major Valley religious groups for the years 1881 and 1941. As in the case of the Ethnicity maps, these maps were created by computer analysis of selected percentage distributions by ID Number. For the most part the maps need no explanation except perhaps to remind readers that Map 23, "PRESBYTERIAN - 1941," shows only those Presbyterians who did not join the United Church, and that in Map 21 "UNITED CHURCH—1941" the United Church category (for 1931 or later) appears elsewhere in this book as "Methodist" or "Meth/UC."

433

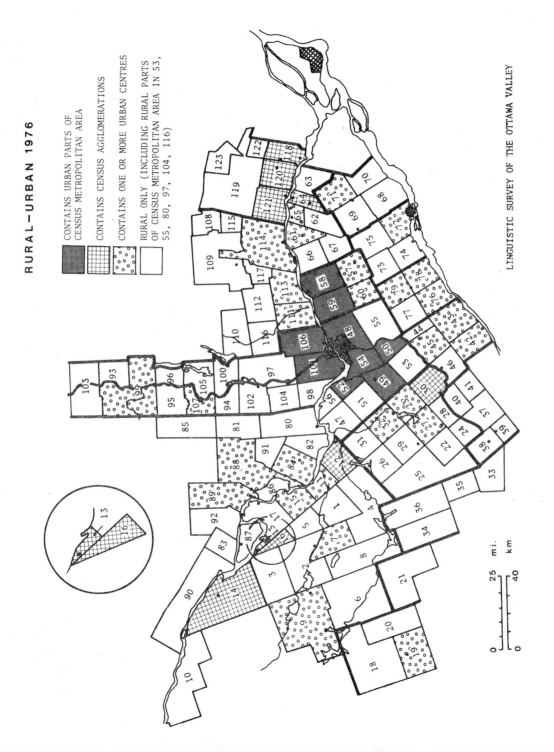

RURAL–URBAN 1976

CONTAINS URBAN PARTS OF
CENSUS METROPOLITAN AREA

CONTAINS CENSUS AGGLOMERATIONS

CONTAINS ONE OR MORE URBAN CENTRES

RURAL ONLY (INCLUDING RURAL PARTS
OF CENSUS METROPOLITAN AREA IN 53,
55, 80, 97, 104, 116)

LINGUISTIC SURVEY OF THE OTTAWA VALLEY

MAP 2

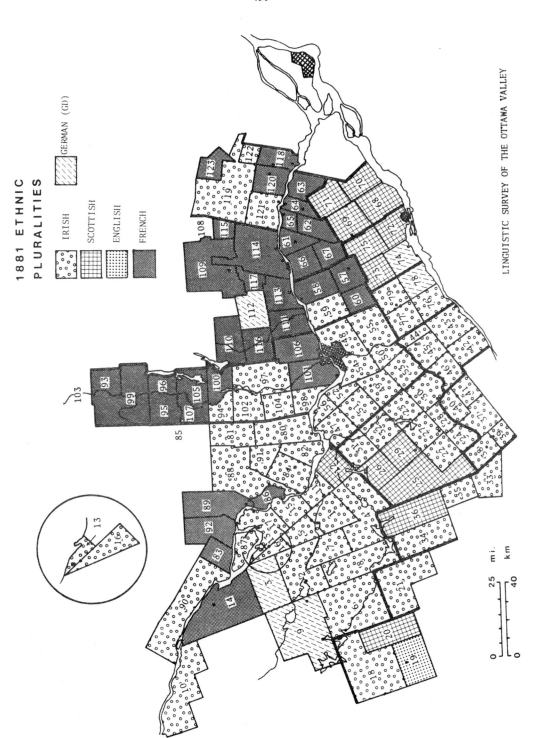

1881 ETHNIC
PLURALITIES

GERMAN (GD)

IRISH

SCOTTISH

ENGLISH

FRENCH

LINGUISTIC SURVEY OF THE OTTAWA VALLEY

MAP 3

25 mi.

km

0

40

0

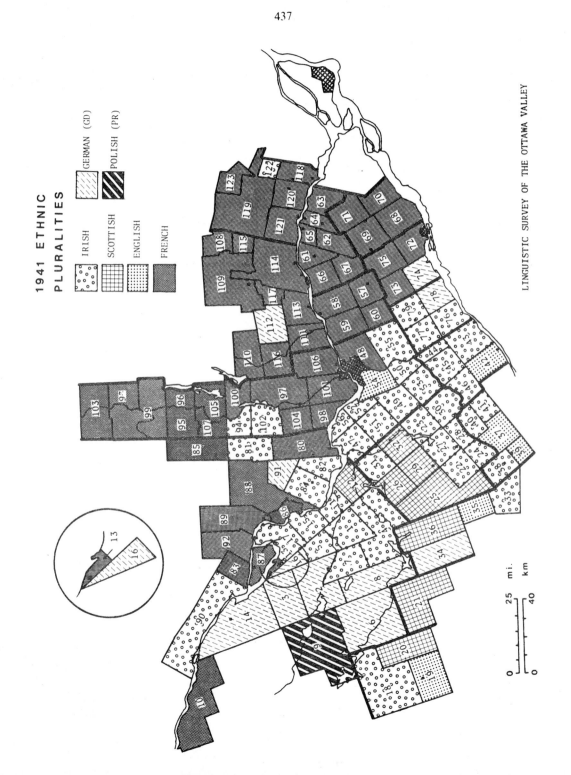

1941 ETHNIC
PLURALITIES

IRISH

SCOTTISH

ENGLISH

FRENCH

GERMAN (GD)

POLISH (PR)

LINGUISTIC SURVEY OF THE OTTAWA VALLEY

MAP 4

mi.

km

25

40

0

0

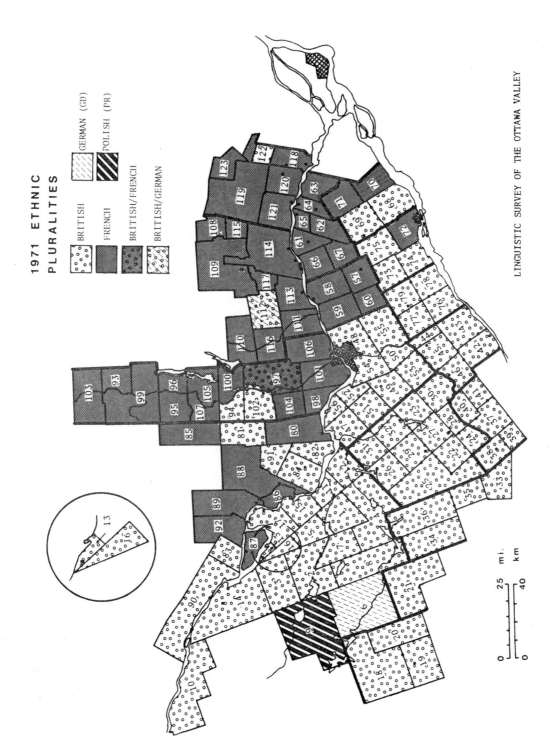

1971 ETHNIC
PLURALITIES

BRITISH

FRENCH

BRITISH/FRENCH

BRITISH/GERMAN

GERMAN (GD)

POLISH (PR)

LINGUISTIC SURVEY OF THE OTTAWA VALLEY

MAP 5

25 mi.

0

40

0

km

441

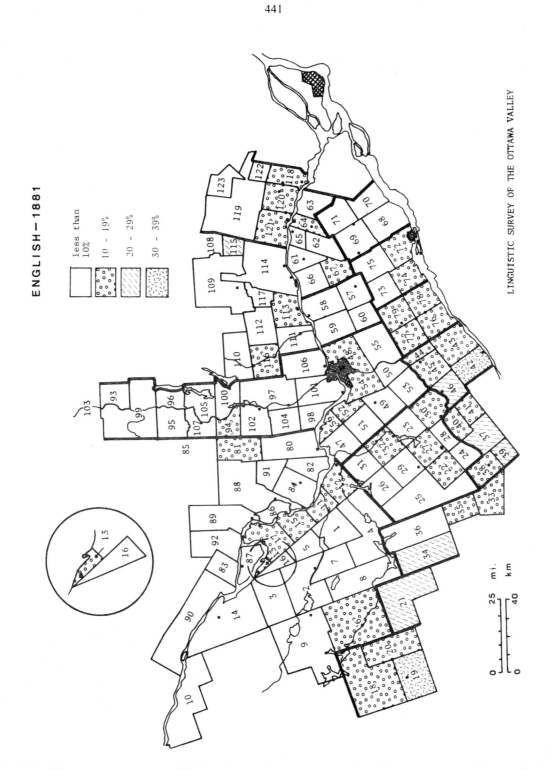

ENGLISH—1881

less than 10%

10 - 19%

20 - 29%

30 - 39%

LINGUISTIC SURVEY OF THE OTTAWA VALLEY

MAP 6

25 mi.

40 km

443

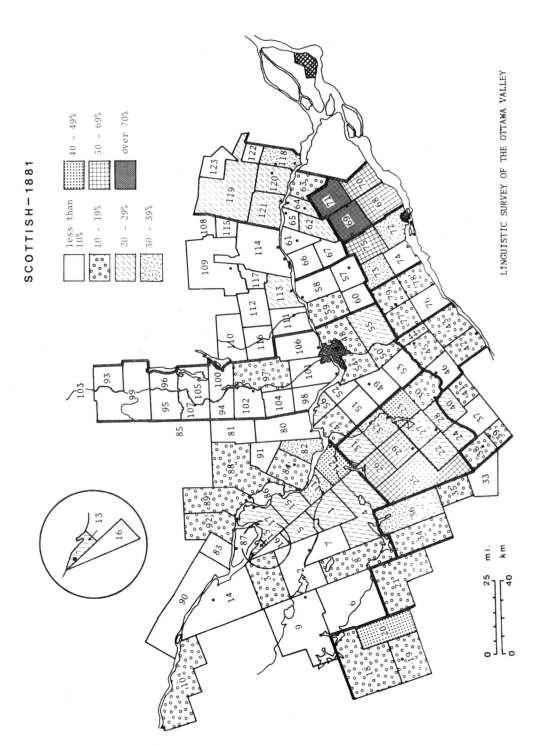

SCOTTISH—1881

less than 10%
10 - 19%
20 - 29%
30 - 39%
40 - 49%
50 - 69%
over 70%

LINGUISTIC SURVEY OF THE OTTAWA VALLEY

MAP 7

25 mi.
40 km

445

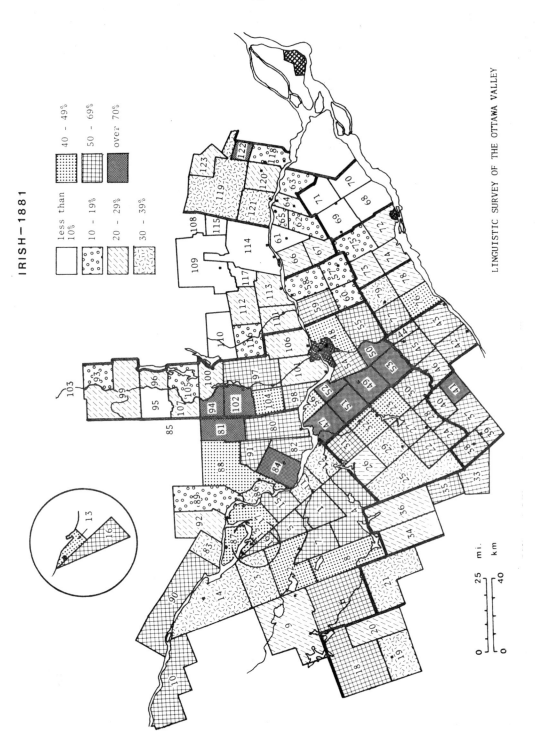

IRISH—1881

less than 10%

10 – 19%

20 – 29%

30 – 39%

40 – 49%

50 – 69%

over 70%

LINGUISTIC SURVEY OF THE OTTAWA VALLEY

MAP 8

25 mi.

40 km

0

0

447

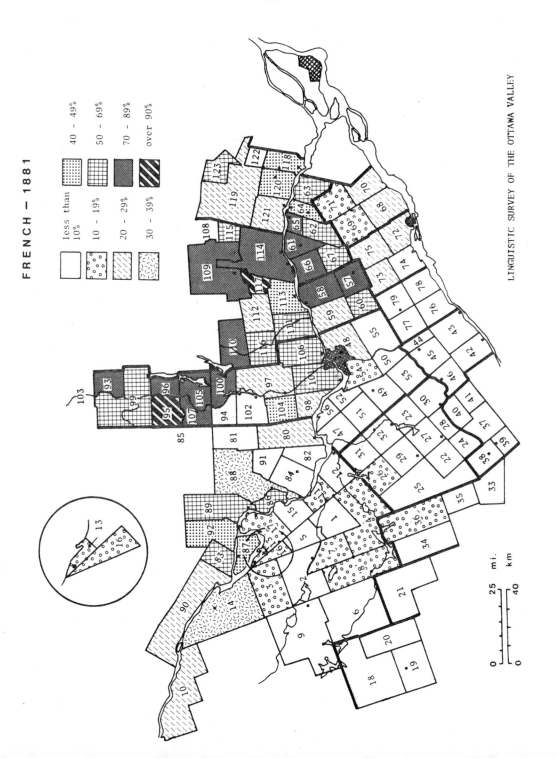

FRENCH – 1881

less than 10%
10 – 19%
20 – 29%
30 – 39%
40 – 49%
50 – 69%
70 – 89%
over 90%

LINGUISTIC SURVEY OF THE OTTAWA VALLEY

MAP 9

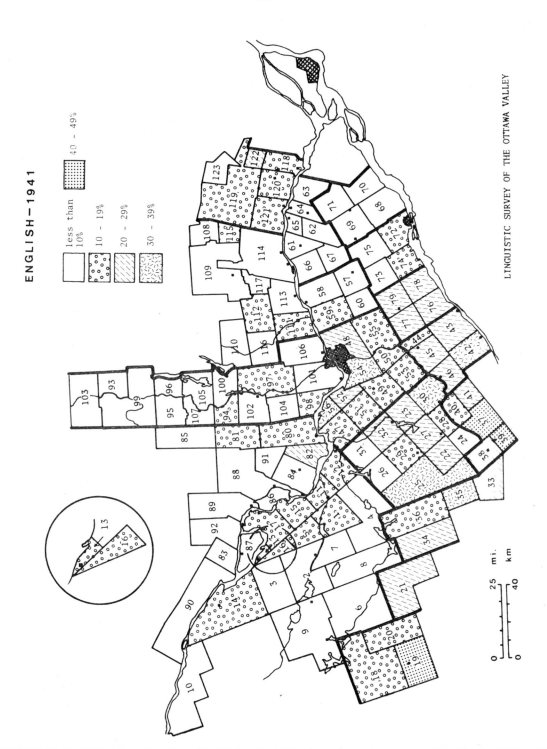

ENGLISH—1941

less than 10%

10 - 19%

20 - 29%

30 - 39%

40 - 49%

LINGUISTIC SURVEY OF THE OTTAWA VALLEY

MAP 10

mi.

km

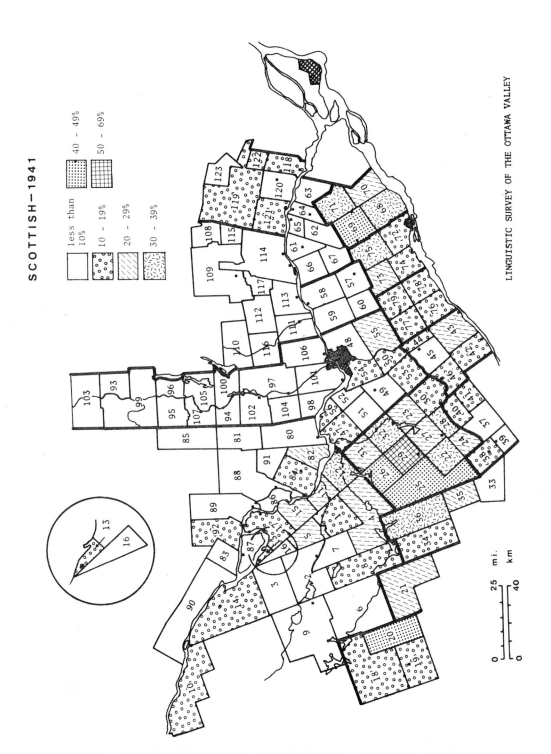

SCOTTISH—1941

less than 10%	40 - 49%
10 - 19%	50 - 69%
20 - 29%	
30 - 39%	

LINGUISTIC SURVEY OF THE OTTAWA VALLEY

MAP 11

mi.
km

0 25

0 40

453

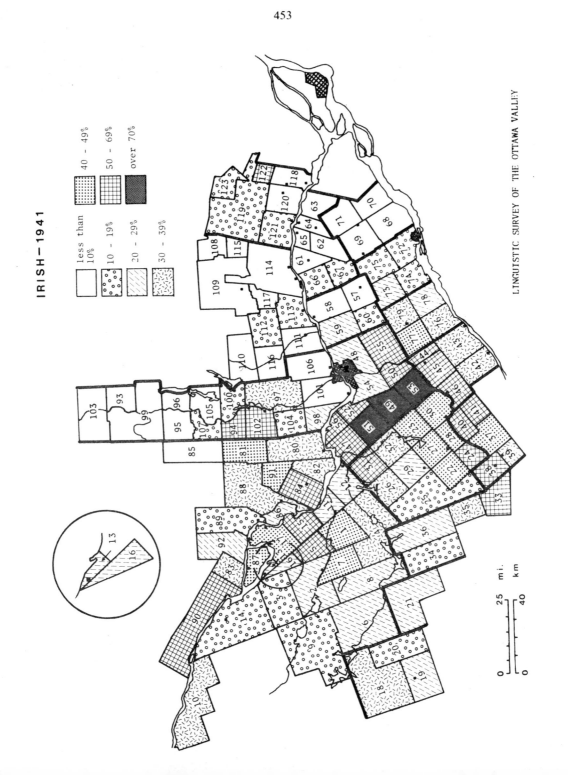

IRISH—1941

less than 10%

10 – 19%

20 – 29%

30 – 39%

40 – 49%

50 – 69%

over 70%

LINGUISTIC SURVEY OF THE OTTAWA VALLEY

MAP 12

455

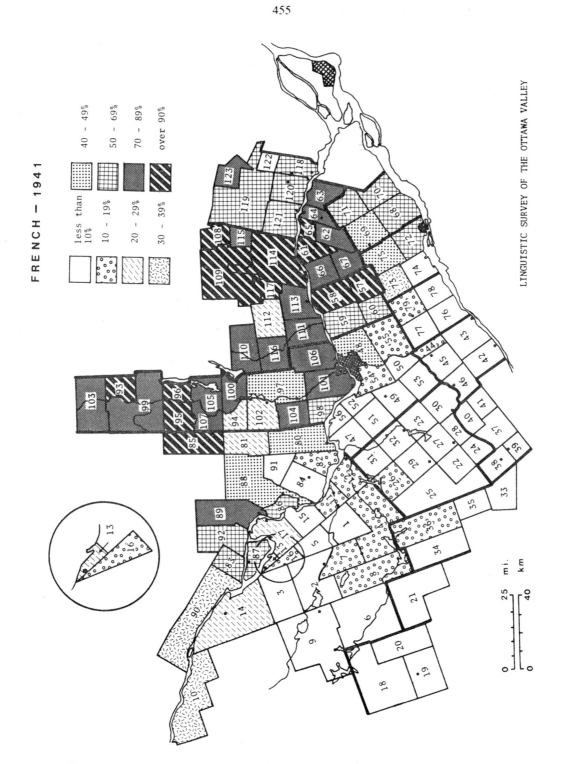

FRENCH — 1941

less than 10%

10 – 19%

20 – 29%

30 – 39%

40 – 49%

50 – 69%

70 – 89%

over 90%

LINGUISTIC SURVEY OF THE OTTAWA VALLEY

MAP 13

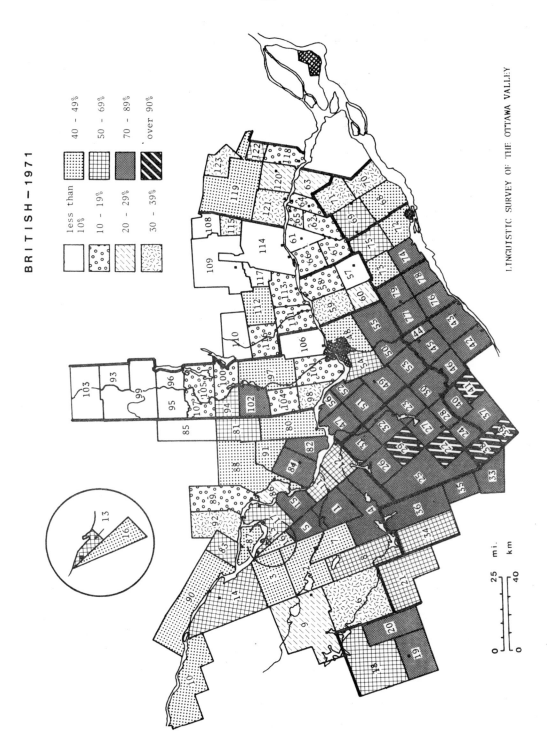

457

BRITISH-1971

less than 10%		40 - 49%
10 - 19%		50 - 69%
20 - 29%		70 - 89%
30 - 39%		over 90%

LINGUISTIC SURVEY OF THE OTTAWA VALLEY

MAP 14

25 mi.

40 km

459

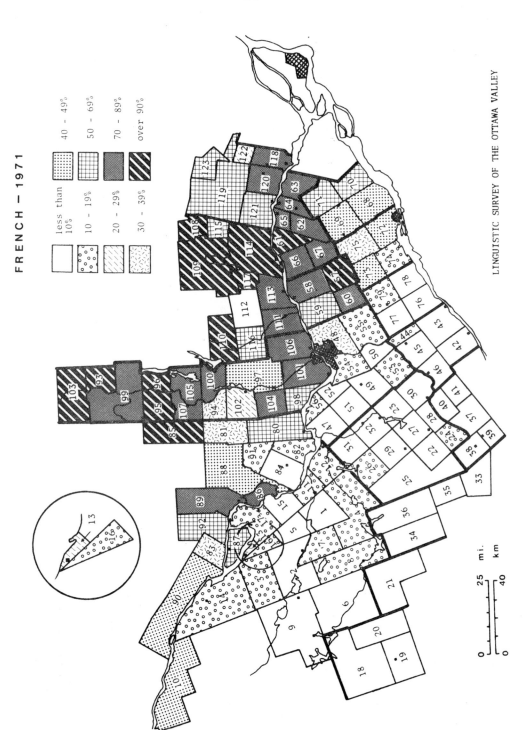

FRENCH – 1971

less than 10%
10 – 19%
20 – 29%
30 – 39%
40 – 49%
50 – 69%
70 – 89%
over 90%

LINGUISTIC SURVEY OF THE OTTAWA VALLEY

MAP 15

25 mi.

40 km

0

461

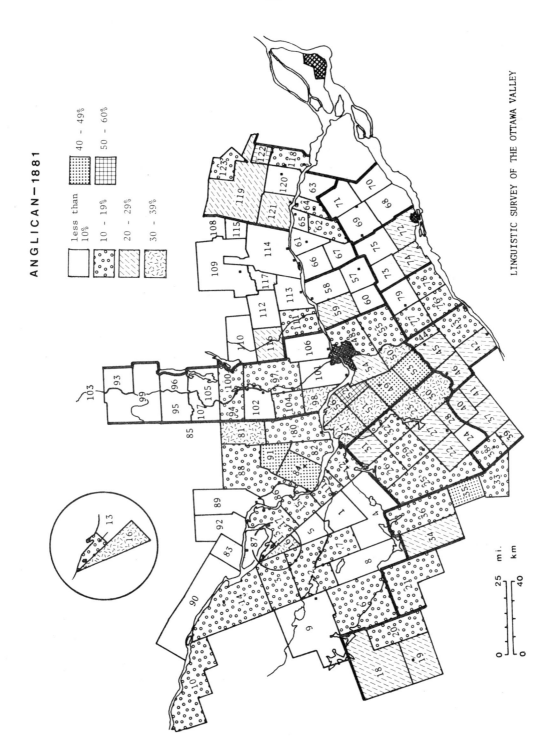

ANGLICAN—1881

less than 10%
10 - 19%
20 - 29%
30 - 39%
40 - 49%
50 - 60%

LINGUISTIC SURVEY OF THE OTTAWA VALLEY

MAP 16

25 mi.
40 km

463

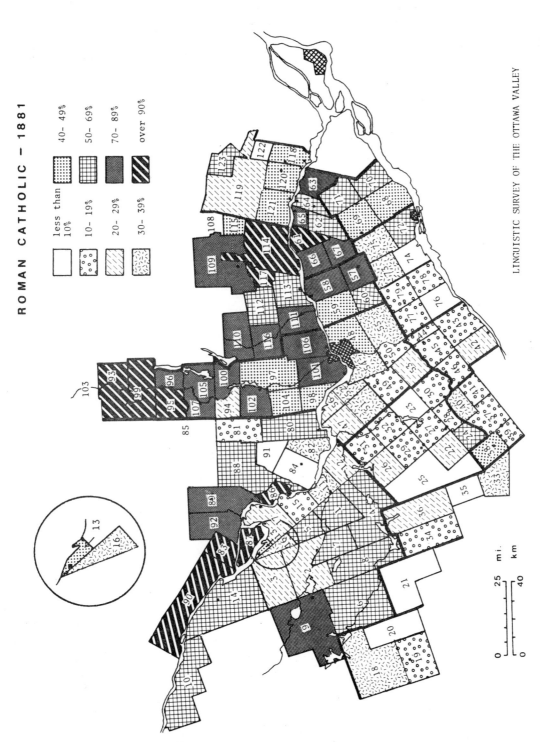

ROMAN CATHOLIC – 1881

less than 10%   40- 49%

10- 19%   50- 69%

20- 29%   70- 89%

30- 39%   over 90%

LINGUISTIC SURVEY OF THE OTTAWA VALLEY

MAP 17

465

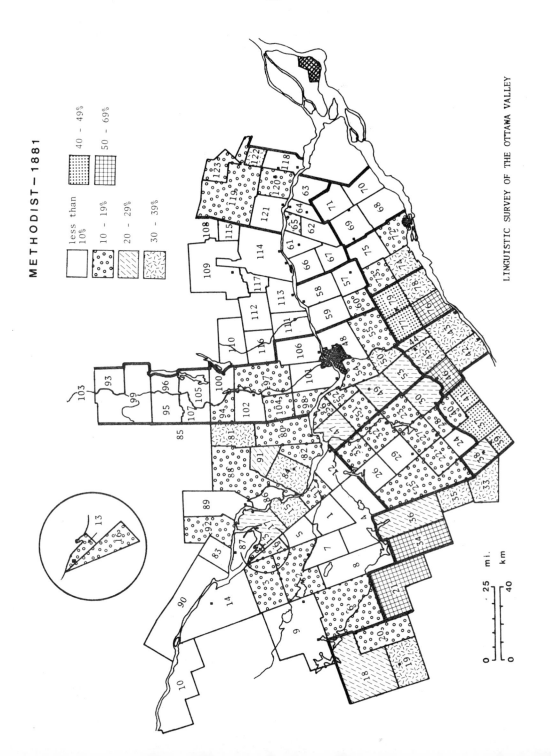

METHODIST—1881

less than 10%

10 - 19%

20 - 29%

30 - 39%

40 - 49%

50 - 69%

LINGUISTIC SURVEY OF THE OTTAWA VALLEY

MAP 18

25 mi.

40 km

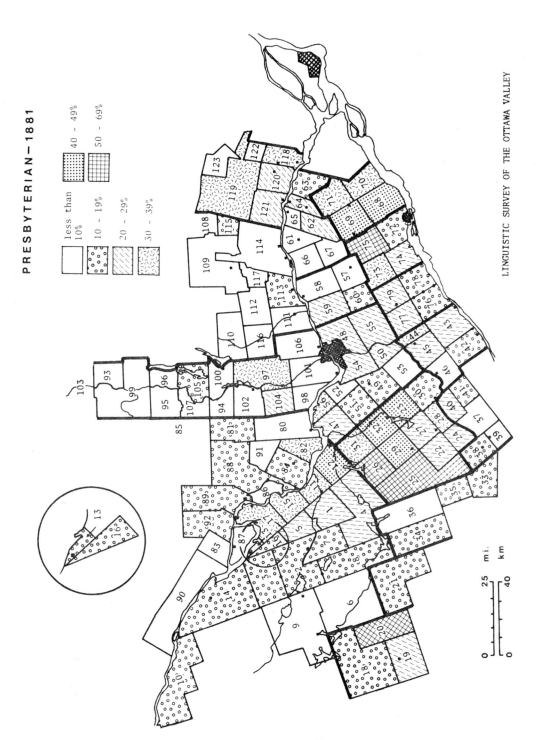

PRESBYTERIAN—1881

less than 10%

10 – 19%

20 – 29%

30 – 39%

40 – 49%

50 – 69%

LINGUISTIC SURVEY OF THE OTTAWA VALLEY

MAP 19

469

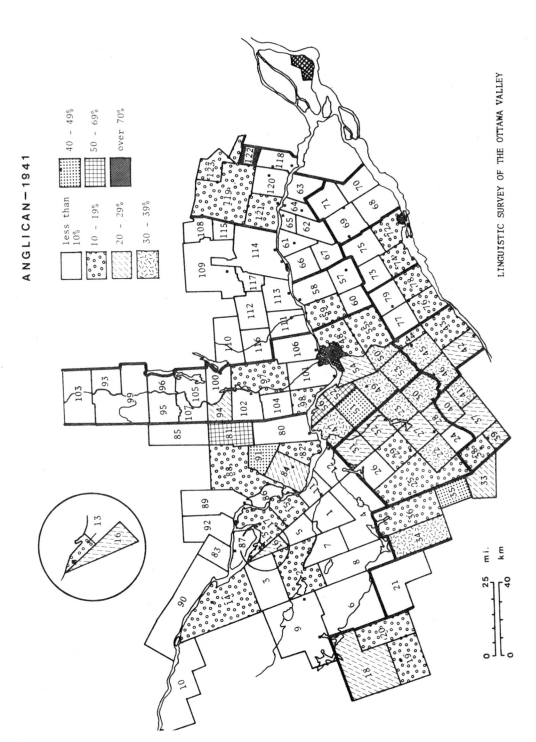

ANGLICAN — 1941

less than 10%
10 - 19%
20 - 29%
30 - 39%
40 - 49%
50 - 69%
over 70%

LINGUISTIC SURVEY OF THE OTTAWA VALLEY

MAP 20

mi.
25
km
40
0

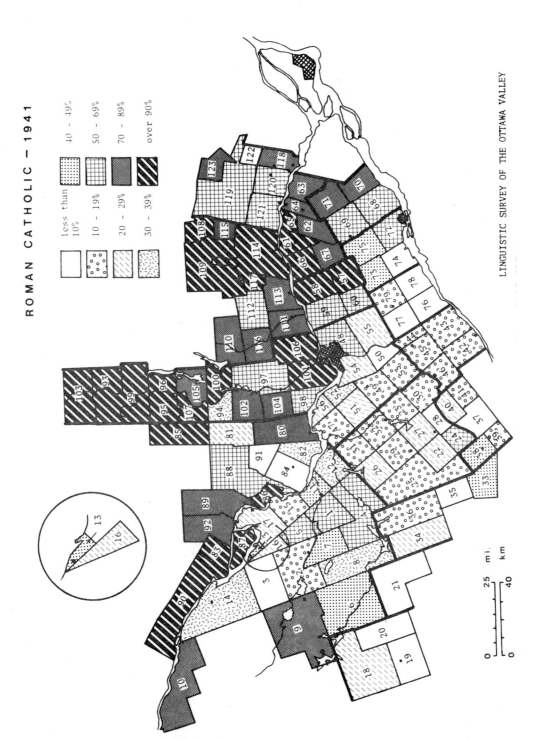

ROMAN CATHOLIC — 1941

less than 10%

10 - 19%

20 - 29%

30 - 39%

40 - 49%

50 - 69%

70 - 89%

over 90%

LINGUISTIC SURVEY OF THE OTTAWA VALLEY

MAP 21

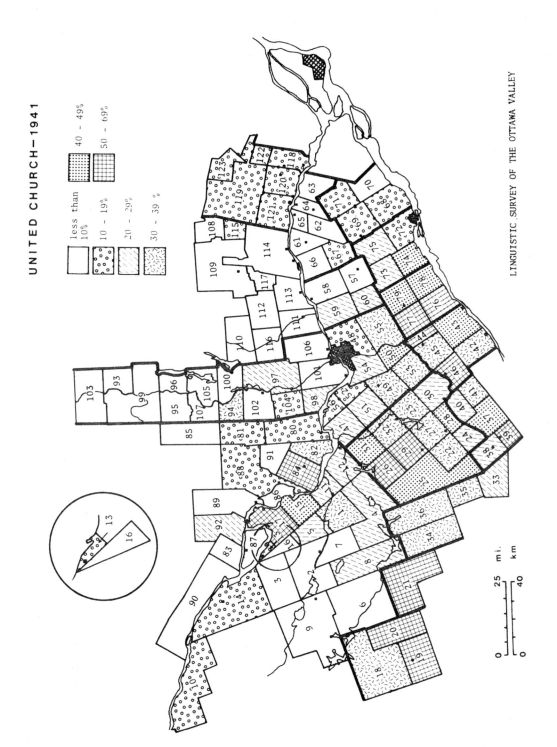

UNITED CHURCH—1941

less than 10%

10 - 19%

20 - 29%

30 - 39%

40 - 49%

50 - 69%

LINGUISTIC SURVEY OF THE OTTAWA VALLEY

MAP 22

25 mi.

40 km

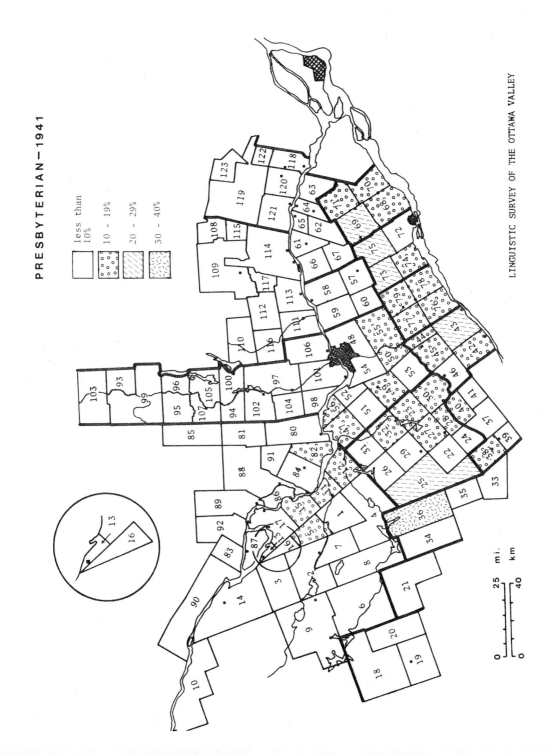

PRESBYTERIAN—1941

less than 10%

10 - 19%

20 - 29%

30 - 40%

LINGUISTIC SURVEY OF THE OTTAWA VALLEY

MAP 23

THE OTTAWA VALLEY:
AN ANNOTATED BIBLIOGRAPHY

A.   BIBLIOGRAPHIES

1.   Aitken, Barbara B., ed. *Local Histories of Ontario Municipalities, 1951-1977: A Bibliography*. Toronto: Ontario Library Association, 1978.

2.   Brault, Lucien. "Bibliographie d'Ottawa," *Revue de l'Université d'Ottawa* 24, no. 3 (juillet-septembre), 1954.

2b.   Emard, M. "Bibliographie des Comtés-Unis de Prescott-Russell, Ontario," *Ontario History* 72 (March 1980), pp. 49-55.

3.   Morley, William F.E., ed. *Canadian Local Histories to 1950: A Bibliography*. vol. III: *Ontario and the Canadian North*. Toronto: The University of Toronto Press, 1978.

4.   National Capital Commission, *History and Heritage Bibliography: National Capital Region* (revised edition). Ottawa: The National Capital Commission, 1978.

4b.   *Ontario since 1867: A Bibliography*. Toronto: Ontario Historical Studies Series, 1973.

5.   St-Amour, Jean-Pierre. *L'Outaouais québécois*. Quebec City: University of Quebec, 1978.

6.   Thibault, Claude, ed. *Bibliographia Canadiana*. Don Mills: Longman Canada, 1973.

B.   GENERAL SOURCES

7.   Adams, W.F. *Ireland and Irish Emigration to the New World*. New Haven: Yale University Press, 1932.

8.   Berry, B.J.L. "Identification of Declining Regions: An Empirical Study of the Dimensions of Rural Poverty," in W.D. Wood and R.S. Thoman, eds. *Areas of Economic Stress in Canada*. Kingston: Queen's University Industrial Relations Centre, 1965.
      - A sophisticated, highly quantitative study of relative rural poverty.

9.   Blake, V.B. and Ralph Greenhill. *Rural Ontario*. Toronto: The University of Toronto Press, 1969.
      - A study of Ontario architecture.

10.   Blanchard, R. *Le Canada Français: Province de Québec*. Paris: Fayard Press, 1960.

11.   Bouchette, J.A. *A Topographical Description of Lower Canada*. London: Longman, Rees, Orme, Brown, Green, 1832.

11b. Brown R. *Ghost Towns of Ontario*. Langley, B.C.: Stagecoach Publishing Co., 1978.

12.   Burnet, Jean R. *Ethnic Groups in Upper Canada*. Toronto: Ontario Historical

Society, 1972.
- General discussion of social attitudes of ethnic groups. Little on immigration and settlement of these groups, or regional variations. Emphasis on social development.

13. Burt, A.L. *The Old Province of Quebec.* 2 vols. Toronto: McClelland and Stewart, 1968.

14. Calvin, D.D. *A Saga of the St. Lawrence: Timber and Shipping Through Three Generations.* Toronto: The Ryerson Press, 1945.

15. Campbell, Wilfred. *The Scotsman in Canada.* vol. I: *Eastern Canada.* Toronto: The Musson Book Co., 1911.

16. Caniff, William. *The Settlement of Upper Canada.* (with a new introduction by Donald Swainson). Belleville: Mika Silk Screening, 1971. (Originally published Toronto: Dudley and Burns, 1869.)
- Focus on the Bay of Quinte area.

17. Careless, J.M.S. *The Union of the Canadas: The Growth of Canadian Institutions, 1841-1857.* Toronto: McClelland and Stewart, 1967.

18. Carruthers, George. *Paper in the Making.* Toronto: The Garden City Press Co-operative, 1947.
- A useful study of the evolution of paper-making and a description of Canadian paper mills.

19. Chapman, L.J. and D.F. Putman. *The Physiography of Southern Ontario.* Toronto: The University of Toronto Press, 1951.
- A geographical study.

20. Charbonneau, R. *Historical Changes in the Organization of Local Municipalities of Quebec.* Ottawa: Dominion Bureau of Statistics, n.d.

21. Clark, S.D. *The Developing Canadian Community.* Toronto: The University of Toronto Press, 1971.
- Chapter on the backwoods society of Upper Canada.

22. Clarke, J. and P.K. MacLeod. "Concentration of Scots in Rural Southern Ontario, 1851-1901," in *The Canadian Cartographer*, 11 (Dec. 1974), pp. 107-113.
- Based on MacLeod's thesis (item 287). Use of the location quotient to suggest a westward movement of Scots out of the Ottawa Valley.

23. Cowan, Helen I. *British Emigration to British North America: The First Hundred Years.* Toronto: The University of Toronto Press, 1961.
- Good examination of the immigration and settlement of Upper Canada. Focus on the policy of emigration, from the British point of view. Some regional limitations as well.

24. Craig, G.M. *Upper Canada: The Formative Years, 1784-1841.* Toronto: McClelland and Stewart, 1963.

25. Currie, A.W. *The Grand Trunk Railway of Canada.* Toronto: The University of Toronto Press, 1957.
- A good railway biography. Little on the Ottawa Valley.

26. Dales, J.H. *Hydroelectricity and Industrial Development in Quebec, 1898-1940.* Cambridge: Harvard University Press, 1957.
- Emphasis upon theory and the development of certain companies. Not a useful source for local historical aspects.

27. Davin, Nicholas Flood. *The Irishman in Canada.* Toronto: Maclean and Co., 1877.
- Discussion of Canadian history, with emphasis placed on the role of Irishmen.

28. Dean, W.G., ed. *Economic Atlas of Ontario.* Toronto: University of Toronto Press, 1969.
- A useful source, with maps illustrating factors from educational attainment to dairy revenue. Many maps broken down to the township level (based on 1961 census, but some change over time shown).

29. Donaldson, Gordon. *The Scots Overseas.* London: Robert Hale, 1966.

30. Dufresne, A.O., B.T. Denis and P.E. Bourrett, articles in *Canadian Mining Journal*, vol. 69 (Oct. 1948).
- Articles on mining in Quebec. Conclusions that there are several mineral deposits, but few have been mined for an extended period.

31. Duncan, Kenneth. "Irish Famine Immigration and the Social Structure of Canada West," in M. Horn and R. Sabourin, eds. *Studies in Canadian Social History*. Toronto: McClelland and Stewart, 1974, pp. 140-163.
- Little on the Ottawa Valley specifically. A qualitative study of Irish immigration.

32. Easterbrook, W.T. and Hugh G.J. Aitken. *Canadian Economic History.* Toronto: Macmillan of Canada, 1975.
- Good general study.

33. Forsey, E. "The Pulp and Paper Industry," in *Canadian Journal of Economics and Political Science*, I (1935), pp. 501-509.
- Problems faced by the pulp and paper industry in the 1930's.

34. Fraser, Alexander. *A History of Ontario: Its Resources and Development.* Toronto: The Canada History Co., 1907.

35. Garon, J.E. *Historique de la colonisation dans la province de Québec de 1825 à 1940.* Quebec City: Quebec Ministry of Colonisation, 1940.

36. Gates, Lillian. *Land Policies of Upper Canada.* Toronto: The University of Toronto Press, 1968.
- A traditional approach to the problem.

37. Gentilcore, R.L., ed. *Ontario.* Toronto: The University of Toronto Press, 1972.
- A collection of geography essays. Essay on settlement most useful for the purposes of the project.

38. Gilmour, James. *Spatial Evolution of Manufacturing: Ontario 1851-1891.* Toronto: University of Toronto Press, 1972.
- Concern with the theoretical framework. Shows that manufacturing in Eastern Ontario declined relative to the rest of the province.

39.   Glazebrook, G.P. de T. *Life in Ontario: A Social History*. Toronto: The University of Toronto Press, 1971.
       - A general social history of Ontario.

40.   Greenhill, Ralph, et al. *Ontario Towns*. Ottawa: Oberon Press, 1974.
       - Ontario architecture.

41.   Guillet, E.C. *Early Life in Upper Canada*. Toronto: The University of Toronto Press, 1963.

42.   Guillet, E.C. *The Great Migration: The Atlantic Crossing by Sailing Ship since 1770*. Toronto: Thomas Nelson and Sons, 1937.

43.   Guillet, E.C. *Pioneer Days in Upper Canada*. Toronto: The University of Toronto Press, 1964.

44.   Guillet, E.C. *Pioneer Settlements in Upper Canada*. Toronto: The University of Toronto Press, 1969.

45.   Hamelin, J. and L. Roby. *Histoire économique du Québec, 1851-1896*. Montreal: Fides, 1971.
       - An excellent economic history, but little on the Ottawa Valley.

46.   Hanks, Carole. *Early Ontario Gravestones*. Toronto: McGraw-Hill, Ryerson, 1974.

47.   Hansen, Marcus Lee and J.B. Brebner. *The Mingling of the Canadian and American Peoples*. New York: Russell and Russell, 1970.

48.   Harris, R.C. and John Warkentin. *Canada Before Confederation*. Toronto: Oxford University Press, 1974.
       - A general historical geography of pre-Confederation Canada.

49.   Hill, Douglas. *The Scots to Canada*. London: Gentry Books, 1972.
       - Broad examination of the Scottish emigrations to British North America. Some detail on the Ottawa Valley area.

50.   Hills, T.L. *The St. Lawrence Seaway*. New York: Frederick A. Praeger, 1960.

51.   Hodgins, Bruce W. *John Sandfield Macdonald*. Toronto: The University of Toronto Press, 1971.

52.   Houston, C. and W.J. Smyth. *The Orange Order in Nineteenth Century Ontario: A Study of Institutional Cultural Transfer*. Toronto: Dept. of Geography, University of Toronto, 1977.
       - Emphasizes the value of Orange lodges in the acculturation of immigrants. Map of lodges.

53.   Hughson, J.W. and C.C.J. Bond. *Hurling Down the Pine*. 2nd edition. Old Chelsea: n.p., 1965.
       - Discusses the timber companies in the Ottawa-Gatineau region. A romantic study, poorly organized.

53b.   Hundey, I., and L. Milberry. *Canada: Part One: Immigrants and Settlers*. Toronto: Macmillan, 1979.

54.   Johnson, J.K., ed. *Historical Essays on Upper Canada*. Toronto: McClelland

and Stewart, 1975.

55. Johnson, Leo A. *History of the County of Ontario, 1615-1875.* Whitby: The Corporation of the County of Ontario, 1973.
   - Best county history produced in Ontario.

56. Johnson, Stanley C. *Emigration from the United Kingdom to North America.* London: George Routledge and Sons, 1913. [reprinted London: Frank Cass Co., 1966.]

57. Jones, Robert Leslie. *History of Agriculture in Ontario, 1613-1880.* Toronto: The University of Toronto Press, 1977.
   - Best study of agriculture in Ontario. Chapters on agriculture and lumbering in the Ottawa Valley.

58. Lamb, W. Kaye. *History of the Canadian Pacific Railway.* New York: Macmillan, 1977.
   - Some information on the CPR's acqustion of local lines in the Ottawa Valley.

59. Langman, R.C. *Patterns of Settlement in Southern Ontario.* Toronto: McClelland and Stewart, 1971.
   - A problem studies text book. Good maps. Case study of Bancroft.

60. Langman, R.C. *Poverty Pockets: A Study of the Limestone Plains of Southern Ontario.* Toronto: McClelland and Stewart, 1975.
   - A text book. Useful charts on farming.

61. Letarte, J. *Atlas d'histoire économique et sociale du Québec, 1851-1901.* Montreal: Fides, 1971.
   - Companion to Hamelin and Roby (item 45).

62. Lewis, H.H. "Population of Quebec Province," in *Economic Geography,* 16 (1940), pp. 59-68.

63. Lower, A.R.M. *Great Britain's Woodyard: British America and the Timber Trade, 1763-1867.* Montreal: McGill-Queen's University Press, 1973.
   - Companion to *The North American Assault on the Canadian Forest*, emphasizing trade with Britain. Minimizes the social disruptiveness of the forest industry. Cf. Cross thesis (item 274).

64. Lower, A.R.M. *The North American Assault on the Canadian Forest: A History of the Lumber Trade Between Canada and the United States.* Toronto: The Ryerson Press, 1938.
   - Emphasis upon Canadian-American trade. Valuable for general information; good on the Ottawa Valley.

65. Lower, A.R.M. *Settlement and the Forest Frontier in Eastern Canada.* Toronto: The Macmillan Co. of Canada, 1936.
   - Deals with generalities.

66. Macdonald, Norman. *Canada, 1763-1841: Immigration and Settlement.* London: Longmans, Green and Co., 1939.
   - Useful study of the British immigration to Canada. Emphasis upon administration of land regulation because it determined the direction and extent

of settlement.

67.   Macdonald, Norman. *Canada: Immigration and Colonization, 1841-1903.* Toronto: Macmillan of Canada, 1968.

68.   Macleod, Betty, et. al. *Patterns and Trends in Ontario Population: An Ontario Population Report.* Toronto: The Ontario Institute for Studies in Education, 1972.
       - A quantitative study of population patterns in Ontario since 1950.

69.   MacRae, Marion. *The Ancestral Roof: Domestic Architecture in Upper Canada.* Toronto: Macmillan of Canada, 1963.

69b.   Makowski, W. *History and Integration of the Poles in Canada.* Niagara Peninsula: Canadian Polish Congress, 1967.

70.   Mannion, John J. *Irish Settlements in Eastern Canada: A Study of Culture Transfer and Adaptation.* Toronto: The University of Toronto Press, 1974.
       - Nothing on the Ottawa Valley.

71.   Middleton, J.E. and Fred Landon. *The Province of Ontario: A History, 1615-1927.* 4 vols. Toronto: The Dominion Publishing Co., 1927.
       - Essentially a political history.

72.   Mills, Edward. *Early Settlement in Ontario.* Parks Canada Report No. 182 (RG 84, vol. 473).
       - Study organized by ethnic group; eg. "German Settlement".

73.   Murray, Florence B. "Agricultural Settlement on the Canadian Shield: Ottawa River to Georgian Bay," in Ontario Historical Society, *Profiles of a Province.* Toronto: Ontario Historical Society, 1967, pp. 178-186.

74.   Nelles, H.V. *The Politics of Development: Forests, Mines, and Hydro-electric Power in Ontario, 1849-1941.* Toronto: Macmillan of Canada, 1975.
       - An excellent study of the relationship between resource development and politics in Ontario.

75.   Ouellet, Fernand. *Le Bas Canada, 1791-1840.* Ottawa: Editions de l'Université d'Ottawa, 1976.

76.   Ouellet, Fernand. *Histoire économique et sociale du Québec, 1760-1850: structures et conjuncture.* Montreal: Fides, 1966.

77.   Paterson, Gilbert C. *Land Settlement in Upper Canada, 1783-1840.* A Report for the Ontario Department of Public Records and Archives for 1920. (Toronto, 1921).
       - An institutional history.

78.   Radecki, H. and B. Heydenkorn. *A Member of a Distinguished Family: The Polish Group in Canada.* Toronto: McClelland and Stewart, 1976.
       - Part of a series dealing with ethnic groups. Focus on Poles in general, rather than specific communities.

79.   Rea, J.E. *Bishop Alexander Macdonnell and the Politics of Upper Canada.* Toronto: The Ontario Historical Society, 1974.

80.   Reaman, G. Elmore. *The Trail of the Black Walnut.* Toronto: McClelland and

Stewart, 1957.
- Examines German settlements in Ontario.

81.   Regehr, T.D. *The Canadian Northern Railway.* Toronto: Macmillan of Canada, 1976.
- Some discussion of branch lines in the Ottawa Valley.

82.   Reid, W. Stanford, ed. *The Scottish Tradition in Canada.* Toronto: McClelland and Stewart, 1977. [published in association with the Multiculturalism Program.]
- Synthesis of previous studies on Scottish settlement in the Ottawa Valley. Articles written by historians, sociologists.

83.   Roy, James A. *The Scot and Canada.* Toronto: McClelland and Stewart, 1947.

84.   Shortt, Adam and A.G. Doughty, eds. *Canada and its Provinces.* vol. 15: *Quebec.* Toronto: Glasgow, Brook and Co., 1914.
- Focus on Montreal and the Eastern Townships. Little on the Ottawa Valley.

85.   Shortt, Adam and A.G. Doughty, eds. *Canada and its Provinces.* vol. 17: *Ontario.* Toronto: Glasgow, Brook and Co., 1914.

86.   Smith, W.H. *Canada: Past, Present and Future ...* Toronto: Thomas Maclear, 1851.
- The book was prepared as a guide for settlers. It provides a picture of Upper Canada in 1850 - the population trends, nature of settlement, economic development, etc. of each county.

87.   Smyth, William J. "The Irish in Mid Nineteenth Century Ontario," in *Ulster Folklife,* 23 (1977), pp. 97-105.
- Discusses the impact of the massive Irish immigration in the 1840's on the social structure of Ontario.

88.   Symington, D.F. "Poverty in Rural Canada," in *Canadian Geographical Journal* 75 (Dec. 1967), pp. 188-197.
- General.

89.   Toye, William. *The St. Lawrence.* New York: Henry Z. Walck, 1959.

90.   Warkentin, John, ed. *Canada: A Geographical Interpretation.* Toronto: Methuen, 1970.
- A general study.

91.   Weaver, Emily P. *The Story of the Counties of Ontario.* Toronto: Bell and Cockburn, 1913.

92.   Wood, J. David. ed. *Perspectives on Landscape and Settlement in Nineteenth Century Ontario.* Toronto: McClelland and Stewart, 1975.

93.   Wood, William. *The Storied Province of Quebec: Past and Present.* vol. II. Toronto: The Dominion Publishing Co., 1931.
- Some information on Argenteuil and Papineau Counties. One of 5 volumes.

94.   Zaslow, M. *The Opening of the Canadian North, 1870-1914.* Toronto: McClelland and Stewart, 1971.
- Academic treatment of the North.

C.   THE OTTAWA VALLEY

I.   BOOKS AND MONOGRAPHS

95.   Aldred, D. *Aylmer, Quebec: Its Heritage.* Aylmer, Aylmer Heritage Association, 1978.
        - A useful source.

96.   Argue, Anne, et al. *Beginnings: A Brief History of Huntley Township, 1819-1930.* Carleton Place: A and B Graphics, 1974.
        - An OFY project, this discusses areas of settlement in Huntley. It utilizes census material, personal interviews, and other available sources, and confirms other examinations of the area.

96b.   Armstrong, C.A. *Away Back in Clarendon and Miller.* N.p.: North Frontenac Press Service, 1976.

96c.   Arnprior Centennial Publications Committee. *Arnprior Centennial, 1862-1962, July 8-14, 1962. Official Programme.* Arnprior: Arnprior Publications Committee, 1962.

97.   (de Barbezieux), Père Alexis. *Histoire de la province ecclésiastique d'Ottawa et de la colonisation dans la vallée de l'Ottawa.* 2 vols. Ottawa: La Cie d'Imprimerie d'Ottawa, 1897.
        - A general ecclesiastical history.

98.   Baskin, Mrs. Alex and Mrs. Gerald Wilson. *The Story of Torbolton Township.* Torbolton Twp.: Centennial Committee, 1967.
        - A local history compiled by non-academic historians; focus upon early settlers, prominent citizens, and local institutions such as churches.

99.   Belden, H. and Co. *Historical Sketch of Carleton County.* (Toronto, 1879). Reprinted, with a new introduction by C.C.J. Bond. Belleville: Mika Silk Screening, 1971.
        - A geographic description of the county in 1879; also a compilation of population figures and important persons.

100.   Belden, H. and Co. *Illustrated Historical Atlas of Carleton County.* (Toronto, 1879). Reprinted by Ross Cumming, editor. Owen Sound: Richardson, Bond and Wright, 1971.

101.   Belden, H. and Co. *Illustrated Historical Atlas of the Counties of Frontenac, Lennox and Addington.* (Toronto, 1878). Reprinted Belleville: Mika Silk Screening, 1971.

102.   Belden, H. and Co. *Illustrated Historical Atlas of Hastings and Prince Edward Counties, Ontario.* (Toronto, 1878). Reprinted Belleville: Mika Silk Screening, 1972.

103.   Belden, H. and Co. *Illustrated Historical Atlas of Lanark County, ... and Renfrew County.* (Toronto, 1880). Reprinted by Ross Cumming, Port Elgin. Owen Sound: Richardson, Bond and Wright, 1972.

104.   Belden, H. and Co. *Illustrated Historical Atlas of Stormont, Dundas and Glengarry Counties.* (Toronto, 1879). Reprinted Belleville: Mika Silk Screening, 1972.

105.   Bennett, Mrs. C.C. *Beckwith Township*. n.p., 1973.

106.   Blanchard, Raoul. *L'Ouest du Canada français: Province de Québec*. vol. 2. Montreal: Beauchemin, 1954.
        - A very good historical geography of the Quebec side of the Ottawa Valley, this discusses immigration and settlement patterns, economic development and industrial change, and so forth.

107.   Bond, C.C.J. *The Ottawa County*. Ottawa: The Queen's Printer, 1968.
        - This discusses the historical development of the National Capital Region. It examines settlement of the area, and its administration and economic development.

108.   Boyce, Gerald E. *Historic Hastings*. Belleville: Hastings County Council, 1967.
        - This emphasizes the southern townships. There is some useful information on settlement.

109.   Brault, Lucien. *Histoire des comtés unis de Prescott et de Russell*. L'Orignal: Conseil des Comtés Unis, 1965.
        - This is a very good history of Prescott and Russell. It discusses administrative and judicial history, politics as well as social and economic development. Adequate local histories are included.

109b.   Brault, L. *Hull 1800-1950*. Ottawa: Editions de l'Université d'Ottawa, 1950.

110.   Brault, Lucien. *Ottawa: Old and New*. Ottawa: Ottawa Historical Information Institute, 1946.

111.   Bretzlaff, J. et al. *Shawville '73*. n.p., 1973.
        - This commemorates Shawville's centennial. A narrative; one of the few sources on Pontiac Co.

112.   Brown, Howard Morton. *Founded Upon a Rock: Carleton Place Recollections*. Carleton Place: 150th Year Festival Committee of Carleton Place, 1969.
        - A local history of the town.

113.   Brown, Jack. *Historical Sketches of Appleton, a Lanark County Village*. Mallorytown: Riverside Press, 1973.
        - A general local history.

114.   Buies, Arthur. *L'Outaouais supérieur*. Quebec: C. Darveau, 1889.
        - A pamphlet favouring French Canadian colonization of the Upper Ottawa Valley.

115.   Burns, A.F. *Bancroft and District Old Home Week, 1961*. Reprinted Lake Ontario Regional Library System, 1976.
        - Useful supplement to other sources.

116.   Burns, Bernard, et al. *March Past*. Kanata: March Township Council, 1972.
        - An OFY project, this examines early settlement and growth. A social history of the township.

117.   Card, D.C. *McClure Heritage*. Picton: Picton Gazette Publishing Co., 1966.
        - Very general.

118. Carsonby Historical Society. *Carsonby: A Community History*. Ottawa: Love Printing Service, 1969.
    - A local history of Carsonby, which focuses upon local families and institutions.

119. Carter, J. Smyth. *The Story of Dundas, being a History of the County of Dundas from 1784 to 1904*. Iroquois: The St. Lawrence News Publishing House, 1905.
    - Based on Croil's book, this brings the political and administrative history to 1904.

120. Centennial Committee of Newboro, Ontario. *The Isthmus: A Historical Sketch of Newboro*. Newboro: n.p. 1967.
    - A local history of Newboro.

121. Chamberland, Abbé Michel. *Histoire de Montebello, 1815-1928*. Montreal: Imprimerie des Sourds-Muets, 1929.
    - A parish history.

122. Chamberland, Abbé Michel. *Histoire de Notre-Dame des Sept-Douleurs de Grenville, P.Q.* Montreal: Imprimerie des Sourds-Muets, 1931.
    - A parish history.

123. *Chapeau Centennial, 1874-1974*. Chapeau: n.p., 1974.
    - Much of the book is taken up by local figures.

123b. Chesterville Women's Institute. *The Time That Was: A History of Chesterville and District*. Chesterville: Chesterville Women's Institute, 1978.

124. Chisamore, Dale, et al. *Brockville: A Social History, 1890-1930*. Brockville: The Waterway Press, 1975.

125. Clarke, A. *A History of Calabogie*. n.p., 1967.
    - A privately published pamphlet; mostly reminiscences.

126. Conwell, James. *Ottawa Valley and Her People*. Toronto: Historical Publishers Association, 1933.

127. Cooper, C.W. *Frontenac, Lennox and Addington*. Kingston: n.p. 1856.

128. Craig, Sarah B. *Hello Nepean*. Ottawa: Mortimer Ltd., 1974.

129. Croil, James. *Dundas; or, A Sketch of Canadian History, and more particularly of the County of Dundas, One of the Earliest Settled Counties in Upper Canada*. Montreal: B. Dawson and Son, 1861.
    - Emphasis on early settlers, and political and judicial history.

130. Dumbrille, Dorothy. *Braggart in my Step: More Stories of Glengarry*. Toronto: The Ryerson Press, 1956.
    - Mostly a series of family narratives and stories of prominent local characters.

131. Dumbrille, Dorothy. *Up and Down the Glens: The Story of Glengarry*. Toronto: The Ryerson Press, 1954.

132. Earle, Evelyn P. *Leeds the Lovely*. Prescott: St. Lawrence Printing CO., 1974.
    - Family narratives.

133. *Early Settlement of Ramsay Township*. (Reprinted from the Almonte Gazette Almanac for 1872). Mallorytown: n.p. 1973.

134.   Eastern Ontario Development Council. *Data Book*. (1971).
         - A booklet designed to attract industry to Eastern Ontario, this consists of industrial information.

135.   Edwardsburg Centennial Committee. *A History of the Township of Edwardsburg*. Spencerville: n.p., 1967.
         - A local history of the township.

136.   Eggleston, Wilfrid. *The Queen's Choice: A Story of Canada's Capital*. Ottawa: The Queen's Printer, 1961.

136b.   Evans, P.M.O. *The Wrights: A Genealogical Study of the First Settlers in Canada's National Capital Region*. Ottawa: National Capital Commission, revised 1978.

137.   Forget, J.U. and Elie J. Auclair. *Histoire de Saint Jacques d'Embrun*. Ottawa: La Cie d'Imprimerie d'Ottawa, 1910.
         - A parish history.

138.   Fraser, Robert J. *As Others See Us: Scots of the Seaway Valley*. Beamsville: The Beamsville Express, 1956.
         - Focus on the settlement of the Fraser Clan in the Seaway Valley.

139.   Gananoque Historical Society. *The Story of Gananoque: Gateway to the 1000 Islands*. Gananoque: n.p., 1970.

139b.   Gard, A.A. *The Pioneers of the Upper Ottawa and the Humors of the Valley*. Ottawa: The Emerson Press, 1906.

140.   Garvey, M. *The History of Killaloe Station*. Killaloe Station: Centennial Committee, 1967.
         - Brief but useful.

141.   Geggie, N. & S. *Lapêche: A History of the Township of Wakefield in the Province of Quebec, 1792-1925*. Lapêche: The Historical Society of the Gatineau, 1974.
         - A short but useful source.

141b.   Gillis, S.J. *The Timber Trade in the Ottawa Valley, 1806-1854*. Ottawa: Parks Canada (Manuscript Report No. 153), 1975.

142   Gourlay, J.L. *History of the Ottawa Valley*. Ottawa: n.p., 1896.
         - A traditional history which offers a goldmine of detailed information on many topics, covering a wide area.

143.   Government of Ontario. Department of Energy and Resources Management. *Mississippi Valley Conservation Report. History*. Toronto: Government of Ontario, 1970.
         - Some social and economic history of the Mississippi Valley.

144.   Graham, Mildred, ed. *Richmond "150": Yesterday and Today, 1818-1968*. Richmond: Love Printing Series, 1968.
         - A narrative of the social and economic development of Richmond.

144b.   Grant, R. *Horse and Buggy Days in Martintown, 1900-1940*. Gardenvale: n.p., 1976.

145.   Gray, Lillian Collier. *Maitland: Seaway Village*. Prescott: The Prescott Journal

(1967?).
- A narrative examining the social and economic development of Maitland.

146.   Greening, W.E. *The Ottawa.* Toronto: McClelland and Stewart, 1961.
- Concern with the settlement and economic development of Ottawa Valley. Focus is the river. Well organized.

147.   Grenville Centennial Committee, *Grenville, 1876-1976.* Grenville: n.p., n.d. (1976).
- A pamphlet done for the town, but containing more on the Chamber of Commerce than on the history of the town.

148.   Haig, Robert. *Ottawa: City of the Big Ears.* [n.p., n.d.].

149.   Hardy, E. "Commissioner's Report: County of Renfrew - City of Pembroke. Restructuring Study." Toronto: Government of Ontario, 1976.
- A study for the regional government containing growth statistics, data on industry, etc.

150.   Harkness, John Graham. *Stormont, Dundas and Glengarry: A History.* Oshawa: Mundy-Goodfellow Printing, 1946.
- The only major history of the 3 counties. The early history is based on Croil; it emphasizes politics, the judiciary and the militia.

151.   Harvey, Anna E. *Lyndhurst: A History.* [n.p., n.d.].

152.   Hawke, H. William. *Historic Gananoque.* Belleville: Mika Publishing, 1974.

153.   Hawkesbury Chamber of Commerce. *Hawkesbury Industrial Survey.* Hawkesbury: Chamber of Commerce, 1957.

154.   Haydon, Andrew. *Pioneer Sketches in the District of Bathurst.* Toronto: The Ryerson Press, 1925.
- A good local history examining important incidents such as Ballyghiblin riots and offering adequate discussion of settlement patterns.

155.   Herrington, W.S. *History of the County of Lennox and Addington.* (1913). Reprinted Belleville: Mika Silk Screening, 1972.
- Little on the northern townships.

156.   Higginson, Miss Maria A. and Mrs. James T. Brock. *The Village of Hawkesbury, 1808-1888: The Era of the Hamilton Brothers.* Hawkesbury: The Ladies Guild of Holy Trinity Church, 1961.
- This pamphlet was a talk to the Hawkesbury Club, based on "notes and memories"; an accurate narrative.

156b. Historical Society of the Gatineau. *Up the Gatineau.* Chelsea: H.S.G., 1975.

157.   *A History of the Founding of the Village of Spencerville, Edwardsburg Township, Ontario.* Prescott: n.p., 1971.

158.   *History of the Rideau Waterway.* Toronto: Department of Energy and Resources Management, Conservation Authorities Branch, 1970.

159.   *Historical Glimpses of Lennox and Addington County.* Lennox and Addington County Council, 1964.

- Little on the northern townships.

159b. Houde, P. *Hull et l'Ouest de Québec*. Montreal: Holt, Rinehart et Winston, 1970.

160. Jamieson, E.L. *The Story of Lanark*. (Reprint of a Historical Souvenir originally published in connection with the centenary of Lanark Village.) n.p., 1974.
   - A narrative concerning the social and economic development of the Lanark area; stresses early settlers, the establishment of churches, etc.

161. Jeacle, Jean C. *To Make a House a Home: The Story of Ingleside, Ontario*. Cornwall: Stormont, Dundas and Glengarry Historical Society, 1975.

162. Keenan, J.W. *Land Use Plan for the Tweed Forest District*. Toronto: Ministry of Natural Resources, 1964.
   - Useful information and maps on agricultural capability of portions of Renfrew, Frontenac, Lanark, Lennox and Addington, and Hastings.

163. Kemptville Centennial Committee. *Historical Review of Kemptville and District*. Smiths Falls; n.p., 1967.

164. Kennedy, Clyde C. *The Upper Ottawa Valley*. Pembroke: Renfrew County Council, 1970.
   - Deals mainly with Renfrew County.

165. Kidd, George Edward. *The Story of the Derry*. Vancouver: n.p., 1943.
   - A good non-academic history examining the development of the community in the Derry.

166. Lajoie, P.G. *Etude Pédologique des Comtés de Hull, Labelle, et Papineau, Québec*. Ottawa: Queen's Printer, 1968.

166b. Lamoureux, G. *Bytown et ses pionniers canadiens-français, 1826-1855*. Ottawa; n.p., 1978.

167. Leavitt, Thaddeus W.H. *History of Leeds and Grenville* (with a new introduction by William F.E. Morley). Originally published in Brockville: Recorder Press, 1879. Republished Belleville: Mika Silk Screening, 1972.
   - A traditional local history, emphasizing biographies of prominent local persons, etc., and containing little social or economic history, but much detailed information.

168. Legget, Robert. *Ottawa Waterway*. Toronto: The University of Toronto Press, 1975.
   - This work focuses upon the Ottawa River, eg. the fur trade. It contains good discussion of settlement in the Valley and is less ancedotal than many histories.

169. Legget, R.L. *Rideau Waterway*. Toronto: The University of Toronto Press, 1955.
   - This book was written for a general audience. Its emphasis is on why the canal was built.

170. Lindsay, Coral. *Kars on the Rideau*. Ottawa: Tweedsmuir History Committee, Kars Branch of the Women's Institute, 1972.
   - A very good history of Kars, this offers substantial analysis of the social and economic development of the area.

171.   Lockwood, G.J.. *Kitley, 1795-1975*. Prescott: St. Lawrence Printing Co., 1974.
       - Discusses prominent families, early churches.

171b. McCallum, J. *Unequal Beginnings: Agriculture and Economic Development in Ontario and Quebec Until 1870*. Toronto: The University of Toronto Press, 1980.

172.   Macdonell, J.A. *Sketches Illustrating the Early Settlement and History of Glengarry in Canada*. Montreal: Wm. Foster, Brown and Co., 1893.
       - Sketches relating principally to the military exploits of the men from Glengarry.

173.   McGiffin, Verna Ross. *Pakenham: Ottawa Valley Village*. Vol. I: *1823-1860*. Pakenham: Mississippi Publishers, 1963. Vol. II: *1860-1900*. Pakenham: Mississippi Publishers, 1967.
       - A good local history, this offers useful analysis of the development of Pakenham.

174.   McGill, Jean S. *A Pioneer History of the County of Lanark*. Toronto: T.H. Best Printing Co., 1969.
       - A good non-academic history of Lanark, this discusses early settlement and provides useful village histories.

174b. McGillivray, R., and E. Ross. *A History of Glengarry*. Belleville: Mika Publishing, 1979.

175.   McKenzie, Ruth. *Leeds and Grenville: Their First Two Hundred Years*. Toronto: McClelland and Stewart, 1967.
       - A very good local history, this offers a useful analysis of the social and economic development of Leeds and Grenville.

175b. Mackinnon, A.D. *The Story of Vankleek Hill*. Belleville: Mika Publishing, 1979.

176.   Maclaren, A. Barnet. *Lumbering on the Rivière du Lièvre: A Saga of Maclarens and Buckingham*. n.p., 1973.
       - Basically a family study, this offers a discussion of the development of Buckingham.

177.   MacNaughton, M.A. et al. *Farm Family Living in Lanark County*. Ottawa: Department of Agriculture, 1950.

178.   Manotick Centennial Committee. *Manotick's Centennial Year Souvenir, 1859-1959*. Manotick: n.p., 1959.
       - Some local history is discussed.

179.   Marcellus, Anna Smith. *Chesterville and District in the Nineteenth Century*. n.p., 1971.

180.   Martyn, Max and Virginia. *The Story of the Lower Rideau Settlement: Merrickville, Burritt's Rapids and District*. Merrickville: Merrickville and District Historical Society, 1976.

181.   Maxville Women's Institute. *History of Maxville and the Community*. Maxville: Maxville Women's Institute, 1967.
       - A useful history of the Maxville area, this offers some discussion of social and economic growth.

182. Morgan, Eleanor W. *"Up the Front": A Story of Morrisburg.* Toronto: The Ryerson Press, 1961.
 - A useful history of the town.

183. Morris, J.A., ed. *Prescott, 1810-1967.* Prescott: The Prescott Journal, 1967.
 - Mostly a collection of reminiscences of Prescott, with a history of the development of the town.

184. *Morrisburg Centennial Anniversary, 1861-1961.* Ottawa: Le Droit, 1961.

185. Municipality of Cardinal. *A History of Cardinal.* Cardinal: Municipality of Cardinal, 1967.
 - Narrative of the early development of Cardinal.

186. Nantel, G.A. *Notre nord-ouest provincial: Etude sur la vallée de l'Ottawa.* Montreal: Eusèbe Senécal, 1887.
 - A colonization study.

186b. Newton, M. *Lower Town Ottawa.* vol. 1: *1826-1854.* (Edited by Robert Naig.) Ottawa: National Capital Commission, 1979.

187. *Le Nord de l'Outaouais.* (R.P. Taché, et al.) Ottawa: Le Droit, 1938.
 - A school text-book.

187c. Osgoode Township Historical Society and Museum. *Glimpses of Osgoode Township: 150 years, 1825-1977.* Vernon: Osgoode Township Historical Society and Museum, 1977.

187v. Ostrum, C. Manuscript History of Alexandria. (Copy in Dunvegan Museum.)

188. *Ottawa Citizen.* Aug. 16, 1926
 - A commemorative issue on Ottawa with sketches of the "lumber kings."

188b. Pembroke Centennial Publicity Committee. *Pembroke Centennial Souvenir Book, 1958, July 6-12.* Pembroke: Pembroke Observer, 1958.

189. Price, C. and C.C. Kennedy. *Notes on the History of Renfrew County.* Pembroke: Renfrew County Council, 1961.

190. Pringle, J.F. *Lunenburgh, or the Old Eastern District: Its Settlement and Early Progress.* Cornwall: The Standard Printing House, 1890.
 - A local history written by Judge Pringle, this amateur history was the basis for many of the later histories, although he used few primary sources.

191. Rigby, G.R. *A History of Lachute.* Lachute: Brownsburg-Lachute Rotary Club, 1964.
 - This useful non-academic history of Lachute offers a narrative of its settlement and economic development.

192. Ross, A.H.D. *Ottawa: Past and Present.* Ottawa: Thorburn and Abbott, 1927.

192b. Rossignol, L. Lapointe, P.L., and Carrière, G. *Hull, 1800-1975: Histoire Illustrée.* Hull: Comité de la grande fête de Hull, 1975.

193. Sadler, Fred. *Fitzroy Township: Centennial Flashback.* [Fitzroy Harbour: n.p., 1967.]

194. Seeley's Bay Centennial Co-ordinating Committee. *Seeley's Bay and District*

Historical Profile. Gananoque: The Gananoque Reporter, 1967.

195. Shortt, Edward, ed. *Perth Remembered*. Perth: Mortimer Ltd., 1967.
    - A collection of documents, articles and memoirs with Perth as its focus.

196. Sim, R.A. *A Study of Lanark County, Ontario*. North Gower: Strathmere Associates, 1963.
    - An examination of population trends in Lanark, with some discussion of the economic base.

197. Skelton, Isabel. *A Man Austere: William Bell, Parson and Pioneer*. Toronto: Ryerson Press, 1947.

198. Smith, A.W., ed. *In These Days: A History of North Hastings and of South Nipissing*. Bancroft: n.p., 1956.

199. Smith, Josephine. *Perth-on-the-Tay*. Ottawa: 1901.

200. Smiths Falls. *75 Years of Progress, 1882-1957*. Smiths Falls: Recorder News Press, 1957.
    - This contains some local history, but mostly a Chamber of Commerce report.

201. Smiths Falls University Women's Club. *The History of Smiths Falls*. Smiths Falls: 1967.

201b. Snyder, M.H. *Nineteenth Century Industrial Development in the Rideau Corridor: A Preliminary Report*. Ottawa: Parks Canada. (Manuscript Report Series, no. 215), 1977.

202. Stevens, G.F. *The United Counties of Leeds and Grenville, 3,000,000 B.C. - 1840 A.D.* Brockville: n.p., 1961.

203. Stittsville Women's Institute. *Country Tales*. Stittsville: Tweedsmuir History Committee, 1963.

203b. Stormont, Dundas and Glengarry Historical Society. *Lectures*. Cornwall: Stormont, Dundas and Glengarry Historical Society. 1977.

204. Tassé, Joseph. *La Vallée de l'Outaouais*. Montreal: Eusèbe Senécal, 1873.
    - A pamphlet favouring colonization in the Ottawa Valley.

205. Thomas, Cyrus. *History of the Counties of Argenteuil, Quebec and Prescott, Ontario from the Earliest Settlement to the Present*. Montreal: John Lovell and Son, 1896.
    - A traditional local history, with emphasis upon prominent settlers and local personages, politics, administration, and so forth.

206. Thompson, Claire. *Township of Lanark, 1820-1970*. Almonte: n.p., 1970.

207. Wales, B.N. *Memories of Old St. Andrews and Historical Sketches of the Seigneury of Argenteuil*. Lachute: Watchman Press, 1934.

208. Walker, Harry J. and Olive. *Carleton Saga*. Ottawa: The Runge Press, 1968.
    - An important history of Carleton County, this emphasizes settlement and economic development in each township.

209. Walker, Harry J. *100 Years: Ottawa and the Valley*. Ottawa: The Ottawa Journal, 1967.

210. Walker, Harry J. *The Ottawa Story: Through 150 Years*. Ottawa: The Journal's Coronation Souvenir Issue, 1953.

211. Warner, H.W. *South Augusta and its Environs*. [A paper read before the Grenville County Historical Society.] n.p., 1964.

211b. Wesche, R., and Kugler-Gagnon, M., eds. *Ottawa-Hull: Spatial Prespectives and Planning*. Ottawa: University of Ottawa Press, 1978.

212. Whitton, Charlotte. *A Hundred Years A Fellin'*. Ottawa: The Runge Press, 1943.
     - This is primarily a history of the Gillies Bros. It makes some generalizations about the timber industry, but is unsystematic.

C.   ARTICLES
     Abbreviations:

CHR   - Canadian Historical Review.
OHSPR - Ontario Historical Society Papers and Records.
WCHSO - Women's Canadian Historical Society of Ottawa.

213. Ahearn, Mrs. M.H. "The Settlers of March Township", *OHSPR* 3 (1901), pp. 97-102.
     - This discusses the early settlers of March Township.

214. Ahearn, Mrs. Thomas. "The Early Settlers of March Township", *WCHSO Transactions* 1 (1901), pp. 46-51.
     - Same as previous article.

214b. Akenson, D.H. "Listening to Rural Language: Ballycarry, Co. Antrim, 1798-1817", in D.H. Akenson, ed., *Canadian Papers in Rural History*, Vol. II. (Gananoque: Langdale Press, 1979), pp. 155-172.

215. Audet, F.J. "The Hon. Thomas McKay, M.L.C., Founder of New Edinburgh, 1792-1855", in *Canadian Historical Association Annual Report* (1932), pp. 65-71.

215b. Blair, E. "Loyalists of Lancaster Township", *Loyalist Gazette* 16, No. 2 (Autumn, 1978), p. 13.

216. Blanchard, R. "Le Pays de l'Ottawa", *Revue de Géographie Alpine* 38 (1949), pp. 1-140.

217. Bond, C.C.J. "Alexander James Christie, Bytown Pioneer: His Life and Times, 1787-1843", *Ontario History* 56 (1964), pp. 16-36.

218. Bond, C.C.J. "The Hudson's Bay Company in the Ottawa Valley", *The Beaver*, (Spring, 1966).

219. Burritt, Mrs. Alexander. "Early Settlement of Grenville County", *WCHSO Transactions* 1 (1901), pp. 57-64.
     - Basically the same article as the one which appeared in OHSPR.

220. Burritt, Mrs. A. "The Settlement of the County of Grenville", *OHSPR* 3 (1901), pp. 102-109.
     - An amateur local history of Grenville, this emphasizes Loyalist settlement.

221. Carnochan, Janet. "Williamstown: An Historic Village", *OHSPR* 17 (1919), pp. 48-58.

222.   Cameron, J.M. "The Role of Shipping from Scottish Ports in Emigration to the Canadas, 1815-55", in D.H. Akenson, ed., *Canadian Papers in Rural History*, vol. II (Gananoque: Langdale Press, 1979), pp. 135-154.

222b. Cameron, Wendy. "Selecting Peter Robinson's Irish Emigrants", in *Histoire sociale - Social History* 9 (May, 1976), pp. 29-46.

223.   Casselman, A.C. "The Highland Scotch United Empire Loyalists", *United Empire Loyalist Association Annual Transactions*, (1901-02), pp. 100-109.

224.   Cole, W.H. "The Local History of the Town of Brockville", *OHSPR* 12 (1914), pp. 32-41.
       - An administrative history.

225.   Cross, M.S. "The Age of Gentility: The Formation of an Aristocracy in the Ottawa Valley", *Canadian Historical Association Annual Report* (1967), pp. 105-117.

226.   Cross, M.S. "The Lumber Community of Upper Canada", *Ontario History* 52 (1960), pp. 213-233.

227.   Cross, M.S. "The Shiners' War: Social Violence in the Ottawa Valley in the 1830's", *CHR* 54 (1973), pp. 1-26.

228.   Cross, M.S. "Stony Monday, 1849: The Rebellion Losses Riots in Bytown", *Ontario History* 63 (1971), pp. 177-190.

229.   Cruikshank, E.A. "The Activity of Abel Stevens as a Pioneer", *OHSPR* 31 (1936), pp. 56-90.

230.   Cruikshank, E.A. "The Adventures of Roger Stevens, A Forgotten Loyalist Pioneer in Upper Canada", *OHSPR* 33 (1939), pp. 11-38.

231.   Cruikshank, E.A. "The King's Royal Regiment of New York", *OHSPR* 27 (1931), pp. 193-323.

231b. Douglas, H.T. "John Burrows Honey (An Early Resident of Bytown)", *WCHSO Transactions* 11 (1954), pp. 24-26.

232.   Dumbrille, John. "A Short History of the Church of England in the Township of Augusta, County of Grenville", *OHSPR* 19 (1922), p. 90.

233.   Dunn, C.W. "Glengarry's Gaelic Heritage", *Dalhousie Review* 42 (1962-63), pp. 193-201.

233b. Elliot, B.S. "The Famous Township of Hull: Image and Aspiration of a Pioneer Community", *Histoire sociale/Social History* 12 (November 1979), pp. 339-367.

234.   Foran, Mrs. T.P. "My Native County—Glengarry", *WCHSO Transactions* 7 (1917), pp. 26-37.

235.   Fraser, Miss M.J.F. "Feudalism in Upper Canada, 1823-1843", *OHSPR* 12 (1914), pp. 142-152.
       - An amateur history of the McNab settlement.

235b. Friel, H.S. "The Rideau Canal and the Founding of Ottawa", *WCHSO Transactions* 1 (1901), pp. 31-35.

236.   Greening, W.E. "Historic Argenteuil County", *Canadian Geographical Journal* 54

(May, 1957), pp. 206-216.
- This contains little that is not in the book (item 146).

237. Griffin, A.C. "Stormont: A Town Unbuilt", *Canadian Magazine* 36, no. 4 (1910-11), pp. 315-324.

238. Hunter, A.F. "The Ethnographical Elements of Ontario", *OHSPR* 3 (1901), pp. 180-199.
- A listing of the various ethnic groups who located in each county of Ontario, this is fairly accurate, for the most part, but does contain some errors.

238b. Jarvis, E. "Military Land Granting in Upper Canada following the War of 1812", *Ontario History* 67 (1975), pp. 121-134.

239. Johnson, J.K. "Col. James Fitzgibbon and the Suppression of Irish Riots in Upper Canada", *Ontario History* 58 (1966), pp. 139-156.
- This discusses the Ballyghiblin riots, and the tensions between Irish canal workers and "the Dutchmen" (the original German-Loyalist settlers) in Cornwall in the 1830's.

240. Joliffe, M.E. "Fitzroy Township", *WCHSO Transactions* 4 (1911), pp. 15-20.
- An amateur local history of Fitzroy Township, this emphasizes prominent settlers.

242. Kinlock, James. "Perth - Solidity and Style", *Canadian Geographic Journal* 79 (Aug. 1969), pp. 40-51.
- A useful analysis of the development of Perth.

243. Kirwan, Mrs. P.T. "The Township of Gloucester", *WCHSO Transactions* 4 (1911), pp. 10-14.

243b. Lapierre, A. "Les francais des milieux ruraux de Prescott-Russell", *Bulletin du Centre de recherche en civilisation canadienne-francaise* 14 (April, 1977), pp. 5-9.

243c. Latchford, L. "Philemon Wright and the Settlement of Hull", *WCHSO Transactions* 8 (1922), pp. 5-19.

244. Lee-Whiting, B. "First Polish Settlement in Canada", *Canadian Geographical Journal* 75 (Sept. 1967), pp. 108-112.
- A brief account of the Wilno-Barry's Bay community.

245. Lee-Whiting, B. "The Opeongo Road - An Early Colonization Scheme", *Canadian Geographical Journal* 74 (1967), pp. 76-83.
- Some information on settlement.

246. Lee-Whiting, B. "Saga of a Nineteenth Century Sawmill", *Canadian Geographical Journal* 74 (Feb. 1967), pp. 46-51.

247. MacDonald, H.S. "Memoir of Col. Joel Stone, A U.E. Loyalist and the Founder of Gananoque", *OHSPR* 18 (1920), pp. 59-90.

248. MacDonald, H.S. "The United Empire Loyalists of the Old Johnstown District", *OHSPR* 12 (1914), pp. 13-32.

249. McDougall, Mrs. Lorne. "Settlement of Part of Leeds County", *WCHSO Transactions* 3 (1910), pp. 73-75.

250. MacKay, B.R. "A Pioneer Community in Beckwith Township, Lanark County, Upper Canada, Locally Known as 'The Derry'", *WCHSO Transactions* 11 (1954), pp. 55-62.

251. Mackay, J.R. "The North Shore of the Ottawa River", *Revue Canadienne de Géographie* 1 (1947), pp. 3-8.
 - Based on the thesis (item 286).

252. Mackay, J.R. "Physiography of the Lower Ottawa Valley", *Revue Canadienne de Géographie* 3 (1949), pp. 53-96.
 - Based on his thesis (item 286).

253. McKenna, Edward. "Unorganized Labour versus Management: The Strike at the Chaudière Lumber Mills, 1891", *Histoire sociale-Social History* 5 (November, 1972), pp. 186-211.

253b. MacLennan, J. "The Early Settlement of Glengarry", *Transactions of the Celtic Society of Montreal* (1887).

253c. MacNab, A. "The Settlement of the Township of Lochiel, Glengarry", *Transactions of the Celtic Society of Montreal* (1892).

254. MacRae, Marion. "Settlement of the Old Eastern District of Upper Canada", *Royal Architectural Institute of Canada Journal* 36, no. 5 (May, 1959), pp.145-47.

255. Mallory, E.S. "Ottawa Lumber Era", *Canadian Geographical Journal* 68 (Feb. 1964), pp. 60-73.

256. Maltby, P.L. and M. "A New Look at the Peter Robinson Emigration of 1823", *Ontario History* 55 (1963), pp. 15-21.

257. Martin, John D.P. "The Regiment de Watteville: Its Settlement and Service in Upper Canada", *Ontario Society* 52 (1960), pp. 17-30.

258. May, John. "Bush Life in the Ottawa Valley Eighty Years Ago", *OHSPR* 12 (1914), pp. 153-163.

259. Morgan, H.R. "The First Tay Canal: An Abortive Upper Canadian Transportation Enterprise of a Century Ago", *OHSPR* 29 (1933), pp. 103-116.

260. Murison, Mrs. R. "The Loyalists of Glengarry", *United Empire Loyalist Association Annual Transactions* (1903-04), pp. 48-58.

260b. Patterson, H. "Benjamin Tett and Bedford Mills", *Historic Kingston* 25 (March, 1977), pp. 60-62.

260c. Parson, H.E. "An Investigation of the Changing Rural Economy of Gatineau County, Quebec", *The Canadian Geographer* 21 (Spring 1977), pp. 22-31.

260d. Parson, H.E. "The Rise and Fall of Farming in a Marginal Area: The Gatineau Valley, Quebec", *Cahiers de Géographie de Québec* 19 (décembre 1975), pp. 573-582.

261. Playter, George F. "The Founding of Three Militry Settlements in Eastern Ontario - Perth, Lanark and Richmond, 1815-18", *OHSPR* 20 (1923), pp. 98-104.
 - A collection of documents.

262. Read, Eva G. "History of the County of Carleton", *WCHSO Transactions* 4

(1911), pp. 5-9.

263. Richards, J.H.B. "Population and the Economic Base in Northern Hastings County, Ontario", *The Candian Geographer* (1958), pp. 23-33.
   - A useful account of the economic history of the northern townships.

263b. Robertson, E. "The Community of Bedford Mills", *Historic Kingston* 17 (January, 1969), pp. 94-96.

264. Seaman, H.S. "The Reverend William Smart, Presbyterian Minister of Elizabethtown, 1811-1876", *OHSPR* 5 (1904), pp. 178-86.

265. Sowter, T.W. Edwin. "The Highway of the Ottawa", *OHSPR* 13 (1915), pp. 42-52.

266. Spragge, G.W. "Colonization Roads in Canada West, 1850-1867", *Ontario History* 49 (1957), pp. 1-18.
   - A general treatment.

267. Spragge, George W. "The Districts of Upper Canada", Ontario Historical Society, *Profiles of a Province* (Toronto: Ontario Historical Society, 1967), pp. 34-42.

268. Sulte, Benjamin. "The Valley of the Ottawa in 1613", *OHSPR* 13 (1915), pp. 31-35.

269. Thorburn, Mrs. C.H. "Ottawa, 1867-1927", *WCHSO Transactions* 10 (1928), pp. 5-29.

270. Young, A.H. "Ottawa a Hundred Years Ago", *OHSPR* 28 (1932), pp. 35-40.

III. THESES

271. Baribeau, Claude. "La Seigneurie de la Petite-Nation de 1802 à 1872", an unpublished M.A. thesis for the University of Ottawa, 1980.

271b. Brozowski, Roman. "Population Changes in Ontario Towns and Villages, 1941-66", an unpublished M.A. thesis for the University of Windsor, 1971.

272. Buckley, D.E. "Perth: Case Study of a Small Town", an unpublished B.A. thesis for Carleton University, 1968.
   - A useful study of the growth of Perth. A geography thesis, emphasizing economic development.

273. Cartwright, Donald G. "French Canadian Colonization in Eastern Ontario to 1910: A Study of Process and Pattern", an unpublished Ph.D. thesis for the University of Western Ontario, 1973.
   - This examines early English-speaking settlement in Prescott and Russell, Stormont and Glengarry, and analyzes French Canadian migration to the area.

274. Cross, M.S. "The Dark Druidical Groves: The Lumber Community and the Commercial Frontier in British North America to 1854", an unpublished Ph.D. thesis for the University of Toronto, 1966.
   - The best study of the economic, social and political development of the Ottawa Valley.

275. Dawes, William G. "Changing Population Patterns in Eastern Ontario, 1931-61", a B.A. thesis for Carleton University, 1968.
 - A geography thesis, this discusses the reasons for the decline of the rural population in Eastern Ontario.

276. Fraser, J.S. "The Renfrew Region in the Middle Ottawa Valley", an M.A. thesis for Clark University, n.d.
 -A geography thesis, this offers a little new information on Renfrew, Carleton and Pontiac Counties.

277. George, V. Alan. "The Rideau Corridor: The Effect of a Canal System on a Frontier Region, 1832-1895", an unpublished M.A. thesis for Queen's University, 1972.
 -This examines the impact of the Rideau Canal upon the growth of the area and concludes that there was little social and economic stimulus in the Rideau Valley, apart from Kingston and Ottawa.

278. Gibson, P.M. "Settlement and Abandonment of Land in the Rouge Valley, Laurentides, Quebec: An Historical Geography", an unpublished M.A. thesis for McGill University, 1967.
 - A good study of the social and economic development of the Rouge Valley.

279. Gilmour, James. "The Economic Geography of the Pulp and Paper Industry in Ontario", an unpublished M.A. thesis for the University of Toronto, 1964.
 - This discusses factors governing location of mills, types of raw materials used.

280. Heathcote, V.M. "Growth and Development of Nepean Township, Ontario", a B.A. thesis for Carleton University, 1973.

281. Hunter, F.G. "The Settlement of the Townships of Lancaster and Charlottenburg in Glengarry County, 1784-1860", a B.A. thesis for Carleton University, 1968.
 - A geography thesis with useful analysis of the settlement and economic development of the two townships.

281b. Khan, J.R. "Changing Patterns of Agricultural Land Use in Renfrew County, 1951-1971", an unpublished M.A. thesis for Carleton University, 1977.

282. Laughton, D.B. "An Historical Geography of Smiths Falls, Ontario", a B.A. thesis for Carleton University, 1970.
 - A geography thesis with useful analysis of Smiths Falls' development.

283. Lindsay, V.H. "The Perth Military Settlement: Characteristics of its Permanent and Transitory Settlers", an unpublished M.A. thesis for Carleton University. 1972.
 - This focuses on Bathurst and Drummond townships and concludes that the more permanent settlers in the areas were civilians, those with families and those on good land. A quantitative study.

284. Lucas, C. Glenn. "Presbyterianism in Carleton County to 1867", an unpublished M.A. thesis for Carleton University, 1973.
 - An institutional examination of Presbyterianism in Carleton County.

285. Lyons, M.E. "Elizabethtown, A Typical St. Lawrence River Township", an

unpublished M.A. thesis for Queen's University, 1935.

285b.   McCallum, J.C.P. "Agriculture and Economic Development in Quebec and Ontario to 1870", an unpublished Ph.D. thesis for McGill University, 1977.

286.   Mackay, John Ross. "The Regional Geography of the Lower Ottawa Valley", an unpublished Ph.D. thesis for the University of Montreal, 1949.
        - A very good geography thesis (though somewhat dated), this offers useful analysis of settlement patterns, economic development, transportation, social changes, plus geography and geology.

287.   MacLeod, P.K. "Gualainn ri Gualainn: A Study of Concentrations of Scottish Settlement in Nineteenth Century Ontario", an unpublished M.A. thesis for Carleton University, 1972.
        - A quantitative study of Scottish settlers which suggests that Scots preferred "clan-like" communities, based on family, occupation or military regiment.

287b.   McRae, J.D. "Recent Changes in Land Ownership. A Case Study in Eastern Ontario", an M.A. thesis for the University of Guelph, 1977.

288.   Morris, W.A. "Pembroke: A Study of the Town and its Industries", an unpublished B.A. thesis for McMaster University, 1956.
        - An unsophisticated study which offers some useful information on Pembroke.

289.   Norton, William. "Agricultural Settlement Patterns in Upper Canada, 1782-1851: A Simulation Analysis", an unpublished Ph.D. thesis for McMaster University, 1973.

289b.   Parson, H.E. "Rural Land Use Change: A Study of the Gatineau Valley of Quebec", an unpublished doctoral thesis for the University of Kentucky, 1976.

290.   Ray, D.M. "Settlement and Rural Outmigration in Easternmost Ontario, 1783 to 1956", an unpublished M.A. thesis for the University of Ottawa, 1961.
        - A geography thesis which analyses the factors producing rural outmigration in the region.

291.   Richards, J.H.B. "Land Use and Settlement Patterns on the Fringe of the Shield in Southern Ontario", an unpublished Ph.D. thesis for the University of Toronto, 1953.
        - A general study with some useful information on agriculture; it disregards ethnicity.

291b.   Sauvé, R.C. "Economic Growth of Eastern Ontario, Trend and Structure Analysis", an unpublished M.A. thesis for the University of Ottawa, 1969.

292.   Sneyd, R.B. "The Role of the Rideau Waterway, 1826-1856", an unpublished M.A. thesis for the University of Toronto, 1965.

293.   Stuart, E. Rae. "Jessup's Rangers as a Factor in Loyalist Settlement", in *Three History Theses*. Toronto: The Ontario Department of Public Records and Archives, 1961.

294.   Turay, Harry. "The Process of Settlement and Land Clearance in Papineau County, Quebec (1800-1967)", an unpublished M.A. thesis for the University of Ottawa, 1969.

295. Zinman, Rosalind. "Lachute, Quebec, French-English Frontier: A Case Study in Language and Community", an unpublished M.A. thesis for Concordia University, 1976.

- A sociology thesis which is concerned with the bilingual character of Lachute.

INDEX

The geographical names which appear in the IU titles are indicated in capital letters. Names which identify entire IU's are followed directly by the IU number: e.g. ADMASTON 0100100. For names which form only part of an IU, the word "in" precedes the appropriate IU number: e.g. ABINGER in 0302100. Many of the IU names are also township names, but this is not universally true, especially in Quebec. See INTRODUCTION p. xii. Counties are listed by name, along with the designation "County." The listing includes the two digit ID prefix for each county (see INTRODUCTION p. xvii): e.g. Renfrew County (01). Cities, towns, villages and unincorporated places are listed along with the ID number of the IU in which they are situated: e.g. Burrits Rapids in 0704599. Geographical or historical places mentioned in the NOTES, such as the Bonnechère River or the Opeongo Line are also included in the index.